[THE GRENVILLITES, 1801–29]

THE GRENVILLITES

1801–29

*Party Politics and Factionalism
in the Age of Pitt and Liverpool*

[James J. Sack]

UNIVERSITY OF ILLINOIS PRESS
Urbana, Chicago, London

Library of Congress Cataloging in Publication Data

Sack, James J   1944–
    The Grenvillites, 1801–29.

    Bibliography: p.
    Includes index.
    1. Great Britain—Politics and government—1800–1837. 2. Grenville family.
3. Political parties—Great Britain—History. I. Title.
DA535.S22   320.9′41′073   78-23288
ISBN 0-252-00713-1

To my parents,
Janet Carroll Sack and Walter J. Sack

[CONTENTS]

[ACKNOWLEDGMENTS]

For permission to quote from or in other ways to utilize documents in their possession, I would like to express my deep appreciation to the authorities of the following institutions: the Bodleian Library, Oxford; the British Library of Political and Economic Science, the London School of Economics; the British Museum; the Central Library, Sheffield; the Department of Palaeography and Diplomatic, the University of Durham; the Huntington Library, San Marino, California; the John Rylands University Library of Manchester; the National Army Museum, London; the National Library of Ireland; the National Library of Wales; the Public Record Office, London; the Sheepscar Library, Leeds; the William R. Perkins Library, Duke University; the University College of North Wales, Bangor; and the Record Offices in Bedfordshire (Bedford); Berkshire (Reading); Buckinghamshire (Aylesbury); Devon (Exeter); Essex (Chelmsford); Hampshire (Winchester); Northamptonshire (Northampton); Staffordshire (Stafford); and Suffolk (Bury St. Edmunds). I would also like to thank the archivists, the librarians, and the staffs of the above-mentioned institutions who by their helpfulness and thoughtfulness made my research a genuine pleasure.

In the preparation of this book, a number of individuals kindly allowed me to examine and quote from their private family papers, and I would like to express my gratitude to them. They include: His Grace the Duke of Grafton, K. G.; the Rt. Hon. the Countess of Sutherland; the Earl Fitzwilliam and his Trustees; the Earl of Harewood; the Earl of Harrowby and the Trustees of the Harrowby MSS Trust; the late Earl Spencer; the Viscount Sidmouth; Lady Charlotte Bonham-Carter; Lady Margaret Fortescue; Sir Richard Proby; George Howard, Esq.; the late Dr. J. G. C. Spencer Bernard; and S. Whitbread, Esq.

I am also obliged to the late Professor William B. Hamilton of Duke University, who kindly put at my disposal the reams of microfilms, transcripts, and notes from his personal collection of Lord Grenville's correspondence, formerly at Boconnoc, Cornwall. The Horace H. Rackham School of Graduate Studies and the Department of History at the University of Michigan, as well as the members of the Chicago Circle Research Board and the Faculty Summer Fellowship Committee at the University of Illinois at Chicago Circle, have been more than generous in their financial support of this project. Mrs. Dawn E. Jackson and Professors Gerald S. Brown, Carolyn A. Edie, Bentley B. Gilbert, D. J. Guth, Scott T. Jackson, D. G. Paz, Bradford Perkins, and William Taylor have helped me in numerous ways. Julie Baskes, Nancy E. Rupprecht, and Rita Zelewsky read and criticized this manuscript at various stages in its preparation, and I would like to thank them for it. Professor Jacob M. Price of the University of Michigan has aided me consistently with such sound advice and invaluable criticism as to put me deeply in his debt.

[INTRODUCTION]

From the Glorious Revolution to the age of Baldwin and MacDonald, perhaps no block of years has received so little attention from political historians (or current political biographers) as the period from 1794 to 1830. The former date saw the near destruction of the old pro-American Whig party, as most of its leading spokesmen under the leadership of the Duke of Portland deserted Charles James Fox and his small knot of friends to lend support to William Pitt and his antirevolutionary Ministry; the latter, the commencement of an age of reform presided over by Fox's political heirs. The intervening thirty-six years were arguably as important for the future of the British people and, indeed, for the Western world as were the years between the Great Divorce and the finalization of the Elizabethan settlement—with one important difference. The entire course of the sixteenth-century Reformation was (insofar as such things ever are) directed from the center of political affairs, the courts of successive sovereigns. The great transformation of British life during the late eighteenth and early nineteenth centuries owed far more to the forges of the Clyde, the traction of George Stephenson's locomotive, or the growing class-consciousness of a Huddersfield weaver than to the state of George III's constitution, Addington's parliamentary fumblings, or even Wellington's victory in 1815. Yet, if for the historian much of the general interest of those years must perforce lie outside Parliament and even outside the confines of the traditional ruling classes, the horror and achievements of those decades of war, industrial revolution, and social transformation were unquestionably reflected in the business and, to a much lesser extent, composition of Parliament.

From the perspective of aggressive political life, Parliament meant the active politicians, as most members of both Houses could generally be counted upon to passively support the King's Government and sustain it in office. However, the composition of that Government, especially the decision as to the identity of the prime minister, was something of a shared responsibility between the King and the chief politicians. No inexperienced Lord Bute was any longer possible; but neither was the chief minister always the necessarily clear-cut choice of the leading members of one party within a two-party structure.

It has now been almost half a century since Sir Lewis Namier presented his novel and classic studies of mid-eighteenth-century British politics as revolving around nonideologically oriented patronage and family connections and local interests, with an almost total absence of that two-party system beloved of the Whig historians.[1] A somewhat anti-Namierite thesis has since then evolved, emphasizing the importance of party and principle in Westminster and local affairs at least after 1780;[2] and it is now quite possible to see the whole period from 1760 to 1830 without adopting the full starkness of Namier's perspective (writing of 1809) that "the basic structure of eighteenth century parliamentary politics" still existed with "no trace of a two party system, or at all of party in the modern sense."[3] Yet, one need not compare the political nation to a straight line moving steadily upward on a graph away from the faction-ridden family and patronage connections of the 1750s toward the Whig and Tory parties of the age of Grey and the Tamworth Manifesto. Rather, a fluctuating line might more logically be used as party (even two party) and principle sometimes seem at the forefront of the political experience, as in the late 1770s, the 1790s, or the early and middle 1820s; while at other times, 1782 to 1784, 1801 to 1812, 1827 to 1829, a revived factionalism seems to predominate, and one must peer deep into the labyrinth to perceive the political principles upon which a North, a Grenville, or a Canning acted.

Outside of the eventually permanent Whigs and Pittite-Tories, the longest lasting of the British political groupings or connections of the period were the members or followers of the Grenville family, and that they were a notorious example of the worst type of factionalism has gone

1. *The Structure of Politics at the Accession of George III* (London, 1929); *England in the Age of the American Revolution* (London, 1930).

2. See especially, for the 1780s, John Cannon, *The Fox-North Coalition, 1782–1784* (Cambridge, 1969), and Donald E. Ginter, ed., *Whig Organization in the General Election of 1790* (Berkeley, 1967). For a later period, see Austin Mitchell, *The Whigs in Opposition, 1815–1830* (Oxford, 1967). For the period as a whole, see Richard W. Davis, *Political Change and Continuity, 1760–1885: A Buckinghamshire Study* (Newton Abbot, 1972), and B. W. Hill, "Executive Monarchy and the Challenge of Parties, 1689–1832: Two Concepts of Government and Two Historiographical Interpretations," *Historical Journal*, XIII, no. 3 (1970), pp. 379–401.

3. *Crossroads of Power* (London, 1962), p. 231.

unquestioned. The nineteenth-century Grenvillites have been basically viewed by historians[4] as one of the last durable factions operating according to the old presuppositions described by Namier and rendered increasingly obsolete by the realities of the new century; in Professor Aspinall's words, they were "a party of placehunters."[5] This unsavory but well-documented picture of the Grenville family, held by many contemporaries and by subsequent historians, is partially true and readily illustrated by the family's vast sinecurial holdings and obvious greed for power that would procure more sinecures, jobs, and pensions. A detailed analysis of the Grenvillites between the years when they acted most independently and most prominently upon the national stage, 1801 to 1829, partially, but only partially, sustains the common criticism of the group. For, flagrantly though they may have acted at times, the Grenvillites were no more immune than the Whigs or the Pittites to that polarization of politics into broader issue-oriented groupings that was the fruit of the American war and, even more sharply, of the French Revolution.

In a sense, the Grenvillites illustrate a dichotomy between two political centuries and almost between two political cultures. They may very well have been the last of the traditional English factions, but that actuality is hardly the end of the story. The Grenvillites should not be viewed as a coherent political group. There was always an inner tension, more serious at some times than at others, between two centers of authority within the party.

On the one hand, George Grenville, first Marquis of Buckingham, and his son, Richard Grenville, first Duke of Buckingham and Chandos, who were landed and parliamentary magnates of the first rank ruling over their interests from the palatial magnificence of Stowe, were of a traditional breed of grandee that put family and personal pride before, ideology or broader loyalties. They looked out for their own and their connection's interest and advancement, favoring coalitions and alliances with any or all groups that appeared to serve their often shortsighted purposes.

On the other hand was quite a different sort of politician: the first Marquis of Buckingham's brother, William Wyndham Grenville,

4. William Ranulf Brock, *Lord Liverpool and Liberal Toryism* (Cambridge, 1941), pp. 78–79; Richard Pares, *King George III and the Politicians* (Oxford, 1953), p. 77; Michael Roberts, *The Whig Party, 1807–1812* (2d ed.; London, 1965), p. 175; David Spring, "Lord Chandos and the Farmers, 1818–1846," *Huntington Library Quarterly*, XXXIII, no. 3 (1970), p. 258.

5. Arthur Aspinall, "The Canningite Party," *Transactions of the Royal Historical Society*, 4th ser., XVII (1934), p. 215.

Baron Grenville, who lived at his Buckinghamshire country home, Dropmore, on a more modest scale than his brother and nephew at Stowe. Lord Grenville's political character was forged in the crucibles of 1793 and 1801, and he was manifestly more than a place-hunter. He was, like all politicians, interested in patronage and honors; but such things were not, as in the case of the Buckinghams, the prime motivating factors of his life. Thus he could and did draw to himself men who were chiefly concerned with the state of Ireland, the French war, the Bank, and the Corn Laws, in contrast with the Stowe Grenvilles, who were chiefly surrounded by toadies who adhered to them in a lord-vassal or patron-client relationship and served their interests in return for sinecures, seats in the House of Commons, and other favors.

Thus it is best to distinguish at the outset between a Grenvillite connection presided over by Buckingham *père* and *fils* and a wider Grenvillite party that, to be sure, usually incorporated the Stowe Grenville group but was led by Lord Grenville. When Grenville retired from active political life in 1817, his wider party ceased to exist. A majority of the former members continued to act with the Whig party, with whom the Grenvillites had coalesced in 1804, though a small number adhered to Lord Liverpool's Tory Ministry. The Stowe Grenville family or patronage connection continued a separate existence at least until 1829, often, as in 1821 and 1827, in opposition to the political line of Lord Grenville himself.

In the following pages I have discussed the rise, development, importance, and decline of the Grenvillites between 1801 and 1829, between the resignation of Pitt's first Ministry over Catholic Emancipation and the eventual passage of the Catholic Relief Bill by Wellington and Peel. From a certain perspective, a Grenvillite group had been in Parliament since at least the early 1780s; therefore the question of origins must necessarily be taken into account. During the 1830s and 1840s, there was also a group of Bucks MPs who followed the first Duke of Buckingham's son, the Marquis of Chandos (after 1839, second Duke of Buckingham and Chandos), in his attempts to forward the agricultural interest. However, to term these individuals Grenvillites or to see them as lineal descendents of the followers of the group that operated from 1801 to 1829 would be misleading and unhelpful, as even the term "Grenvillite" had by then passed from the national political vocabulary.

No systematic study of the Grenvillites has ever before been attempted. Thus, I have tried to ascertain their fluctuating numerical strength as well as discuss their self-perception, their relationship with other national political groups, and their over-all contribution to the tenor of British political life during the age of the Napoleonic wars and the Industrial Revolution. From the point of view of the general political historian, probably the most significant aspect of this study will concern the structure of the Grenville-Foxite coalition and the relationship between the Grenvillites and the Foxite-Whigs during the years between 1804 and 1817. It was during this period that Lord Grenville, perhaps unwittingly, performed his chief service to the nineteenth-century two-party tradition by leading back to the Whig party many of the Portland Whigs who had deserted it during 1793 and 1794.[6] Yet, hopefully, one will also find elucidated a sense of the quality of English political life during the early years of the last century, both in terms of the cement of political activity that bound together leaders and followers of one of the most famous—or infamous—of contemporary parties and in terms of the infinite complexity in relationships that made the Grenvillites anything but a well-organized body of politicians.

6. E. A. Smith, in his study of Lord Fitzwilliam's politics, would place more emphasis than I upon that Earl's role in the Whig reunion. *Whig Principles and Party Politics* (Manchester, 1975), p. xi.

[ABBREVIATIONS]

Althorp Papers	Althorp, Northamptonshire, England, Spencer Papers
Auckland	*Journal and Correspondence of William Eden, Lord Auckland,* ed. George Hogge (4 vols.; London, 1860–62)
Bodleian	Oxford, England, Bodleian Library
BM, Add. MSS.	London, England, British Museum, Additional Manuscripts
BRO	Aylesbury, England, Buckinghamshire Record Office
Castle Howard Papers	Castle Howard, Yorkshire, England, Carlisle Papers
Correspondence of Prince of Wales	*Correspondence of George, Prince of Wales,* ed. Arthur Aspinall (8 vols.; London, 1963–71)
Court and Cabinets of George III	Richard Plantagenet Temple Nugent Brydges Chandos Grenville, Second Duke of Buckingham and Chandos, *Memoirs of the Court and Cabinets of George the Third: From Original Family Documents* (2d ed., 4 vols.; London, 1853–56)
DRO	Exeter, England, Devonshire Record Office
DNB	*Dictionary of National Biography* (1st ed.; 1885–1901)

Dropmore   Great Britain, Parliament,
                               Historical Manuscripts Commission,
                               Walter Fitzpatrick, ed., *Report on the*
                               Manuscripts of J. B. Fortescue,
                               Preserved at Dropmore, Vol. I, 13th
                               appendix, pt. 3 (London, 1892).
                               Vol. II, 14th appendix, pt. 5
                               (London, 1894). Vols. III–IX
                               (London, 1899–1915).
                               Great Britain, Historical
                               Manuscripts Commission, Francis
                               Bickley and Walter Fitzpatrick, eds.,
                               Report on the Manuscripts of J. B.
                               Fortescue, Preserved at Dropmore,
                               Vol. X (London, 1927)

Duke   Durham, North Carolina, U.S.A.,
                               Duke University, Perkins
                               Library

Dunrobin Castle   Dunrobin Castle, Sutherland,
   Papers   Scotland, Sutherland Papers

Durham Papers   Durham, England, Durham
                               University, Grey of Howick Papers

ERO   Chelmsford, England,
                               Essex Record Office

Elton Hall   Elton Hall, Huntingdonshire,
   Papers   England, Proby Papers

HRO   Winchester, England,
                               Hampshire Record Office

HEH-STG   San Marino, California, U.S.A.,
                               Henry E. Huntington Library,
                               Stowe-Grenville Papers

HMC   Historical Manuscripts
                               Commission

JRL   Manchester, England, John
                               Rylands Library

Later Correspondence   *Later Correspondence of George III,*
   of George III   ed. Arthur Aspinall (5 vols.;
                               Cambridge, England, 1962–70)

Leeds Papers   Leeds, England, Sheepscar Library,
                               Canning (Harewood) Papers

LSE   London, England, London
                               School of Economics

Memoirs of the Regency	Richard Plantagenet Temple Nugent Brydges Chandos Grenville, Second Duke of Buckingham and Chandos, *Memoirs of the Court of England during the Regency, 1811–1820: From Original Family Documents* (London, 1856)
Memoirs of George IV	Richard Plantagenet Temple Nugent Brydges Chandos Grenville, Second Duke of Buckingham and Chandos, *Memoirs of the Court of George IV: From Original Family Documents* (London, 1859)
Namier and Brooke	Sir Lewis Namier and John Brooke, *The History of Parliament: The House of Commons, 1754–1790* (London, 1964)
NAM Papers	London, England, National Army Museum, Nugent Papers
NLI	Dublin, Ireland, National Library of Ireland
NLW	Aberyswyth, Wales, National Library of Wales
NRO	Northampton, England, Northamptonshire Record Office
Parl. Debates	Thomas Curson Hansard, ed., *The Parliamentary Debates*
Parl. History	William Cobbett, ed., *Cobbett's Parliamentary History of England: From the Earliest Period to the Year 1803*
PRO	London, England, Public Record Office
RO	Record Office
Sedgwick	Romney Sedgwick, *The History of Parliament: The House of Commons, 1715–1754* (New York, 1970)
Sheffield Papers	Sheffield, England, City Library, Wentworth Woodhouse Muniments, Fitzwilliam Papers

Spencer Bernard   Nether Winchendon,
    Papers   Buckinghamshire, England,
                                 Spencer Bernard Papers

SRO   Stafford, England,
                                 Staffordshire Record Office

UCNW   Bangor, Wales, University
                                 College of North Wales

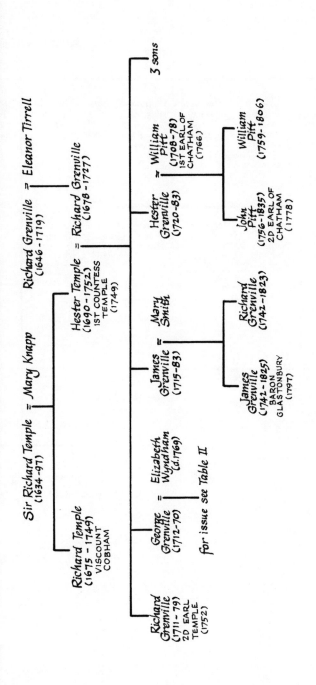

TABLE I

The Grenville and Temple Families
in the Eighteenth Century

Sir Richard Temple = Mary Knapp
(1634-97)

Richard Grenville = Eleanor Tirrell
(1646-1719)

Richard Temple
(1675-1749)
VISCOUNT
COBHAM

Hester Temple = Richard Grenville
(1690-1752)   (1678-1727)
1ST COUNTESS
TEMPLE
(1749)

Richard Grenville
(1711-79)
2D EARL
TEMPLE
(1752)

George Grenville = Elizabeth Wyndham
(1712-70)   (d.1769)

for issue see Table II

James Grenville = Mary Smith
(1715-83)

Hester Grenville = William Pitt
(1720-83)   (1708-78)
                    1ST EARL OF
                    CHATHAM
                    (1766)

3 sons

James Grenville
(1742-1825)
BARON
GLASTONBURY
(1797)

Richard Grenville
(1742-1823)

John Pitt
(1756-1835)
2D EARL OF
CHATHAM
(1778)

William Pitt
(1759-1806)

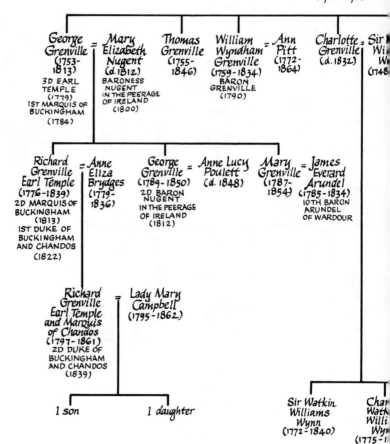

George Grenville
(1712 – 70)

George Grenville (1753-1813) 3D EARL TEMPLE (1779) 1ST MARQUIS OF BUCKINGHAM (1784) = Mary Elizabeth Nugent (d. 1812) BARONESS NUGENT IN THE PEERAGE OF IRELAND (1800)

Thomas Grenville (1755-1846)

William Wyndham Grenville (1759-1834) BARON GRENVILLE (1790) = Ann Pitt (1772-1864)

Charlotte Grenville (d. 1832) = Sir Wi W (1748

Richard Grenville Earl Temple (1776-1839) 2D MARQUIS OF BUCKINGHAM (1813) 1ST DUKE OF BUCKINGHAM AND CHANDOS (1822) = Anne Eliza Brydges (1779-1836)

George Grenville (1789-1850) 2D BARON NUGENT IN THE PEERAGE OF IRELAND (1812) = Anne Lucy Poulett (d. 1848)

Mary Grenville (1787-1854) = James Everard Arundel (1785-1834) 10TH BARON ARUNDEL OF WARDOUR

Richard Grenville Earl Temple and Marquis of Chandos (1797-1861) 2D DUKE OF BUCKINGHAM AND CHANDOS (1839) = Lady Mary Campbell (1795-1862)

Sir Watkin Williams Wynn (1772-1840)

Cha Wat Willi Wy (1775-1

1 son   1 daughter

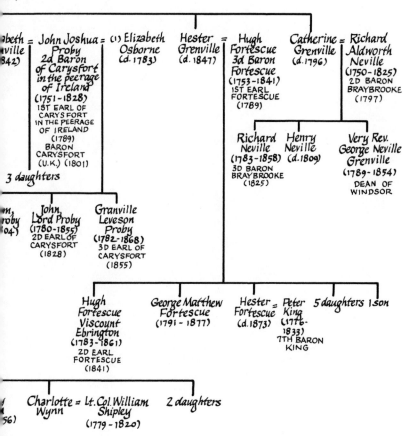

h Wyndham
769)

abeth = John Joshua = (1) Elizabeth
ville   Proby   Osborne
842)   2d Baron   (d. 1783)
      of Carysfort
      in the peerage
      of Ireland
      (1751-1828)
      1ST EARL OF
      CARYSFORT
      IN THE PEERAGE
      OF IRELAND
      (1789)
      BARON
      CARYSFORT
      (U.K.) (1801)

3 daughters

Hester = Hugh   Catherine = Richard
Grenville Fortescue   Grenville   Aldworth
(d. 1847) 3d Baron   (d. 1796)   Neville
      Fortescue   (1750-1825)
      (1753-1841)   2D BARON
      1ST EARL   BRAYBROOKE
      FORTESCUE   (1797)
      (1789)

      Richard Henry   Very Rev.
      Neville Neville   George Neville
      (1783-1858) (d.1809) Grenville
      3D BARON   (1789-1854)
      BRAYBROOKE   DEAN OF
      (1825)   WINDSOR

m,   John,   Granville
roby Lord Proby   Leveson
04) (1780-1855)   Proby
    2D EARL OF (1782-1868)
    CARYSFORT 3D EARL OF
    (1828)   CARYSFORT
            (1855)

Hugh   George Matthew Hester = Peter 5 daughters 1 son
Fortescue Fortescue   Fortescue King
Viscount (1791-1877)   (d.1873) (1776-
Ebrington   1833)
(1783-1861)   7TH BARON
2D EARL   KING
FORTESCUE
(1841)

Charlotte = Lt.Col.William 2 daughters
56)   Wynn   Shipley
           (1779-1820)

TABLE II
The Issue of George and Elizabeth Grenville

[THE GRENVILLITES, 1801–29]

[CHAPTER I]

The Grenville Family Connection

BETWEEN the middle of the eighteenth century and the first decade of the nineteenth, the three most visible English political families were the Pitts, the Foxes, and the Grenvilles. From within these families, two succeeding generations of politicians—the elder and the younger Pitt, Henry and Charles Fox, and George and William Grenville— seemed to belie the old superstition that fathers rarely pass on their abilities to their sons; though none of these sons had issue to challenge fortune a second time. The younger Pitt and Charles James Fox, as much as anyone, midwifed the birth of something resembling the nineteenth-century Tory and Whig parties and, even more consider- ably, represented in their persons the principles of conservatism and liberalism that are still dear to *homo politicus*. The Grenvilles, on the contrary, nursed the origin of no party and in their activities, accom- plishments, and failures basically serve to remind one—not always fairly—of more traditionally oriented politics based on family loyalty and wealth; for to all Grenvilles the family and not the Burkean concept of desirability of party was usually paramount.

The Grenvilles of Wotton, Buckinghamshire, were a not particularly noted middling gentry family until, in 1710, an advantageous marriage took place between Richard Grenville and Hester Temple, the ultimate heiress of the Temples of Stowe, Buckinghamshire. When their eldest son, Richard Grenville, second Earl Temple (1711–79), inherited the not inconsiderable estates and fortune of his mother's family in 1752, he was reputedly the richest man in England.[1] This Temple, however, had no children; and, upon his death in 1779, the eldest son and namesake of his brother George, the first Grenville Prime Minister (1763–65), inherited the lot, including the title of third Earl Temple.

The elder George Grenville, in 1749, married Elizabeth Wyndham,

1. Sedgwick, II, 85. For information on the first greatly active political generation of the Grenvilles, see Lewis Wiggin, *The Faction of Cousins* (New Haven, 1958).

the daughter of a prominent Tory, Sir William Wyndham. Years later, after the death of Elizabeth Grenville in 1769, her youngest and most illustrious son, a second Grenville Prime Minister (1806–7), paid tribute to the concern she had expended in supervising the education of her children in spite of a "long and painful disease."[2] George Grenville's death followed his wife's by a year. The couple left seven surviving children: three sons and four daughters.

The sons—George (1753–1813), who was heir to his uncle Temple's peerage and property; Thomas (1755–1846); and William Wyndham (1759–1834)—trod their father's path to Eton[3] and Christ Church, Oxford. George was elected to the House of Commons for Bucks in 1774. That same year Thomas entered Lincoln's Inn; but law was apparently not his forte, and in 1778 he joined the army as an Ensign in the Coldstream Guards. William, who was the only one of the three to receive a B.A. from Christ Church, entered Lincoln's Inn in 1780.

Each of the four Grenville daughters was wed: the eldest, Charlotte (d. 1832), in 1771, to Sir Watkin Williams Wynn of Wynnstay in Denbighshire; the youngest, Catherine (d. 1796), in 1780, to Richard Aldworth Neville (later the second Baron Braybrooke) of Billingbear and Stanlake, Berkshire, whose chief seat after 1797 was Audley End, Essex; the third, Hester (1758–1847), in 1782, to Hugh Fortescue of Castle Hill, Devonshire, heir to his father, the second Baron Fortescue; and the second, Elizabeth (d. 1842), in 1787, to John Joshua Proby, second Baron Carysfort of Elton Hall, Huntingdonshire, an Irish peer.

The extended Grenville family was close-knit and visited each other frequently. Thus, for almost half a century there was a semiconstant progress to and from the Wynns at Wynnstay, the Fortescues at Castle Hill, the Probys at Elton Hall, the Nevilles at Audley End, the Grenvilles proper at Dropmore and Butleigh, and, as a sort of grand finale, Stowe. Perhaps the loss of their parents while they were still in or near childhood caused the Grenville children to cleave to one another in a more than normal manner. At least one member of the family, Lord Carysfort, felt that the coldness and reserve for which the entire Grenville family was so justly celebrated proceeded not from arrogance but from shyness at having to associate with the world in general rather than

2. Duke, Boconnoc-Hamilton Papers, Box 150, Lord Grenville, "Commentaries of My Own Political Life and of Public Transaction Connected With It" (copy).

3. The importance of the old school tie in determining the composition of political groupings has often been recognized. Contemporaries of George and Thomas Grenville at Eton who later acted with them in politics included R. A. Neville, H. Fortescue, G. C. Berkeley, and W. Young. William Grenville's two closest friendships at Eton were with the future Marquis Wellesley and J. Newport. Richard Arthur Austen-Leigh, ed., *The Eton College Register, 1753–1790* (Eton, 1921).

just the family. He warned his daughter about "the Abuse which flows from so good a Source. The great love of the Grenvilles, Brothers & Sisters, for each other, has led them to exclude the World a great deal too much."[4]

As is not unnatural at any time, and most emphatically was not in the patriarchal world of the eighteenth-century British landed classes, the social camaraderie among the Grenvilles had its counterpart in the political activities of the family. The nucleus of the Grenvillite political group was always the basic family unit—the sons, sons-in-law, grand-children, and nephew (in the case of James Grenville, Baron Glaston-bury) of George and Elizabeth Grenville. This meant, in effect, that a relatively numerous group could normally be counted upon to follow the political line of the first Marquis of Buckingham (the title attained by the younger George Grenville in 1784) and William Wyndham Grenville, Baron Grenville.

There were, however, exceptions. Thomas Grenville and Sir Watkin Wynn supported the Whigs during the 1780s. Lords Braybrooke and Glastonbury, perhaps in gratitude for their recent peerages, followed Pitt's politics from 1801 to 1806. But looking at the period from 1780 to 1817 as a whole (or in the case of the Wynns to 1825), what is remarkable is not the occasional truancy but rather the general political cooperation that existed within the family circle—a cooperation which made the Grenvillites the most successful family-oriented group of the period.

1. *George Grenville, Third Earl Temple and*
First Marquis of Buckingham

George Grenville (MP for Bucks, 1774–79), the third Earl Temple after 1779 and the first Marquis of Buckingham after 1784, was the touchiest and most pompous nobleman in Britain. He irritated most of the leading politicians of the period by his uncanny ability to allow small, even trivial issues, to affect his judgment.[5] During his short second tenure as Lord Lieutenant of Ireland (1787–89), he threatened three times to resign over a minor patronage question. He harassed Pitt unmercifully during his first Ministry, expecting him to drop all to attend to his petty desires. He threatened to withdraw his support from

4. Elton Hall Papers, Carysfort to Lady Charlotte Proby, March, 1812 (copy).
5. He was not universally popular at Eton either, and one of his younger contem-poraries found him full of "false pomp and pride . . . obstinate and passionate." *Auckland,* Cooke to Eden, July 25, 1782, I, 333.

his own brother in February, 1806, only a few days after Lord Grenville went to the Treasury, because he, unlike the Prime Minister, was not made an assistant mourner at Pitt's funeral.[6] He took offense at such matters as the familiarity of style used by the Home Secretary in addressing him as Irish Lord Lieutenant.[7] The story of the mad George III, in November, 1788, remarking in one of his soliloquies, "I hate nobody, why should anybody hate me?" and then reflecting a moment and adding "I beg pardon, I do hate the Marquis of Buckingham"[8] is notorious and, even if apocryphal, no doubt accurately describes the feelings of the King.

There has been a continuing and controversial literature on the subject of the resignation of Temple (as he then was) as Secretary of State for Foreign Affairs from Pitt's new and seemingly precarious Government in December, 1783. Yet, whether the action was taken from a cowardly fear of impeachment[9] or was a prudent recognition of his own liability to the Prime Minister,[10] George III, at least, had no doubt that his conduct was "base."[11] A few days after his leave-taking, Temple wrote to Pitt and Sydney, the Home Secretary, to request a mark of approbation of his earlier Irish Lieutenancy (1782–83).[12] Sydney, at least, was disgusted at the request and wrote Temple's successor in Dublin of the Earl's "egregious absurdity."[13]

Yet, absurdity or not, within the year Temple received the Marquisate of Buckingham and straightaway began to press for the Garter and a dukedom.[14] The order was forthcoming in 1786, but despite frequent solicitation during the remainder of Pitt's first Ministry for, at best, an elevation in the English and, at worst, an Irish dukedom, the Mar-

---

6. HEH-STG, Box 174, Grenville to Buckingham, Feb. 20, 1806.

7. *Court and Cabinets of George III*, Sydney to Buckingham, Feb. 6, 1788, I, 353–54.

8. *Auckland*, Sheffield to Eden, Nov. 22, 1788, II, 244.

9. Arthur Aspinall in his preface to *Later Correspondence of George III*, I, xxvii.

10. E. Anthony Smith, "Earl Temple's Resignation, 22 December 1783," *Historical Journal*, VI, No. 1 (1963), 91–97. See also in the same journal: P. J. Jupp, "Earl Temple's Resignation and the Question of a Dissolution in December 1783," XV, No. 2(1972), 309–13; Paul Kelly, "The Pitt-Temple Administration: 19–22 December 1783," XVII, No. 1 (1974), 301–28.

11. *Later Correspondence of George III*, George III to Pitt, April 12, 1789, I, 408.

12. *Court and Cabinets of George III*, Temple to Pitt, Dec. 29, 1783, I, 291–93.

13. Great Britain, Parliament, Historical Manuscripts Commission, H. C. Maxwell Lyte, ed., *Report on the Manuscripts of His Grace the Duke of Rutland Preserved at Belvoir Castle* (4 vols.; London, 1888–1905), Sydney to Rutland, March 3, 1784, III, 78.

14. *Dropmore*: Temple to Grenville, Oct. 3, 1784, I, 239; Grenville to Temple, Oct. 7 or 8, 1784, I, 240. HEH-STG, Box 12, Grenville to Buckingham, n.d.

quis of Buckingham remained just that.[15] He did, however, finally prevail upon Pitt and Lord Grenville to persuade the King to grant his wife an Irish Baronage with a remainder to their second son, Lord George Grenville.[16]

George Grenville (the future Buckingham) had, in 1775, married Mary Elizabeth Nugent, daughter and heiress of the Anglo-Irish poet-politician Robert Nugent, who was created Earl Nugent of Ireland in 1776. A Roman Catholic convert since 1772, Mary Elizabeth brought the seeds of religious tension into her new family. The three children, two sons and a daughter, born to this union were educated in their father's Anglican faith. However, three years before her mother's death in 1809, the daughter, Lady Mary Grenville, was received into the Church of Rome.

The Buckinghamshire property, which was chiefly pasture and butter-producing acreage over which the senior Grenvilles presided, included estates yielding an annual value (by an 1823 estimate) of £23,927.[17] The Stowe Grenvilles also owned property in Northamptonshire, valued by the same estimate at £2,608; in Warwickshire, at £4,172; and in Somersetshire, at £5,581.[18] The first Marquis of Buckingham in 1788 inherited from his father-in-law, Earl Nugent, estates heavily burdened with annuities in Ireland, Essex, and Cornwall.[19] By 1823, the Irish estates, located in counties Clare, Longford, and Westmeath, were worth around £6,939 per annum.[20] The Gosfield estate in Essex in 1788 was not worth more than £1,500 per annum, subject to £700 in annuities. It remained in the Grenville family until 1824, inhabited by émigré nuns in the 1790s and for eighteen months in 1807 and 1808 by Louis XVIII. In 1824, the first Duke of Buckingham succeeded in selling it and purchasing additional Bucks property, which, he claimed, raised his annual rent roll by £3,000.[21] The Cornish estates included some 1,836 acres yielding

15. *Dropmore*, Buckingham to Grenville: Oct. 3, 1789, I, 526–27; July 21, 1800, VI, 273–74.

16. Ibid., Buckingham to Grenville, July 21, 1800, VI, 273–74; *Later Correspondence of George III*, Pitt to George III, Dec. 17, 1800, III, 452.

17. Spencer Bernard Papers, PFD6/36.

18. Ibid.

19. *Dropmore*, Buckingham to Grenville: Oct. 18, 1788, I, 358; Oct. 29, 1788, I, 360.

20. HEH-STG, Box 11, Temple to Buckingham, Jan. 22, 1813; Spencer Bernard Papers, PFD6/36.

21. *Dropmore*, Buckingham to Grenville, Oct. 29, 1788, I, 360; BM, Wellesley Papers, Add. MSS. 37310, Buckingham to Wellesley, Oct. 9, 1810; *Correspondence of Charlotte Grenville, Lady Williams Wynn*, ed. Rachel Leighton (London, 1920), Lady Wynn to Henry Wynn, Oct. 9, 1824, pp. 323–24.

£1,386 per annum and some nonproductive copper mines. Their prime importance lay in the political control they permitted over St. Mawes borough.[22]

As early as 1786, when the lady in question was six years old, negotiations had commenced to wed Earl Temple, the heir of the first Marquis of Buckingham, to Anne Eliza Brydges, daughter and heiress of the third and last Duke of Chandos.[23] The wedding took place in due course in 1796. The Chandos seat was at Avington, north of Winchester, in Hampshire. In 1805 the rental value of Lady Temple's Hampshire property was £2,789, but fifteen years later her husband purchased additional land in that county, so that by the 1830s the Hants estates were producing £5,846 per annum.[24] The Chandos interest also included some £4,000 of annual rents in county Queens;[25] £3,627 in Somersetshire;[26] and £4,000 in Jamaica.[27] Both the Grenville and Brydges (Chandos) families owned property in the London area: Buckingham House, calculated at bringing £32,000 on the market in 1827; Chandos House, rented at £1,000 per annum around 1823; and assorted odds and ends to over £4,000 rental per annum in Middlesex.[28]

In 1798, the English and Irish estates of the first Marquis of Buckingham were charged with annual payments of £7,400, effected by the late Lord Temple, his uncle, George Grenville, his father, Lord Nugent, his father-in-law, and himself.[29] Out of the Bucks estates, Thomas Grenville had a life annuity of £600, Lord Grenville one of £500 (which Lady Grenville received after his death),[30] Lord Nugent (Buckingham's younger son) one of £1,500,[31] and Lady Arundel (Buckingham's daughter) one of £750.[32] The more impecunious

---

22. HEH-STG, Box 225, Ledbrooke to Robson, Jan. 3 and 17, 1830; David Spring, *The English Landed Estate in the Nineteenth Century: Its Administration* (Baltimore, 1963), p. 16.

23. *Dropmore*, Buckingham to Grenville, May 7, 1786, I, 259.

24. HRO: 5M43/63. "Rental of the Hampshire Estates in 1805"; 5M48/67, "An Estimate of the Annual Income of the Avington Estate," Oct. 5, 1832.

25. HEH-STG, Box 11, Temple to Buckingham, Jan. 22, 1813.

26. Spencer Bernard Papers, PFD6/36.

27. HEH-STG, Box 11, Temple to Buckingham, Jan. 22, 1813.

28. HEH-STG, Box 153, Sloane to the Duchess, Aug. 24, 1827; Spencer Bernard Papers, PFD6/36.

29. BM, Thomas Grenville Papers, Add. MSS. 41851, Buckingham to Thomas Grenville, Feb. 3, 1798.

30. Ibid., Jan. 31, 1798; Add. MSS. 47458A, George Fortescue to Buckingham, Dec. 31, 1846.

31. HEH-STG, Box 335, Nugent to Buckingham, Dec. 29, 1841.

32. F. M. L. Thompson, "The End of a Great Estate," *Economic History Review*, 2d ser., VIII, No. 1 (1955), p. 43.

among the Grenvilles were further aided by outright gifts. Thomas Grenville received £600 per annum,[33] Lord Nugent, £1,000 per annum,[34] and Lady Mary Grenville, Lady Arundel, £25,000 as part of her dowery.[35]

In toto, the annual rental value of the Stowe Grenvilles' estates around 1823 was £64,051.[36] The property was valuable, not only in the money raised from rents that (coupled with the lucrative Grenville sinecure, the Tellership of the Exchequer) enabled the family to revel in a high standard of living, but also in the direct political influence it gave the Grenvilles over nominations to the House of Commons.

Stowe was, of course, after 1749, the capital mansion of the senior branch of the Grenville family.[37] The estate had formed the patrimony of the Temple family since the reign of Elizabeth, and the eighteenth century saw its architectural apotheosis, as successive Cobhams, Temples, and Grenvilles made it a fit habitation for a family that believed it would have mounted the throne of England if the will of Henry VIII had been recognized. Horace Walpole saw a pomposity or lack of taste both in the grounds with their temples, memorials, and obelisks and in the mansion, which possessed a frontage of 1,000 feet. Yet even Walpole found that "the vastness pleases me more than I can defend." Generations of British and French royal families, famous travellers, and architects came to marvel and to be entertained by successive owners of Stowe. But the political aspect was seldom absent even from the architecture. Walpole compared old Cobham's Temple of Friendship with yet another Temple—that of Janus—"sometimes open to war, and sometimes shut up in factious cabals."[38]

2. *Thomas Grenville*

Already an Ensign in the Coldstream Guards, Thomas Grenville succeeded his elder brother as MP for Bucks in 1779 when George was

33. BRO, Fremantle Papers, 51, Buckingham to Fremantle, Nov. 20, 1789.

34. HEH-STG, Box 335, Nugent to Buckingham, Dec. 29, 1841.

35. BM, Thomas Grenville Papers, Add. MSS. 41851, Buckingham to Thomas Grenville, Oct. 17, 1810; HEH-STG: Box 4, East to the Duchess, March 11, 1829; Box 225, Ledbrooke to Robson, Jan. 17, 1830. In 1839, out of the Bucks estates the first Marquis's two surviving sisters, Lady Fortescue and Lady Carysfort, had outstanding portions of £10,000 each, as had his two late sisters, Lady Wynn and Catherine Neville. Thompson, "End of a Great Estate," p. 43.

36. Spencer Bernard Papers, PFD6/36.

37. For a description of the magnificence of Stowe, see William Page, ed., *A History of the County of Buckingham*, Victoria History of the Counties of England (4 vols.; London, 1908–27), IV, 229–32.

38. Clement Shorter, *Highways and Byways in Buckinghamshire* (London, 1910), pp. 265–70.

called to the Lords. He was again returned at the general election of 1780. Thomas was an early partisan of Fox and the Rockingham Whigs, coming into Parliament at a period of some cooperation between those opposing Lord North's Ministry. When the youngest Grenville brother, William Wyndham, entered Parliament in February, 1782, the three brothers were united politically for the last time before the 1790s and the crisis occasioned by the French Revolution. It was this opposition to the North Ministry and the American war that, on the surface at least, provided Thomas with a rationale to abandon—permanently, as it turned out—his military career. Yet, considering Thomas's developing scholarly predilections and his retiring disposition, it is difficult to envision him as enjoying a military role. Lieutenant Grenville resigned from the army in February, 1780, telling the House, on Fox's prodding, that because of political bias on the Government's part he had four times been refused the normal promotion, even when the Duke of Rutland raised a corps and offered him a captaincy.[39]

When North resigned in 1782 and Fox became Foreign Secretary in the Rockingham Administration, he sent Thomas Grenville as his representative to Paris for the Anglo-American peace negotiations. The Fox-Grenville attachment caused a definite coolness between Thomas and Temple, who unlike Thomas, not only supported Shelburne as Prime Minister following Rockingham's death, but was also under pressure to succeed the outgoing Fox as Foreign Secretary. Had this office materialized and Thomas persevered in his intention to resign with Fox, it would have placed Temple in an invidious position both as a politician and as a man. And Temple had little patience with a brother who placed private friendship before fraternal ties.[40]

Thomas Grenville's friendship with Fox was stronger than his relationship with his elder brother and was only broken by the storms arising from the French Revolution. If Fox's 1783 India Bill had gone through, Thomas was probably slated to go to India as Governor General.[41] As it happened, however, rather than assuming an office on the Ganges, he became, in essence if not strictly in fact, one of Fox's Martyrs and was out of Parliament until the general election of 1790. In December, 1783, Thomas had voted as a Bucks MP for a motion

39. *Annual Register*, LXXXVIII (1847), 305–12 passim; John Debrett, ed., *The Parliamentary Register*, XVII (April 11, 1780), 135–36.

40. *Court and Cabinets of George III:* Thomas Grenville to Temple, July 9, 1782, I, 57–58; Temple to Thomas Grenville, July 12, 1782, I, 59–63.

41. See: Sir Denis Le Marchant, *Memoir of John Charles Viscount Althorp, Third Earl Spencer* (London, 1876), p. 22; Elizabeth Jane Savile, *The Rt. Hon. Thomas Grenville* (n.p., 1908), p. 7; *Annual Register*, LXXXVIII (1847), 306.

implying censure of Temple for relaying messages from the King to the Lords on the East India Bill. Temple wrote his brother, not in the heat of anger, but after a year's reflection, that "when you joined in the vote which impeached my honour, and possibly my life, you forgot the feelings of a brother, and dissolved the ties between us. I loathe the looking back, still less do I mean to reproach: my heart is still alive to those feelings which nature and religion dictate to me."[42]

In 1790, Fitzwilliam used his influence with another Whig devotee to procure Thomas a parliamentary borough, Aldeburgh.[43] Once returned to the House of Commons, Thomas's prominent younger brother, Lord Grenville, used him as a trusted go-between in March, 1791, over discussions on the advisability of a coalition between Pitt's Ministry and the Foxite Opposition—the type of role that Thomas played with much skill after 1803 but proved abortive in 1791.[44]

Thomas, a man of a deeply conservative nature, was one of the Whigs most susceptible to anti-French sentiments after 1789. Loyalty to the political friends with whom he had acted for so many years precluded any desire on his part for a precipitous dissolution of the Whig party; thus, despite his agreement with Burke's antirevolutionary principles, he thoroughly reprobated the great man's habit of denouncing France in the Commons without consultation with Fox and other Whigs.[45] Throughout 1792 and 1793, however, Thomas increasingly made public his dissatisfaction with the foreign and domestic repercussions of the Revolution.[46] Finally, on December 29, 1793, Grenville sat down and wrote to Fox, "with an impression of greater uneasiness and anxiety than has ever yet belonged to any letter from me to you," on their points of difference,

the one is respecting the war with France which you condemn and oppose

42. Namier and Brooke, III, 584; *Court and Cabinets of George III,* Buckingham to Thomas Grenville, Feb. 1, 1785, I, 309–10.

43. Donald E. Ginter, ed., *Whig Organization in the General Election of 1790* (Berkeley, 1967), Portland to Adam, Oct. 13, 1789, p. 104; HEH-STG, LIOF2, memorandum of Thomas Grenville, Nov., 1789.

44. HEH-STG, LIOF2, memorandum of Thomas Grenville, March 8 and 13, 1791. The negotiations broke down ostensibly over Pitt's remaining at the head of the Government. Lord Grenville had envisioned Lord John Cavendish at the Exchequer, Fox at the Admiralty or as a Secretary of State, and possibly Fitzwilliam as Lord President—all three in the Cabinet. He and Pitt were to serve as Secretaries of State under Chatham at the Treasury. BRO, Grenville Papers, 632, Grenville to Thomas Grenville, March 28, 1791.

45. Sheffield Papers, FII5d–55–1, Thomas Grenville to Fitzwilliam, April 22, 1791.

46. *Later Correspondence of George III,* Pitt to George III: April 30, 1792, I, 590; May 26, 1792, I, 596; Jan. 5, 1793, I, 650; Feb. 13, 1793, II, 6.

while I think it the greatest of all duties to support and maintain it to the
utmost; the other respects an apprehension which I entertain of there
being principles & designs in this country adverse to the constitution of
it, which makes me feel it to be my duty to resist whatever can give to
such designs either strength, opportunity or countenance while you on
the other hand believe in no such designs & believe the danger to arise
from there being too little of free inquiry & resistance in the minds of the
people of the country.[47]

In the summer of 1794, with the accession of the Portland Whigs
to the Government, Thomas Grenville went, with his closest friend
and fellow Portland Whig, Earl Spencer, to Vienna as Minister Extraordinary. In 1799, he served on a special Embassy to Berlin. He refused the Chief Secretaryship of Ireland in 1798.[48] Had negotiations
commenced with France at Lunéville after the battle of Marengo in
1800, it was the decided wish of George III that Thomas Grenville
should conduct them.[49]

Thomas Grenville was, for well over sixty years, one of the best
regarded figures in the upper reaches of English society. His amiability
considerably eased the delicate social relations between the Grenvillites
and Foxites after the union of 1804. He had been an adventurous youth
who had taken part in the Keppel riots; but decades before Greville
described him as such in 1838, he had already mellowed into a mild,
refined, and venerable man.[50] Thomas was a bachelor, and some of his
friends surmised that he had no sexual interest in women.[51] Greville
recounts that Thomas Grenville in his youth, like so many of his Whig
contemporaries, had fallen in love with Spencer's sister, Georgianna,
Duchess of Devonshire, and remained unmarried because he could find
no other woman to compare with her.[52] Whatever Thomas's sexual
preferences, the love and attention that under other circumstances
might have been expended on wife or children was in his case poured out
upon his books. Indeed, his chief interest, even before his political
retirement in 1809, was literary; and by the time of his death he had

47. BM, Thomas Grenville Papers, Add. MSS. 42058, Thomas Grenville to Fox,
Dec. 29, 1793 (copy).
48. *Correspondence of Charles, First Marquis Cornwallis*, ed. Charles Ross (2d ed.;
London, 1859), Thomas Grenville to Cornwallis, Nov. 27, 1798, III, 9.
49. *Later Correspondence of George III*, George III to Grenville: July 17, 1800, III,
376; Aug. 30, 1800, III, 405–6.
50. Charles Fulke Cavendish Greville, *The Greville Memoirs, 1814–1860*, ed. Lytton
Strachey and Roger Fulford (London, 1938): III, 78–80; IV, 43.
51. *The Diaries of Sylvester Douglas, Lord Glenbervie*, ed. Francis Bickley (London,
1928), I, 5–6.
52. Greville, *Memoirs*, V, 366–68.

accumulated a library of over 20,000 volumes, its worth computed at over £50,000. The library, left in Thomas's will to the British Museum, included the second Caxton edition of Chaucer's *Canterbury Tales,* the folio copy of the first edition (1623) of Shakespeare's collected works, a 1469 edition of Livy that may have belonged to Pope Alexander VI, numerous Homers, scarce Spanish and Italian poems and romances, and invaluable early editions of Ariosto.[53]

3. *William Wyndham Grenville, Baron Grenville*

When William Grenville became the Chief Secretary in Lord Temple's Irish Administration in September, 1782, he assumed a post that, with the permanent residence of the Lord Lieutenant in Ireland, had grown in political importance, an eventuality that his predecessor William Eden was one of the first to grasp.[54] William Grenville, who was twenty-three, had been in the Commons only since February, and inevitably his lack of experience as a "man of business" drew some adverse comment.[55] The Temple viceroyalty lasted less than a year. The general thread of a liberal policy, at a time when the Renunciation question was agitating the Dublin scene, is distinct on the part of both brothers and clearly points toward their relatively enlightened Irish views in 1801 and thereafter.[56] Grenville resigned his post with Temple on the advent of the Fox-North coalition and returned to Lincoln's Inn.

During the early 1780s, both William and Temple were coming more and more into the orbit of their first cousin, William Pitt. The origin of the personal relationships between the children of George Grenville and those of Lord Chatham is somewhat difficult to document exactly. Grenville and Chatham had not been political allies during the boys' formative years, and they had not attended the same schools. Lord Holland, writing many years later, stated that Pitt knew nothing of his first cousins until they came into Parliament; and he mentioned that Thomas Grenville told him he had never been in Pitt's company until 1793, which Holland admitted "seems incredible." Lord Erskine told

53. Savile, *Thomas Grenville,* pp. 7–9.
54. Edith M. Johnston, *Great Britain and Ireland, 1760–1800* (Edinburgh, 1963), pp. 34–44 passim.
55. *Auckland,* Cooke to Eden, Oct. 16, 1782, I, 336; Great Britain, Parliament, Historical Manuscripts Commission, *Report on the Manuscripts in Various Collections,* Vol. VI: *Manuscripts of H. V. Knox, Esq.* (London, 1909), Sackville to Knox, n.d., p. 187.
56. *Court and Cabinets of George III,* Grenville to Temple: Nov. 30, 1782, I, 70–72; Dec. 7, 1782, I, 83–84; Dec. 15, 1782, I, 87.

Holland that once when the young William Grenville entered Alice's Coffee House, Pitt did not know his identity.[57] Pitt never visited Stowe before July, 1783. In 1780, both Pitt and William Grenville (as well as three later Grenvillites: Althorp, Euston, and Robert Smith) were associated with Goosetree's Club, and it was possibly in these environs that they embarked upon that reading of Adam Smith which was so to color their subsequent economic thinking.[58]

William's swift ascent in Pitt's Ministry was probably retarded by the fact that he sat for an expensive county constituency and thus could not afford those continual reelections upon taking a new office that were demanded by the Act of 1707. In 1784, he was made a Paymaster General (1784–89) and a member of both the Boards of Control (1784–93) and Trade (1784–89). He served as Vice President of the Board of Trade under Hawkesbury (1786–89) and succeeded Sydney as President of the Board of Control (1790–93). He was Speaker of the House of Commons for five months in 1789, resigning in June to enter the Cabinet as Home Secretary. On November 25, 1790, he was called to the Lords as Baron Grenville to take the lead in that House, and seven months later he succeeded the Duke of Leeds at the Foreign Office.[59]

In 1792, Lord Grenville married Anne Pitt,[60] daughter of Thomas Pitt, first Baron Camelford, owner of the Boconnoc estates in north-western Cornwall. At the time of his marriage, Grenville had a private fortune worth £30,000 or rather £1,350 per annum, as well as a sinecure, the Rangership of Parks, valued at about £1,000 per annum. Thomas Grenville stated that Camelford gave Anne a marriage settlement of £20,000 down and £11,000 at his death.[61] A year before his

57. Henry Richard Vassall Fox, Third Baron Holland, *Memoirs of the Whig Party during My Time*, ed. Henry Edward Vassall Fox, Fourth Baron Holland (2 vols.; London, 1852–54), II, 43.

58. John Ehrman, *The Younger Pitt: The Years of Acclaim* (London, 1969), pp. 106–7, 110, 132.

59. For an account of Grenville at the Home Office, see R. R. Nelson, *The Home Office, 1782–1801* (Durham, North Carolina, 1969). For Grenville's tenure at the Foreign Office, see Ephraim Douglass Adams, *The Influence of Grenville on Pitt's Foreign Policy, 1787–1798* (Washington, D.C., 1904). Grenville was created a peer solely to undertake the leadership of the Lords. This seems to have marked the institutionalization of that position. J. C. Sainty, "The Origins of the Leadership of the House of Lords," *Bulletin of the Institute of Historical Research*, Vol. XLVII, No. 115 (1974), pp. 62–63.

60. According to Thomas Grenville, Camelford wanted his daughter to marry William Pitt and Grenville was a second choice. Anne, on whatever grounds, initially refused William Grenville. HEH-STG, LIOF2, memorandum of Thomas Grenville, Aug. 23 and Sept. 8, 1790.

61. *Dropmore*, Buckingham to Grenville, Dec. 15, 1791, II, 240; HEH-STG, LIOF2, memorandum of Thomas Grenville, Aug. 23, 1790.

marriage, with Buckingham's aid, Grenville purchased the six-hundred-acre Dropmore estate near Burnham in southern Bucks.[62] In 1804, the second Lord Camelford was killed in a duel; and his sister, Lady Grenville, inherited the Boconnoc estates and Camelford House in London.

William Grenville was not a popular or well-liked politician. William Cobbett, the publicist and political activist, who hated all Grenvilles, related a story that the Baron was so stiff that he refused to allow a tailor to touch him when being measured for clothes.[63] Such hyperbole, related through the medium of the *Weekly Political Register,* must have sounded a responsive cord in many of Cobbett's more conservative contemporaries, for Grenville's personality struck many as cold and reserved. Unlike Pitt he does not seem to have had an intimate circle of friends with whom he could boisterously open up; and, compared with Fox, Holland, or Canning, he was positively morose. Tierney, indeed, thought him dull.[64] None doubted his extraordinary talents (like his father's) for business or finance or his ability to see to the core of the great issues of the day; but, not only his reserve, but what many thought was obstinacy put people off. George III, who had a longer political memory than most, compared him with his father, in that "George Grenville never could be reasoned out of or driven from any point; that Lord Grenville takes up his opinions entirely from himself and never will listen to arguments against them."[65]

A devotee of the solitary out-of-doors life, Grenville preferred nursing trees, gardens, and horses to the camaraderie derived from political activities.[66] His love of Greek scholarship was the polestar of his life, and he was as at home in discussing the character of Medea or his admiration for Sophocles[67] as in the interstices of the Irish question or cash payments. Between April, 1801, and April, 1802, a time of extensive political activity connected with the peace of Amiens, he read the *Illiad* twice in Greek with, as he put it, "considerable attention," as

62. *Dropmore,* Buckingham to Grenville, Dec. 15, 1791, II, 240.

63. *Cobbett's Weekly Political Register,* Vol. 77, No. 6 (Aug. 11, 1832).

64. BM, Holland House Papers, Add. MSS. 51585, Tierney to Lady Holland, Aug. 24, 1813.

65. *Diaries of Glenbervie,* I, 149–50.

66. *Auckland,* Eden to Auckland, Autumn, 1807, IV, 314; Emma Eleanor Elizabeth (Hylsop) Elliot-Murray-Kynynmound, Countess of Minto, *The Life and Letters of Sir Gilbert Elliot, First Earl of Minto* (London, 1874), Minto to Lady Minto, Aug. 12, 1805, III, 357–58; *Correspondence of Prince of Wales,* Princess Elizabeth to Prince, Sept. 11, 1808, VI, 309.

67. Duke, Boconnoc-Hamilton Papers, Grenville to De Lewas, March 20, 1809 (copy).

well as the fourteen first books of the *Odyssey* once. Grenville was not a
man who in his correspondence with family, friends, or political
acquaintances dwelt, like Wilberforce or Gladstone, upon personal
religious convictions. But his private journal makes clear that he
combined his rigorous adherence to secular Greek literature with Len-
ten and Passiontide readings from the Greek New Testament.[68]

Occasionally another side of this reserved and careworn man becomes
evident. When at Oxford, Grenville was said to have gutted a man's
room in four and a half minutes for a wager.[69] And when Richard Colley
Wellesley, then Earl of Mornington, his dearest friend since their Eton
days, was absent on the continent in 1791 for reasons of health,
Grenville visited his several young illegitimate children, despite the
fact that Mornington had never mentioned their existence to him. The
Earl was duly grateful, as his own brother, Wellesley Pole, would have
nothing to do with them.[70]

4. *The Extended Family*

Charlotte Grenville, the eldest daughter of George and Elizabeth
Grenville, in 1771 married Sir Watkin Williams Wynn (1748–89) of
Wynnstay in Denbighshire. Wynn, who was the representative of one
of the leading landowning families in north Wales, served as MP for his
home county from 1774 until his death. Like the Grenvilles, he stood in
opposition to North from 1778 to 1782; and, unlike most of his wife's
English relations, he opposed both the Shelburne and Pitt
Administrations.[71] His two sons, however, Sir Watkin (MP for Denbighshire, 1796–1840) and Charles Williams (MP for Montgomeryshire, 1799–1850), were firm Grenvillites. However, Sir Watkin, a
pleasure-seeking, irresponsible youth and a friend of Beau Brummell's,
was rightfully never taken seriously by the Westminster political community, which gave him the nickname of "Bubble."[72] Charles, on the

68. Ibid., Grenville's Journal, 1801–2, M.F. reel 16.

69. John Cam Hobhouse, First Baron Broughton, *Recollection of a Long Life*, ed.
Charlotte Carleton (Hobhouse), Baroness Dorchester (6 vols.; New York, 1909–11),
III, 52.

70. *Dropmore*, Mornington to Grenville, Jan. 18, 1791, II, 18.

71. Namier and Brooke, III, 672; Ian R. Christie, *The End of North's Ministry,
1780–1782* (London, 1958), p. 403.

72. *The History of White's with the Betting Books from 1743 to 1878 and a List of
Members from 1736 to 1892* (1892), I, 173–74; *Lord Granville Leveson Gower, First Earl
Granville: Private Correspondence, 1781 to 1821*, ed. Castalia Rosalind (Campbell)
Leveson-Gower, Countess Granville (London, 1916), Leveson Gower to Susan Leveson
Gower, Nov. 5, 1792, I, 56–57; Great Britain, Historical Manuscripts Commission,

other hand, was a Grenville by temperament and intellect, as well as by his political views, which were influenced by his maternal uncles, Thomas and William.

Richard Aldworth Neville (1750–1825) of Stanlake and Billingbear, Berkshire, married Catherine Grenville in 1780. From the first Baron Braybrooke (d. 1797) he inherited the peerage and the Griffin family estates, which centered at Audley End in Essex.[73] Neville, despite his Northite politics, was returned as MP for his antiwar brother-in-law's borough of Buckingham at the general election of 1780. He resigned in February, 1782, over "a difference in public politics" concerning support of North's Government; although, as Buckingham later put it, they continued "good friends."[74] By 1784 and the advent of Pitt's Ministry, the political differences with the Grenvilles came to an end. There was always a sense, however, in which Neville (or Braybrooke, as he was known after 1797) was less a member of the Grenvillite connection than his other brothers-in-law, Fortescue and Carysfort, and between 1801 and 1806 he firmly opposed their political course. As a result, Buckingham was not concerned with furthering Neville's career; and when Neville applied to Pitt in 1791 for the Lieutenancy of Berks and it was refused, the Marquis of Buckingham did not display the type of violent outburst that normally accompanied the dismissals of Grenville patronage applications.[75]

Hugh Fortescue (1753–1841), son of the second Baron Fortescue, of the prominent Devon family, married Hester Grenville in 1782. Upon his father's death in 1785, he was called to the Lords; and in 1789, probably through Grenville influence, he was created the first Earl Fortescue. He possessed no overly ambitious nature; and, when about 1788 through Buckingham's means he was offered the Treasurership of the Household, he refused because of the necessity of frequent court attendance.[76] He loyally supported the Grenvillite political line in the Lords, though he was not always eager to leave Castle Hill for London.[77]

Neither the Nevilles nor the Fortescues held pocket boroughs or

---

Francis Bickley ed., *Report on the Manuscripts of Earl Bathurst, Preserved at Cirencester Park* (London, 1923), Bathurst to Bathurst, May 28, 1814, p. 278.

73. Richard Griffin, Third Baron Braybrooke, *The History of Audley End* (London, 1836), pp. 52–53.

74. Reading, Berkshire RO, Braybrooke-Glastonbury Papers, D/EZ6/1, Braybrooke to Glastonbury, Sept. 13, 1806.

75. ERO, Braybrooke Papers, D/DBY/C5, Pitt to Neville, Oct. 5, 1791.

76. HEH/STG, LIOF2, memorandum of Thomas Grenville, Aug., 1790.

77. His eagerness to come to town in December, 1788, at the time of the Regency crisis, William Grenville makes clear, was an exception. *Court and Cabinets of George III,* Grenville to Buckingham, Dec. 9, 1788, II, 40.

a decisive interest in their home counties, hence their dependence upon "Uncle Buckingham's" largesse. Only after much pruning was Braybrooke's son, Richard Neville, returned for Berks in 1812, and Fortescue's son, Viscount Ebrington, for Devon in 1818.[78]

Elizabeth Grenville, in 1787, became the second wife of John Joshua Proby (1751–1828), second Baron Carysfort in the Irish peerage. By his first marriage, Carysfort had had three sons, and his second wife bore him as many daughters. The sons were always treated as nephews by Elizabeth's brothers. Lord Grenville was closer to Carysfort politically than to any of his other brothers-in-law, and Carysfort's loyal support of the Grenvilles' Irish policies earned him an Irish Earldom in 1789 and a United Kingdom Baronage in 1801.[79] Also through the influence of Lord Grenville, he was sent as Ambassador to Berlin in 1800.[80]

The chief estates of the Proby family centered around Elton Hall in Huntingdonshire and Glenart Castle, Arklow, county Wicklow. The family had electoral designs in both counties, which the Grenvilles did all in their power to aid. But the Montague domination of Hunts and the Fitzwilliam preeminence in Wicklow precluded any long-lasting electoral success. Only in 1806, when Lord Grenville was Prime Minister, and in 1814, when the shire was in a peculiarly chaotic situation, was a Proby returned for Hunts.[81] And in Wicklow, only after Earl Fitzwilliam and Carysfort had been allied politically for fifteen years in the Grenvillite-Whig union did Fitzwilliam lend his considerable interest to a Proby.[82]

A more distant connection of the sons of George Grenville who often acted with them in politics was their first cousin, James Grenville (1742–1825), first Baron Glastonbury after 1797 and MP for Buckingham (1770–90) and Bucks (1790–97). Glastonbury, whose seat was at Butleigh Court in Somersetshire, did not always support the Grenville political line after 1801; and, when forced to choose between two cousins in 1804, he followed Pitt. After Pitt's death in 1806, however, he supported the Grenvillites. Of his Grenville first cousins, he was

78. NLW, Charles Wynn Papers, 10,804D, Charles Wynn to Saxton, June 8, 1807; DRO, Fortescue Papers, 1262M/15.
79. *Correspondence of Cornwallis,* Cornwallis to Portland: June 3, 1800, III, 244; June 17, 1800, III, 264.
80. HEH-STG, Box 173, Grenville to Buckingham, Feb. 19, 1800.
81. Sheffield Papers, 50a/49/63, Carysfort to Fitzwilliam, Oct. 16, 1806; *Dropmore,* Thomas Grenville to Grenville: June 2, 1814, X, 387; June 5–6, 1814, X, 388.
82. Sheffield Papers: F82c/9, Fitzwilliam to Carysfort, March 2, 1815 (copy); F82c/25, Ponsonby to Fitzwilliam, Nov. 24, 1815.

closest to Thomas, who like himself was a bachelor and to whom he left his estates, with remainder to one of Braybrooke's sons. [83]

The Grenville family in its widest sense was considered as a group by Buckingham several decades before 1801. Temple (as he then was) was careful to let his father-in-law, Lord Nugent, and his brothers-in-law, Fortescue, Neville, and Wynn, know his measures during the political crisis of 1783 which resulted in the fall of Shelburne's Administration. [84] Lord Bulkeley, Buckingham's closest friend, also considered them as acting together in a special sense, over and above their combined support of Pitt's Ministry. [85] In this, the Grenvillites were similar to a number of connections, groups, or small factions that clustered around the commanding figure of the younger Pitt. However, the resignation of the Prime Minister in 1801 and the preliminary negotiations leading up to the peace of Amiens gave the Grenvillites a reason or an excuse to emerge as an independent force to bid for support beyond a constricted circle of family and political dependents.

83. For an account of James Grenville's political career during the 1770s and 1780s, see Namier and Brooke, II, 546–47. For the terms of Glastonbury's will, see ERO, Braybrooke Papers, D/DBY/F–42.

84. *Dropmore*, Temple to Grenville, March 20, 1783, I, 203.

85. *Court and Cabinets of George III*, Bulkeley to Buckingham, Dec. 11, 1788, II, 51.

CHAPTER II

The Grenvillite Faction: The Uses of Patronage

1. The Grenvilles as Parliamentary Patrons

At the general election of 1812, the last of his lifetime, the first Marquis of Buckingham was able to return in his own interest six members of the House of Commons: one for his home county, two for Buckingham borough, two for St. Mawes, and one for Aylesbury. Only six United Kingdom peers controlled or influenced more seats than the Stowe Grenvilles.[1]

By the end of the eighteenth century, the Grenvilles, returning in their interest one knight of the shire and three borough representatives, were the leading political family in Bucks. From 1774 to 1839, they consistently returned one county member. After 1784, there was no contested election for Bucks until the Reform fight of 1831. As befitted the premier seat under their control, whenever possible the eldest male heir of the Grenville peerage sat for the county, which during the latter part of the eighteenth century had around 4,000 voters in a population of 107,900.[2] Only when the heir was underage, as was the case from 1779 to 1797 and from 1813 to 1818, was it necessary to farm out the county to a close relative (Thomas Grenville, 1779 to 1784 and 1813 to 1818; William Grenville, 1784 to 1790; and James Grenville, 1790 to 1797).

Like most contemporary aristocratic families, the Grenvilles had no hesitation under normal conditions in uniting with political opponents to keep the "peace of the county," thus ensuring that no vast sum of money be spent in contested elections. Only under conditions of such extreme national disharmony as that during the general election of 1784, when the country was divided between warring Foxite Whigs

---

1. Thomas Hinton Burley Oldfield, *The Representative History of Great Britain and Ireland* (London, 1816), VI, 285–98 passim.

2. William Page, ed., *A History of the County of Buckingham*, Victoria History of the Counties of England (4 vols.; London, 1908–27), II, 96.

and supporters of the King and Pitt, was a Grenville sent forth to do expensive (and successful) battle against the Foxite enemy. That general election, however, was an aberration and involved conditions not repeated for nearly half a century. Even uncontested Bucks elections cost between £600 and £700 during the late eighteenth century.[3] During the 1780s, a constant motif in the relationship of Lord Buckingham and his politically rising youngest brother, William Grenville, a county member, involved the expense of those reelections which by law William would have to undergo should he accept higher office. And, indeed, William's career was temporarily retarded due to a reluctance to force the issue with the Marquis.[4]

The cost of uncontested elections rose considerably during the nineteenth century, coming to over £1,000 in 1807 and to over £3,000 ten years later.[5] This may have been due to heightened levels of expectations on the part of the freeholders. By 1818, vast public breakfasts for hundreds of freeholders were costing as much as the entire election forty years before.[6] At the general election of 1826, the Marquis of Chandos, heir to the first Grenville Duke of Buckingham and county member since 1818, in an effort to curtail these expenses, entered into an agreement with Robert Smith, the other member, not to canvass. Since Chandos had scores of bills from the elections of 1818 and 1820 still owing, he also meant to give no dinners. Smith, however, wrote circulars to the freeholders, which Chandos thought broke the agreement, and the normal melee occurred with Chandos running up a bill for £2,500 for what his disgusted father called "a quiet election for the County."[7] During the frequent elections of the early 1830s—three in as many years—with the Grenville fortune dissipated, Chandos was running up bills of over £10,000. However, both in 1831 and 1832, indicative of the rise of extraparliamentary pressure groups, the burden was alleviated by the West Indian interest, which favored the proslavery Chandos, and by private subscriptions.[8]

During the general election of 1826, Chandos told his father that he desired to quit the county at the next election to return for Buckingham

3. *Dropmore,* Buckingham to William Grenville: Oct. 30, 1786, I, 273; Nov. 9, 1786, I, 274.
4. Ibid.: Buckingham to William Grenville, June 7, 1788, I, 333–34; William Grenville to Buckingham, June 11, 1788, I, 335.
5. HEH-STG, T3–00–3.
6. Ibid.: L7G3, Browne to Ledbrooke, March 20, 1820; T3–00–3; T3–00.
7. Ibid.: Box 330, Chandos to Buckingham, n.d.; Box 326, Chandos to Lady Chandos, n.d.; ST. 98, Buckingham's private diary, May 20, 1827.
8. Ibid., T3–00, Newman's account of the 1830–33 elections; BRO, Fremantle Papers, 139, Newman to Thomas Fremantle, May 17, 1831.

borough, as "really the situation is *not worth* all the trouble expense & inconvenience."[9] In 1828, he owed £3,000 in election debts (a mere trifle of his financial embarrassments) and again the subject of abandoning the county was raised. Buckingham, who had closed Stowe and was in Italy for several years due to his own dim economic straits, agreed to aid Chandos financially, to pay his election and other debts, and to settle on him all his own unsettled estates, making as a sine qua non of the whole affair that Chandos should never give up the county. "I consider him doing it [standing], as vital to the Interests of his family," Buckingham wrote, "and should he not comply with my wish I feel that the Interest must [illegible] & the County lost, which his Grandfather obtained by perseverance & personal popularity & exertion & which I retained through perilous & doubtful times, I trust & believe with advantage to my family & certainly by great sacrifice of every sort.[10]

Both seats for Buckingham borough, two miles from Stowe, had been firmly in the hands of the Grenvilles since 1747.[11] Buckingham was a nomination borough with the right of election vested in twelve self-elected burgesses, of whom in the 1820s five were Grenville tenants.[12] The parish and borough of Buckingham in the census of 1821 contained 3,465 persons, of which number 1,495 lived in the town proper and 1,970 in outlaying hamlets.[13] The population included a substantial number of Dissenters, especially Quakers, who generally opposed the Stowe interest after the Reform Bill. The chief industries were Stowe-oriented, as the Reformers found to their disgust at the general election of 1832, when Sir Thomas Francis Fremantle, the Duke of Buckingham's nominee and a Tory, was returned as one of the members under the enlarged franchise as he had been in 1827, 1830, and 1831 under the restricted one. Some disgruntled Whigs published a poll of the Buckingham electors, which showed that the Grenville influence still operated on voters who were tenants, butchers, druggists, or whatever to the family that still overshadowed the borough.[14]

Between 1747 and 1780, Grenville was the surname of both Bucking-

9. HEH-STG, Box 330, Chandos to Buckingham, n.d.

10. Ibid.: Box 4, East to the Duchess, March 15, 1828; Box 145, Buckingham to East, May 3, 1828.

11. Sedgwick, I, 197.

12. *A Poll of the Electors of Buckingham and its Boundary Parishes taken on the 10th of December, 1832: with a Preface on the supposed influence which operated on the Votes of the Electors who Supported Sir Thomas Francis Fremantle* (Buckingham, 1833).

13. J. Pigot, *Dictionary of Bucks* (n.p., 1830), p. 76.

14. *A Poll of the Electors of Buckingham.* For an excellent analysis of Buckingham, see R. W. Davis, "Buckingham, 1832–1846: A Study of a 'Pocket Borough,'" *Huntington Library Quarterly,* XXXIV, No. 2 (1971).

ham members. Once the nephews of the first Marquis of Buckingham and Lord Grenville came of age, Buckingham became a safe haven for them—a place where they might earn their parliamentary spurs or a way station where they might remain while their ambitious fathers developed electoral interest elsewhere. Indeed, before 1806, both Buckingham and his uncle Temple had made an effort to recommend only Grenville relatives to the burgesses. Such a tradition broke down permanently in 1806, when Lord Grenville was Prime Minister and on the lookout for safe seats for ministerial supporters.[15]

During the first decade of the nineteenth century, the cost of a single election for Buckingham hovered around £80.[16] By the late 1820s and early 1830s, due to rising election expenses similar to those in the county, the Duke of Buckingham's candidate, Sir Thomas Fremantle, was paying around £150 in the nomination borough. At the 1832 general election, the first under the enlarged franchise, three candidates were in the field: Sir Harry Verney for the Whigs; George Morgan as an independent vaguely backed by the Duke of Buckingham's politically wayward son, Lord Chandos; and Sir Thomas Fremantle, the only candidate representing the orthodox Grenvillian interest. Fremantle estimated that his expenses might run as high as £300 to £500, more than he could afford, though he was fully prepared to continue paying about £150. Buckingham agreed to pay a small part of the expenses; but he would authorize no ribbons, colors, or treating; and he refused to pay for a dinner should Fremantle be elected. Fremantle was furious; he stated to the Duke that he was fighting for the true Grenville interest against its enemies and threatened to withdraw if the Duke failed to pay his share. Buckingham finally capitulated and agreed to pay £300, Fremantle to pay the balance.[17]

The capital seat of Buckinghamshire, Aylesbury, a town famous for the fine quality of its lace, had a population of 3,186 in 1801 and 5,021 in 1831.[18] A parliamentary borough whose right of election was contained in its inhabitant householders, it had about 500 voters in the late eighteenth century. Its reputation for venality was legendary, even in a political nation hardly accustomed to a thorough investigation of local electoral irregularities. John Wilkes, the famous radical

15. *Dropmore*, Buckingham to Lord Grenville, July 23, 1806, VIII, 240–42.
16. HEH-STG, T3–00–3.
17. BRO, Fremantle Papers, 130: Buckingham to Thomas Fremantle, Nov. 18 and 27, 1832; Buckingham to Parrott, Nov. 18, 1832; Thomas Fremantle to Buckingham, Nov. 21 (draft), Nov. 26 (copy), 1832; William Fremantle to Thomas Fremantle, Nov. 22, 1832. The total election bill was £520, but it is unknown exactly how the money was split. Davis, "Buckingham, 1832–1846," p. 168.
18. Page, ed., *History of Buckingham*, II, 101–6.

agitator, reputedly paid £5 apiece to his supporters in the 1750s;[19] and his successor, Anthony Bacon, paid 5s. to his prospective voters every Christmas.[20]

The first Marquis of Buckingham, who had long had his eyes on the borough, had, sometime before 1789, extracted promises from some citizens to support Scrope Bernard, his private secretary and the son-in-law of a wealthy London banker, at a general election due most probably in 1790.[21] When the sitting member died in 1789, Bernard, at a cost of more than £1,500, was chosen to represent Aylesbury after winning a bitter electoral battle with General Gerard Lake, a friend of the Prince of Wales.[22] In preparation for the general election of 1790, Bernard was dealing in sums over £5,000, and Buckingham's contribution was well over £1,000.[23] Yet, before 1802, at Aylesbury, the senior Grenvilles were dealing with a candidate (Scrope Bernard) who had some wealth and financial connections of his own; after that date, the full expense of keeping one seat at Aylesbury seems to have come out of the exchequer at Stowe. It is difficult to see that the results were worthwhile.

There may always have been an antiaristocratic element among the voters,[24] and they were certainly often open to seduction by wealthy strangers. Twice during the thirty years before the passage of the first Reform Bill, the Grenvilles lost a contested election at Aylesbury. In 1802, Buckingham's two candidates, Scrope Bernard and Thomas Francis Fremantle, lost an expensive election to a wealthy Liverpool merchant and a large Bucks landowner;[25] and in 1804, Thomas Grenville was successfully opposed by the Cavendish interest.[26]

19. Archibald Philip Primrose, Fifth Earl of Rosebery, *Miscellanies, Literary and Historical* (4th ed.; London, 1921), II, 335.

20. Spencer Bernard Papers, PFE3/15(d), Draft of Bernard on the Aylesbury election.

21. Ibid.

22. BRO, Fremantle Papers, 54, Bernard to Fremantle, April 21, 1789; Spencer Bernard Papers, PFE3/15(d), Draft of Bernard on the Aylesbury election.

23. *Dropmore*, Buckingham to William Grenville, May 6, 1789; PRO, Chatham Papers, 30/8/117, Bernard to Buckingham, Sept. 2, 1792.

24. Richard W. Davis suggests that the opposition to the Grenville interest in Aylesbury in 1802 had an ancient lineage and was motivated to an extent by dislike for aristocratic domination of one seat for the borough. For a study of that opposition see *Political Change and Continuity, 1760–1885: A Buckinghamshire Study* (Newton Abbot, 1972), pp. 44–48.

25. For information on the 1802 general election, see Robert Gibbs, *The Bucks Miscellany* (Aylesbury, 1891), p. 274.

26. BM, Thomas Grenville Papers, Add. MSS. 41851, Buckingham to Thomas Grenville, June 29, 1804.

As a result of the well-documented electoral peccadillos of Aylesbury, the House of Commons in 1804 ordered the three hundreds of Aylesbury to be admitted to the borough's voting right: this led to quite considerable expense, as the first Marquis of Buckingham spent several thousand pounds creating 40s. freehold property within the new franchise.[27] In 1804, just the expense of a Grenville-sponsored Aylesbury election petition cost Buckingham nearly £1,000;[28] and by the second decade of the nineteenth century, the control of one seat at Aylesbury cost the Stowe Grenvilles more than the control of one seat for the county. Lord Nugent, the impecunious brother of the second Marquis of Buckingham, spent £5,222 of his brother's money at the general election of 1818 for Aylesbury—and he came in at the head of the poll—while his nephew, Lord Temple, spent only £3,021 for Bucks.[29]

The scant political rewards that flowed from this increasing expense made it difficult to justify. At the general election of 1812, the first Marquis of Buckingham, several months before his death, ensconced his younger son, Baron Nugent of Ireland, in the Aylesbury seat. But within a few years of a new regime at Stowe, the second Marquis of Buckingham and his brother Nugent were taking opposite political lines. Nugent ostentatiously refused to join the conservative Grenvillites in their break with the Whig party in 1817, and the content of Nugent's whiggery was of the more advanced persuasion. Therefore, subsequent to the general election of 1820, Nugent, now hoisting the liberty cap on his election colors, never received election funds from his brother.[30] Indeed, at the general election of 1826, he successfully ran on his Whig principles and did not even canvass, spending only £33.[31]

Buckingham's dilemma was made even more acute by the problem of whether to give support to Nugent at Aylesbury. It was one thing to refuse to pay election expenses but quite another to support alternative candidates to one's own brother. In 1823, 1825, and during the late 1820s, the toryish Buckingham was so angry about Nugent's political activities that he resolved to oppose him or, at best, to remain neutral.

---

27. NLW, Charles Wynn Papers, 10,804D, Charles Wynn to Temple, Nov. 27, 1807; Robert Gibbs, *A History of Aylesbury* (Aylesbury, 1885), pp. 276–77.

28. HEH-STG, L7G3, general expenses.

29. Ibid., L7G3, Browne to Ledbrooke, March 20, 1820.

30. BRO, Fremantle Papers, 51, Buckingham to Fremantle, June 15, 1826.

31. *Bucks Chronicle* (Aylesbury), June 3 and 24, 1826. This was an unusual circumstance for Aylesbury, and Nugent became celebrated in song as "George, the people's choice/A pure choice and free." *Bucks Chronicle,* May 31, 1828.

In the event of the general elections of 1826 and 1830, however, blood proved thicker than principles, and fraternal good will was expressed.[32]

The Reform election of 1831 in Aylesbury was contested, with Nugent and William Rickford, an Aylesbury banker and Whig, for the Bill, and Viscount Kirkwall against it. Rickford received the second votes of the parties of the two other candidates. Lord Chandos, Buckingham's Tory son, concurrently fighting the first contested election for Bucks since 1784, came out decidedly for Rickford and Kirkwall; therefore, his uncle Nugent supported Chandos's two county opponents, John Smith and Pascoe Grenfell. Chandos and Nugent were both returned.[33] Perhaps in retaliation for Chandos's policy, Nugent in 1832, when appointed Governor of the Ionian Islands by the Whig Administration, chose the brother of the advanced reformer, John Cam Hobhouse, to run as his Aylesbury successor at the post-Reform election. He even canvassed with him, although, as Hobhouse lost the election, to no political avail, save to cause a rise in the Duke of Buckingham's blood pressure, which perhaps was reason enough.[34] From that year, for the first time since the death of their father in 1813, the Duke ceased to give Nugent a yearly gift of £500.[35]

St. Mawes in southwestern Cornwall, a fishing village and freeman's borough of about 100 persons, had an electorate of about twenty-five.[36] Robert Nugent, the first Marquis of Buckingham's father-in-law, returned one member for the borough from 1741 until his death in 1788. The interest then reverted to the Grenvilles. Hugh Boscawen controlled the other seat and, sometime before the general election of 1790, sold his interest to Buckingham, who thereafter returned both members.[37]

Buckingham had no positive feeling that the MPs for St. Mawes, like those for Buckingham, should be related to him. The only kin of his who ever sat for the borough were three nephews, whose cumulative span only amounted to about four years. The average representative tended to be a personal friend or protégé of one or another of the Stowe Grenvilles, or a political ally within a broader Grenvillite party.

32. HEH-STG, ST. 95, Buckingham's private diary, Jan. 25, 1823; *Memoirs of George IV*, Thomas Grenville to Buckingham, Sept. 27, 1825, II 282–83; HEH-STG: Box 8, Nugent to Buckingham, May 29, 1826; Box 238, Parrott to Buckingham, June 4, 1829; Box 326, Chandos to Lady Chandos, n.d.

33. *Bucks Gazette* (Aylesbury), May 7, 14, 21, 1831.

34. Ibid., Aug. 18, 1832; BRO, Grenville Papers, 632, Buckingham to Thomas Grenville, Nov. 14, 1832.

35. HEH-STG, Box 335, Nugent to Buckingham, Dec. 29, 1841.

36. W. G. Lewis, *A Peep at the Commons* (London, 1820), pp. 3–5.

37. Sedgwick, I, 219; Namier and Brooke, I, 239.

Before 1790, when the borough influence was divided between the not always harmonious[38] Nugent and Boscawen interests, the election bills may have been higher than during the long Grenville tenure. At least the 1784 election cost Nugent £217, while the double election of Scrope Bernard and William Shipley in 1807 was only £129.[39] Between 1817 and 1830, the amounts spent on both double and single elections varied between £62 and £104.[40] In 1831, when in response to an election petition the wider scot and lot franchise was restored to the borough and a contested election took place, the bill for the Grenville nominees rose to £278.[41] As to the payment of these expenses, men of some means paid their own bills, while those less able paid only part, depending upon the circumstances, the patron paying the rest.[42]

One of the chief problems for any Cornish borough monger was the presence of other gentlemen of the same sort who lay in wait to gobble up one's holdings. After 1808, the Grenvilles were especially nervous that the Buller family, who at one time or another controlled the members for four neighboring boroughs, had their eyes on St. Mawes and were not above offering bribes to the freemen and inaugurating litigation as to the correct voting rights of the borough.[43] Before the general election of 1826, Buckingham, in expectation of vigorous opposition from one of the younger Bullers, saw to it that a number of his Bucks and Hants friends were qualified as electors at St. Mawes.[44] Buller apparently took the hint, for, despite sending out literature exhorting the citizens to rebel against the tyrant Buckingham, he failed to materialize on the day of the election.[45]

In 1830, at the first contested election for St. Mawes since the Grenvilles acquired proprietary rights, C. E. Carrington and Grenville Pigott, Buckingham's candidates, were opposed by W. Haldimand and R. W. Edgell. Among the voters present who alleged to be qualified, the two new claimants won by 28 votes to 13, but the Mayor disqualified many of the Haldimand-Edgell voters, and Carrington and Pigott

38. Namier and Brooke, I, 239.

39. Spencer Bernard Papers, PFE4/8, Bernard and Shipley to Ball; HEH-STG, T3–00.

40. HEH-STG, Box 284, Jago to Pigott, Aug. 23, 1831.

41. Ibid.

42. Ibid.: Box 284, Morland to Buckingham, May 14, 1813; Box 228, Pigott to Ledbrooke, May 22, 1830.

43. BRO, Fremantle Papers, 46, Buckingham to Fremantle, Feb. 23, 1808; NLW, Coedymaen Papers, 22, Buckingham to Charles Wynn, June 2, 1822.

44. HEH-STG: Box 330, Chandos to Buckingham, n.d.; T3–00.

45. Ibid.: Box 285, Bates to Morland, Sept. 26, 1825; L7G3, Buller's election address, 1826; Box 284, Morland to Buckingham, June 8, 1826.

were returned. Dr. Lawrence Boyne, a radical surgeon who had given Buckingham trouble since 1818, and several others presented a petition to the Commons asking for a return to a scot and lot franchise.[46] In December, 1830, a House committee obliged them, though it also permitted Buckingham's nonresident freeholders to vote.[47]

In 1831, two reformers, S. T. Spry and H. B. Ker, stood unsuccessfully under the new franchise against Buckingham's candidates, Pigott and Sir Edward Sugden (28 votes to 18). The local press asserted that, as in 1830, the anti-Grenvillite candidates received the votes of the majority of the resident electors. Shortly after the election, fourteen electors of St. Mawes who had voted against the Grenville interest presented a petition to the Lords, praying for the removal of the franchise from St. Mawes, as they, tenants of the Duke of Buckingham, had been "warned" from their homes by the Duke's agents and had been forced to build new houses in another part of town. If the petitioners were accurate, which the Duke denied in Parliament, it marked a sorry ending to the Grenvilles' influence in this parliamentary borough that was abolished by the first Reform Bill.[48]

The Grenvilles had retained control over their St. Mawes freemen for over forty years by acting both as landlords and as patrons. The leading families of the borough expected and received, whenever politically feasible, naval promotion and customs positions from the Stowe Grenvilles, who took such responsibilities seriously. When the Grenvilles had no government patronage to dispense, the electors had no qualms in pressing for and receiving private employment in Buckinghamshire.[49] As an example of how religiously the Grenvilles aided the electors, when one Robert Jago, a tide surveyor at St. Mawes, wished a superannuation in 1822, the two MPs for the borough, Scrope Bernard Morland and Joseph Phillimore both pressed the Government in his behalf and also requested that his son, William, be appointed to succeed him. When the Treasury rendered an unfavorable ruling on the younger Jago's claims, Buckingham, who had given his allegiance to Liverpool's Tory Administration only six months earlier, threatened to withdraw all his

46. *Falmouth Packet* (Falmouth), Aug. 7, 1830; HEH-STG, Box 282, Morland to Jago, Jan. 21, 1822.

47. HEH-STG, L7G3.

48. The petitioners named those who had warned them out of their homes. This incident may also have been an example of the excess of agents rather than a decision on the Duke's part. *Cornubian* (Falmouth), May 6, 1831; *Falmouth Packet* (Falmouth), May 7, 1831; *Bucks Gazette* (Aylesbury), June 2, 1832.

49. HEH-STG: Box 285, Ball to Bernard, Sept. 3, 1806; Box 285, Ball to Bernard, Jan. 20, 1808; Box 285, Jago to Bernard, May 24, 1808.

support from the Government. A compromise was reached only when a vacant tide surveyorship in London was found for young Jago.[50]

The last Duke of Chandos maintained one of the two leading interests in the borough of Winchester during the last part of the eighteenth century. He was the owner of the Avington estate within five miles of the borough. Winchester was officially a freemen borough, with non-resident freemen entitled to vote. Its electorate, however, became progressively smaller as it took on more and more of the features of a corporation borough.[51]

During the late 1790s, a division occurred within the Chandos interest when a dispute arose between the corporation of Winchester and the testy Earl Temple, son of the first Marquis of Buckingham, who, in 1796, had married the daughter and heiress of the late Duke of Chandos.[52] Though Temple had some powerful potential support within the corporation in the person of James Henry Leigh, High Steward of Winchester and the maternal uncle of Lady Temple, the Grenville-Chandos interest was dormant until 1812. At that general election, Lady Temple desired to start for Winchester, Leigh's son Chandos, her first cousin. He commenced a canvass, but withdrew before the polling. Two MPs in the interest of the Pittite Mildmay family (who had controlled one seat at Winchester since 1802) were returned, Henry Carew Mildmay and Richard Meyler. Chandos Leigh, in an address endorsed significantly from Temple's estate of Avington, announced his firm intention of standing again at the earliest opportunity.[53] However, a locally prominent Whig Hants family, the Barings of Stratton Park, challenged, albeit unsuccessfully, the hold of the Pittite Mildmays over both Winchester seats in 1812. Since it was clear that the Barings contemplated trying again, the alacrity with which the Mildmays reached an accommodation with the

50. Ibid.: Box 284, Morland to Harrison, May 22, 1822 (copy); Box 285, Phillimore to ?, n.d. NLW, Coedymaen Papers, 22, Buckingham to Charles Wynn, June 2 and 5, 1822.

51. Sedgwick, I, 256, estimates the number of freemen at 85 before 1754; Namier and Brooke, I, 302, at around 70 between 1754 and 1790; and Joshua Wilson, *A Biographical Index to the Present House of Commons* (London, 1806), p. 227, writes in 1806 of Winchester's right of election as "vested in a mayor, recorder, aldermen, bailiffs, and corporation, in number thirty-four.

52. *A Biographical List of the House of Commons, Elected in October,* 1812 (London, 1813), p. 57.

53. NLW, Aston Hall Papers, 2504, Lady Temple to Louisa Lloyd, Oct. 6, 1812; *Hampshire Chronicle* (Winchester), Oct. 5, 12, and 19, 1812; Oldfield, *Representative History of Britain,* III, 498–99.

Grenvilles—now split from their own Whig connections—in 1818 probably reflected both a similarity of purpose on the national level and a remembrance of a bitterly fought election against the Barings in 1812.[54]

When Richard Meyler died in 1818, Thomas Baring wasted no time in writing to the corporation to propose his brother, Henry Baring, as successor. This time the second Marquis of Buckingham (as Temple had become in 1813) was ready. Brushing aside those on the corporation who wished to place the Marquis's son, Earl Temple, in the vacant seat, he sent Temple to Winchester to propose Chandos Leigh. Leigh turned out to be unacceptable to the corporation due, apparently, rather to his irregular sexual life than to political reasons; but his father, the High Steward, J. H. Leigh, stood. Baring withdrew and the Mildmays agreed to Buckingham's nominee, allowing the Marquis to elect a new batch of freemen in his interest. In 1819, Temple was elected Mayor of Winchester.[55]

The Grenvilles had no trouble returning one MP for Winchester until, at the general election of 1831, there was a contest between two supporters of the Reform Bill, Paulet St. John Mildmay and William Bingham Baring, and an antireformer, James Buller East, who was the Grenville nominee. The election had the surface bearings of ideological warfare against the Grenville candidate, but Chandos, the Duke of Buckingham's son, now High Steward of Winchester, reminded Mildmay of the thirteen-year-old electoral compact between their two families, and Mildmay felt obliged to support East. He made a public declaration, however, that in the future the Grenville-Mildmay arrangement was terminated. In the event, East managed to squeak through: Mildmay 69 votes, East 39, Baring 34.[56] But in the first election after passage of the Reform Bill in 1832, Winchester had 531 voters; and, despite a great exertion on Buckingham's part, Baring and Mildmay were returned, and East declined on the day before the poll.[57]

In 1818, Buckingham gloated insufferably[58] over the fact that he now controlled seven seats in the Commons instead of six, but he seems never to have been popular in Winchester. Both his friends

54. *Hampshire Chronicle* (Winchester), Oct. 12, 1812.

55. Ibid., March 9, Sept. 27, 1819; NLW, Coedymaen Papers, 20, Buckingham to Charles Wynn, n.d.; BRO, Fremantle Papers, 55, Buckingham to Fremantle, March 12, 1818.

56. *Hampshire Chronicle* (Winchester), May 2 and 9, 1831.

57. BRO, Fremantle Papers, 130, William Fremantle to Thomas Fremantle, Dec. 4, 1832; *Hampshire Chronicle* (Winchester), Dec. 10 and 17, 1832. East was reelected in 1835 and sat until 1864.

58. BRO, Fremantle Papers, 55, Buckingham to Fremantle, March 12, 1818.

and enemies, even on the hustings, stated at various times that the corporation looked to the Duchess of Buckingham, not to the Duke,
as the patron.[59]

The Grenville property in Somersetshire, Northhamptonshire, and
Ireland yielded scant electoral influence. The family, of course, gave aid
to its political allies of the moment but showed no real inclination to
play a more concrete role.[60] When Temple succeeded to the peerage in
1813, he wished to embark upon a rather ambitious policy of making
freeholders on his estates in Westmeath and possibly Longford. But his
agent, Edward Box, thought it would be too much trouble and expense
for its worth.[61] The Grenvilles were, however, on the lookout for
English or Welsh boroughs that might be added to their five or six.
Lord Grenville made an abortive attempt to take over Bodmin in
Cornwall, where his father-in-law, Lord Camelford, had been patron,
but he lost out to Lord de Dunstanville.[62] Unfortunately, the decade
(the 1820s) when the Stowe Grenvilles gave their foremost consideration to acquiring new boroughs (and the first Duke of Buckingham gave
semiserious consideration to Callington,[63] Beaumaris,[64] Wendover,
Hedon, and Lincoln[65]) was the very decade when the family's financial
situation began to decline.

The Stowe Grenvilles' major attempt, after 1790, to acquire a new
borough—that of Saltash in Cornwall—ended in an expensive failure.
There was a generations-old dispute at Saltash between the corporation
and the burgage-holders as to the right of election, and the borough-
hungry Buller family had traditionally championed the rights of the
latter, of whom they controlled a suitable number.[66] However, in
1806, Buckingham, with his brother Prime Minister, attempted to

59. William Fremantle maintained this. BRO, Fremantle Papers, 130, William
Fremantle to Thomas Fremantle, Dec. 4, 1832. Sir James Mackintosh stated the same
thing. BM, Mackintosh Papers, Add. MSS. 52445, Mackintosh's Journal, Feb. 10,
1823. So did one of East's most important supporters in 1832 and on the hustings.
Hampshire Advertiser (Southampton), Dec. 15, 1832.

60. See, for example, BRO, Fremantle Papers, 46, Buckingham to Fremantle,
Nov. 18, 1806.

61. HEH-STG, Box 123, Box to Buckingham, Aug. 14, 1813.

62. Oldfield, *Representative History of Britain*, III, 249–50; *The Croker Papers: The
Correspondence and Diaries of the Late Right Honourable John Wilson Croker, 1809 to 1830*,
ed. Louis J. Jennings (London, 1885), I, 165.

63. HEH-STG, ST. 95, Buckingham's private diary, May 9, 1823.

64. BRO, Fremantle Papers, 46, Buckingham to Fremantle, Jan. 11, 1824.

65. Spencer Bernard Papers, PFD8/4, Buckingham to Morland, Sept. 17, 1824;
HEH-STG: Box 157, East to Buckingham, April 14, 1826; Box 330, Chandos to
Buckingham, May 10, 1826.

66. Sedgwick, I, 219; Namier and Brooke, I, 239.

reassert the rights of the corporation. He was initially able to assure key members of the corporation that their Admiralty patronage did not come through the Bullers[67] and to ensure that no Treasury patronage should be given save on his recommendation.[68] The general election of 1806 saw the return of John Buller's two members, who were supported by his thirty-eight burgage-holders, rather than Buckingham's nominees, William Fremantle and Richard Neville, who were supported by the corporation. But an election petition to the Commons on February 19, 1807, was successful, and the Buller members were unseated.[69] Grenville's Administration fell shortly thereafter, however, and James Buller entered Portland's Government as a Lord of the Admiralty. Two Grenville supporters, William Fremantle and Admiral Thomas Fremantle, were returned at the general election of 1807 but were unseated by a subsequent election petition.[70] The election expenses incurred by Buckingham between 1806 and 1808 on this business totaled over £15,000.[71]

The first Marquis and the first Duke of Buckingham expected those who represented their parliamentary interest to hew to the Grenville political line. Considering the fact that the boroughs were always cheap—and in some instances cost the nominees nothing—it seemed only just that political support should follow. It was considered proper etiquette for a member to give his patron more than general support on important national issues and to resign in case of a conflict over them. During the early 1780s, both Thomas Grenville, MP for Bucks, and Richard Neville, MP for Buckingham, lost Grenville patronage when they refused to follow the politics of their near relation; Neville, in fact, resigned in the middle of the parliamentary session in a dispute over the American war. Buckingham had a long memory, and when giving Neville's son, his own nephew, a seat in 1806, he made it abundantly clear that he wanted no repetition of such ingratitude.[72] Lady Buckingham's nephew, Charles Edmund Nugent, MP for Buckingham, actually committed the lese majesty of voting against the Grenville side on the Regency issue in 1789 and then refusing a demand from his irate

67. Durham Papers, Buckingham to Howick, April 6 and May 19, 1806; *Court and Cabinets of George III,* Howick to Buckingham, May 31, 1806, IV, 32.

68. BRO, Fremantle Papers, 54, Buckingham to Fremantle, July 22, 1806.

69. Oldfield, *Representative History of Britain,* III, 142.

70. *Parl. Debates,* X (Feb. 22, 1808), 691.

71. HEH-STG, T3–00–3.

72. Reading, Berkshire RO, Braybrooke-Glastonbury Papers, D/EZ6/1, Braybrooke to Glastonbury, Sept. 13, 1806.

uncle to resign the borough. Needless to say, Buckingham was never forward in pressing Nugent's naval career.[73]

On the whole, the first Marquis of Buckingham, who was perhaps a more formidable figure than his ducal son and was certainly more sure of his friends, was rarely embarrassed by the defection of his own MPs. He also seems to have initiated fewer preelection pledges from his members. The first Duke's entire career, on the other hand, characterized as it was by political zigzags, was one long trial for his members. When Francis Horner was offered a seat at St. Mawes in 1813, stipulations were made as to a potential resignation, which caused Horner acute anxiety in 1815, during the Hundred Days, when he found himself opposed to Buckingham's pro-war line.[74] When Sir Edward Hyde East came into Parliament for Winchester in 1823, and Sir C. E. Carrington for St. Mawes three years later, they practically took a pledge of allegiance to the Duke.[75] In 1826, William Fremantle assured the worried Duke, who was undergoing one of his frequent changes of political sentiment, that should the Grenvillites cease support of the Government—an action to which Fremantle could never consent—he would immediately resign Buckingham, a pledge he kept in 1827. Sir Edward Sugden entered into an agreement with the politically erratic Duke in 1831 that he would *not* have to resign from St. Mawes if his opinion in support of Peel remained consistent even though Buckingham's changed.[76]

A true prince of virtue would resign his seat (or offer to do so) at a time of political strife with his patron without waiting to be asked. A normal man would no doubt wait, conscious of a patron's dislike of appearing odious to his contemporaries by expelling a dissenter from Parliament. A cad would refuse to resign at all. With relatives the problem was, of course, greater. Sons, brothers, nephews, and cousins might take liberties with a patron's patience, conscious of a strong blood tie that argued against dismissal from a seat. The first Duke of Buckingham tolerated all sorts of opposition from his son Lord Chandos, his brother Lord Nugent, and his cousin Lord Ebrington, which

---

73. *Court and Cabinets of George III,* William Grenville to Buckingham, Jan. 19, 1789, II, 93–94; HEH-STG, Box 9, Buckingham to his wife, Sept. 7, 1791.

74. *Memoirs and Correspondence of Francis Horner, M.P.,* ed. Leonard Horner (Boston, 1853), Fremantle to Horner, March 16, 1813, II, 130.

75. BRO, Fremantle Papers, 46, Buckingham to Fremantle, Sept. 16, 1822; JRL, Carrington Papers, 1/6a, Buckingham to Carrington, Sept. 20, 1825.

76. BRO, Fremantle Papers: 46, Fremantle to Buckingham, May 27, 1826 (copy); 139, memorandum of a conversation between Buckingham and Sugden, April 22, 1831.

he would never have allowed from a non-Grenville; then, only after extraordinary pressure, did he elbow Ebrington, but not Chandos or Nugent, into resigning his seat.

2. *The Preeminent Sinecurists*

If one of the sources of Grenvillite political strength was the ability to reward partisans with seats in the Commons, at first glance it might appear that an almost equally important prop involved the sophisticated use of sinecurial and other patronage under the family's purview. That, however, was not necessarily the case. In an age before the expansion of communications, transportation, bureaucracy, and industry so characteristic of Victorian society, the avenues of social and economic advancement were necessarily constricted. One way for a generally hard-working and ill-paid politician to provide for his children or dependents was through the statutory grant of public money, generally in return for a nominal service to the state. Such sinecures were a tolerated, if not always approved, aspect of Georgian political life. Needless to say, a grasping and powerful minister or court favorite could easily abuse the tenuous nature of such a system. By almost all accounts, both of sinecurial and nonsinecurial holders, the Grenville family was the most notorious national example of such abuses. Thus what most regarded as their overaccumulation of public money both weakened trust in their good faith and left more than a vague air of corruption hovering about their causes.

In 1764, the then Prime Minister, George Grenville, acquired for his eldest son and namesake the lucrative post of one of the four Tellerships of the Exchequer. The Tellers' fees were paid from the Exchequer, being in the nature of a poundage on the issued money. For the ordinary service of the army, the Tellers received 7s. 6d. on every hundred pounds issued and for the extraordinary service 3s. 9d. They received 8d. in the hundred for what was issued for the navy and 12d. for the ordnance. The largest fee they received was on pensions and annuities, which amounted to 2½ percent.[77]

The result of such a system of payment insured that in time of war the fees of the Tellers skyrocketed: before the American war, young George Grenville averaged less than £3,000 per annum; at the height of the war, £7,000.[78] As a concession to the economical reform movement that gathered steam after the British defeat at Yorktown, Parliament in

77. *Parl. Debates,* XXIII (May 7, 1812), 73.
78. HEH-STG, ST. 65.

1782 limited the emoluments of future—but not current—Tellers to
£2,700 per annum.[79] Thus the average yearly fees of the first Marquis of
Buckingham during the ten years of peace prior to 1793 were £3,949
and between the commencement of the French war in 1793 and 1812
£14,471.[80] As the war years passed, the amounts naturally grew; and in
1808 (before the commencement of the Peninsular war), the Committee on Public Expenditure reported that the two surviving pre-1782
Tellers, Buckingham and Camden, each received £23,000.[81]

Each Tellership gave to its holder considerable patronage power, for a
deputy Teller and four minor clerks were dependent upon his good will.
Buckingham seems generally to have chosen Bucks allies to serve him in
office.[82] Then the fees payable to the deputy Teller and the second clerk
went directly to Buckingham, who allotted back to those individuals
what he desired. Thus, between 1791 and 1805, the fees payable to the
two clerks totaled an average of £2,065 per annum. Yet, Buckingham
allowed William Fremantle, his deputy Teller, less than 20 percent of
his yearly salary. Indeed, part of Thomas Grenville's yearly £600 gift
from Buckingham came from the fees of Fremantle's office.[83]

Sheridan and Fox in 1797 mounted a parliamentary attack upon
useless places and sinecure offices.[84] Partly in response to their attack
and partly on a request from Pitt, each year from 1797 to the peace of
Amiens in 1802, Buckingham took only £2,700 of his fees (the
post-1782 regulated sum) and gave his surplus to the public.[85] Following the resumption of the French war in 1803, however, Buckingham
did not revert to the 1797–1802 practice. He probably no longer feared
an attack in the House, as the Foxites were aligned with the Grenvil-

79. *Parl. Debates,* XXIII (May 7, 1812), 74.

80. HEH-STG, Box 117, Camden to Buckingham, Oct. 25, 1812.

81. Great Britain, Parliament, *Sessional Papers* (House of Commons) *Third Report of
the Committee on the Public Expenditure, etc. of the United Kingdom,* III (1808), 257–79
passim.

82. For example, J. Sealey of Buckingham, W. Fremantle, and Captain Browne of
the Bucks Militia. *Dropmore,* Buckingham to William Grenville, June, 1789, I, 262;
P. F. McCallum, *Le Livre Rouge or a New and Extraordinary Red Book* (London, 1810), pp.
64–65.

83. BRO, Fremantle Papers: 46, Buckingham to Fremantle, March 19, 1797; 47,
Buckingham to Fremantle, April 3, 1800; 47, "Abstract of the sums I have paid Lord
Buckingham, 1791–1805 inclusive"; Great Britain, Parliament, *Sessional Papers* (House
of Commons) *Account of the Marquis of Buckingham's Salary, Fees, & Gratuities,* 1794–96,
XLV, No. 920 (1797); HEH-STG, Box 171, Thomas Grenville to Buckingham, April
4, 1807.

84. *Parl. History,* XXXIII (March 13, 1797), 77–107.

85. PRO, Dacres Adams Papers, 30/58/3, Buckingham to Pitt, April 3, 1800;
BRO, Fremantle Papers, 48, Fremantle to Vansittart, May 26, 1819 (draft).

lites after 1804 and relations between the two groups were difficult enough without making an issue of his sinecure.

In 1810, Thomas Creevey, an ally of Samuel Whitbread, the leader of the more left-wing Whigs and an enemy to the Grenville-Foxite alliance, agitated the Tellership issue in the Commons. Thereupon, Lord Grenville informed Holland and Lauderdale that if important Whigs took up the question, he would resign as party leader. Lauderdale gave Grenville assurances. When Creevey again raised the matter in 1812 by giving notice of a motion on the subject, Grenville reiterated his threat.[86] Thus, only thirty-eight members joined Whitbread and Creevey in the minority on the motion.[87]

Buckingham himself desired to keep the question of his sinecure as much as possible out of the discussions of the newly elected Commons of 1812. He thus suggested to Lord Camden that starting on April 5, 1813, they both agree to give one-third of their profits, over £8,000 each, as a voluntary contribution to the public. This was gratefully accepted by the Treasury, but Buckingham cheated the public even in this, as he died in February, 1813.[88] Creevey estimated in the Commons in 1812 that Buckingham and Camden had between them received more than the interest of £1,000,000 sterling from their offices.[89] In toto, by 1812, Buckingham's Tellership appears to have amounted to around 30 percent of the annual income of the Stowe Grenvilles.

Buckingham's two brothers likewise feasted from the public trough. In 1800, Thomas was granted for life the sinecure post of Chief Justice of Eyre, south of Trent, valued at £2,316 per annum.[90] Buckingham's second tenure as Lord Lieutenant of Ireland (1787-89) involved an intricate search for a lucrative sinecure for his brother William. Only a few weeks after arriving in Ireland, the Marquis assured William, "You have not for a moment been out of my mind, and the reason for not doing anything hitherto has been the difficulty of getting exact accounts of those great offices." Buckingham was especially eager to procure the dying Richard Rigby's Mastership of the Rolls (£2,000 per annum), and the two brothers kept a ghoulish death watch for three

86. *Dropmore*, Lord Grenville to Grey, April 12, 1812, X, 235-36.

87. *Parl. Debates*, XXIII (May 7, 1812), 88.

88. HEH-STG: LIOF2, Buckingham to Camden, Nov. 5, 1812 (copy); Box 117, Harrison to Camden and Buckingham, Dec. 15, 1812.

89. *Parl. Debates*, XXIII (May 7, 1812), 73.

90. *Later Correspondence of George III*, Pitt to George III, July 14, 1800; McCallum, *New Red Book*, p. 89.

months around his sickbed.[91] When problems arose over an Englishman taking an Irish law office and William refused the offer, Buckingham disapproved of such scruples.[92] There followed a futile two-year search through the maze of lucrative Irish sinecures, offices, and reversions until in 1791 Lord Grenville accepted from Pitt the then vacant English Rangership of Parks at £1,000 per annum.[93] In 1794, the Auditorship of the Exchequer, fixed by Parliament in 1783 at £4,000 per annum, fell vacant and Pitt gave it to Grenville, who gave up the Rangership, but he did not accept the income of his new sinecure until his resignation as Foreign Secretary in 1801.[94] This sinecure proved particularly embarrassing to the Whigs in 1806 when Grenville took office and in 1811 when it appeared he would do so, because he was responsible for auditing his own accounts as First Lord of the Treasury. Of particular distaste to the radicals was the annual pension of £1,500 that George III granted Lady Grenville in 1801—to take effect upon her husband's death. Even though Lady Grenville inherited her paternal estates in 1804, the family refused to give up the pension until 1820.[95]

Other sinecures, places, and pensions came to those closely associated with the Grenvilles; and their closest Bucks allies, the Bernards and the Fremantles, were almost suffocated with them. But it was the Grenville family per se that stirred the public wrath. Through Grenville influence Lord Carysfort, Buckingham's brother-in-law, received the Irish Mastership of the Rolls, valued at £1,307 per annum in compensation after the Union.[96] General Richard Grenville, Buckingham's first cousin, was Ranger and Keeper of the House and Park at Windsor, valued at £600 yearly, and Clerk of the Privy Seal, valued at £358 per annum.[97] Sir George Nugent, Lady Buckingham's nephew, was Governor of St. Mawes Castle at £109 yearly.[98] Henry Wynn, the youngest son of Buckingham's eldest sister and a former Minister to Dresden, received,

91. *Dropmore,* Buckingham to William Grenville: Jan. 26, 1788, I, 299; March 19, 1788, I, 311.

92. Ibid.: April 11, 1788, I, 319; April 16, 1788, I, 321.

93. Ibid.: Dec. 11, 1791, II, 237; Dec. 15, 1791, II, 240.

94. HEH-STG, Box 173, Lord Grenville to Buckingham, Feb. 27, 1794.

95. *Court and Cabinets of George III,* Lord Grenville to Buckingham, Feb. 20, 1801, III, 138–39; *Dropmore,* Thomas Grenville to Lord Grenville, Nov. 8, 1812, X, 306; BM, Liverpool Papers, Add. MSS. 38384, Lord Grenville to Liverpool, April 29, 1820.

96. *Dropmore,* Buckingham to William Grenville, July 7, 1789, I, 482; *The Black Book* (London, 1820), p. 26.

97. *Dropmore,* Buckingham to Lord Grenville, Dec. 10–15, 1793, II, 478; *Black Book,* p. 47.

98. *Black Book,* p. 68.

as one of the last acts of Lord Grenville's Ministry, a pension for life, at
£1,200 per annum. In 1822, after the Grenvillites gave their support
to Lord Liverpool's Administration, Wynn was sent as Minister to
Switzerland at a yearly salary of £4,000.[99] Lord Braybrooke, another
Grenville brother-in-law, had held since 1762 the sinecure of Pro-
vost Marshall of Jamaica, worth £2,100 yearly. While this office had
nothing to do with the influence of Buckingham or Lord Grenville,
it became associated in the public mind with the sinecures of the rest
of the family.[100]

The Grenvilles were by no means unique in their places, pensions,
and reversions. Yet, they received the most attention during the longest
time span, on the hustings, in the press, and from the Commons. As
early as the general election of 1796, Horne Tooke was singling out
Lord Grenville as the preeminent sinecurist.[101] By the time of the Spa
Fields riots of 1816, lists of sinecurists were circulated in London with
the Grenvilles at their heads.[102] Thus their family name had become
almost synonymous with "place-hunter." Perhaps this was an inevitable consequence of their role as a swing group. The Pittites lambasted
them for a decade after 1804, the Whigs after 1821, and the Radicals continuously.

The *Courier,* the best edited Pittite daily, at the commencement of
Lord Grenville's premiership in 1806, described the Grenville family as
"gorged with places and pensions" and Buckingham specifically as one
who "can scarcely walk under the weight of his enormous sinecures."[103]
For the rest of his political life, Lord Grenville and his allies of the
moment had to sustain an almost monthly barrage of criticism of the
sinecures from the respectable press.[104] For example, in January, 1810,
when Grenville, as opposition leader, made a speech on the opening day
of the session on Britain's financial crisis, the *Courier* wondered how a
country whose revenues were so exhausted could afford to succor Spain

99. *Later Correspondence of George III,* Howick to George III, March 23, 1807, IV,
535–36; John Wade, *The Extraordinary Black Book* (London, 1831), p. 248, has a
vicious attack on Wynn's pension.

100. McCallum, *New Red Book,* p. 90. For an attack on the late Lord Braybrooke,
see Wade, *Extraordinary Black Book,* pp. 204–5.

101. See Tooke's speech to the Westminster electors, June 9, 1796, in *The Extraordinary Red Book* (London, 1816), p. vii.

102. Castle Howard Papers, Book 133, Lady Stafford to Carlisle, Dec. 6, 1816.

103. *Courier* (London), Jan. 27, 1806. See also June 17 and Oct. 6, 1806.

104. During the first six months of 1807, there are attacks on the Grenville
sinecures in the *Courier* on March 16, March 25, April 11, May 2, and July 4. During
the 1808 parliamentary session, the sinecures were attacked on March 2, April 1,
April 6, and April 9.

and Portugal, contend alone against France, and continue to support "an enormous interior expense, of which the sinecures of the *Grenville* Family are not the least."[105] Following the Grenvillite union with Liverpool's Tory Government in December, 1821, the Whig press attacked the family and made lists that showed which members got what public money.[106]

On at least two occasions, extremely embarrassing attacks against the Grenvilles' accumulation of public money took place in Parliament: in 1812, over the profits of Buckingham's Tellership,[107] and in 1822, on Henry Wynn's mission to Switzerland.[108]

The Grenville nephews, upon leaving the security of their uncle's boroughs, often found hostility directed against them, not on political grounds per se, but because of the ever-present sinecures. During the general election of 1812, when Richard Neville, the eldest son of Lord Braybrooke, ran successfully for Berks—the first time a Neville had been returned from his ancestral county since 1710—"all the Grenville heaps" were struck upon placards, causing much comment. Again, at the general election of 1818, the Grenvilles were the cause célèbre in Berks, causing James Grenville, Lord Glastonbury, to comment to Neville's father, "What had the Grenville pensions & sinecures to do with Dick's Election? Such arguments were wholly irrelevant to the Berkshire poll."[109]

When Lord Ebrington, Fortescue's eldest son, ran at a special election for Devon in May, 1816, he was attacked by his opponent "because some of his Relatives have obtained Places and Pensions, Marquisates, Earldoms, and Baronies." Ebrington's supporters asked in a circular letter whether it was fair to reject the young Viscount because "his Grandfather's Great Uncle's Cousin's Cousin's Relation, Jeroboam, made Israel to sin?" Eventually Ebrington pledged himself to advocate in Parliament for the abolition of all sinecures "WHOEVER Holds

---

105. *Courier* (London), Jan. 25, 1810.
106. *Traveller* (London), Jan. 10 and March 29, 1822. Wynn wrote the Duke of Buckingham of "the general disposition of the Press to impute rapacity etc. to all of us, which really has now been done for so many years unintemporately that they have established it almost as an acknowledged point in public belief." HEH-STG, Box 183, Nov. 24, 1823.
107. *Parl. Debates,* XXIII (May 7, 1812), 73–88.
108. *Parl. Debates:* N.S., VII (May 15, 1822), 604–53; N.S., VII (May 16, 1822), 659–70, *Traveller* (London), March 29, 1822.
109. Reading, Berkshire RO, Braybrooke-Glastonbury Papers: D/EZ6/2, Braybrooke to Glastonbury, Nov. 3, 1812; D/EZ6/1, Glastonbury to Braybrooke, July, 1818.

Them," but he was still defeated. He evidently learned his lesson, and by the time he ran successfully for Devon at the general election of 1818, he had severed all political ties with his mother's family.[110]

The effect of this incessant criticism upon the Grenville sinecure holders became evident as the years passed, and alternated between obstinacy and defensiveness. Buckingham regarded his Tellership to be as much his property as the crown was the King's.[111] Lord Grenville threatened to resign as the opposition leader in 1810 and 1812 should any of his important Foxite allies attack the Tellership, but he was not totally deaf to the argument that Buckingham's sinecure was extravagant. When in November, 1812, Buckingham proposed to give up one-third of the profits of his office and Thomas Grenville wondered whether he and Lord Grenville should do the same, Lord Grenville refused, stating that Buckingham's office differed from most others. He wrote: "The increase in profit rising with the public expenditure, & the just feeling that this actual amount far exceeds what could have been intended when the proportion of the fee was fixed, or even when the existing grants were made, do afford an equitable claim on the proprietors for some concession—& I always wished that this had been earlier felt & acknowledged."[112]

In 1817, both surviving Grenville brothers were careful to approach the Chancellor of the Exchequer with the suggestion that they be included in what they understood to be a desire on the part of Ministers during the distress to give up 10 percent of their incomes.[113] In 1830, when the Whigs came to power, Lord Grenville decided to give up his "invidious and envied office," apparently under the mistaken notion that there would be an attack upon him in the Commons. Both his brother, Thomas Grenville, and his nephew, Charles Wynn, Secretary at War in the new Administration, persuaded him to reconsider, Wynn reassuring his aged and ill uncle that not a voice in the new Parliament save possibly Orator Hunt's would be raised against him.[114] But that

110. DRO, Fortescue Papers, 1262M/13: "To the Independent Freeholders of the County of Devon," May 11, 1816; "Facts against False Assertions," May 6, 1816.

111. *Dropmore,* Buckingham to Lord Grenville, Jan. 28, 1812, X, 195–96.

112. *Dropmore,* Thomas Grenville to Lord Grenville, Nov. 15, 1812, X, 309; BM, Thomas Grenville Papers, Add. MSS. 41853, Lord Grenville to Thomas Grenville, Nov. 13, 1812.

113. BM, Thomas Grenville Papers, Add. MSS. 41858, Lord Grenville and Thomas Grenville to Vansittart, Feb. 12, 1817 (draft); NLW, Coedymaen Papers, 12, Charles Wynn to Mrs. Wynn, Feb. 13, 1817.

114. BRO, Grenville Papers, 632: Lord Grenville to Thomas Grenville, Dec. 16, 1830; Lord Grenville to Thomas Grenville, Feb., 1831. NLW, Charles Wynn Papers, IX, Charles Wynn to Lord Grenville, Feb. 12 and 14, 1831 (copies).

Lord Grenville was bitter about the whole business can be seen in a letter from his sister, Lady Wynn, who quotes him as remarking that under the new system a man could not look to office supporting him "with any means of providing either for himself or his family, & is to expect to retire from it, with less provision for his old age than a Chelsea Pensioner."[115] Thomas Grenville decided at the end of his long life to leave his valuable library, which he had purchased chiefly from the profits of his sinecure, to the British Museum, because "the impression of a debt & obligation which I owe to the publick has recently but irresistibly overpowered in my mind all other considerations."[116]

3. *The Grenvillite Faction before 1801*

The parliamentary boroughs and sinecures that the first Marquis of Buckingham and, to a lesser extent, Lord Grenville were instrumental in obtaining for their political followers gave them a fairly firm hold upon a number of individuals by 1801. Some members of the group seemed chiefly moved by these accountings; others had, perhaps, less material concerns. The Youngs, Bernards, Fremantles, and Nugents can be described as general place-hunters without doing their characters an injustice. Lord Bulkeley seemed primarily motivated in politics by personal friendship with the first Marquis of Buckingham. Some of the extended family may have acted with their Grenville relations out of a sense of tribal loyalty, a sentiment which could pull in more than one direction, as when two first cousins, William Pitt and Lord Grenville, ceased seeing eye to eye after 1801. Yet tribal loyalty implicitly involved more than disinterested attachment, and one of the Marquis's brothers-in-law once evoked an image of an expansive Buckingham, who promised him reversions and cabinet positions upon some future assumption of power.[117] Thus, besides members of the Grenville family, Buckingham had, before 1801, a small phalanx of one peer and several on-and-off members of the House of Commons whom he could assume were his particular friends.

Thomas James, seventh Viscount Bulkeley in the Irish peerage (1752–1822), of Baron Hill in Anglesey, was granted an English Baronage by Pitt in 1784. His chief estates were in Anglesey, which he

115. *Correspondence of Charlotte Grenville, Lady Williams Wynn*, ed. Rachel Leighton (London, 1920), pp. 276–77.
116. BM, Thomas Grenville Papers, Add. MSS. 47458A, Thomas Grenville to Buckingham, Oct. 25, 1845 (copy).
117. Reading, Berkshire RO, Braybrooke-Glastonbury Papers, D/EZ6/1, Braybrooke to Glastonbury, July 2, 1804.

served as an MP from 1774 to 1784, and in Carnarvonshire, where his half-brother and heir, Sir Robert Williams sat as MP, usually as a Grenvillite, from 1790 to 1826.[118] Bulkeley was an early friend of young George Grenville (later first Marquis of Buckingham): they took the Grand Tour together in 1773 and 1774,[119] and they acted together in opposition to North's Ministry after 1779.

When members of Bulkeley's own family were not available to represent his pocket borough of Beaumaris, he farmed it out to the Grenville connection: in 1784 to Hugh Fortescue and in 1794 to Sir Watkin Wynn. He faced the problem of his half-brother Sir Robert Williams's dislike of steady parliamentary attendance—a situation the Grenvilles would face from most of their Welsh adherents. Bulkeley, for example, wrote Williams on January 30, 1801, at a critical moment in party fortunes, to "pray come to Town & shew yourself in Parliament your hounds should not prevent you from doing a little public duty . . . & considering how many favors I ask for our countrymen it makes it very awkward for me your scarce ever appearing or voting in Parliament."[120]

An early Eton friend of Buckingham was William Young (1749–1815) of Delaford, Bucks, an author, fellow of the Royal Society, and MP for St. Mawes from 1784 to 1806 and for Buckingham from 1806 to 1807.[121] When Buckingham was in Ireland as Lord Lieutenant, with sections of the Irish Exchequer at his disposal, he gave Young provisions "most essential" to his "family subsistence."[122] Young was a testy man, well liked perhaps by the Marquis of Buckingham, but despised by others in the Grenvillite group.[123]

Scrope Bernard (1758–1830), of Nether Winchendon, Bucks, near Aylesbury, son of a colonial Governor of New Jersey and Massachusetts Bay, struck up a friendship with William Grenville at Oxford during the 1770s. When William's brother Temple went to Ireland as Lord Lieutenant in 1782, he took Bernard as his permanent private secretary.[124] Bernard and his family profited both from the Grenville connection and from his marriage to the daughter of a wealthy London banker, William Morland, whose surname Bernard added to his own in 1811.

118. Namier and Brooke, I, 459.

119. William James Smith, ed., *The Grenville Papers* (4 vols.; London, 1852–53), George Grenville to Temple, March 26, 1774, IV, 555.

120. UCNW, Baron Hill Papers, 6160, Bulkeley to Williams, Jan. 30, 1801.

121. HEH-STG, Box 18, Young to Buckingham, April 8, 1813.

122. *Court and Cabinets of George III,* Young to Buckingham, Nov. 30, 1788, II, 25–26.

123. *Dropmore,* Bernard to William Grenville, Feb. 14, 1788, I, 303.

124. Sophia Elizabeth Napier Higgins, *The Bernards of Abington and Nether Winchendon: A Family History* (4 vols.; London, 1903–4): II, 232; III, 44.

During the first Grenville viceroyalty, Bernard was made Examiner of the Hearth Money Collection in Ireland at £300 per annum; during the second, Usher of the Black Rod (held from 1787 to 1789) at £608 per annum, and Agent for Irish Half Pay at £600 per annum (which ultimately passed to a Bernard offspring).[125] When William Grenville was joint Paymaster in 1785, he procured Bernard the job of joint Agent and Solicitor of Invalids, a situation that was not compatible with Parliament, so Bernard gave it to his brother, Thomas. When Lord Grenville was at the Treasury twenty years later, he enabled Scrope's son, Francis, to succeed his uncle.[126]

When Grenville was Home Secretary from 1789 to 1791, Bernard served as his Under Secretary, and in 1792, he received a pension of £554 per annum upon his retirement after only three years in office. He gave the pension to his wife, Harriet, to be settled on her father, William Morland, for his life, and then to revert to Mrs. Bernard. When she died long before her husband, he lost the pension. The first Duke of Buckingham, who more or less inherited Bernard with his estates and emoluments, once remarked that Bernard's "sole object has been . . . to fasten the Bernard family on the Country for the longest possible space of time."[127]

William Grenville was eager to forward Bernard's political career. From 1785 to 1788, Bernard acted as secretary of a commission of inquiry into the conduct of public offices.[128] He entered Parliament from Aylesbury in 1789, and served Grenville and Dundas as Under Secretary at the Home Office. He proved less than successful as a politician. He remained in the Commons, with two brief exceptions, until his death in 1830.

After 1792, his chief preoccupation centered about the private concerns of Buckingham, whom he served as banker, political agent, and general vicegerent.[129] The country's loss may not have been the Grenvilles' gain, however. Bernard's own career as a Buckinghamshire and

125. *Dropmore:* Temple to William Grenville, March 12, 1783, I, 202; Bernard to William Grenville, Dec. 27, 1787, I, 294–95. *Black Book,* p. 58; HEH-STG, Box 183, Charles Wynn to Buckingham, Dec. 5, 1823.
126. PRO, Chatham Papers, 30/8/113/Pt. 2, Bernard to Pitt, July 13, 1796; HEH-STG, ST. 18, Bernard to Temple, Feb. 24, 1806; NLW, Coedymaen Papers, 23, Buckingham to Charles Wynn, Dec. 10, 1823.
127. PRO, Chatham Papers, 30/8/117, Bernard to Buckingham, Sept. 2, 1792; NLW, Coedymaen Papers, 23, Buckingham to Charles Wynn, Dec. 10, 1823.
128. Higgins, *The Bernards,* William Grenville to Bernard, Dec. 23, 1785, III, 74–75.
129. HEH-STG, Boxes 284 and 285; Spencer Bernard Papers, PFE3/5. Bernard's memorandum on the Aylesbury election; HRO, Wickham Papers, 38M49/6/10, Bernard to Wickham, April 27, 1805.

London banker, which leads from prosperity to near financial collapse, prefigures the careers of the latter Grenvilles at least enough to call into question his ability and Buckingham's wisdom in employing him. The historian of the Bernard family feels that Scrope's neglect of his business duties precipitated the near ruin of the Bernard-Morland family by the 1830s.[130]

The Fremantle family of Aston Abbots, Bucks, like the Bernards, feasted from the Grenville largesse but gave far more astute service in return. The head of the family, John Francis Fremantle, was a friend of the first Marquis of Buckingham. When Fremantle died suddenly in 1786, Buckingham assured his four sons of his protection and support.[131] John Fremantle, the third son, thought Buckingham "the most extraordinary man living," and well he might if the number of sinecures and favors the family procured from its mentor was a good indication.[132] The eldest son, Thomas Francis Fremantle, the future Admiral and one of the most distinguished naval officers of the period, made no effort to conceal the fact that he considered Buckingham, through his influence with two First Lords of the Admiralty, Chatham and Spencer, responsible to the greatest extent for his early promotions.[133]

William Henry Fremantle (1766–1850), who of Fremantle's sons was Buckingham's favorite, entered the army and went to Ireland in both 1782 and 1787, during the Grenville viceroyalties, as aide-de-camp to the Lord Lieutenant. From such a favored position in the Irish establishment, Fremantle was allowed to purchase a troop of Yeoman cavalry, the 58th, which Buckingham compelled a Captain of Dragoons to sell to him at the regulated price. Apparently it was a rather shady deal, as a year later, with Buckingham's concurrence, Fremantle was prepared to sell his company at a "very advanced price." The King, who was ever watchful of Buckingham's "jobs," got wind of the affair and refused to allow it. This royal interference caused Buckingham to threaten Pitt with his resignation, as was his normal operating procedure; but it was Fremantle who, in 1789, disposed of his company and quit the service.[134]

130. Higgins, *The Bernards*, IV, 312–16.

131. ERO, Braybrooke Papers, D/DByC5/11, Neville to Bulkeley, May 19, 1786.

132. BRO, Fremantle Papers, 45, John Fremantle to William Fremantle, n.d.

133. Ibid., Thomas Fremantle to William Fremantle, Nov. 11, 1790, and June 26, 1791; *Court and Cabinets of George III*, Fremantle to Buckingham, March 7, 1800, III, 42.

134. BRO, Fremantle Papers, 45: John Fremantle to William Fremantle, n.d., and Aug. 24, 1790. PRO, Chatham Papers, 30/8/325/Pt. 2, Buckingham to Pitt, Aug. 30 and Sept. 8, 1788.

In addition to his deputy Tellership of the Exchequer, William Fremantle held the positions of joint Resident Secretary to the Lord Lieutenant of Ireland in London, for which he received £632 sterling per annum in compensation after the Union,[135] and joint Solicitor in Great Britain for Irish Affairs at £391 per annum. His sister-in-law was Keeper of the Irish House of Commons at £722 per annum.[136] Throughout the 1790s, Fremantle, like Scrope Bernard, was an agent of Buckingham's, and like Bernard he married an heiress, Selina Hervey, in 1797, worth £5,000 a year, who settled on him £6,000 in bank annuities and her London house.[137] It may have been his marriage that first gave Fremantle an entrée to the court circle around George III. Sometime in the late 1790s, William Fremantle and his wife purchased a home in Englefield Green, Surrey, near Windsor; and Fremantle's letters, for the rest of his life, abound with the activities of the royal family. He seems to have been on particularly intimate terms with the Duke of Kent, although nearly all of the family corresponded with him.[138]

At Buckingham's instigation, during Lord Grenville's premiership in 1806, Fremantle was made a joint Secretary of the Treasury. Thomas Grenville for one was somewhat sceptical of how the new office would "accord with . . . Englefield Green, & all the luxuries to which he is so long accustomed."[139] Fremantle came to the House of Commons for the first time in 1806, sitting for Harwich; he represented Kirkwall in Scotland, on Lady Stafford's interest, from 1808 to 1812, and Buckingham from 1812 to 1827. He was the consummate courtier, on excellent terms with Buckingham *père* and *fils* and with Georges III and IV—neither a mean accomplishment. Upon his late arrival in the Commons, he quickly became a major power in the Grenvillite group.

Another prominent member of the Grenvillite group was Lady Buckingham's half-brother's illegitimate son, George Nugent (1757–1849), MP for Buckingham (1790–1802 and 1818–32) and Aylesbury (1806–12). Nugent's relationship with Buckingham combined an amalgam of family ties and dependency; none of the Marquis's other nephews were ever so beholden to him, as they had their own relatively wealthy fathers to sustain them. A Lieutenant-Colonel in the Army,

135. BRO, Fremantle Papers, 47, Hardwicke to Buckingham, Nov. 15, 1801.

136. McCallum, *New Red Book*, p. 137; *Black Book*, p. 42.

137. BRO, Fremantle Papers, 50, Buckingham to Fremantle, Aug. 9, 1797.

138. Ibid., 51, Kent to Fremantle, April 29, 1806.

139. *Dropmore:* Fremantle to Buckingham, Jan. 25, 1806, VII, 342–43; Thomas Grenville to Lord Grenville, Feb. 8, 1806, VIII, 20. HEH-STG, Box 170, Thomas Grenville to Buckingham, July 21, 1806.

Nugent, like William Fremantle, went to Ireland in 1787 as aide-de-camp to the Marquis of Buckingham.[140]

In the spring of 1788, Buckingham desired to give Nugent a vacant Lieutenant-Colonelcy that was within his patronage. George III, however, with no previous communication with the Marquis, appointed his own aide-de-camp to the post, and only William Grenville's entreaties dissuaded Buckingham from resignation.[141] When a similar position fell vacant in March, 1789, Buckingham again wished it to go to Nugent; but the King, claiming disgust with Buckingham's conduct in 1783 when he resigned as Secretary of State at the commencement of Pitt's Ministry, once more disregarded the wishes of his viceroy. Since Buckingham had but recently and most decisively taken George's part during the bitter Regency struggle in Ireland, he was understandably furious. For the third time within a year, he announced his resignation; and this time William Grenville, who was as indignant as his brother, also decided to give up his own office, a decision that galvanized Pitt into action. After some initial blustering, George III allowed his Prime Minister to work out a satisfactory compromise, whereby Nugent received the Lieutenant-Colonelcy of the 4th Dragoon Guards in Ireland.[142] In 1790, he was exchanged into the Coldstream Guards as a Lieutenant-Colonel.

Not quite a year after the French war commenced, Nugent applied to Lord Amherst, the Commander in Chief, and persuaded Buckingham to second his request for permission to raise a regiment with himself as Colonel. In return, he offered to give up his Lieutenant-Colonelcy in the Guards without sale and to allow the Government to nominate officers in the projected regiment. Buckingham thought the whole notion "extravagant" but urged it on Lord Grenville.[143] The proposal at first encountered the opposition of Lord Amherst. Nugent then decided he would like to become an aide-de-camp to the King, and again Grenville was drafted to push Pitt on the subject. Grenville did his best, but as he remarked to Buckingham, "I am sure you know that the King's Ministers do not name his aides-de-camp; and that the pressing such a

140. See the memoir of Nugent included in Claud Nugent, *Memoir of Robert, Earl Nugent* (London, 1898), pp. 272–89.

141. PRO, Chatham Papers, 30/8/325/Pt. 2, Buckingham to Pitt, June 27 and July 8, 1788; *Court and Cabinets of George III*, William Grenville to Buckingham, July 1, 1788, I, 403–7.

142. *Dropmore*, Buckingham to William Grenville, April 11, 1789, I, 449–50; *Court and Cabinets of George III*, William Grenville to Buckingham, n.d., II, 133; *Later Correspondence of George III:* Pitt to George III, April 11, 1789, I, 407; George III to Pitt, April 12, 1789, I, 408; George III to Pitt, April 18, 1789, II, 410.

143. *Dropmore*, Buckingham to Lord Grenville, Oct. 9, 1793, II, 441.

request beyond a certain point, makes difficulties in his mind, instead of removing them." Grenville thought the possibility of a corps for Nugent was a more likely prospect than the latter request.[144]

Buckingham, however, then began to bother Pitt himself about the aide-de-camp matter and, as frequently happened on such matters, received no answer from the Prime Minister.[145] In the meantime, Nugent, in perhaps unwarranted anticipation of his appointment, had quit the Guards, making the situation even more tense. Then, one morning in late December, 1793, the Grenville brothers picked up the *Gazette,* and found the announcement of six new aide-de-camps and no mention of Nugent among them. By January, 1794, the War Office yielded to Grenville pressure, and Nugent was allowed to raise a regiment, which on January 31 was 520 strong. Concerning it, Buckingham wrote, "I have recruited 90 men for him and, by the bye, have bought three commissions in it rather than *ask more favours.*"[146]

Lord Grenville's problems with Buckingham over Nugent went on and on. In November, 1794, he received a letter from the Marquis stating that Nugent meant to quit the service because his commission as Colonel had been dated on March 5, 1794, and other officers "over whom he had bought his rank" had commissions dating from March 1, 1794, even though some of them were three years below him in service. Grenville promised to look into the matter, and apparently some agreeable solution was reached.[147] Then, in September, 1795, Buckingham approached his brother with a desire that Nugent be made a Major-General, which was refused at that moment though granted in the subsequent year.[148]

Despite the headaches Nugent caused officialdom, he was a conscientious and adequate commander. He certainly distinguished himself, during the 1798 Irish rebellion, both for his ability as a commander and for the tact he displayed in conciliating Belfast. Lord Cornwallis, the Lord Lieutenant, was an unabashed admirer of his conduct[149] and,

144. *Court and Cabinets of George III,* Lord Grenville to Buckingham, Nov. 21, 1793, II, 246.

145. *Dropmore,* Buckingham to Lord Grenville, Dec. 22, 1793, II, 482.

146. PRO, Chatham Papers, 30/8/140/Pt. 1, Lord Grenville to Pitt, Dec. 21, 1793; *Dropmore,* Buckingham to Lord Grenville, Jan. 31, 1794, II, 501.

147. *Dropmore:* Buckingham to Lord Grenville, Nov. 24, 1794, II, 647–48; Lord Grenville to Buckingham, Dec. 5, 1794, II, 649–50.

148. Ibid.: Buckingham to Lord Grenville, Sept. 13, 1795, III, 134; Buckingham to Lord Grenville, Sept. 27, 1795, III, 136.

149. *Correspondence of Charles, First Marquis Cornwallis,* ed. Charles Ross (2d ed.; London, 1859): Cornwallis to Dundas, July 12, 1799, III, 115; Cornwallis to Ross, Aug. 14, 1799, III, 123–24.

indeed, was so loth to lose his services in Ireland that he persuaded the Government not to name him Lieutenant Governor and Commander in Chief of Jamaica. It was not until Cornwallis resigned over the Catholic question in 1801 that Nugent was appointed to Jamaica, where he remained until 1806.[150]

Buckingham continued to press Nugent's case even when the Grenvilles were out of office and power. On May 16, 1804, only a few days after the Grenvillite party had definitively broken with Pitt and stood in decided opposition to his second Ministry, he had the temerity to request his continuation at Jamaica;[151] and just a few days after the start of the Regency in 1811, he successfully petitioned the Prince to send Nugent to India as Commander in Chief.[152]

Buckingham came to Nugent's defense for the last time in 1812. The Regent's old friend, Lord Moira, was appointed both Governor General and Commander in Chief in India, thus necessitating Nugent's subordination to Moira. Buckingham, however, prodded the President of the Board of Control, Lord Buckinghamshire, who owed him favors dating from a previous generation, to enable Nugent to continue drawing the full salary of his initial position.[153] Such a conciliatory measure did not impress Nugent, who promptly resigned his commission on the grounds that to stay in India with reduced powers and patronage would be demeaning. He did, however, request of the Liverpool Ministry the government and command of the Cape of Good Hope.[154]

The death of the Marquis of Buckingham in 1813, wrote finis to Nugent's effective career, as he failed to receive the African station and was equally unsuccessful in attempts to receive the command of the army in Ireland and a peerage.[155] However, in 1848, at the age of ninety-one, he was made a Field Marshal.

150. BM, Liverpool Papers, Add. MSS. 38278, Nugent to Liverpool, July 17, 1819.

151. *Later Correspondence of George III,* Buckingham to Camden, May 16, 1804, IV, 180.

152. *Correspondence of Prince of Wales,* Buckingham to the Regent, Feb. 13, 1811, VII, 232.

153. *The Letters of King George IV, 1812–1830,* ed. Arthur Aspinall (Cambridge, England, 1938), McMahon to the Regent, Nov. 12, 1812, I, 179–80; *Dropmore,* Buckingham to Lord Grenville, Nov., 1812, X, 319; HEH-STG, LIOF2, Buckingham to Buckinghamshire, Nov. 13, 1812.

154. NAM Papers, 6807/181, Nugent to Buckinghamshire, Nov. 1, 1813 (copy).

155. BM, Liverpool Papers, Add. MSS. 38278, Nugent to Liverpool, July 17, 1819; BRO, Fremantle Papers, 51, Buckingham to Fremantle, Aug. 21, 1822.

[CHAPTER III   ]

The Development of the Grenvillite Party, 1801–4

ON March 14, 1801, after seventeen years at the helm, William Pitt surrendered the Treasury seals to his sovereign as a result of their irreconcilable view on the Catholic emancipation issue, thus concluding the longest and most stable Ministry since Walpole's. His successor, Henry Addington, would then preside over one of the least steady. Accompanying Pitt in his resignation were: Lord Grenville, the Foreign Secretary; Henry Dundas, Secretary for War; Earl Spencer, First Lord of the Admiralty; William Windham, Secretary at War; Lord Camden, a Minister without portfolio; Lord Cornwallis, Lord Lieutenant of Ireland; and Lord Castlereagh, the Irish Chief Secretary. Others in important sub-Cabinet offices who also resigned included: George Canning, Pitt's special friend; two of his fellow "Canningites," Lords Granville Leveson Gower and Morpeth; Earl Temple, elder son of the Marquis of Buckingham; George Rose; and Lord Gower. Of those who demonstrated this loyalty to Pitt in 1801, Spencer, Windham, Morpeth, Temple, and Gower (as second Marquis of Stafford) were by 1805 attached politically to Lord Grenville in his opposition to Pitt's second Administration.

Theories abounded in the sophisticated political world of Westminster as to the "true" reason for Pitt's resignation.[1] A goodly number of the theories settled upon the relationship between Lord Grenville and Pitt. Either Pitt had tired of Grenville, wanted to be rid of him, and found his own resignation the easiest way out;[2] or Grenville and Dundas, both wishing to retire, though not alone, had contrived to persuade Pitt to press the Catholic question in such a way as to involve

1. For a good summary of these views, see Richard E. Willis, "William Pitt's Resignation in 1801: Re-examination and Document," *Bulletin of the Institute of Historical Research,* XLIV, No. 110 (1971), 239–57.

2. For the views of Thomas Pelham, Lord Chichester, and Glenbervie, see *The Diaries of Sylvester Douglas, Lord Glenbervie,* ed. Francis Bickley (London, 1928), I, 262–63.

his pride in not giving way to George III.[3] Lord Uxbridge remarked upon the prevailing tendency at Court to blame the whole affair upon the Grenvilles, especially upon the Marchioness of Buckingham, who was a Roman Catholic.[4] Charles Abbot, likewise, reported the rumor that Lord and Lady Buckingham had "impelled" Grenville to act as he had on the Catholic question.[5] To my knowledge not a shred of evidence exists which supports these rather convoluted theories, although the anti-Grenvillian hostility they illustrate was real enough. By 1801, for a variety of reasons—among them the overaccumulation of sinecures, Buckingham's sly patronage grabs, and Lord Grenville's coldness of manner—the Grenville family was one of the most disliked in the kingdom. This situation was aggravated rather than tempered by the events of the ensuing months.

1. *The Stowe Grenville and Fitzwilliam*
Connections in 1801

Both in private and in public Lord Grenville professed his intention to support the King's new Ministers. He informed both Buckingham and George III of this fact, and he persuaded his brother-in-law, Lord Carysfort, to remain at his Berlin embassy.[6] In the Lords, when the Earl of Carlisle refused to commit himself to support the new Government and spoke disparagingly of a "ricketty administration," Grenville and Spencer immediately stood up and plighted their troth to Addington.[7] In private, however, Grenville was much less effusive, as he considered the Ministers "not in every instance exactly such as might be wished."[8]

The Marquis of Buckingham and members of his immediate coterie, on the other hand, vented their disgust over recent events in a more public manner. The Marquis, thinking the new Ministers a group of "vapid dregs," marshaled part of his forces in the Commons to vote against them at the first opportunity, in February.[9] On March 20, when

3. The alleged view of Addington in November, 1801, *after* the peace preliminaries were signed. Ibid., I. 277.

4. *Diaries and Correspondence of James Harris, First Earl of Malmesbury*, ed. James Howard Harris, Third Earl of Malmesbury (London, 1844), IV, 9.

5. *The Diary and Correspondence of Charles Abbot, Lord Colchester*, ed. Charles Abbot, Second Baron Colchester (London, 1861), I, 243.

6. *Court and Cabinets of George III*, Lord Grenville to Buckingham, Feb. 4, 1801, III, 136; *Later Correspondence of George III*, Lord Grenville to George III, Feb. 5, 1801, III, 486; *Dropmore*, Lord Grenville to Carysfort, Feb. 6, 1801, VI, 436–37.

7. *Parl. History*, XXXV (Feb. 10, 1801), 945–46.

8. *Dropmore*, Lord Grenville to Carysfort, Feb. 17, 1801, VI, 450.

9. *Courier* (London), Feb. 21, 1801.

Lord Darnley moved in the Lords for a committee on the state of the nation, a traditional opposition strategy, Buckingham himself came down, along with his crony Bulkeley, to speak for it. Five days later in the Commons, on a similar motion by the Foxite Whigs, Buckingham's son, Temple, announced that the Ministry was "a thing of shreds and patches" in which he could have no confidence. He alluded to the sorrow he felt in having to differ at this stage from his normal allies; avowed suitable anti-Foxite sentiments; and then added, with regard to those ancient enemies, that "yet, setting out from different points, led by different impulses, and following different routes, they might agree in arriving at the same conclusion."[10]

The exact motivation of the Stowe Grenville family in these transactions is somewhat obscure. There is no solid evidence that they actually worked for some type of Grenville-Foxite alliance at this early date, though Glenbervie heard that Buckingham was planning an Administration with Moira and the Prince of Wales at Carlton House.[11] His plan may have been a result of the King's sudden bout of illness during the late winter of 1801, for it can be argued that Buckingham envisioned smoothing the path for the entrance of the Grenville connection into a new King's or Regent's Administration. But this action was more likely an expression of anger on Buckingham's part at a recent turn of events that had deprived his connection of offices and patronage. The flirtation with the Foxite opposition was brief, however, and for the Stowe Grenvilles proved a major embarrassment. Temple discovered the difficulties of attempting to work in concert with those who spoke of the Rights of Man in the Commons.[12] He made one last slashing attack on Addington on May 6, comparing him with Caliban and Trinculo "whose situations were so equivocal that it was impossible to distinguish their heads from their legs"; then he retired to Avington for trout fishing.[13] By this point, Lord Grenville, the King, Pitt, and, of course, the new Prime Minister were furious with the Stowe Grenvilles; and Bulkeley wrote of them that "their unpopularity is beyond all descrip-

10. BM, Wellesley Papers, Add. MSS. 37308, Buckingham to Wellesley, Feb. 10, 1801; *Parl. History*, XXXV: (March 20, 1801) 1190–94 and 1200, (March 25, 1801) 1106–07. *Courier* (London), March 27, 1801.

11. *Diaries of Glenbervie*, I, 205. Aspinall comments that in Feb., 1801, the Prince consulted with Buckingham. But he also consulted with Pitt and Spencer, and neither Buckingham's name nor the names of any of his followers can be found on the proposed Cabinet list which the Prince had drawn up and which, of several such lists, Aspinall thinks is the most definitive. *Correspondence of Prince of Wales*, IV, 183–85.

12. NLW, Coedymaen Papers, 20, Temple to Charles Wynn, March 31, 1801.

13. *Parl. History*, XXXV (May 6, 1801), 1403; *Dropmore*, Buckingham to Lord Grenville, May 17, 1801, VII, 20.

tions with the Ins and the Outs and with all Parties." Even an old oppositionist told Bulkeley that unless Buckingham joined the Whigs "head & soul they would not give a farthing for his vote."[14]

However, what made this curious opposition to Addington on the part of the Stowe Grenvilles potentially more significant than might at first meet the eye was not solely the temporary union of Buckingham and the Whigs but the stance of certain followers and friends of the second Earl Fitzwilliam. William Wentworth Fitzwilliam (1748–1833), as the nephew and heir of Rockingham and the patron of Edmund Burke, was practically the living embodiment of the conservative Whig tradition. He, of course, countenanced the break-up of the old Whig party in 1793 and 1794 and supported Pitt in opposition to French revolutionary principles and French aggression. Fitzwilliam's imprudent actions as Lord Lieutenant of Ireland in 1794 and 1795 led to his recall by the Prime Minister; but though embittered, he continued to give general support to the Government.

Charles James Fox, who was less hysterical concerning his perceptions of the French Revolution, was crushed by the separation from Fitzwilliam, of whom he wrote at the time that he was his most affectionate friend and the person "in the world of whom decidedly I have the best opinion."[15] Thus despite a personal as well as political break with Portland, Spencer, Windham, Thomas Grenville, and other apostates from whiggery, Fox kept up a close friendship with Fitzwilliam, though they sometimes avoided political subjects.[16] By 1800, Fox was discussing the best way to detach Fitzwilliam, who opposed the Irish Union, from the Government and musing to Grey that the Whigs must play down parliamentary reform as a subject abhorrent to the conservative Earl. To Fox's delight, Fitzwilliam was receptive to these overtures and, even before the news of the fall of Pitt was generally known, consented to move the amendment to the address on February 2, 1801.[17] Thus when, in March, the motions were made in both Houses for a committee on the state of the nation, the Fitzwilliamites

14. *Dropmore,* Lord Grenville to Carysfort, March 24, 1801, VI, 475; UCNW, Baron Hill Papers, 6168, Bulkeley to Williams, May 23, 1801.

15. Loren Reid, *Charles James Fox* (London, 1969), pp. 305–6, as quoted from BM, Add. MSS. 47571.

16. NRO, Fitzwilliam Papers, 58, Fox to Fitzwilliam, Feb. 1, 1801. For a recent political and intellectual biography of Fitzwilliam which highlights his role as the conservator of Rockinghamite Whig orthodoxy, see E. A. Smith, *Whig Principles and Party Politics* (Manchester, 1975).

17. BM, Fox Papers, Add. MSS. 47565, Fox to Grey, n.d.; NRO, Fitzwilliam Papers, 58, Fox to Fitzwilliam, Feb. 1, 1801; *Parl. History,* XXXV (Feb. 2, 1801), 887.

and the Grenvillites connected with Stowe were already voting in
unison against Pitt and Addington, eight months before the vote on the
preliminary peace treaty.

During the first decade of the nineteenth century, Fitzwilliam controlled or influenced the return of seven, and at times eight, members of
Parliament.[18] The two most important, in terms of their weight in the
Commons, were French Laurence (1757–1809) and William Elliot (d.
1818). Laurence and Elliot were Burke's James and John. The former, a
prominent lawyer, Admiralty judge, and Regius Professor of Civil Law
at Oxford, helped Burke in preparing his preliminary impeachment
case against Hastings and served as his literary executor.[19] Fitzwilliam,
indeed, originally gave Laurence a Commons seat in 1796 to gratify
Burke.[20] Elliot, who was from county Roxburgh and a cousin of the
first Earl of Minto, had been a friend of Richard Burke, who introduced
him to his father.[21] In 1801, one month after the reaction against the
preliminary peace treaty had led to the formation of the Grenvillite
opposition, Fitzwilliam, based upon his knowledge of Elliot's views on
the efficacy of the French war, offered him a seat in the Commons. At
that time, Elliot sent the Earl a statement of his principles, which serves
as a document of the neo-Burkean ideology of the Fitzwilliam group
throughout the period. He subscribed to Burke's views on the French
Revolution, admitted the necessity of Pitt's restrictions on civil liberties, and opposed both parliamentary reform and any sudden abolition
of the slave trade.[22]

In addition to Buckingham, Bulkeley, and Fitzwilliam, eight other
peers who had supported the French war and were thus not generally
found on opposition division lists voted in the minority on Darnley's
motion on the state of the nation on March 20, 1801: Bute, Carlisle,
Carnarvon, Darnley himself, Dundas, Fife, Romney, and Yarborough.[23] Dundas, who was Fitzwilliam's brother-in-law, Carlisle,
Carnarvon, Fitzwilliam, and Yarborough had been members of the
united Whig party before divisions of the early 1790s. Carnarvon
and Fitzwilliam were connected with the new opposition under Lord

18. Thomas Hinton Burley Oldfield, *The Representative History of Great Britain and Ireland* (London, 1816), p. 287.
19. *The Correspondence of Edmund Burke*, ed. Alfred Cobban and Robert A. Smith, VI (Cambridge, England, 1967), p. 65.
20. Sheffield Papers, F32C, Fitzwilliam to Burke, Aug. 30, 1796.
21. *Gentleman's Magazine*, LXXXVIII, N.S. (1818, Pt. 2), 467.
22. NRO, Fitzwilliam Papers, 59, Elliot to Fitzwilliam, Dec. 8, 1801.
23. *Parl. History*, XXXV (March 20, 1801), 1203.

Grenville's leadership by November, 1801; Carlisle by January, 1802; Yarborough by June, 1803; and Bute and Dundas shortly thereafter.

2. *The Founding of the Grenvillite Party, 1801–3*

On October 14, 1801, only two weeks after the signing of the peace preliminaries between France and Britain, Grenville wrote to Addington that he intended to oppose the treaty in Parliament.[24] The question of whether to support, resist, or remain silent on the peace preliminaries was for Grenville but the culmination of six years of tortuous self-questioning as to the proper method of fighting the war against France and Jacobinism. The one difference for him in 1801 was that he held no official responsibility. There was never a doubt in Grenville's mind as to the issues at contention in the war. Britain was fighting for her constitution, her social system, and her religion against French "monsters."[25] Grenville was not, like Windham or Burke, fighting per se to restore the Bourbons, though he might not have found such a solution to be undesirable. He was, on occasion, enough of a Burkean to see the war in Armageddonish terms, yet he was realistic enough to dislike the doling out of subsidies to ineffective continental allies.[26] The various peace moves of 1796 and 1797, which centered around Malmesbury at Lille and Hammond at Vienna, left Grenville, who wanted peace offers made only to unite public opinion at home, in a despondent state, contemplating resignation, yet at the same time politically sensitive to the pressing domestic clamor for peace.[27] He never seriously contemplated acceptance of the New Year's letter sent by Bonaparte to the King in 1800, in which he called for a negotiated peace, and even after Marengo wanted, if not a secure and permanent peace, an "advantageous and honourable" one.[28] This, he quickly decided, the 1801 preliminaries were not.

24. *Dropmore*, Lord Grenville to Addington, Oct. 14, 1801, VII, 59–60.

25. PRO, Chatham Papers, 30/8/140/Pt. 1, Lord Grenville to Pitt, Oct. 8, 1797; *Court and Cabinets of George III*, Lord Grenville to Buckingham: Sept. 17, 1794, II, 303; May 26, 1801, III, 161.

26. He threatened to resign from the Cabinet in February, 1795, when Pitt announced interest in a new Prussian subsidy. *Dropmore*, III: Pitt to Lord Grenville, Feb. 20–28, 1795, 25; Lord Grenville to Pitt, March 2, 1795, 30.

27. BM, Thomas Grenville Papers, Add. MSS. 41851, Lord Grenville to Thomas Grenville, June 15, 1797; PRO, Chatham Papers, 30/8/140/Pt. 1, Lord Grenville to Pitt, Oct. 8, 1797.

28. *Court and Cabinets of George III*, III, Lord Grenville to Buckingham: Jan. 1, 1800, 4; June 24, 1800, 84.

During the month prior to the parliamentary debates on the preliminaries—November 3 in the Lords, November 3 and 4 in the Commons—the great and minor chiefs of Pitt's late Ministry took sides in arguing the proper course to pursue in the face of a peace most thought inadequate. Camden and Dundas, who agreed in reprobating the preliminaries, decided to stay away from Parliament and not to enter into opposition.[29] Pitt himself was hardly joyous about parting with the Cape of Good Hope and Malta, but he saw the peace as "fortunate for the country" because of the scant prospect of a British victory.[30]

Several days after Lord Grenville received news of the preliminaries, he wrote to Earl Spencer, former First Lord of the Admiralty, suggesting that they meet sometime before the parliamentary session was scheduled to resume on October 29. Spencer, who firmly disagreed with the terms of the preliminaries, agreed to come to Dropmore on Monday, October 25. He could see no reason why Britain should give up the Cape or, indeed, any other hard-won French or Dutch colony without French reciprocity.[31] All three Grenville brothers were united in abhorrence of the preliminaries—Thomas allegedly having remarked that he would sooner have put his hand in the fire than have signed them.[32] But other members of the Grenville connection who had supported the family political line for almost two decades equivocated on this issue. Grenville wrote his brother-in-law, Lord Braybrooke, on October 14, denouncing the peace; but upon the advice of Lord Glastonbury, a Grenville cousin, Braybrooke refused to come to Parliament for the debates, admitting that had he done so the conviction in William's arguments "might have tempted me to join the family in a vote which will be looked upon as factious." Glastonbury, too, declined to attend.[33] Lord Bulkeley, who had willingly opposed Addington the previous March but was always worried about his interest in Carnarvonshire, upon learning that Carnarvon had illuminated for the peace,

29. *Dropmore*, Dundas to Lord Grenville, Oct. 10, 1801, VII, 56–58; Great Britain, Historical Manuscripts Commission, Francis Bickley, ed., *Report on the Manuscripts of Earl Bathurst, Preserved at Cirencester Park* (London, 1923), Camden to Bathurst, Nov. 2, 1801, pp. 28–29.

30. *Dropmore*, Pitt to Lord Grenville, Oct. 5, 1801, VII, 49–50.

31. Ibid.: Lord Grenville to Spencer, Oct. 9, 1801, VII, 53–54; Spencer to Lord Grenville, Oct. 9, 1801, VII, 56. Althorp Papers, 42, Spencer to Camden, Oct. 14, 1801.

32. *Diaries of Glenbervie*, I, 269.

33. Reading, Berkshire RO, Braybrooke-Glastonbury Papers, D/EZ6/1, Braybrooke to Glastonbury, Oct. 16 and Nov. 1, 1801; *Dropmore*, Thomas Grenville to Lord Grenville, Oct. 23–31, 1801, VII, 66–67.

instructed his half-brother, Sir Robert Williams, to vote for the peace.[34]

Sometime before October 23, Thomas Grenville saw William Windham, the former Secretary at War, and learned that he was prepared to actively resist Addington.[35] The members of the small group that followed Fitzwilliam's politics were likewise communicating with each other and agreed to attend the session to oppose Ministers.[36] One potential source of support for the Grenvillite position on the preliminaries quickly dried up. George Canning, whose heart was with his old chief at the Foreign Office, visited Grenville on October 18. Afterward, he told John Hookham Frere of his joy at talking with a person who was not infatuated with the peace, and commenting, "What a comfort it would be, if I were in a situation to act with such!"[37] Yet Canning feared embarrassing an even dearer captain, William Pitt, and chose silence as a proper alternative to opposition.[38] Canning's small knot of friends (Lord Boringdon, Lord Granville Leveson Gower, and, temporarily, Lord Morpeth) were equally unavailable to the Grenvilles.[39]

In the Lords' debate on November 3, Grenville gave the main speech for the opposition, addressing the peers, whom he had dominated for a decade as leader, in his usual concise, nonflorid, solid oratory. He followed two main lines of argument: the first, clearly to protect his own credibility, denied that the treaty of 1801 could be viewed in the light of 1797; the second pointed out the errors in the preliminaries. In 1797, the Bank stoppage, the defection of Britain's allies, and the naval mutinies all had caused the general malaise that had made the peace negotiations at Lille defensible. But in 1801, with the navy supreme and colonial conquests multiplied, there was no such excuse to give France a period of peace in which to further her commerce and create a navy. Other provisions in the Lille negotiations included retention of

34. UCNW, Baron Hill Papers, 6176, Bulkeley to Williams, Oct. 21, 1801; Dropmore, Buckingham to Lord Grenville, Oct. 25, 1801, VII, 66.

35. Dropmore, Thomas Grenville to Lord Grenville, Oct. 23–31, 1801, VII, 66–67.

36. NRO, Fitzwilliam Papers, 59: Laurence to Fitzwilliam, Oct. 11, 1801; Carnarvon to Fitzwilliam, Oct. 25, 1801.

37. BM, Canning–Frere Papers, Add. MSS. 38833, Canning to Frere, Oct. 18, 1801, where on the preliminaries Canning wrote of Pitt, "God forgive P. for the hand that he has had in them!"

38. PRO, Granville Papers, 30/29/8/70, Canning to Leveson Gower, Oct. 14, 1801.

39. BM, Morley Papers, Add. MSS. 48226, Morpeth to Boringdon, Nov. 8, 1801; Leeds Papers, 65, Leveson Gower to Canning, Oct. 17, 1801; PRO, Granville Papers, 30/29/9/1/56, Boringdon to Leveson Gower, Nov. 15, 1801.

the Cape and Cochin, and stipulations for Portugal and the Prince of Orange, none of which were obtained in the preliminaries.[40]

In the Commons, during the debate on the preliminaries, the new opposition took seats on the opposition bench at the bar end of the House, where Burke sat after his separation from Fox.[41] Windham carried the main thrust of the attack in a peroration that concerned basically, as befitted a Burkean, much more ethereal questions than those of the more pragmatic Grenville: loss of national character, Britain's reputation, the French drive for universal empire, the irreligion and immorality associated with the Revolution. He castigated those who, like Hawkesbury, the Foreign Secretary, failed to see that, while Bonaparte may have trampled on the Rights of Man at home, he still exported such ideals abroad. "Nothing," he remarked, can be more idle than the "hope of the extinction of Jacobinism," though now the Jacobin orators "are not to be looked for in the clubs at Paris, but in the clubs of London."[42]

The defense of the peace used against the Grenville-Windham arguments drew weight both from the caliber of such speakers as Pitt, Nelson, and St. Vincent and from the intrinsic merit of their case. Given the contemporary stance of Bonaparte and the state of France in 1793 and 1801, it was difficult to get away with the argument that he represented Jacobinism triumphant. Nelson, who should have known if anyone did, maintained that Minorca was of little value and that Malta was of no consequence to naval security unless it was in French hands, which the treaty stipulated against. Nelson viewed the Cape as a mere "tavern on the passage" to the East, which served often to "delay the voyage." Pitt felt that the loss of certain colonies was unfortunate but that, as they only added a degree to Britain's wealth and that at the price of more war, "a little more wealth would be badly purchased by a little more war." Running through many of the pro-peace speeches was the question of what Britain could do even if the war did continue. Could she restore the Bourbons, given all the good will in the world? Did anyone really advocate or see the possibility of a successful third coalition after the failure of the other two? If so, with whom? Both Mulgrave and Pitt pointed out that, since historically Malta and Minorca were usually controlled by the strongest naval power anyway, in the event of a resumption of war, Britain could no doubt retake them.[43] All in all, the Government position supported by the King and Pitt, seemed more

40. *Parl. History,* XXXVI (Nov. 3, 1801), 163–71.
41. *Courier* (London), Nov. 5, 1801.
42. *Parl. History,* XXXVI (Nov. 4, 1801), 86–140.
43. Ibid., (Nov. 3 and 4) 29–157 passim.

impressive than the opposition rhetoric, and there was no division in the Commons on the debate.

The House of Lords, however, divided 114 to 10. The minority consisted of the Marquis of Buckingham; the Earls Carnarvon, Fitzwilliam, Pembroke, Radnor, Spencer, and Warwick; the Barons Grenville and Gwydir; and the Bishop of Rochester.[44] Pembroke, Gwydir, and Rochester were among this group by fluke and could hardly be considered permanent oppositionists; they did not even oppose the definitive treaty of Amiens in May, 1802. Neither Warwick nor Radnor was ever a firm Grenvillite, and the former supported Pitt after 1804, while the latter had no connection.[45] Henry Herbert, first Earl of Carnarvon (1741–1811), an extremely close friend of Fitzwilliam, had a political career whose hallmark was its unpredictability. He supported both the American and French wars, took a hand in the foundation of the Association of the Friends of the People, opposed the Irish Union, and had an erratic voting record. However, he was a solid supporter of the new opposition during and after 1801.[46]

A mainstay of the new opposition from the beginning was George John, second Earl Spencer (1758–1834), a Rockinghamite and Portland Whig. Thomas Grenville paid Spencer the ultimate compliment in 1805 when he urged his closest friend to come to Stowe to celebrate the visit of the Prince of Wales: "I cannot upon the present occasion offer you any other inducement than that of the real pleasure which the three brothers will have in the presence of the 4th."[47] Spencer ultimately brought his small family connection into the new opposition: his brother-in-law, Richard Bingham, second Earl of Lucan (though not on the peace issue); his cousin, William Stephen Poyntz; and his son, Viscount Althorp (who entered Parliament in 1804).

William Windham (1750–1810), who was in effect the leader of the new opposition in the Commons from 1801 to 1806, was an able parliamentarian yet a difficult individual with whom to coalesce, as Fox, Pitt, and Grenville each discovered in turn. A favorite of both Samuel Johnson and Edmund Burke, and a Foxite Whig, Windham never faltered in the struggle against the principles of the French Revolution and against those Whigs who betrayed a softness toward

44. Ibid., (Nov. 3) 191.
45. BM, Liverpool Papers, Add. MSS. 38359, list of peers; *Later Correspondence of George III*, V, 357–58.
46. Leslie G. Mitchell, *Charles James Fox and the Disintegration of the Whig Party* (Oxford, 1971), p. 177; *Parl. History*, XXXV (May 7, 1800), 171–72.
47. Althorp Papers, 59, Thomas Grenville to Spencer, Aug. 3, 1805.

them.[48] He was the great defender of the French nobility and royalists and, naturally, as Secretary at War, opposed the 1796 and 1797 peace negotiations, though he perversely relished the thought of Pitt being thrown out by Fox, Fox by Sheridan, Sheridan by Horne Tooke, etc., and then meeting the Duke of Bedford and Coke of Norfolk at a continental exile.[49] In line with his hard-nosed character, Windham defended bullbaiting as an aid to the populace in resisting Jacobinical doctrines, and he expressed doubt whether a single bullbaiter had ever joined a corresponding society.[50] At the general election of 1802, Windham lost his Norwich seat and was returned from the Marquis of Buckingham's borough of St. Mawes.

Windham brought two MPs with him into the new opposition: William Pleydell-Bouverie, Viscount Folkestone (1779–1869), son of the second Earl of Radnor; and William Edwardes, second Baron Kensington of Ireland (1777–1852). Folkestone served as a Windham lieutenant in the Commons, frequently speaking on issues germane to the new opposition. Kensington seldom spoke, but he regarded himself, and was regarded by Windham, as the latter's man. Folkestone, who at this period was an intense royalist (although later in the decade he became a follower of Whitbread), in May, 1803, conceived the rather curious idea of moving a resolution that Parliament should proclaim its intention of restoring Louis XVIII, inviting him to England, giving him a royal establishment and "the means of raising an army—making him the Principal, & ourselves only the auxiliaries, giving him assistance in troops, in Money, in Ships—but letting them be at his disposal & under his command." Windham, who was himself more royalist than George III, was put into a state of "consternation" by this news, and the motion was not made.[51]

Windham was also responsible for the appearance of William Cobbett as the new opposition's semiofficial journalist. When Cobbett returned from the United States in 1800, he started a pro-Government London daily, the *Porcupine,* for which he probably received £3,000 from the Ministry through Windham.[52] Despite this initial support,

48. Archibald Philip Primrose, Fifth Earl of Rosebery, *The Windham Papers* (London, 1913), Windham to Mrs. Crewe, Oct. 5, 1793, I, 159.

49. Ibid., Oct. 31, 1796, II, 24–25.

50. *Parl. History,* XXXVI (May 24, 1802), 831–44.

51. BM, Windham Papers, Add. MSS. 37881, Folkestone to Windham, May 31 and June 1, 1803. For an account of Kensington, see E. Tangye Lean, *The Napoleonists: A Study in Political Disaffection, 1760–1960* (London, 1970), pp. 18–39.

52. Arthur Aspinall, *Politics and the Press* (London, 1949), p. 79; BM, Windham Papers, Add. MSS. 37853, Cobbett to Windham, Aug. 4, 1800.

however, in February, 1801, Cobbett broke with his benefactors, vehemently denounced Catholic emancipation, and urged his readers to rally round the Church and the King.[53] But the *Porcupine* opposed the preliminary treaty with France, and in November, 1801, Cobbett was forced to transfer, at some loss, his shares in the newspaper to supporters of Addington.[54] Then a triple negotiation began—between Cobbett and Windham, Windham and the Grenvilles, and the Grenvilles and other political allies—to obtain financial backing for a weekly journal to be edited by Cobbett, who estimated that £600 would be required to commence publication. The monetary contributions were divided into £50 shares: Buckingham took three; Fitzwilliam and Spencer, two; Lord Grenville, Thomas Grenville, Temple, and Windham, one; and Laurence and Cobbett, one-half each.[55] On January 18, 1802, the first number of *Cobbett's Weekly Political Register* appeared. Lord Grenville used this occasion to attempt to bind Canning closer to the new opposition by asking for his assistance for the paper; but, although Canning wished the project well, he politely refused.[56]

It is probably safe to assume that the Grenvilles or, for that matter, Windham never exercised a very firm grasp upon Cobbett's editorial policy. From conviction, Cobbett supported their anti-Amiens policy and the Grenville-Foxite coalition.[57] But as early as the spring of 1804, he was engaging in violent diatribes against the financial and diplomatic policies of Pitt's first Ministry in terms that Lord Grenville could hardly approve.[58] When the Talents took office, Cobbett almost immediately went into a semiradical opposition. In a rather revealing letter to Windham from that period, Cobbett lamented that the Grenvilles had never socialized with him, and he contrasted their reserved conduct with the civility and kindness he had met from the Foxites. He soon afterward quarreled with Windham too over a minor patronage matter, and this terminated their personal relationship.[59]

Lord Grenville's attendance at Parliament during the first four months of 1802 was deliberately spotty, much to the chagrin of some

53. *Porcupine* (London), Feb. 9, 10, 11, 1801.

54. BM, Windham Papers, Add. MSS. 37853, Cobbett to Windham, Nov. 24, 1801.

55. Ibid.: Cobbett to Windham, n.d.; Cobbett to Windham, Jan. 17, 1802. *Correspondence of Prince of Wales,* Thomas Grenville to Spencer, Jan. 5, 1802, IV, 372.

56. Leeds Papers, 63: Lord Grenville to Canning, Jan. 12, 1802; Canning to Lord Grenville, Jan. 12, 1802 (draft).

57. *Cobbett's Annual Register:* May 15–22, 1802; Dec. 24–31, 1803.

58. Ibid., May 19, 1804.

59. BM, Windham Papers, Add. MSS.: 37853, Cobbett to Windham, Feb. 10, 1806; 37883, Windham to Laurence, March 12, 1806.

members of the new opposition.[60] He may have been motivated by a desire to appear less factious when the definitive treaty of Amiens was brought forward, and he may have reasoned that his attempts to entice Pitt into some type of opposition to the peace might better be done in noncontroversial surroundings. However, in his refusal to heed the activist desires of Laurence, Windham, and Thomas Grenville, who were aggressively attacking Addington in the Commons, Lord Grenville displayed the first inkling of that attachment to a country life that so infuriated the more forward oppositionists after 1807.[61]

A few adherents to the new opposition came forward that winter and spring of 1801–2. Lord Grenville's brother-in-law, Lord Carysfort, returned from Berlin in November, 1801, as did Gilbert Elliot, first Baron Minto (1751–1814), from Vienna. Elliot, a Northite and Portland Whig (who was raised to the peerage in 1798), was, along with Windham, Laurence, and his cousin, William Elliot, a particular devotee of Edmund Burke. He fully accepted the need for Catholic emancipation and, after the February, 1801, resignations, indicated that he wished to resign his Vienna embassy as soon as he was relieved.[62]

On the first day of the resumed parliamentary session, January 19, 1802, Frederick Howard, fifth Earl of Carlisle (1748–1825), the old Northite and Portland Whig, who had not attended the Lords during the previous autumn, arose to announce his dissatisfaction with the foreign policies of the Ministry and, in effect, signified his general agreement with the new opposition.[63] Carlisle was generally in ill health from a nervous disorder during most of the last twenty years of his life, and the illness precluded his taking a decided part in Parliament after 1805 or his accepting office at appropriate times.[64] One of his most important contributions to the new opposition lay simply in his family connections: his son, Lord Morpeth, was a Grenvillite by 1802; his brother-in-law, Lord Stafford, by 1805; and his son-in-law, John Campbell, first Baron Cawdor (1755–1821), by 1802.

In the Commons, in March, 1802, William Baker (1743–1824), an old Whig who had adhered to Pitt during the war and supported the

60. BM, Thomas Grenville Papers, Add. MSS. 41852, Lord Grenville to Thomas Grenville, March 1, 1802.

61. NRO, Fitzwilliam Papers, 60, Laurence to Fitzwilliam, Feb. 12 and 24, 1802; *Court and Cabinets of George III,* Thomas Grenville to Buckingham, March 2, 1802, III, 194–95; *Parl. History,* XXXVI (March 3, 1802), 332–45.

62. *Dropmore,* Minto to Lord Grenville, Feb. 15, 1801, VI, 448; BM, Windham Papers, Add. MSS. 37852, Minto to Windham, March 6, 1801.

63. *Parl. History,* XXXVI (Jan. 19, 1802), 312–13.

64. BM, Morley Papers, Add. MSS. 48226, Morpeth to Boringdon, Sept. 21, 1805.

Government on the preliminaries in November, announced that, due to Bonaparte's aggressive stance in Italy, Louisiana, and the West Indies, "the country must still be considered as in a state of war." Baker's tenure with the new opposition was short, however, as he lost his seat at the general election of 1802.[65]

During the several months preceding the vote on the definitive treaty, both the Grenville brothers and George Canning sought to detach Pitt from his pro-ministerial line. The Grenvilles found Pitt shaken by French actions in Italy and Louisiana yet scarcely prepared to desert Addington.[66] Canning made an ineffective attempt to divide Addington, a defender of the slave trade, and Pitt, an opponent of it, on a mildly antislavery motion in the House of Commons.[67] He also managed a birthday dinner for Pitt on May 28, at the Merchant Taylor's Hall, celebrating the glories of the previous Administration, with a program full of implied slurs on the current Ministers. Yet, although Pitt may have been gratified by the performance, the ultimate and unintentional outcome may have served to further solidify the new opposition—who "entered the Hall and marched up it in a body"—as a corporate group separate from the rest of the old Pittite party.[68]

The full debate on the formal treaty of Amiens took place in both Houses of Parliament on May 13, 1802. During the previous weeks, among the various members of the new opposition who had moved for papers relative to the treaty, thus giving themselves ample time to discuss those contingent questions which most bothered them, were: Carlisle on the Netherlands, Elliot on Portugal, Temple and Spencer on Malta, and Laurence on India.[69]

Few original arguments were presented in the Lords, and sixteen peers[70] voted in the antipeace minority. Among these were ten definite members of the new opposition: Buckingham, Carlisle, Carnarvon, Carysfort, Cawdor, Fitzwilliam, Fortescue, Grenville, Minto, and Spencer; four peers who occasionally lent their votes to the Grenvillites

65. *Parl. History*, XXXVI: (Nov. 4, 1801) 151, (March 3, 1802) 340.

66. *Court and Cabinets of George III*, III: Thomas Grenville to Buckingham, Feb. 27, 1802, 190; Lord Grenville to Buckingham, March 12, 1802, 200.

67. See the article on this issue by Patrick C. Lipscomb, "Party Politics, 1801–1802: George Canning and the Trinidad Question," *Historical Journal*, XII, No. 3 (1969), pp. 442–66.

68. BM, Canning-Frere Papers, Add. MSS. 38833, Canning to Frere, April 26, 1802; Emma Eleanor Elizabeth (Hyslop) Elliot-Murray-Kynynmound, Countess of Minto, *The Life and Letters of Sir Gilbert Elliot, First Earl of Minto* (London, 1874), Minto to his wife, May 29, 1802, III, 250.

69. *Parl. History*, XXXVI (May, 1802), 659–86 passim.

70. Ibid. (May 13, 1802), 686–738 passim.

but were not members of the party in any formal way—Kenyon, Mansfield, Radnor, and Warwick; the Duke of Richmond, who told the House of Lords that he had no intention of entering an opposition;[71] and the Earl of Darlington, a follower of the Prince of Wales.[72]

Only one novelty in Windham's antipeace arguments in the Commons was not present the previous November: he now criticized Pitt, if with gentlemanly rhetoric, for failure to take the ideological aspects of the war seriously enough during his own Ministry.[73] This incident caused little comment at the time, though it was certainly indicative of the way in which at least one section of the new opposition was leaning, as Lord Folkestone, a Windham follower, was likewise making anti-Pittite noises in the Commons at this time.[74]

The vote in the Commons was 276 to 20, the minority excluding the two tellers, Temple and Isaac Gascoyne, the latter a proslavery MP concerned with the seemingly precarious position in which the treaty had left Jamaica.[75] The twenty MPs[76] included five followers of Fitzwilliam: Bryan Cooke, Charles Lawrence Dundas, William Elliot, F. F. Foljambe, and French Laurence; four members of the direct Grenville connection: Thomas Grenville, the Wynn brothers, and Sir William Young; Windham and his two supporters, Folkestone and Kensington; Spencer's representative, W. S. Poyntz; William Baker, who may have been a connection of Spencer's; Carlisle's son, Lord Morpeth; and five individuals who were not permanent members of the new opposition: Lord Bruce, Charles Lennox, and Charles Ellis—all of whom supported Pitt after 1804; and William Chamberlayne and George Ellis, who were not returned at the general election of 1802.

Not all of the Marquis of Buckingham's six members or those connected with him before 1801 signified opposition to the definitive treaty: General Nugent, MP for Buckingham, was in Jamaica; Scrope Bernard, MP for Aylesbury, was in a desperate reelection contest and probably found a vote against a popular peace unappealing; Jeremiah Crutchley, MP for St. Mawes, was never a Grenvillite and probably bought his seat at the general election of 1796.[77] Buckingham's closest friend, Lord Bulkeley, and his brother-in-law, Lord Braybrooke, actually came to Parliament and voted in favor of the peace. His first cousin,

71. Ibid., 731.
72. *Correspondence of Prince of Wales,* V, 12, list of the Prince's party, May, 1804, taken from the Chatham Papers.
73. *Parl. History,* XXXVI (May 13, 1802), 748–49.
74. Ibid., (May 7) 655.
75. See the article on Gascoyne in the DNB.
76. *Parl. History,* XXXVI (May 14, 1802), 828.
77. Namier and Brooke, II, 283.

Lord Glastonbury, who in March, 1802, was soured on the treaty, either voted in favor of the peace or, more probably, remained at Butleigh.[78] Braybrooke, Glastonbury, Bulkeley, and Bulkeley's half-brother, Sir Robert Williams, failed to follow the Grenville political line until Pitt's death in January, 1806. Buckingham was hurt and furious, and even ceased calling his cousin Glastonbury "Jemmy." Braybrooke, who did not see the Stowe Grenvilles again until December, 1803, had no doubts that certain promises made to him by the Grenville family, such as the Admiralty and reversionary rights for his sinecure, would not be forthcoming.[79] Despite the family political reunion of 1806, no offices or jobs were given to these apostates during Lord Grenville's Ministry. Buckingham's nephew, Charles Wynn, also had his doubts as to the correctness of the Grenville line, but he swallowed them to the great advantage of his subsequent political career.[80]

The new opposition per se made only one permanent convert to its Commons bench during the last six months of 1802: Admiral George Cranfield Berkeley (1753–1818), Lady Buckingham's half-brother, who had such powerful Pittite connections that he was generally preferred by whichever party governed.[81] Likewise entering the opposition but certainly not following Grenville or Windham were a few of Canning's friends and a group of country gentlemen.[82] This small rise in parliamentary dissatisfaction was probably related to a changing national perception of peace prospects. By the commencement of the first session of the new Parliament on November 16, 1802, with further French aggression in Switzerland, northern Italy, and Germany, it appeared highly unlikely that the peace of Amiens would be more than a short truce. Indeed, Lord Grenville's parliamentary comments upon Ministers—comparing them with Ethelred the Unready—were more violent than during the preceding year.[83] But with renewed war a probability, important Grenvillites began to cast their eyes about for supporters in their effort to see the conflict managed by capable hands.

Although, in late 1802, the primary motivation of the leader of the new opposition, Lord Grenville, seemed to be to return Pitt to office

78. HEH-STG, Box 9, Buckingham to his wife, May 7, 1802; *Dropmore*, Thomas Grenville to Lord Grenville, March 13, 1802, VII, 89.

79. Reading, Berkshire RO, Braybrooke-Glastonbury Papers, D/EZ6/1, Braybrooke to Glastonbury: Sept. 13, 1802, Dec. 5, 1803.

80. NLW, Coedymaen Papers, 20, Temple to Charles Wynn, April 9, 1802.

81. Namier and Brooke, II, 85.

82. *Diary of Colchester*, I, 411–12; Durham Papers, Tierney to Grey, Dec. 4, 1802.

83. *Parl. History*, XXXVI (Nov. 23, 1802), 944–45.

forthwith, the relationship between Pitt and Grenville between 1801 and 1804 is complex and tangled. Pitt was at least surrounded by pro-Grenvillites, especially Camden and Canning, who wished for the return of both chiefs to their old stations; of Grenville's group only Carlisle appeared eager for such an event. In both camps, however, were those who greatly preferred that each leader go his own way: on Pitt's side, Viscount Melville (as Henry Dundas was created in December, 1802); and on Grenville's, Buckingham, Windham, and Fitzwilliam. What Grenville and Pitt themselves desired was thus often swayed by consideration for their allies.

The political and personal relations between the two cousins were not always easy after 1794, even though once the peace of Amiens was signed they no longer had any profound differences of opinion. How deeply their discussions went and how candidly they dealt with each other, however, is sometimes difficult to gauge. During these years when Pitt was not at his physical best, Canning had to warn Grenville on at least one occasion to avoid any reference to the late troubles over the peace so as not to upset his health.[84] And, in 1804, when Thomas Grenville revealed to Fox that in 1801 Pitt had concealed from Lord Grenville that he had made an offer to the King to waive Catholic emancipation for the rest of the reign, Fox expressed amazement at this breach between the two men.[85]

In late 1802, partly on the initiative of Canning, Grenville visited Pitt from October 18 to 21 at Walmer. The French question was no longer a stumbling block, the Catholic issue had seemingly been shelved for the moment, and the two men discussed positively the possibility of Pitt's return to office at the head of a Government that would include Pittites, Addingtonians, and Grenvillites.[86] After Grenville's return home, Buckingham was aghast at the prospect of a coalition with Addington, at the quasi-abandonment of the Catholic question, and—indicative of the way in which his mind was moving —at the scant room for possible new accessions to the Ministry, such as the Foxite Whig, Charles Grey. Thomas Grenville, who agreed with Buckingham, quickly arranged a conference with Spencer at Stowe; and to Canning's horror, Lord Grenville wrote Pitt and more or less an-

84. Leeds Papers, 63, Canning to Lord Grenville, Oct. 3, 1802 (copy).

85. BM, Fox Papers, Add. MSS. 47581, Fox to Fitzpatrick, Jan. 29, 1804.

86. Leeds Papers, 63, Canning to Lord Grenville, Oct. 3, 1802 (copy); *Diaries of Malmesbury,* IV, 79, 82; *Court and Cabinets of George III,* III, Lord Grenville to Buckingham: Oct. 20, 1802, 211–13; Nov., 1802, 214–15. *Dropmore,* Buckingham to Lord Grenville, Nov. 1, 1802, VII, 117–22.

nounced the termination of their projected arrangements.[87] The proposed union with Pitt created little more excitement among Laurence, Windham, and Minto, who were not in attendance at the inhibiting Stowe congress; only Carlisle seemed eager to follow in that direction.[88]

A new note of cooperation with Pitt crept into Lord Grenville's activities, however, after the parliamentary session began in November. Whatever his own future, Grenville informed Canning and wrote Pitt that he fully agreed that Pitt should be placed at the head of an administration to save the country.[89] Thomas Grenville echoed this view in the Commons.[90] But by this time Pitt's own followers were confused: Lord Camden thought Grenville's return to office was essential to Pitt, whereas George Rose felt quite the opposite.[91] Probably Tierney was closer to the true state of affairs than anyone when he wrote to Grey that "the State of Parties . . . is more curious than ever and the new House of Commons more loose and unsettled, if possible, than the last."[92]

Grenville seemed, in general, to desire to cooperate more fully with his cousin, but he was deterred by the negative views of certain key members of his party. This, of course, begs the question of whether he privately welcomed the proffered advice against joining Pitt and Addington. There is no real evidence that he did. He may have felt, however, that as a party leader he was no longer totally a free agent and that he must, from honor and necessity, place some degree of reliance upon the opinions of those he led—the vast majority of whom, from 1802 to 1804, argued against too close a relationship with Pitt.

When Pitt and Grenville met in early January, 1803, and their opinions seemed to coalesce on the issues, as usually happened during their private meetings, Grenville felt relatively optimistic about Pitt's line at the resumption of the parliamentary session after the Christmas recess. But Pitt was not a free agent either; and later in the month, after

87. *Dropmore*, ibid.; *Court and Cabinets of George III*, Thomas Grenville to Buckingham, Nov. 3, 1802, III, 215–16; *Dropmore*, Lord Grenville to Pitt, Nov. 8, 1802, VII, 123–24; *Diaries of Malmesbury*, Canning to Malmesbury, Nov. 9, 1802, IV, 90–91.

88. NRO, Fitzwilliam Papers, 61, Laurence to Fitzwilliam, Nov. 15, 1802; Minto, *Life of Minto*, Minto to his wife, Nov. 26, 1802, III, 260–61; *Dropmore*, Thomas Grenville to Lord Grenville, Nov. 15, 1802, VII, 128–29.

89. *The Diaries and Correspondence of the Right Hon. George Rose*, ed. Leveson Vernon Harcourt (London, 1860), I: 491–92; Canning to Rose, Nov. 20, 1802, 456–57, 499–500.

90. *Parl. History*, XXXVI (Dec. 9, 1802), 1100.

91. Edmund Phipps, *Memoirs of the Political and Literary Life of Robert Plumer Ward, Esq.* (London, 1850), Ward to Mulgrave, Nov. 24, 1802, I, 91; *Diaries of Rose*, I, 503.

92. Durham Papers, Tierney to Grey, Dec. 4, 1802.

several Pitt-Addington meetings, Grenville again despaired of any meaningful and active involvement on Pitt's part in the overthrow of the Government.[93] Pitt's own line in Parliament during the winter and spring months of 1803 was to give Addington as little trouble as might be consistent with his own honor, due to the increasingly tense situation vis-à-vis war or peace with France.[94] Grenville's policy, too, similar to his inactivity during the winter months of 1802 and backed up this time by Thomas Grenville and Canning, was to stay low.[95]

Between March 20 and April 13, 1803, the Pittites and Addingtonians discussed intensively a governmental change that would either replace Addington with Pitt's brother, Lord Chatham, while both Pitt and Addington served as Secretaries of State (which Pitt rejected out of hand), or replace Addington directly with Pitt. The stumbling blocks in the Prime Minister's eyes, and still more in the view of his colleagues, and the chief reason for the ultimate failure of the negotiations, centered around whether the Grenvillites should be included in the Ministry at once (Addington was quite prepared to see them enter after a month or so) and whether in the change the current Ministry should be viewed as having been merely reconstructed or as having come to an end. George Rose thought it absolutely necessary that Grenville and Spencer come back; Melville took the opposite line.[96]

Throughout the negotiations, Grenville and Pitt were in communication by personal contact and by letter. Grenville insisted upon freedom of action on the Catholic question, upon license to state in public his disagreement with public policy since 1801, and upon the necessity for a new Government rather than a reconstruction of the current one. Grenville also thought Pitt should form a Ministry that would include all four of the great parties of the state, thereby admitting Grey, Moira, and Tierney (though not Fox) into office.[97] Pitt told Addington during discussions on April 10 and 11 that it was his intention, if he took office, to submit the names of Grenville and Spencer to the King for inclusion in the Cabinet. Addington, unhappily, agreed to the terms, but his Cabinet did not, and the Prime Minister terminated the

93. *Court and Cabinets of George III*, Lord Grenville to Buckingham: Jan. 10, 1803, III, 242–43; Jan. 24, 1803, 245–46.

94. BM, Rose Papers, Add. MSS. 42772, Pitt to Rose (two letters), March 2, 1803.

95. *Court and Cabinets of George III*, Lord Grenville to Buckingham, III: Jan. 30, 1803, 248; Feb. 15, 1803, 251.

96. *Diaries of Rose*, II, 36; BM, Rose Papers, Add. MSS. 42772, Rose to Pitt, n.d.; BM, Melville Papers, Add. MSS. 40102, Melville to Pitt, June 16, 1803; Philip Ziegler, *Addington* (London, 1965), pp. 176–80.

97. *Court and Cabinets of George III*, memorandum of Lord Grenville, III, 282–90 passim.

discussions.[98] Whether Windham was to be offered a place in the projected Government was ambiguous,[99] though the question may have been academic, as Minto wrote that he, Windham, and William Elliot were opposed to joining a Pitt-Addington-Grenville coalition anyway.[100]

This tension within the new oppositon over the 1802 and 1803 negotiations illustrates a problem that was faced by Grenville as party leader. That he was the leader was never in contention. His past career and long experience both in office and as a general man of business marked him out for a political prominence that even Fox never questioned, much less Windham and Fitzwilliam or (later) Holland and Grey. Yet, the individuals he was leading were used to going their own political way and were not drawn to him by the charisma that a Pitt, Fox, Canning, Peel, or Gladstone could exercise over followers. Nor did he attempt to exercise such authority. Lord Grenville came somewhat reluctantly, as his correspondence shows, to view himself as a party leader, but there was never any false modesty in the role he knew he was constitutionally incapable of playing.[101] His position was made much easier by the fact that his popular brother, Thomas, was able to serve as a bridge to the more austere William for the use of both the new opposition and (later) the Foxites. At moments of great political tension—in January, 1804, when the Grenville-Foxite coalition was formed; in February, 1806, when the Talents took office; in January, 1811, when the Grenvillites and the Whigs negotiated to form a new Government—and over issues of less moment, Thomas was the medium of communication both to and from Lord Grenville concerning any embarrassing or difficult situation. Grenville's burden was further eased after Pitt's death, when lifelong friends like Auckland, Carrington, Essex, and Hardwicke adhered to him.

The French war resumed in May, 1803, and so did parliamentary warfare. The Grenville group was, of course, in decided opposition. Pitt, in the words of Canning, was "completely, avowedly, unmistakeably & irrecoverably separated" from Addington but, significantly, "not in direct hostility to him" through "consideration" for the King.[102] Since a war detested by the Foxite Whigs had resumed, that body had fewer motives for lending general support to the Government.

98. *Diaries of Rose*, II, 38; Ziegler, *Addington*, pp. 178–79.

99. See, for example, *Diary of Colchester*, I, 415, and *Diaries of Rose*, II, 38.

100. Minto, *Life of Minto*, Minto to his wife, April 18, 1803, III, 284–85.

101. He wrote in 1807, "I am not competent to the management of men. I never was so naturally, and toil and anxiety more and more unfit me for it." *Court and Cabinets of George III*, March 7, 1807, IV, 133.

102. BM, Canning-Frere Papers, Add. MSS. 38833, Canning to Frere, June 9, 1803.

In early June, 1803, Fitzwilliam and Colonel Patten introduced in Parliament resolutions that accused the Government of timidity and worse in its conduct of foreign policy. William Pitt did not deem it the proper moment to take a stand and attempted to pursue a neutral course between the position of the war hawks and that of the Prime Minister. He moved for the reading of the orders of the day. The Ministry opposed Pitt's motion. Even Canning, for the first time in his life, as he informed the House, voted against his friend's position. Pitt, after receiving 56 of 333 votes cast, left the House. On the least controversial section of the resolutions, which condemned Ministers for withholding from Parliament evidence of French intentions, Charles Fox wanted to support the new opposition, even if such action might entail a Whig junction with Pitt or Grenville; but he was overruled by his friends.[103] The definite supporters and more distant sympathizers of Lord Grenville in the Commons then obtained 34 votes (excluding Canning and Temple as tellers) out of 275 cast.[104]

At this point, Fox, extrapolating from the voting patterns of the entire spring of 1803, calculated that there were in the Commons 69 Foxites, 58 Pittites, and 36 Grenvillites.[105] Fox certainly took a broad view in his definition of a Grenvillite and obviously included under that umbrella anyone actively dedicated to the destruction of the Addingtonian regime. George Canning, who was perhaps more attuned to the divisions within the conservative ranks, divided the party labeled by Fox as Grenvillite into four groups: (1) the "Grenvilles and Windhams"—Windham, Thomas Grenville, Watkin and Charles Wynn, Elliot, Laurence, Folkestone, Kensington, Temple, Berkeley, Young, and "one more . . . of this description . . . whom I cannot recall" (probably Lord Proby); (2) the "Ld. Fitzwills"—Foljambe, Cooke, and the three sons of Lord Dundas: Charles Lawrence, Lawrence, and Philip; (3) "Us or P[itt]'s friends"—Leveson Gower, Morpeth, Cartwright, Sturges Bourne, John Osborne, Mildmay, Lawley, Dent, Patten, Gregor, Dillon, Gascoyne, Sir William Eliot, and Canning himself; and (4) the "Straglers"—Porchester, Codrington, Hippisley, Beresford, and Henry Holland.[106]

In the Lords, on the same opposition motions, 18 Pittites emerged, 10 Foxites and 13 Grenvillites broadly construed.[107] The latter in-

103. BM, Fox Papers, Add. MSS. 47575, Fox to Holland, June 6, 1803.
104. *Parl. History*, XXXVI (June 3, 1803), 1533–71.
105. BM, Fox Papers, Add. MSS. 47575, Fox to Holland, June 6, 1803.
106. Sturges Bourne, Mildmay, and Eliot, also voted with Pitt on the division of 56. BM, Canning-Frere Papers, Add. MSS. 38833, Canning to Frere, June 9, 1803.
107. *Parl. History*, XXXVI (June 2 and 6, 1803), 1571–73; *The Times* (London), June 3 and 7, 1803; BM, Fox Papers, Add. MSS. 47575, Fox to Holland, June 6, 1803. Lord Cawdor was apparently voting by proxy.

cluded, as definite and permanent members of the new opposition: Carlisle, Carnarvon, Carysfort, Cawdor, Fitzwilliam, Fortescue, Grenville, Minto, Spencer, and Yarborough; and three other peers not permanently connected with the group: Kenyon, Mansfield, and Warwick.[108] Charles Anderson Pelham, first Baron Yarborough (1749–1823), was a Portland Whig who had generally supported Pitt's Government after the outbreak of the war, except on Irish questions. He, along with Buckingham and Fitzwilliam, had signified a distaste for Addington as early as March, 1801, but not until his 1803 vote did he enter into unqualified support for the new opposition.[109]

3. The Formation of the Grenville-Foxite Coalition

In October, 1803, Fox laid out to Charles Grey the four options open to the Whigs: (1) attack both present and past Ministers, (2) support Addington, (3) join the new opposition, (4) do nothing. Fox himself inclined toward the third option, which was based upon Catholic emancipation, the one great issue common to both the Grenvillites and the Foxites.[110] His mind, however, had long since been moving in that direction.

The union of the Foxites and the Grenvillites at first seemed as bizarre to contemporary English opinion as had the celebrated and much denounced coalition of Fox and Portland with Lord North in 1783. But the two situations differed crucially in several ways. The Fox-North coalition had burst like a storm upon a generally unprepared public, whereas the Fox-Grenville coalition was the culmination of several years of subtle preparation and management. Since the latter coalition did not take ministerial shape until Pitt's death in 1806, the King and the people had time to get used to the rather novel idea. Then, too, Pitt himself, during the spring of 1804, was acting with Fox and Grenville and was quite prepared, until forbidden by the King, to admit Fox into his second Administration. Thus, if Pitt was prepared to do this, who could complain too strongly if Grenville did the same? Also, the 1804 Grenville-Foxite coalition was basically a reunion of friends who had

108. *The Times* (London), June 7, 1803; *Parl. History*, XXXVI (June 6, 1803), 1573.

109. Namier and Brooke, II, 22–23. Buckingham was so ill during 1803 that Grenville urged him to curtail his political activities. *Court and Cabinets of George III*, Lord Grenville to Buckingham, Feb. 1, 1803, III, 249–50; *Dropmore*, Buckingham to Lord Grenville, Oct. 9, 1803, VII, 189–90.

110. *Memorials and Correspondence of Charles James Fox*, ed. Lord John Russell (reprint of 1853–57 ed.; New York, 1970), Fox to Grey, Oct. 19, 1803, III, 428–29.

acted together during the 1770s, 1780s, and early 1790s and had been separated by differences over the French Revolution and war but nevertheless obviously pined for each other's company.

During the 1790s, certain questions had separated the Foxites from the mainstream of the body politic, but these were no longer pressing concerns in 1803 and for years thereafter. Among these issues, those involving parliamentary reform and civil liberties were being held in abeyance for any number of reasons and were no more likely to be raised by the increasingly conservative Whig leadership than by any other section of the ruling class. When the legitimate civil liberties of Englishmen, an issue on which the Foxites and Grenvillites did differ, again became a burning concern after 1816, the Grenvillites manfully parted from their Whig allies. The two groups were in total agreement—in principle if not always in tactics—on the most pressing domestic concerns of the day: Catholic emancipation and a genuine reform of the Irish social and political establishment. On economic issues such as the Bank payment question, Lord Grenville was not a conservative. In May, 1803, he supported the Foxite Lord King's motion in the Lords for a committee to examine the financial state of the country, and the following December he made a long and impressive speech on the noxious implications (as he saw them) of the great increase in paper currency.[111]

Throughout the first decade of the new century, a subtle change had been taking place in the way certain people perceived the nature of the war against France and the character of Napoleon. Already in May, 1802, Cobbett had viewed favorably the proclamation of Bonaparte as First Consul for life on the grounds that whiggish elements in England who had supported the Rights of Man and other rhetorical paraphernalia of the new order would become increasingly disenchanted with the regal and ancient régime aspects of Napoleon's rule. He saw quite correctly that the friendship of the *Morning Chronicle* for France would increase or diminish in exact proportion to the French Government's espousal of democratic or monarchical privileges and that if Bonaparte should become "Emperor of the Gauls, it [would] hate him as cordially as we do."[112]

It had long been difficult for the Foxites to view France as being in any way the beleaguered fortress defending freedom against the forces of reaction. Perhaps the great tragedy of the last years of Fox's life was that Bonaparte was not Washington. When the war seemed likely to resume

111. *Parl. History*, XXXVI (May 13, 1803), 1252–58; *Parl. Debates*, I (Dec. 13, 1803), 1824–31.

112. *Cobbett's Annual Register*, May 15–22, 1802.

in 1803, both Fox and Grey favored the continuance of peace, but in spite of their inclination, Grey remarked, "We ought not to show ourselves backward in offering to support the most vigorous exertions for the prosecution of the War. . . . I think we should take care to obviate the charge . . . that we are insensible to the honor of the Country, and always disposed to underrate . . . the aggressions of France."[113] By 1808 and 1809, a powerful section of the Whigs, under the leadership of Fox's favorite nephew, Lord Holland, were as much in favor of the Peninsular war as were Pitt's heirs—if for slightly different reasons. Even George III, in 1806, agreed to send Lord Lauderdale, the "Citizen Maitland" of other days, to attempt to negotiate a peace with France.

But, if the Foxites were moving decidedly toward the political center on foreign policy issues, they were hardly alone in this. As Bonaparte came more and more to discard the trappings of St. Just and Carnot and to replace them with those of Richelieu and Louis XIV, he became in the eyes of some Englishmen more the traditional enemy, though to be resisted, and less the Anti-Christ. The "French Republic is as much destroyed as its bitterest Enemy could have wished," Grenville wrote in 1807.[114] Armageddon had become Blenheim and Gog, Louis XIV. Even Windham himself allegedly apologized to Sidmouth in 1809 for his opposition to the 1801 peace.[115] Problems still arose—for example, after Austerlitz—but they were capable of conciliation. Even after 1813, when some of the original questions implicit in the war had resumed a prominent place in the political discussion, the Grenvillite and Whig arguments that commenced were divisive but not immediately critical. The parties had always had an explicit understanding that their differing views on the origins and conduct of the 1793 war need not be kept hidden, and neither side hedged much on the matter.[116]

The Grenville-Foxite coalition certainly had nothing inevitable about it. It was just as conceivable that Fox might have aligned with Addington, as some of his erstwhile followers had done in 1803, or that Grenville might have swallowed his pride and coalesced with Pitt and Addington in 1804. That neither of the latter possibilities occurred was the result chiefly, it seems, of circumstances that were not necessarily crucial or in any way immutable obstacles to another course of action.

113. Durham Papers, Grey to Fox, March 15 and 19, 1803.
114. BM, Thomas Grenville Papers, Add. MSS. 41852, Lord Grenville to Thomas Grenville, Dec. 10, 1807.
115. Ziegler, *Addington*, p. 147.
116. Durham Papers, Grey to Holland, Jan. 17, 1817.

For, on the one hand, most of the leading members of Grenville's circle and, on the other, Fox and Grey—assuming a certain decent amount of political agreement could be found—were personally drawn more toward each other than to any other party.

One aspect of prime importance that affected both Grenville's position as party leader and the relationship of his group to the more orthodox Pittites was the fact that Grenville was essentially leading a party of Portland Whigs. Lords Carlisle, Carnarvon, Cawdor, Fitzwilliam, Minto, Spencer and Yarborough and William Baker, Thomas Grenville, and William Windham had been followers of Fox, North, and Portland in the 1780s; and William Elliot, French Laurence, and Sir Watkin Wynn, while not then in Parliament, had been socially associated with that group. Whatever the circumstances, they had then joined Pitt to oppose the principles of the French Revolution and not from any personal admiration for or loyalty to him. But after Pitt acquiesced in what was to them a shameful peace, they felt no vestigial loyalty to him as a person, to cause them to jump at his beck and call. The French situation had led them to break with friends—in particular, with Charles James Fox and his circle—and habits of a lifetime over a war that was conceived of in near-apocalyptic terms; and the genuine sorrow caused by the break with Fox and whiggery was too intense and personal to permit them to follow Addington and Pitt in a retreat from their former position. When the battle had resumed and Pitt had shown himself a less than able general, they no longer had any reason to support him. Not that any of them looked upon Fox as an alternate general—Grenville could perform that role admirably; but if the old opposition evidenced a desire to coalesce with them on terms that were not inadmissible to the war effort, why resist? The avidity with which they resumed the old social relations once the new alliance was effected probably testifies to the fact that they sorely missed those relationships. The remnants of the Portland Whigs were about to experience once again a long-sacrificed harmony between their political principles and personal relationships.

There is no doubt that the prime instigator of the Grenville-Foxite coalition was Charles James Fox himself. He began warily to throw out the possibility of such an alliance to his chief lieutenant, Charles Grey, as early as November, 1802, not as something to be expected at an early date, but as an ultimate option nevertheless.[117] Similarily, at the commencement of the first session of the 1802 Parliament, the leading Whig newspaper, the *Morning Chronicle,* gave Thomas Grenville a warm endorsement should he be proposed by the new opposition as

117. *Memorials of Fox,* Fox to Grey, Nov. 29, 1802, III, 374–76.

Speaker of the House of Commons.[118] Besides his old and dear social relations with so many of the new opposition, what Fox particularly admired about the group was their willingness to act in a concerted party opposition, as he put it, "not dissimilar to my own."[119] After resumption of the war, Fox used, as his argument to justify the desire that his followers not attack the Grenvillites in Parliament or in the press, that the Ministers were more to be blamed for starting a wicked war than the powerless Grenvilles were to be blamed for talking against peace.[120]

But Fox was not the only actor on the stage who envisioned the idea of a Grenville-Foxite coalition with something akin to satisfaction. The Prince of Wales, who was a Portland Whig of sorts, also greatly desired such a juncture; and Fox used his enthusiasm as an excuse to open up the idea during the summer of 1803 to at least two other prominent Whigs, Adair and Lauderdale.[121] At first Fox was somewhat disposed to use the Catholic question as the wedge with which to pry open the door to the alliance, but he found the Grenvillites unenthusiastic about such agitation at that precise moment.[122] Then, too, the Prince's opposition to such a course was known, and Emmet's Rebellion in Ireland probably clinched the matter.

The alternative of a concerted Grenville-Foxite attack on the Government's defense system, Fox felt, would serve as well. Apparently after discussions with key leaders among the Grenvillites, Fox and Windham avowed similar sentiments on December 9, during the annual debate on army estimates. Fox, who was worried that many of his followers might blanch at the prospect of cooperation with the Grenvillites, took advantage of the formal annual occurrence to convey the impression that the concurrence of opinion was accidental rather than deliberately planned; and now, as in the future, he was careful to lead his followers slowly toward Stowe and Dropmore.[123] The *Morning Chronicle* during this period gave its blessing to the coalition.[124] It was up to the Grenvilles to make the next move.

118. *Morning Chronicle* (London), Nov. 15, 1802.

119. *Memorials of Fox*, Fox to Grey, March 12, 1803, III, 398–99.

120. Ibid., Fox to O'Brien, June 26, 1803, IV, 8–9.

121. BM, Fox Papers, Add. MSS.: 47564, Fox to Lauderdale, July 7, 1803; 47565, Fox to Adair, n.d.

122. *Memorials of Fox*, III: Fox to Grey, Nov. 27, 1803, 434–35; Fox to Fitzpatrick, Dec. 6, 1803, 441; Fox to Holland, Dec. 17, 1803, 321. BM, Thomas Grenville Papers, Add. MSS. 48156, Fox to Thomas Grenville, Dec. 20, 1803.

123. BM, Fox Papers, Add. MSS. 47581, Fox to Fitzpatrick, Nov. 30 and Dec. 2, 1803.

124. *Morning Chronicle* (London), Dec. 28 and 30, 1803.

As of early January, 1804, Lord Grenville had made no definite decision on the advisability of a junction with Fox. On January 10, 12, and 13, he had long conversations with Pitt, who assured his cousin that he fully felt the inadequacies of the present system and that if he were asked to form a Government, he would seek to include "as much as possible of the talents & weight of the Country." Pitt refused, however, to enter into a traditional and systematic opposition, though he said he would, if necessary, oppose individual bills.[125] On January 11, Grenville saw Windham and informed him of his wish to enter into a more vigorous opposition than hitherto. In addition, he sought the views of Buckingham, Carysfort, and three Portland Whigs: Thomas Grenville, Spencer, and Carlisle. All agreed that a Grenville-Foxite junction of some type must be formed—Buckingham especially, who likened the situation to the anti-North coalition during the last days of the American war. Buckingham, indeed, was prepared to countenance a Foxite Ministry as opposed to a continuation of Addington's Government.

Grenville decided that his brother Thomas was the proper person to approach Fox with their proposal.[126] Thomas, who agreed to take on the task, went to his home on Cleveland Square in London; and from there he encountered Fox, who was probably staying at Holland House. Fox agreed to meet his old friend on January 26, "half-way" between the two residences, for a morning ride in the park. During this meeting a proposal was discussed and agreed to. The only decisions made at the time were that Addington must be brought down and that a nonexclusive "ministry of talents" must succeed him. Lord Grenville immediately wrote and informed Pitt of the success of the negotiations.[127]

On February 2, Windham, the champion of the émigrés, wrote to Fox, the extoller of the Revolution, requesting an interview but allowing that "after an interval of twelve years or more; for such I am afraid it. is; there must be thus much of ceremony before former habits can be resumed, but in all that relates to personal regards & feelings, things will be found, I trust, as exactly in their places. . . ."[128]

125. BM, Thomas Grenville Papers, Add. MSS. 41852: Lord Grenville to Buckingham, Jan. 11, 1804; Lord Grenville to Thomas Grenville, Jan. 13, 1804.

126. Ibid., Lord Grenville to Buckingham, Jan. 15, 1804; *Dropmore*, VII: Thomas Grenville to Buckingham, Jan. 13, 1804, 206–7; Buckingham to Lord Grenville, Jan. 14, 1804, 208.

127. *Dropmore*, VII: Thomas Grenville to Lord Grenville, Jan. 25, 1804, 210; Lord Grenville to Pitt, Jan. 31, 1804, 211–12. BM, Fox Papers, Add. MSS. 47581, Fox to Fitzpatrick, Jan. 29, 1804.

128. BM, Windham Papers, Add. MSS. 37843, Windham to Fox, Feb. 2, 1804 (copy).

[CHAPTER IV]

The Grenville-Foxite Coalition: Part One

---

1. The Grenvillite Party, 1804–6

During the months subsequent to the commencement of the Grenville-Foxite alliance, it was Fox's task to reconcile the old opposition to the new state of affairs. The divisions within the old Whig party between 1793 and 1804 were by no means limited to a split between Foxites and Portland Whigs over the French Revolution. The Foxites themselves experienced quasi-schismatical problems that were aggravated by Fox's secession from Parliament in 1797, by the peace of Amiens, and between 1797 and 1804 by the often erratic conduct of the Prince of Wales, himself a reclaimed Portland Whig of sorts.[1] The personal differences between Grey and Sheridan and between Fox and Tierney, the distrust of Foxite leadership for the Prince's line, the wrath of Fox when the Duke of Norfolk, Tierney, Sheridan, Hobhouse, and others supported Addington in 1803 all had combined by 1804 to reduce the old opposition to a confused and incohesive group with triple loyalties—to Fox, to the Prince, and (in a nonpersonal sense) to Addington—that were sometimes difficult to sort out.[2] It was a tribute to Fox's genius as a party leader that he was able to reunite the loyalties of the three groups by June, 1804, when, with both the Prince's friends and Addington in opposition, the stragglers returned to the fold. By the end of 1804, Fox was able to write with some satisfaction, "Opposition *seems* now restored, at least to what it was before the Duke of Portland's desertion, and other adverse circumstances of those times."[3]

---

1. One of the best current accounts of the internal state of whiggery during these years is in the various introductions (by years) to *Correspondence of Prince of Wales*, Vols. III to V. See also Richard E. Willis, "Fox, Grenville and the Recovery of Opposition, 1801–1804," *Journal of British Studies*, XI, No. 2 (1972), p. 24.

2. Durham Papers, Grey to Fox, Dec. 17, 1802, and March 15, 1803; BM, Fox Papers, Add. MSS. 47581, Fox to Fitzpatrick, June 6, 1803.

3. *Memorials and Correspondence of Charles James Fox*, ed. Lord John Russell (reprint of 1853–57 ed.; New York, 1970), Fox to Grey, Dec. 17, 1804, IV, 71.

A number of Fox's friends, including William Plumer, Lord Lauderdale, Samuel Whitbread, and Richard Brinsley Sheridan, made it abundantly clear to either Fox or Grey that they were not overjoyed by a union with the Grenville family.[4] Grey, who was himself having second thoughts, recalled that Lauderdale had told him he considered the Grenvilles "the most corrupt Politicians that ever existed," that he believed "their Strength to be contemptible," and that he foresaw "the worst popular affects in such a coalition."[5] Faced with such criticism, Fox wisely temporized and began to emphasize the limited nature of the coalition, making it clear that in not immediately seeking a closer connection he was acting only out of deference to his supporters.[6] In his ultimately successful campaign to convince Lauderdale of the efficacy of acting with the Grenvillites, Fox laid great emphasis on his old bugaboo, the increasing power of the crown; thus, he pointed out, only through coalitions with "obnoxious Persons" were groups formed powerful enough to resist Charles II, James II, and George III.[7]

Lord Grenville, on the other hand, had few such problems. The only member of the new opposition who expressed the least reservation about the way events had moved was Lord Minto, who informed Grenville that he assented only to a loose form of opposition with the Foxites. However, by 1805, having been seduced in part by Holland House dinners, he was as enthusiastic about the coalition as were his friends.[8]

Between March 12 and April 25, ten major divisions took place in the House of Commons, in all but a few of which the Grenvillites, Foxites, and Pittites united to confound Addington. Such victories as the Government won were Pyrrhic, and it was obvious then, as it would be in 1940, that the Prime Minister would have increased difficulty in sustaining his position. The Grenvillites made up about 10 percent of the entire opposition in the Commons that brought down Addington's Ministry.

On April 18, discussions began between Pitt and the King (through the Lord Chancellor), and Pitt kept both Grenville and Fox fully

4. BM, Fox Papers, Add. MSS.: 47581, Fox to Fitzpatrick, Feb. 24, 1804; 47564, Fox to Lauderdale, Feb. 17, 1804. *Memorials of Fox*, Fox to Fitzpatrick, Feb. 25, 1804, IV, 23; *The Diary and Correspondence of Charles Abbot, Lord Colchester*, ed. Charles Abbot, Second Baron Colchester (London, 1861), I, 181.

5. Durham Papers, Grey to Fox, Feb. 2, 1804.

6. *Memorials of Fox:* Fox to Grey, Feb. 15, 1804, III, 453; Fox to Fitzpatrick, Feb. 25, 1804, IV, 23; Fox to Holland, March 19, 1804, III, 242; Fox to Lauderdale, March 30, 1804, IV, 35. BM, Fox Papers, Add. MSS. 47569, Fox to Smith, March 12, 1804.

7. BM, Fox Papers, Add. MSS. 47564, Fox to Lauderdale, April 9, 1804.

8. Emma Eleanor Elizabeth (Hylsop) Elliot-Murray-Kynynmound, Countess of Minto, *The Life and Letters of Sir Gilbert Elliot, First Earl of Minto* (London, 1874), Minto to his wife: Feb. 20, 1804, III, 303–4; Feb. 24, 1804, III, 304–5; Sept. 9, 1805, III, 369.

informed. On May 2, Pitt told the King indirectly of his desire to form a
nonexclusive Ministry, and he made it clear that the Catholic question
would not be raised during George's reign.[9] Despite rhetorical hedging, both Grenville and Fox seemed to concur in the temporary abandonment of that full grant of emancipation, which they both claimed
was crucial.[10] While the King refused to accept Fox as a Minister, he
agreed to send him to a foreign embassy and to tolerate some of his
friends in office.

Grenville, on the evening of May 7, hosted a meeting at Camelford House that was attended by Buckingham, Carlisle, Carnarvon,
Dundas, Fitzwilliam, Spencer, Thomas Grenville, and Windham.
Despite Fox's denial of any debt owed him by the new opposition, the
Grenvillites agreed not to enter the new Ministry without the Whig
leader.[11] On May 8, Grenville informed Pitt of this decision.[12] Thus
ended, in the words of Charles Yorke, "the history of Pitt and Grenville
connection, the latter having at last publicly abandoned his near kinsman
and ancient colleague for his most ancient and inveterate rival and
political antagonist."[13]

Lord Grenville was in an unenviable position, open to charges of
dishonor and baseness whatever his course of action. Perhaps with a
backward glance at the increasingly infirm King, he chose the line
favored by most of his family, his closest friends, and political supporters (and incidentally by the Prince of Wales), a line from which he
veered only at the end of his active political life. In any event, since he
was prepared to defer the Catholic question, Grenville was unable to
cast a believable mantle of political virtue over his decision; and,
needless to say, he impressed few by dragging out before the public the
old corpse of a broadbottom government. He certainly forgot all about
his nonexclusive principles when he himself came to power in 1806 and
refrained from requesting the services of the Pittites.

Sometime during the spring of 1804, after Pitt entered office,
Charles Long and George Rose drew up a list of strengths of some of the

9. *Court and Cabinets of George III,* Lord Grenville to Buckingham, April 19, 1804,
III, 348–50; *The Diaries and Correspondence of the Right Hon. George Rose,* ed. Leveson
Vernon Harcourt (London, 1860), II, 113–14; Philip Ziegler, *Addington* (London,
1965), pp. 214–16.

10. Leeds Papers, 63, Lord Grenville to Canning, n.d.; BM, Fox Papers, Add.
MSS. 47569, Fox to Lord Grenville, April 20, 1804; *Memorials of Fox,* Fox to Grey,
April 19, 1804, IV, 45.

11. *Morning Post* (London), May 10, 1804; *Diary of Colchester,* I, 507.

12. *Court and Cabinets of George III,* Lord Grenville to Pitt, May 8, 1804, III,
352–53.

13. *Later Correspondence of George III,* Yorke to Hardwicke, May 8, 1804, IV, 157.

opposition groups in the Commons. They estimated that out of a total of 658 members 79 followed Fox; 68, Addington; 41, the Prince of Wales; 23, Grenville; leaving 29 whose leadership was doubtful.[14] Those in the House of Commons whom they regarded as Grenvillites were: Lord Althorp, Admiral G. C. Berkeley, Colonel Robert Craufurd, John Dent, H. A. Dillon, William Elliot, Lord Folkestone, Pascoe Grenfell, Thomas Grenville, John Coxe Hippisley, Henry Holland, Lord Kensington, French Laurence, Sir John Newport, Peter Patten, Charles Anderson Pelham, W. S. Poyntz, Lord Proby, Lord Temple, William Windham, Charles Wynn, Sir Watkin Wynn, and Sir William Young.[15]

The list erred (in my opinion) in seven names. Dent and Patten were never followers of Lord Grenville per se and by 1805 generally supported Pitt; Dillon was unattached politically;[16] Holland and Hippisley were, as Canning aptly called them, "Stragglers" in politics and not Grenvillites;[17] Craufurd was in substantial agreement with Windham on military policies,[18] but that appears to have been the extent of his association with the formal Grenvillite party. That Pelham, who had only recently arrived in the House of Commons and was a connection of a mildly Grenvillite peer, Lord Yarborough, ever considered himself a member of the new opposition is problematic.

Long and Rose evidently did not consider Carlisle's son, Lord Morpeth, or the majority of Fitzwilliam's MPs—Bryan Cooke, the three Dundas brothers, and F. F. Foljambe—as Grenvillites. However, any wishful thinking on the part of the Pittites that Morpeth would follow the politics of his friends, Canning and Pitt, rather than his Grenvillite father's, was soon dashed. Fitzwilliam (as will be discussed below) occupied a peculiar position in party politics, but it is probably best to regard his members as an integral part of the new opposition at least until 1805.

The Grenvillite section of the opposition in the Commons acquired three new additions during the winter of 1803–4, Lord Porchester, Pascoe Grenfell, and Sir John Newport. Henry George Herbert, Lord Porchester (1772–1833), was the eldest son of a prominent member of the new opposition, Lord Carnarvon. Canning had not regarded Por-

14. *Diaries of Rose,* II, 119.
15. PRO, Chatham Papers, 30/8/234/, fol. 50–58, as seen at Duke, Grenville-Hamilton Papers, Box 151.
16. BM, Liverpool Papers, Add. MSS. 38359, list of Commons members, 1805.
17. BM, Canning-Frere Papers, Add. MSS. 38833, Canning to Frere, June 9, 1803.
18. Joshua Wilson, *A Biographical Index to the Present House of Commons* (London, 1806), pp. 150–51.

chester as connected with the new opposition a year earlier,[19] but he was certainly following his father's line by 1804; and, indeed he told Lord Grenville that he was acting under his banner.[20] Pascoe Grenfell (1761–1838) of Taplow Court in Bucks, who was a parliamentary watchdog of the Bank of England, was certainly never a pronounced party man; but, insofar as he acted with any group, it was, as Thomas Grenville put it, "with us."[21] Simon John Newport (1765–1843), Grenville's "earliest Private and Public Friend"[22] at Eton and Lincoln's Inn, was the son of a Waterford banker. The Grenvilles always aided him: Buckingham procured an Irish Baronetcy for him in the 1780s, and Lord Grenville used his influence to obtain Government support for him at Waterford for the general election of 1802, although a long and involved election petition prevented him from taking his seat until December, 1803.[23] Newport was a fervent supporter of Catholic emancipation; and this, as well as his old friendship with Lord Grenville, caused him to adhere somewhat to Grenville's politics until 1817. Following the fall of the Talents in 1807, however, Newport was one of the many so-called Grenvillite MPs in whom it is difficult to distinguish any significant differentiation from the general mass of the Whig party.

There were three adherents in the Commons to the Grenvillite section of the opposition between the formation of Pitt's second Ministry and early 1805. Two of them, the sons of Grenvillite peers, who had just entered Parliament for the first time, were Hugh Fortescue, Viscount Ebrington (1783–1861), Lord Grenville's nephew; and John Charles Spencer, Viscount Althorp (1782–1845), Earl Spencer's son. The third individual, William Baker, MP for Herts, had supported the new opposition against the peace of Amiens. He was not returned at the general election of 1802, but in early 1805 both Lord and Lady Spencer aided him at a special successful election for his old constituency.[24]

The strength of the Grenvillites in the Lords during the spring of 1804, in proportion to the entire strength of the combined opposition,

19. BM, Canning-Frere Papers, Add. MSS. 38833, Canning to Frere, June 9, 1803.
20. Duke, Grenville-Hamilton Papers, Box 156, Carnarvon to Grenville, n.d. (transcript).
21. Duke, Grenville-Hamilton Papers, Box 149, Wickham to Lord Grenville, Nov. 15, 1807 (transcript); Dropmore, Thomas Grenville to Lord Grenville, Jan. 27, 1816, X, 412.
22. Duke, Newport Papers, Newport to Lord Grenville, March 30, 1815.
23. HRO, Wickham Papers, 38M49/5/32, Newport to Wickham, Feb. 27 and Dec. 7, 1803.
24. Althorp Papers, 58, Baker to Spencer, Feb. 6, 1805.

varied from 18 to 25 percent.[25] Two new Grenvillite peers had appeared on the scene—though neither appears to have had any close personal or public relationship to any member of the Grenville family. Both were Portland Whigs who owed their recent English peerages to Pitt: Richard Bingham, second Earl of Lucan (1764–1839), Spencer's brother-in-law; and Thomas Dundas, first Baron Dundas (1741–1820), Fitzwilliam's brother-in-law.

The most important member of the House of Lords to adhere to Grenville during the course of Pitt's second Ministry was George Granville Leveson Gower, second Marquis of Stafford (1758–1833). His wife, the Countess of Sutherland, was a prominent Scottish land-owner, and between them they influenced the return of at least six MPs.[26] Stafford was a member of the Pittite wing of the combined opposition to Addington during the spring of 1804, but he opposed the King's exclusion policy and refused to accept any office in Pitt's second Ministry.[27] The loss of Stafford's parliamentary support during the early months of 1805 is a good example of the Prime Minister's declining authority and his general lackadaisical conduct during the last year of his life. Both Canning and Hawkesbury urged Pitt to cultivate the politically powerful Marquis, but he declined even to inform Stafford of his reconciliation with Addington in December, 1804; and when Stafford made known his desire for the Garter, the honor went elsewhere.[28]

As children Stafford and Grenville had attended a school at East Hill near Wandsworth, and Grenville was more attentive to his old friend than Pitt had been. But Stafford had other personal motivations for adhering to the Grenvillites; as his wife acknowledged, by 1805 at least half of Stafford's closest friends, including his brother-in-law, Lord Carlisle, were voting with the Grenville group.[29] Although Stafford did not immediately pledge himself wholeheartedly to the new opposition, by March, 1805, he voted for an opposition motion on the defense

25. *Parl. Debates:* II (April 19, 1804), 165; II (April 24, 1804), 256.
26. Thomas Hinton Burley Oldfield, *The Representative History of Great Britain and Ireland* (London, 1816), IV, 286, 294.
27. Dunrobin Castle Papers, Lady Stafford to Gower: HeP6b/2/1/13, May 10, 1804; HeP6b/2/1/14, May 14, 1804.
28. PRO, Dacres Adams Papers, 30/58/6, Hawkesbury to Pitt, Jan. 6, 1805; PRO, Granville Papers: 30/29/8/3, Canning to Leveson Gower, Feb. 25, 1805; 30/29/6/5/39, Morpeth to Leveson Gower, Feb. 25, 1805.
29. Dunrobin Castle Papers, HeP6b/2/1/31, Lady Stafford to Gower, Feb. 24, 1805; James Loch, *Memoir of George Granville, Late Duke of Sutherland, K.G.* (London, 1834), p. 6.

of the country, and by September Fox, Lauderdale, Thomas Grenville, and Lord and Lady Stafford were working together to influence Scottish burgh affairs.[30] The switch from Pittite to Grenvillite wrought havoc within the Leveson Gower boroughs, as their six MPs had been among the most aggressive supporters of Canning and Pitt in the overthrow of Addington's Ministry.[31] Yet, by the time of Lord Grenville's Ministry, in February, 1806, the entire connection—including Canning's friend, Lord Granville Leveson-Gower—supported it.[32]

By 1805, besides Stafford, at least one lay peer and one bishop were acting with Grenville's wing of the opposition: Henry Fleming Lea, fourteenth Viscount Hereford (1777–1843), and William Cleaver, Bishop of Bangor (1742–1815). Hereford was an unimportant parliamentary addition who followed Grenville's line from that period.[33] Cleaver, who had tutored the children of the first Marquis of Buckingham,[34] had been made Bishop of Chester in 1787, probably through Grenville influence, and was translated to Bangor in 1800. He was the only bishop who stood in decided opposition to Pitt's Ministry in 1805.[35]

Two other peers who later became firm followers of Grenville were Lords Auckland and Bute, both of whom acted in a qualified manner with the Grenvillites in 1805. William Eden, first Baron Auckland (1745–1814), had a reputation, like some bishops, for nodding toward the rising sun. Auckland, a sometime supporter of the Fox-North coalition whose subsequent desertion was particularly resented by many Whigs, was one of Pitt's financial and diplomatic experts in the years after 1785. Because of an old interest in the House of Orange, Auckland very reluctantly supported the peace of Amiens; and, due to a too loquacious tongue on that matter, he nearly lost his Postmaster Generalship.[36] Although during 1805 Auckland was not in declared opposition to Pitt, who had removed him from his office, he was careful

---

30. *Parl. Debates,* III (March 8, 1805), 828–29; BM, Fox Papers, Add. MSS. 47564, Fox to Lauderdale, Sept. 3, 17, and Oct. 10, 1805.

31. SRO, Sutherland Papers, D868/11/18, Villiers to Stafford, May 16, 1805.

32. Dunrobin Castle Papers, HeP6b/2/2/9, Lady Stafford to Gower, Feb. 13, 1806; PRO, Granville Papers, 30/29/8/4/157, Canning to Leveson Gower, Dec. 6, 1806.

33. Leeds Papers, 78A, Charles Wynn to Canning, April 21, 1827.

34. William James Smith, ed., *The Grenville Papers* (4 vols.; London, 1852–53), IV, 257.

35. BM, Liverpool Papers, Add. MSS. 38359, list of peers, 1805.

36. BM, Auckland Papers, Add. MSS. 34455: Auckland to Rosslyn, Oct. 28, 1801; Addington to Auckland, May 7, 1802; Auckland to Addington, May 7, 1802 (copy).

to keep up a working relationship with Grenville.[37] John Stuart, first Marquis of Bute (1744–1814), son of George III's earliest friend, was a Portland Whig and in 1804 was generally considered to be a follower of the Prince of Wales.[38] Unlike most members of that faction, however, who gradually drifted back into the main body of the Foxite Whigs between 1804 and 1807, Bute appears to have adhered to Lord Grenville personally at some point during or after 1805. Grenville frequently held his proxy, successfully cultivated him personally, and sent him sensitive political correspondence.[39]

During the twenty months of Pitt's second Administration, two major irritants clouded the Grenville-Foxite coalition: the impeachment proceedings against Lord Melville for speculating with public funds, and differing views on the correct policy to pursue in the face of continental war disasters. Lords Grenville and Spencer sympathized with Melville's predicament from the beginning.[40] But on April 8, 1805, twenty Grenvillite MPs, including Thomas Grenville, Lord Temple, and Lord Althorp, voted for Samuel Whitbread's motion of censure against Melville.[41] Indeed, the whole proceedings exhibited for all to see that Grenville neither was a strong party leader nor had particularly firm control over his following. He readily admitted that on this question he differed from all with whom he was connected (except for Spencer); and to Buckingham he poured out his view: that he had "no pretensions to be the head of a party, but if I had, it would certainly be a most extraordinary party, whom I can influence in nothing, but am expected to follow in hunting down the measures and character of a government, of which I certainly was no more the head than I am of the opposition now, but of which I could not well deny that I was often considered as the next most responsible member."[42]

A similar situation arose six months later as the news of Austerlitz trickled back to England while the opposition was considering the advisability of an amendment to the address at the opening of the fourth

37. *Parl. Debates,* IV (May 13, 1805), 822–29; BM, Auckland Papers, Add. MSS. 34456, Lord Grenville to Auckland, March 23 and 31, 1805.

38. *Correspondence of Prince of Wales,* V, 12.

39. Sandon Hall, Stafford, Harrowby Papers, Lord Grenville to Bute, Vol. XXI: Nov. 18, 1805, fol. 42; Sept. 30, 1809, fols. 45–46; Jan. 6, 1812, fol. 56; July 6, 1813, fol. 54. Althorp Papers, 78, Lord Grenville to Spencer, Feb. 15, 1809.

40. *Dropmore,* Thomas Grenville to Lord Grenville, April 1–7, 1805, VII, 255.

41. See the list, probably more accurate than Cobbett's list in the *Parl. Debates,* in Wilson, *A Biographical Index,* pp. 612–14.

42. *Court and Cabinets of George III,* Lord Grenville to Buckingham, May 27, 1805, III, 421–22.

session of Parliament. In early December, 1805, before the result of the battle was known, the two wings of the opposition were unable to agree on the efficacy of the continental connections with Russia and Austria. Indeed, some thought was given to attempt no common line on that divisive subject but rather to allow both groups to avow their differing sentiments on the war.[43] Thomas Grenville, who favored a soft line toward Ministers while the Austrian war held some hope of success, discarded his previous opinion when the full impact of the disaster at Austerlitz was known and, by January 6, 1806, advocated Fox's anti-ministerial position. In this line he had the support of—in Lord Grenville's words—"all my friends whom I most love." But Grenville's reaction, as in the Melville case and, probably, in remembrance of his own disappointments in continental allies, was full of sympathy for Pitt. In unburdening himself to Buckingham, he said he doubted that, even if he and Fox were to form a Ministry, they could agree "on the very first day" in the Cabinet.[44]

Buckingham himself concurred with his brother on the war, but his opinion of Pitt was so low that he was a de facto member of the group that was pushing Lord Grenville to an accommodation with Charles James Fox, who was described by the Marquis at this time as a man of "whose talents, & correctness I think so highly."[45] Fox himself had no intention of allowing an important fissure to appear in a coalition to whose development and maintenance he had devoted so much energy. He privately thought Grenville an obstinate man who mouthed "absur-dities," but he did everything possible to draw up an amendment to which both groups could adhere.[46] He invited Thomas Grenville to St. Anne's Hill and literally enveloped him in conciliation. He then made plans to visit Lord Grenville on January 17 at Camelford House, taking with him the sketch of an amendment, and he told Grey that he would be "very practicable about any alterations" Grenville might wish.[47] But when the meeting was held and the amendment readied, events closer to home proved to be of more immediate interest than either the state of Austria or the resistance of Russia.

43. Althorp Papers, 58, Buckingham to Spencer, Dec. 9, 1805.

44. *Court and Cabinets of George III:* Thomas Grenville to Buckingham, Jan. 6, 1806, IV, 5–6; Lord Grenville to Buckingham, Jan. 7, 1806, IV, 8–9.

45. BM, Thomas Grenville Papers, Add. MSS. 41851, Buckingham to Thomas Grenville, Jan. 9, 1806.

46. BM, Fox Papers, Add. MSS. 47575, Fox to Holland, Jan. 1, 1806.

47. *Court and Cabinets of George III:* Thomas Grenville to Buckingham, Jan. 12, 1806, IV, 11–12; Lord Grenville to Buckingham, Jan. 13, 1806, IV, 13. Durham Papers, Fox to Grey, Jan. 14, 1806.

2. *All the Talents, 1806–7*

When William Pitt died at half past four on the morning of January
23, 1806, Mulgrave wrote that "the world was deprived of its greatest
ornament and the country of its best protector."[48] Pitt's final illness and
death affected his cousin, Lord Grenville, deeply; and, indeed, Wellesley found Grenville so overcome that he could scarcely speak.[49] Others
with less fond memories of Pitt than Grenville's, however, intervened
to cause Grenville a major embarrassment on the eve of office. When, on
January 27, prominent Pittites supported a motion for suitable public
memorials to honor the late statesman, Lord Grenville asked Fox as a
personal favor not to oppose the motion. Fox, who was no hypocrite
whatever his sins, minded his own conscience and refused. In speaking against the motion, he was joined by two Grenvillites, Windham
and Folkstone; and to make matters worse, Sir William Young,
Buckingham's member for St. Mawes, and Thomas Grenville were
conspicuously absent on the day of the vote. Lord Temple, however, in a
speech written by Canning, approved the motion and made it clear that
he spoke for his uncle in another place.[50]

There was little question that the rump of Pitt's weak Ministry was
able to carry on the King's business, and Portland, Hawkesbury, and
Castlereagh quickly informed their sovereign of this fact.[51] On January
27, Lord Grenville, whom few in any group doubted was Pitt's logical
successor, was instructed in an audience with the King to submit a list
of Ministers. The following day Grenville, Spencer, Fox, Grey, and
Windham met at Spencer House to confer, as Fox put it, "chiefly to
Men."[52] During the next week, Grenville learned the difficulties inher-
ent in attempting to form a governing coalition in a form satisfactory to
his own loose party as well as to the Foxites, the Carlton House group,
and the Addingtonians.

Two particular personnel problems immediately concerned Grenville. Windham, who was slated for the Secretaryship for War and the

48. Great Britain, Parliament, Historical Manuscripts Commission, J. J. Cartwright, ed., *Report on the Manuscripts of the Earl of Lonsdale* (London, 1893), Mulgrave to Lowther, Jan. 23, 1806, p. 157 (hereinafter referred to as HMC *Lowther*).
49. [Archibald Philip Primrose, Fifth Earl of Rosebery, ed.,] *The Wellesley Papers*
(London, 1914), Wellesley to Bathurst, Jan. 22, 1806, I, 190.
50. *Parl. Debates*, VI (Jan. 27, 1806), 41–73; *Diary of Colchester*, II, 31; *Diaries
of Rose*, II, 241; *Later Correspondence of George III*, Canning to his wife, Jan. 28, 1806,
IV, 386.
51. *Later Correspondence of George III*, Cabinet minute, Jan. 24, 1806, IV, 382.
52. BM, Windham Papers, Add. MSS. 37843, Fox to Windham, Jan. 28, 1806.

Colonies, pointed out to Grenville his own obligations to his followers, Folkestone and Kensington, and the desire of his fellow Burkean, French Laurence, for a seat on the Admiralty Board. Folkestone was given a place at the Admiralty Board; and upon his refusal of it, the position went to Kensington. When Laurence received nothing, Windham was so distraught that he claimed to hope that the entire negotiation might break off.[53] Following so soon upon the difference of opinion over Pitt's memorial, this incident further aggravated the tension between Grenville and Windham. Fitzwilliam wanted the Privy Seal for himself and the Postmastership for his nephew, Charles Lawrence Dundas; but he himself had to accept instead the Lord Presidency, and the Postmastership went to Lord Carysfort, Grenville's brother-in-law.[54]

The disappointment of both Windham and Fitzwilliam raises the question of the correctness of labeling them as Grenvillites in 1806. They, certainly, among the former Portland Whigs, had the closest social relationship with Fox and the general Holland House set. Unlike Spencer, Carlisle, Minto, or Elliot, neither seems to have been personally close to any member of the Grenville family except Thomas. Contemporaries were divided as to their exact political positions. George Rose, who in 1804 considered Windham but not Fitzwilliam a Grenvillite, counted both men in the Foxite wing of the 1806 Administration.[55] The *Courier,* the leading antiministerial newspaper, within a three-day period during February, 1806, labeled both men Foxites and Grenvillites.[56] Lady Stafford thought that Fitzwilliam "probably" acted with Fox and Windham "probably" with Grenville.[57] Lady Holland dated Windham's separation from Grenville from as late as March, 1807.[58] The few historians who have considered the matter at all are as divided as were the contemporary observers. Alan Frederick Fremantle, writing of 1806, thought of Windham as a Foxite and of Fitzwilliam as a Grenvillite. Keith Feiling considered both men Foxites. J. Steven Watson counted Windham (and also Spencer) as a follower of Fox.[59]

53. Ibid., 37847: Windham to Lord Grenville, Jan. 29, 1806; Lord Grenville to Windham, Feb. 5, 1806. Archibald Philip Primrose, Fifth Earl of Rosebery, ed., *The Windham Papers* (London, 1913), Windham to Laurence, Feb. 1, 1806, II, 285.
54. NRO, Fitzwilliam Papers, 68, Fox to Fitzwilliam, Feb. 4, 1806.
55. *Diaries of Rose,* II, 252.
56. *Courier* (London), Feb. 4 and 7, 1806.
57. Dunrobin Castle Papers, HeP6b/2/2/7, Lady Stafford to Gower, Feb. 14, 1806.
58. *The Journal of Elizabeth Lady Holland, 1791–1811,* ed. Giles Stephen Holland Fox-Strangeways, Sixth Earl of Ilchester (London, 1908), II, 225.
59. Alan Frederick Fremantle, *England in the Nineteenth Century* (New York, 1929),

Windham probably considered himself a Grenvillite, if only at the commencement of the Ministry, since he asked Lord Grenville and not Fox for patronage. Also, upon the vacancy of Pitt's Cambridge seat, Windham supported Spencer's son Althorp in his unsuccessful contest against a leading Foxite, Lord Henry Petty.[60] After his disappointment over Laurence's being denied an office, however, Windham did everything possible during the remainder of the Talents' Ministry to make Lord Grenville and the Marquis of Buckingham miserable.

On the political spectrum, Fitzwilliam was far more conservative than was Lord Grenville; hence, at least until Peterloo and Fitzwilliam's late transfiguration into a liberal hero, they agreed on certain sensitive issues. Yet it is doubtful whether after 1804 or 1805 Fitzwilliam acted as a personal follower of Lord Grenville. Unlike any Grenvillite, the Earl's family was associated with the Whig Club;[61] and, by heritage and private friendships (and forgetting ideology, which the conservative Foxites were not always averse to do), he was such a Whig among Whigs that it is difficult to view him—the man who stood next to Lords Holland and Howick at Fox's funeral bier—as anything but a Foxite Whig. Lord Grenville himself probably regarded Fitzwilliam as such in 1806. He indicated on February 5, 1806, (before Folkestone refused office) that he had ten personal supporters in important positions in the new Ministry: Spencer, Minto, Carysfort, Carnarvon, Temple, Morpeth, Folkestone, Elliot, Windham, and Wickham.[62] The list is interesting for the inclusion of Windham and Folkestone, of Fitzwilliam's close friend Carnarvon and his MP William Elliot, and for the exclusion of the Earl himself.

Other Grenvillites in the Administration included: Spencer, Home Secretary; Minto, President of the Board of Control; William Elliot, Chief Secretary for Ireland; Temple, joint Paymaster and Vice-President of the Board of Trade; Althorp, a Lord of the Treasury; Charles Wynn, Under Secretary at the Home Department; Sir John Newport, Chancellor of the Irish Exchequer; and Carnarvon, Master of the Horse. Auckland, who had played his normally shifty game throughout 1805, upon ascertaining that Grenville would probably form a Ministry, wrote him a flattering letter begging to be of "some

II, 146, 150; Keith Feiling, *The Second Tory Party, 1714–1832* (London, 1938), p. 248; J. Steven Watson, *The Reign of George III,* The Oxford History of England, Vol. XII (Oxford, 1960), p. 435.

60. BM, Windham Papers, Add. MSS. 37906, Windham to Amyot, Jan. 23, 1806.
61. *Morning Chronicle* (London), May 4, 1808.
62. BM, Thomas Grenville Papers, Add. MSS. 41852, list of names, Feb. 5, 1806.

little use" and received the lead at the Board of Trade.[63] Carlisle, in pique because he had not been invited to the January 28 meeting at Spencer House, when offered an office refused on grounds of ill health; however, his son Morpeth became a member of the Board of Control.[64] Stafford, without solicitation on his part, was given Lord Cornwallis's vacant Garter, the lack of which order had in part caused his split with Pitt one year earlier.[65] Of Lord Grenville's own closest connections, neither the Marquis of Buckingham nor Thomas Grenville received any office in the new Ministry.

Two of Lord Grenville's personal friends who were not hitherto active in partisan politics, John King (1760–1830) and William Wickham (1761–1840), were rewarded with important posts. King, who was the son of a chaplain of the Irish House of Commons, had attended Christ Church, Oxford, with William Grenville. When Grenville was at the Home Department, King had served as his Under Secretary and had retained that position until 1806. When Grenville became Prime Minister, King transferred to the Treasury as a Secretary. Six months later, he gave up that post and received a lifetime appointment to the Comptrollership of Army Accounts, and was succeeded in his old post by Buckingham's protégé, William Fremantle.[66] Like King, Wickham had known William Grenville at Christ Church and, during the 1790s when Grenville was Foreign Secretary, had served him as his chief diplomatic agent.[67] In 1802, Wickham had been sent by Addington to Dublin as Chief Secretary, and he was in residence during the ill-fated Emmet's Rebellion. In January, 1804, he resigned his Irish office officially for reasons of health but from an actual motive of even more interest in that it shows the sympathetic climate of feeling within Grenville's innermost circle toward the Irish nationalists. Quite simply, Wickham came under Emmet's spell, identified with him to an intense degree, viewed him as an Irish patriot fighting in a righteous cause, and nearly suffered a nervous breakdown when Emmet, on the morning of his execution, sent him a letter acknowledging his kindness.[68]

63. BM, Auckland Papers, Add. MSS. 34456, Auckland to Lord Grenville, Jan. 26, 1806.
64. Castle Howard Papers, Thomas Grenville to Morpeth, n.d.; BM, Thomas Grenville Papers, Add. MSS. 41856, Morpeth to Thomas Grenville, n.d.
65. Dunrobin Castle Papers, HeP6b/2/2/7, Lady Stafford to Gower, Feb. 14, 1806.
66. R. R. Nelson, *The Home Office, 1782–1801* (Durham, North Carolina, 1969), pp. 34–36.
67. Harvey Mitchell, *The Underground War against Revolutionary France: The Missions of William Wickham, 1794–1800* (Oxford, 1965).
68. NLI, Plunket Papers, PC923, Wickham to Armstrong, n.d.; HRO, Wickham

On January 29, Henry Addington, Viscount Sidmouth, who according to the Pittite whips controlled perhaps sixty-three members of the Commons[69] and had opposed Pitt since July, 1805, met twice with Fox and Grenville to discuss the possibility of his entering the Ministry.[70] Sidmouth had some original objections to the novel notion, but they were overcome largely through the persuasion of an intimate, the Earl of Buckinghamshire, who also was a close friend of the Marquis of Buckingham.[71] The agreement propelled two Addingtonians into the Cabinet: Sidmouth as Lord Privy Seal and Chief Justice Ellenborough as a member without portfolio. Other members of the group also obtained offices: John Hiley Addington and John Sullivan at the Board of Control, Buckinghamshire as joint Postmaster General, Nathaniel Bond as Judge Advocate, and Nicholas Vansittart as Secretary to the Treasury. The adherence of the once despised Addingtonians to the Ministry not unnaturally caused qualms in various quarters. Thomas Grenville expressed a "disgust that I cannot conceal or disguise" and intimated that he could never work directly with such individuals.[72] Some of Pitt's friends, of course, professed shock that Grenville had resorted to a connection with Sidmouth without even approaching them for support.[73]

While among the Grenvillites French Laurence, Windham, Carlisle, and Thomas Grenville were bothered by the compromises endemic in forming a stable coalition, the Foxites too had doubts concerning their share in the proceedings. They had held no offices since the Rockingham and Portland Ministries of the early 1780s; therefore, the accumulated desires of a quarter century of official impotence were legion. Albermarle, Darnley, and Derby, for example, all wanted Ireland.[74] On January 27, Fox conceded the Treasury to Grenville, but a problem arose immediately concerning Grenville's sinecure, the Auditorship of the Exchequer. The holder of both the Treasury and the Auditorship would be placed in the invidious position of having to audit his own

---

Papers: 38M49/1/45, "extract of a letter from Mr. Wickham written at Geneva," Aug., 1836; 38M40/1/56, memorandum of Wickham, 1837.

69. BM, Liverpool Papers, Add. MSS. 38359, list of Commons members, 1805.

70. BM, Auckland Papers, Add. MSS. 34456, Buckinghamshire to Auckland, Jan. 29, 1806.

71. DRO, Sidmouth Papers, 152M, Sidmouth to Buckinghamshire, Sept. 4, 1806.

72. Althorp Papers, 62, Thomas Grenville to Spencer, Feb. 7, 1806.

73. Cartwright, ed., HMC *Lowther:* Camden to Lowther, Feb. 3, 1806, p. 160; Long to Lowther, March 13, 1806, pp. 177–78.

74. BM, Holland House Papers, Add. MSS. 52204A, Allen's Journal, loose papers; BM, Thomas Grenville Papers, Add. MSS. 41856, Fox to Thomas Grenville, Jan. 28, 1806.

accounts. Grenville briefly considered Spencer for the Treasury, but eventually an arrangement was worked out whereby Fox introduced a bill that would allow Grenville to hold both positions but would authorize a deputy to discharge his auditorial duties.[75] Yet, when the issue was still in doubt and Fox suggested Charles Grey for the Treasury, the abrupt manner in which the Grenvilles discarded the proposal hurt Fox deeply. The Grenvilles also objected to Derby as Lord Lieutenant of Ireland and to Lauderdale as President of the Board of Control because of his disapproval of the late Indian Administration of Lord Grenville's friend, Lord Wellesley. The objection to Lauderdale especially irritated Fox, and he told Thomas Grenville outright that there is "something . . . that I do not quite like. . . . There does not seem to be a proper feeling that having conceded the enormous point that the Treasury should be in your hands, I have a right in return, to every thing in arrangement that can lend to take off the unfavourable impression this circumstance will make among my friends."[76] Eventually, in a compromise worked out on the Indian question, a Grenvillite, Lord Minto, went to the Board of Control and Lauderdale was scheduled to go to Bengal as Governor General.[77]

By February 4, disagreements between Fox and Lord Grenville over individuals (though not over public issues) caused talk of breaking off the negotiations. Fox, above all, did not desire this to happen, and he approached Thomas Grenville to mediate the quarrel. Thomas agreed and by February 5 a Ministry was arranged.[78] If one includes Fitzwilliam, the Foxites in the Cabinet numbered five. They and the posts they held were: Fox himself as Foreign Secretary; Lord Henry Petty, Chancellor of the Exchequer; Lord Erskine, Lord Chancellor; Charles Grey, First Lord of the Admiralty; and Fitzwilliam, Lord President. Other non-Cabinet Foxite Ministers included: Lord Derby, Chancellor of the Duchy; General Fitzpatrick, Secretary at War; R. B. Sheridan (who was more a follower of the Prince of Wales than of Fox), Treasurer of the Navy; Lord John Townshend, joint Paymaster General; Sir Arthur Pigott, Attorney General; and Sir Samuel Romilly, Sollicitor General. Foxites serving in Ireland were the Duke of Bedford as Lord Lieutenant and George Ponsonby as Lord Chancellor.

75. *Parl. Debates*, VI (Feb. 4, 1806), 148; BM, Thomas Grenville Papers, Add. MSS. 41852, Lord Grenville to Thomas Grenville, Jan. 29, 1806; *Court and Cabinets of George III*, Lord Grenville to Buckingham, Jan. 30, 1806, IV, 15–16.

76. BM, Thomas Grenville Papers, Add. MSS. 41856, Fox to Thomas Grenville, Jan. 28, 1806.

77. BM, Holland House Papers, Add. MSS. 51469: Lord Grenville to Fox, June 23, 1806; Lauderdale to Fox, June 6, 1806.

78. BM, Thomas Grenville Papers, Add. MSS. 41856: Fox to Thomas Grenville, Feb. 4, 1806; Thomas Grenville to Fox, Feb. 5, 1806 (copy).

Counting Windham as a Grenvillite for the moment, the eleven-member Cabinet included three Grenvillites, five Foxites, two followers of Sidmouth, and one direct representative of the Prince of Wales (Lord Moira at the Ordnance). However, of the top-rank Cabinet positions, the Grenvillites held the Treasury and two out of the three seals. Of the various Boards, the Treasury was heavily weighted in favor of the Grenvillites, the Admiralty in favor of the Foxites. The Board of Control had no Foxites, possibly a tribute to Grenville's desire to protect Wellesley from too close a scrutiny. The Grenvillites picked up additional strength within the Ministry when in July, 1806, Lord Minto, who was serving in a non-Cabinet position at the head of the Board of Control, went to India (to replace Lauderdale, who had encountered difficulties in his confirmation by the Court of Directors) and Thomas Grenville succeeded him with a Cabinet seat.

The Foxites, who numerically formed one of the largest blocs in the House of Commons, in general complained little about a quasi-Grenvillite predominance in office. Everybody knew that with Pitt's death, Lord Grenville was his natural and obvious successor, a sentiment in which even some Pittites—Melville, Camden, Rose, Canning —momentarily acquiesced.[79] Had Grenville desired to lead a coalition of Pittites and Addingtonians, nothing could have stopped him, and the Foxites probably realized this as much as anyone else. The Foxites certainly knew that during George III's reign they would have no chance of forming an exclusive Ministry. Therefore they faced the choice of standing in second place in Grenville's Ministry or of resigning themselves to a further period in the political wilderness. In the long run they probably made a wise choice, for their association in office with Grenville and Spencer gave them, after a period of discredit, a chance to achieve a degree of respectability that had been denied them since 1793. It also gave to Grey and Althorp (the latter of whom was not a Foxite in 1806)—both of them too young to have acquired office in 1782 or 1783—their only taste of official position until the crisis of 1830 made the one a Reform Prime Minister and the other Chancellor of the Exchequer and leader of the House of Commons.

Despite an overabundance of Grenvillites in important offices, Lord Grenville almost immediately experienced three serious problems that greatly shook his faith in his efficacy as a party leader and in his ability to keep together a strong Ministry. The problems involved the Marquis of Buckingham, the Marquis Wellesley, and William Windham.

Buckingham, who had spent the last five years of Pitt's life in decided

---

79. BM, Huskisson Papers, Add. MSS. 38737, Melville to Huskisson, Jan. 28, 1806; Cartwright, ed., HMC *Lowther,* Camden to Lowther, Feb. 3, 1806, p. 160; *Diaries of Rose,* II, 247–48, 264.

opposition to his cousin's line and had written, on January 9, 1806, that his opinion of Pitt as a Minister was so low that it was "hopeless to look to any Govt. in which he is to bear a part,"[80] was furious that Pitt's brother, Lord Chatham, had designated Lord Grenville but not himself as an assistant mourner at Pitt's funeral. Buckingham informed Thomas Grenville indirectly that he saw this as "a severe piece of unkind behaviour" from Lord Grenville, and both he and his son Temple more or less threatened a public break with the new Prime Minister. Lord Grenville then wrote Chatham and declined the role of assistant mourner.[81] Three months later, Buckingham was again so upset that he, backed by Temple, was again contemplating withdrawal of support, because Lord Grenville had ceased paying close attention to him. Although the dispute had blown over within a month, Lord Grenville was so hurt by these periodic explosions by those with whom he was so closely connected that he fairly warned his relatives that if they did withdraw their support, he would resign the Treasury.[82] When Thomas Grenville was appointed First Lord of the Admiralty in the governmental reshuffle following Fox's death, all problems with the testy Marquis quickly ceased; for with a brother at the Admiralty, Buckingham, who always fancied himself a military genius, poured his energies into strategical advice to Thomas, requests for patronage, and suggestions for the transfer of naval commanders.[83]

Grenville's handling of the Wellesley problem, however, was more tragic and less capable of solution than that concerning the somewhat humorous fumblings of Lord Buckingham. Richard Colley Wesley, first Marquis Wellesley, brother of the future Duke of Wellington, in his youth and early manhood, had been William Grenville's closest friend. During his early parliamentary career, he was a Grenville protégé; and, luckily, because he was in India as Governor General from 1797 to 1805, he was not called upon directly to take sides in the post-1801 factional struggles. Indeed, some of the politicians at home were in doubt as to whose line he did follow.[84] When Pitt wrote

80. BM, Thomas Grenville Papers, Add. MSS. 41851, Buckingham to Thomas Grenville, Jan. 9, 1806.

81. Ibid., 41854, Temple to Thomas Grenville, Feb. 21, 1806; HEH-STG, Box 174, Lord Grenville to Buckingham, Feb. 20, 1806; PRO, Chatham Papers, 30/8/364, Lord Grenville to Chatham, Feb. 21, 1806.

82. Durham Papers, Buckingham to Howick, April 6, 1806; *Court and Cabinets of George III:* Lord Grenville to Buckingham, May 9, 1806, IV, 29–31; Thomas Grenville to Temple, n.d., IV, 37–38. BM, Thomas Grenville Papers, Add. MSS. 41854, Temple to Thomas Grenville, May 10 and June 14, 1806.

83. BM, Thomas Grenville Papers, Add. MSS. 41851, Buckingham to Thomas Grenville, Nov., 1806, to Feb., 1807, passim.

84. BM, Fox Papers, Add. MSS. 47575, Holland to Fox, Feb. 8, 1805.

Wellesley in 1804 in the hope of securing his future political support, the Governor General responded diplomatically that, while he wished for the reunion of all his friends, he imagined that illness would preclude an active political life after his return to Britain. [85]

Wellesley arrived home in January, 1806, to find a dying Prime Minister. In gratitude to Sidmouth for supporting him while he was in India, he at least considered the idea of refusing a position in a Ministry that was constructed with an anti-Addingtonian bias. [86] However, he informed Grenville of his desire to be included in the new Cabinet, though not at the Board of Control. Yet Wellesley's return to England was marked by the attempt of several MPs—most prominently James Paull and Philip Francis, the latter a Foxite who was closely involved in the attempt to impeach Hastings twenty years earlier,—to prosecute him for his conduct of native wars and for certain financial transactions of his Government. On January 27, Francis and Paull began a long parliamentary campaign and were supported indirectly—so Wellesley informed Grenville—by Windham, another principal in Burke's long-past struggle against Hastings. [87] Grenville thus found it impossible to include his closest friend in the new Government, but he promised him a post at the first opportunity. Both Buckingham and Temple guaranteed Wellesley their parliamentary support in the face of the attacks. [88]

The parliamentary attacks on Wellesley lasted throughout Grenville's premiership, and three of the most forward participants were Windham, Laurence, and Folkestone, whom by this time it would have been impossible to categorize as Grenvillites in any way. [89] During this difficult period Lord Grenville showed his faith in Wellesley by employing him on delicate political missions to George Canning, [90] yet it was probably inevitable that personal relations between the two men would eventually sour. Too many of the men with whom Grenville was politically aligned were involved to some degree in opposing him. When Portland succeeded Grenville in 1807 and offered the Foreign seals to Wellesley, the Marquis declined, although he pledged support

85. PRO, Dacres Adams Papers: 30/58/5, Pitt to Wellesley, Dec. 21, 1804 (copy); 30/58/6, Wellesley to Pitt, May 18, 1805.

86. BM, Wellesley Papers, Add. MSS. 37295, Wellesley to Sidmouth, Jan. 23, 1806.

87. [Rosebery, ed.,] *The Wellesley Papers*, Wellesley to Lord Grenville, Jan. 25, 1806, I, 203; BM, Thomas Grenville Papers, Add. MSS. 41852, Lord Grenville to Thomas Grenville, Jan. 25, 1806; *Parl. Debates*, VI (Jan. 27, 1806), 36–37.

88. DRO, Sidmouth Papers, 152M, Sidmouth to Buckinghamshire, Oct. 8, 1806; *Court and Cabinets of George III*, Wellesley to Buckingham, March 12, 1806, IV, 26–27.

89. *Parl. Debates*, VII (July 6, 1806), 925–38.

90. BM, Rose Papers, Add. MSS. 42773, Canning to Rose, Sept. 3, 1806.

for the new Government.[91] Thereafter Wellesley and Grenville were never intimate, and only the passage of decades allowed some degree of cordiality to reenter their relationship.

The problems involved in the Wellesley case illustrate only one facet of the Grenvilles' declining relationship with Windham, the former chief of the new opposition in the Commons who also sat for a Grenville borough. Windham wanted his electoral freedom from Buckingham at the first opportunity, however, and he received it at the general election of 1806. Then he and Buckingham had words about the long delay in granting a Grenvillite MP, Sir William Young, colonial patronage within Windham's purview.[92] Windham also continued to press Grenville to find an office for French Laurence, hopefully the Judge Advocateship. Grenville consistently refused, however, because of Laurence's anti-Wellesley activities in the House of Commons, and thereby provoked Windham's ire.[93]

Grenville and Windham quarreled constantly over colonial patronage at the Cape, and eventually the Prime Minister made appointments without consulting the Secretary. When Windham left office in March, 1807, he left a memorandum with his chief clerk testifying that he had never consented to Grenville's patronage claims.[94] During the September, 1806, ministerial reshuffle, Grenville had desired that Windham, while keeping his office, move to the Lords. Windham categorically refused, maintaining that he would sooner retire from office.[95] Grenville's motivation in this may have resulted in part from a desire to remove Windham from a position of responsibility in the Commons. This is supported by Buckingham's reminder to Thomas Grenville that, considering the illness of Earl Grey and the likelihood

91. BM, Wellesley Papers, Add. MSS. 37309, Portland to Wellesley, March 24, 1807; [Rosebery, ed.,] *The Wellesley Papers,* Wellesley to Portland, April 21, 1807, I, 234–46.

92. BM, Windham Papers, Add. MSS. 37883, Buckingham to Windham, Feb. 10, 1806; *Court and Cabinets of George III,* Windham to Buckingham, Feb. 19, 1806, IV, 22–23.

93. *Dropmore:* Lord Grenville to Windham, June 4, 1806, VIII, 174; Windham to Lord Grenville, June 4, 1806, VIII, 175–76. Another source of the Grenville-Windham problem was the War Minister's hostility to the Volunteers, beloved especially by the Marquis of Buckingham. A. D. Harvey, "The Ministry of All the Talents: The Whigs in Office, February 1806 to March 1807," *Historical Journal,* Vol. XV, No. 4 (1972), p. 628.

94. BM, Windham Papers, Add. MSS. 37847: copies of letters from Windham to Lord Grenville, June 9, 16, Sept. 2, 27, 1806; Lord Grenville to Windham, June 11, Sept. 5, 27, 1806; memorandum of Windham, March 25, 1807.

95. Ibid.: Lord Grenville to Windham, Sept. 19, 1806; Windham to Lord Grenville, Sept. 19, 1806.

of the removal of Lord Howick (as Charles Grey had become in April, 1806) from the Commons, nothing would be more "mischievous . . . [than] the abandonment of the H of C to Windham." By this time the Marquis of Buckingham regarded his MP from St. Mawes as the possessor of "the most capricious mind, the worst judgment, the most insulated opinions, & the most systematik unpopularity" in the House.[96]

Windham, according to Lord Holland, spoke so bitterly against "the grasping spirit" of the Grenville family, while waiting in the outer room to deliver his insignia of office to George III upon the fall of the Talents in March, 1807, that Holland feared the Lords of the Bedchamber might hear him.[97] At the general election of 1807, Windham was returned from Fitzwilliam's borough of Higham Ferrers, where he sat until his death in 1810. Laurence regarded this formal connection between Windham and Fitzwilliam "as an union of all who remained more immediately representing the sentiments of Lord Rockingham & Mr. Burke."[98]

In retrospect, the Talents' Ministry was a typical example of the weak and brief series of governments that existed from 1801 to 1812 under Addington, Pitt, Grenville, Portland, and Perceval. It was probably saved the ignominious fate of Portland's Government—resignations on the part of its most effective members—only by George III's refusal to countenance even the possibility of future action on the Catholic question. It had one outstanding credit to its fame, the abolition of the slave trade.[99] Despite the vacillations and confusions of February and March, 1807, it had the dubious distinction, perhaps even honor, of leaving office at least in part because of a measure that was designed to improve the lot of Irish Catholics—a fate it shared with Pitt, Peel, and Gladstone.

The opportunity for maneuver in foreign affairs during the year following the battle of Austerlitz was not great; and, under the Talents, the campaigns in South America and southern Italy and the naval action at the Dardanelles were probably no more badly handled than was Walcheren in 1809. Neither did these actions add anything of a

96. BM, Thomas Grenville Papers, Add. MSS. 41851, Buckingham to Thomas Grenville, Sept. 7, 1806.

97. Henry Richard Vassall Fox, Third Baron Holland, *Memoirs of the Whig Party During My Time,* ed. Henry Edward Vassall Fox, Fourth Baron Holland (2 vols.; 1852–54), II, 204–5.

98. NRO, Fitzwilliam Papers, 72, Laurence to Fitzwilliam, May 3, 1807.

99. See Roger Anstey, "Re-interpretation of the Abolition of the British Slave Trade, 1806–1807," *English Historical Review,* LXXXVII, No. 343 (1972), pp. 304–32.

permanent nature to British security; nor did they reflect well on British military and political judgment. The Talents sought to better relations with the United States by adopting a generally more conciliatory policy, and the Administration could not be blamed if President Jefferson and Secretary Madison did not recognize its efforts as such.[100] Their attempt to negotiate a peace with France was finally abandoned when they found it impossible to secure honorable terms.

In any event, the Grenville-Foxite alliance bore up rather well in office. Both groups learned the value of compromise; thus, the Grenvillites acquiesced in sending Lauderdale to India, and in return the main body of Foxites countenanced no support for Paull's attacks on Wellesley.[101] Problems of a minor nature occasionally arose between the groups: the patronage grabbing Grenvilles were hardly enamored with the idea of a reversion bill,[102] and the Grenville family worked with the Staffords to keep Scottish patronage out of the hands of Lord Lauderdale and his "demagogue connexions."[103] Yet, with a few exceptions,[104] even disputes involving parliamentary seats and patronage were few.

The most personally divisive issue to threaten the coalition in terms of both the inner stability of the Ministry and the long-range prospects of a unified party concerned the ministerial prospects of Samuel Whitbread, the brother-in-law of Lord Howick. The Talents' handling of Whitbread certainly betrayed an absence of sensitivity, but the chief culprit was not Lord Grenville. At the time of the formation of the Talents' Ministry, Whitbread, one of the more powerful speakers in the Commons, was given no office. Charles Grey (soon to become Lord Howick), Whitbread's relative, discussed with Fox the possibility of giving him a peerage; but when Whitbread was informed of this, he contemptuously told Grey that he wanted neither a peerage nor an

100. For a discussion of Anglo-American relations during the Talents' Ministry, see Bradford Perkins, *Prologue to War: England and the United States, 1805–1812* (Berkeley, 1961), pp. 101–39.

101. C. H. Philips, *The East India Company, 1784–1834* (Manchester, 1940), p. 145.

102. Grenville thought Petty might have informed him of his intention to move for limiting the granting of reversions, though Grenville himself was not opposed to limiting the reversions to one life beyond that of the current holder. BM, Holland House Papers, Add. MSS. 51468, Lord Grenville to Fox, Feb. 28, 1806.

103. Dunrobin Castle Papers, Lady Stafford to Gower: HeP6b/2/2/9, Feb. 13, 1806; HeP6b/2/2/7, Feb. 4, 1806.

104. For one, though, see BM, Holland House Papers, Add. MSS. 52055A, Allen's Journal, Sept. 9, 1806.

office—the second part of which disclaimer Grey seems to have taken too seriously.[105]

After Fox's incapacitation, Howick attempted to secure for Whitbread Fitzpatrick's non-Cabinet office of Secretary at War, but the old General failed to resign, putting Howick in an embarrassing position.[106] On January 5, 1807, Howick informed the Commons that the French peace neotiations had failed because of the injustice and ambition of France. Whereupon Whitbread arose, expressed his total disagreement with Howick's speech, and intimated that Fox would have taken a different line.[107] This appeared to preclude office or a Cabinet seat for Whitbread insofar as Grenville was concerned. Yet Howick told his chief in February that it was "essential to his comfort" to conciliate Whitbread, though Grenville felt that "such amity is not to be purchased except at a price which I am not disposed to give for it."[108] Howick's arguments evidently wore him down, however, and on March 5, a few days before the King delivered his coup de grace, Grenville told Canning that Whitbread would enter the Cabinet as Secretary at War.[109]

The manner of Grenville's conduct following Fox's collapse in July, 1806, endeared him at least to the conservative Whig leadership. Both Howick and Holland, in private correspondence and memoirs, lauded the Prime Minister's utter rectitude and fairness to the Foxite remnants. Holland, indeed, made the obvious point that had Grenville so desired he could have brought in some Pittites, conciliated George III, and fixed himself permanently in office, but that he did not do so "was a proof of the directness of his intentions, and of his inflexible steadiness in political connection."[110] Holland's wife, who had her own personal reasons for disliking the Grenvilles, and his librarian, John Allen, questioned this lofty view of Grenville's motivation. Both felt that he preferred a continued union with the Whigs rather than with Hawkes-

105. HRO, Tierney Papers, 31M70/72c, Whitbread to Tierney, Dec. 25, 1806; Roger Fulford, *Samuel Whitbread, 1764–1815* (London, 1967), pp. 144–45.

106. BM, Holland House Papers, Add. MSS. 52204A, Allen's Diary, Aug. 30, 1806; BM, Windham Papers, Add. MSS. 37847, Lord Grenville to Windham, Sept. 19, 1806; Fulford, *Whitbread*, pp. 154–57.

107. *Parl. Debates*, VIII (Jan. 5, 1807), 305–76.

108. BM, Thomas Grenville Papers, Add. MSS. 41852, Lord Grenville to Thomas Grenville, Feb. 23, 1807.

109. Julian R. McQuiston, "Rose and Canning in Opposition, 1806–1807," *Historical Journal*, XIV, No. 3 (1971), 522.

110. Durham Papers, Howick to Ponsonby, Aug. 26, 1806; Holland, *Memoirs of the Whig Party*, II, 50–51.

bury or Castlereagh, because he could trust the former but not the latter in a quarrel with the King.[111]

At Fox's death the Cabinet changes included: Sidmouth replacing Fitzwilliam as Lord President; Holland replacing Sidmouth as Privy Seal; Howick supplanting Fox at the Foreign Department; and Thomas Grenville replacing Howick at the Admiralty. Fitzwilliam remained in the Cabinet without office. Among the new Cabinet of twelve, three (Lord Grenville, Thomas Grenville, and Spencer) were definite Grenvillites, five (Petty, Erskine, Howick, Fitzwilliam, and Holland) were Foxite Whigs, two (Sidmouth and Ellenborough) were Addingtonians, one (Moira) represented the Prince of Wales, and Windham followed no political leader. Three great patronage offices—the Treasury, Admiralty, and Home Office—were firmly under Grenvillite control.

Lord Grenville maintained cordial relations, up to a point, with the two other groups within the Talents' Ministry—the Addingtonians and the Prince's party. Sidmouth himself expressed full satisfaction in his private correspondence with his brother.[112] However, during the winter of 1807, when Grenville opened talks with Sidmouth's old nemesis, George Canning, the Viscount felt that a Canningite accession to the Ministry, coupled with proposed Catholic concessions, must lead to a break between his party and the Talents.[113]

Relations with the Prince of Wales, Moira, and Sheridan were likewise relatively good.[114] The Prince was motivated in his political persuasions by personal questions, chiefly relating to his wife, his daughter, his father, and money. His long career was an adventure in self-deception, and he was under the delusion that he was the "sheet anchor" of the Talents' Ministry, that his support was greatly instrumental in its formation, and that he could sustain it in power. Therefore, George was not in the least impressed by what he regarded as the desultory manner of the Government's (and especially Grenville's) handling of the so-called "delicate investigation" of his wife's amatory affairs.[115] However, when in March, 1807, he was faced with the prospect of a Portland Ministry that included two special friends of the Princess of Wales—George Canning and Spencer Perceval—he

111. BM, Holland House Papers, Add. MSS. 52004A, Allen's Journal, Sept. 19, 1806; *Journal of Lady Holland,* II, 182–83.
112. DRO, Sidmouth Papers, 152M, Sidmouth to J. H. Addington, Sept. 18 and 20, 1806.
113. *Dropmore,* Holland to Howick, March 6, 1807, IX, 67.
114. *Correspondence of Prince of Wales:* Moira to the Prince, Sept. 16, 1806, V, 436; Sheridan to the Prince, Sept. 22, 1806, V, 451.
115. Ibid.: Moira to the Prince, Nov. 5, 1806, VI, 38–39; the Prince to Moira, Nov. 7, 1806, VI, 41–42.

flayed the Talents for leaving office and thereupon announced his political neutrality.[116]

One of the great disappointments of Grenville's experience as a party leader was the failure of Thomas Grenville to emerge as a successful House of Commons man. When Francis Horner first heard Thomas speak in the Commons in 1804, at a period when he was making an effort to take a decided part in the debates, he confided to a friend: "He is very sensible, distinct and acute in his matter; but after the first twenty minutes, his delivery becomes unpleasant. His indiscriminate emphasis . . . comes to have no more effect in one respect, than no emphasis at all . . . at the same time . . . your attention is fretted & worried by . . . misplaced phrases & emphasis upon nothings."[117] During the Talents' Ministry, it became obvious to friends and enemies of the Administration that Thomas Grenville's lack of attendance, his ineffective debating when he did attend, and his surface coldness of character precluded him from occupying the one role his brother desired him to play, that of leader of the Grenvillites in the House of Commons. Lord Grenville himself, by the conclusion of his Ministry, finally faced this fact.[118] At the general election of 1807, Thomas even desired to retire from Parliament and unsuccessfully requested that the Marquis of Buckingham give his seat at Buckingham borough to George Tierney.[119]

The failure of Thomas Grenville as a parliamentarian and the obvious fact that Howick, Lord Grenville's Foxite friend, would soon succeed his ailing father in the Lords, presented the Talents in general and Grenville in particular with a problem that remained unresolved throughout the course of the Ministry and well beyond it. The Grenvillite party was essentially a House of Lords group. With Thomas Grenville's increasing ineffectiveness and Windham's break with the Grenvillites, Lord Grenville was left with no strong voice to enunciate his views in the Commons. For obvious reasons, certain powerful Foxite commoners, like Whitbread or Tierney, failed to qualify for such a role. The only other possibility from within the new opposition, William Elliot, was respected by the House and did give "life & spirit" to Lord

116. Ibid., Carysfort to Lord Grenville, March 25, 1807, VI, 155; HRO, Tierney Papers, 31M70/67b, Prince to Tierney, March 20, 1807.

117. LSE, Horner Papers, Vol. II, Horner to Murray, Feb. 28, 1804.

118. Sandon Hall, Stafford, Harrowby Papers, Vol. XII, fols., 72–76, Bathurst to Harrowby, June 2, 1806; *Journal of Lady Holland,* II, 182–83, 208; Holland, *Memoirs of the Whig Party,* II, 196–97; *Court and Cabinets of George III,* Lord Grenville to Buckingham, March 2, 1807, IV, 129.

119. *Court and Cabinets of George III,* Thomas Grenville to Buckingham, April 26, 1807, IV, 171–72.

Grenville's views, but he lacked self-confidence as well as good health.[120] Therefore, on numerous occasions in 1806 and early 1807, Lord Grenville attempted to secure the adherence to his Ministry of a few key men of business from the opposition benches.[121] The Pittite group to which Grenville looked for aid had itself, of course, since 1801, been seriously fragmented, roughly between those who had resigned with Pitt and those who had served Addington on Pitt's request. This split, which was papered over in 1804, was still a living reality in 1806.[122]

The Pittites, following the formation of the Talents' Ministry, were in a curious and distraught state. They were bitter that the Administration contained none of their talent, yet they felt bound to support the King's choice, at least until the Government's line deflected from Pitt's principles. Canning and his friends, who had been amenable to the new opposition since 1801, for the moment looked upon Grenville as their true leader, deserving of support against the Foxite elements of his own Ministry; and they even indulged in daydreams of a Grenville-Foxite split, with Grenville leading the Pittites in opposition.[123] But after a few days of inaction almost all of the Pittites found ample excuse to oppose the Talents on grounds ranging from Ellenborough's joint position as Cabinet member and Chief Justice to Windham's new military policy.[124]

Grenville fruitlessly approached Canning at least five or six times, directly or indirectly, during the summer of 1806, using his friend Wellesley and his brother-in-law Carysfort as conduits.[125] Canning, perhaps overestimating the Administration's weakness following Fox's collapse, would not enter the Ministry without a suitable Pittite adherence. Apparently the highest Lord Grenville was prepared to raise his ante was to offer Canning a Cabinet position, Spencer Perceval a

120. Duke, Grenville-Hamilton Papers, Box 156, Wickham to Lord Grenville, Nov. 8, 1818 (transcript); Duke, Newport Papers, Lord Grenville to Newport, Dec. 29, 1818.

121. See McQuiston, "Rose and Canning," pp. 503–37.

122. *Diaries of Rose*, II, 247–48; Cartwright, ed., HMC *Lowther*, Canning to Lowther, Feb. 9, 1806, pp. 164–65.

123. BM, Rose Papers, Add. MSS. 42774B, Eldon to Rose, n.d.; *Diaries of Rose*, II, 256–57, 262–64, and 312–14; Cartwright, ed., HMC *Lowther*, Canning to Lowther, Feb. 9, 1806, pp. 164–65.

124. BM, Morley Papers, Add. MSS. 48219, Boringdon to Canning, Feb. 28, 1806; Cartwright, ed., HMC *Lowther*, Canning to Lowther, April 8, 1806, p. 182.

125. Leeds Papers, 63: Lord Grenville to Canning, June 30 and July 1, 1806; Canning to Lord Grenville, July 1, 1806 (copy). McQuiston, "Rose and Canning," pp. 508–10; BM, Rose Papers, Add. MSS. 42773: Lincoln to Rose, Aug. 6 and 10, 1806; Rose to Lincoln, Aug. 8, 1806 (draft); Canning to Rose, Aug. 9 and 10, 1806.

non-Cabinet professional arrangement, and George Rose a Pay-mastership.[126] Some Pittites, on the other hand, talked in terms of six Cabinet seats,[127] and Canning himself, who was genuinely fond of Grenville, thought five positions for the Pittites not an unwarranted number.[128] The arrangements in favor of new offices for Howick and Holland were by this point reaching fruition, and nothing was decided for the moment in terms of a Pittite junction.[129]

The Ministry's position was outwardly strengthened by the outcome of the 1806 general election; and Canning, who could read election results if anyone could, met with Grenville three times during March, 1807. If the Talents' Ministry had continued in office, it seems proba-ble that Canning, who had become less firm in his determination to enter office only with the rest of the Pittites, would quickly have succeeded to a Cabinet seat, possibly taking Thomas Grenville's posi-tion at the Admiralty. But when the Catholic Bill became an issue, Canning was equally receptive to Portland, a position which paid off when the new Prime Minister offered him the Foreign seals.[130]

126. BM, Morley Papers, Add. MSS. 48219, Canning to Boringdon, Aug. 29, 1806; Leeds Papers, 61, Wellesley to Canning, Sept. 2, 1806; BM, Rose Papers, Add. MSS. 42773, Canning to Rose, Sept. 15, 1806.

127. BM, Rose Papers, Add. MSS. 42773, Rose to Canning, Sept. 16, 1806 (draft).

128. BM, Canning-Frere Papers, Add. MSS. 38833, Canning to Frere, Sept. 21, 1806.

129. Leeds Papers, 61, observations by Wellesley on Canning's letter to Lowther, Oct. 2, 1806.

130. McQuiston, "Rose and Canning," pp. 521–24; BM, Morley Papers, Add. MSS. 48219, Canning to Boringdon, March 15, 1807; Holland, *Memoirs of the Whig Party*, II, 196–97.

[CHAPTER V]

The Grenville-Foxite Coalition: Part Two

---

1. The Grenvillite Party, 1806–7

If the main body of the Pittites remained aloof from an arrangement with the Talents' Ministry, a few supporters of the late Prime Minister adhered to Lord Grenville in 1806 or 1807 and acted with him even after Portland formed a predominately Pittite Government. Among the Grenville relatives and friends who had opposed the family's political persuasion since the peace of Amiens but now returned to their former allegiance were: a brother-in-law, Lord Braybrooke; a cousin, Lord Glastonbury; Buckingham's closest friend, Lord Bulkeley; and Bulkeley's half-brother, Sir Robert Williams.

Two old friends of Pitt and Grenville, Lords Carrington and Euston, refused to enter the opposition organized by the Pittite remnants in 1806. Robert Smith, first Baron Carrington (1752–1838), owner of the Wycombe Abbey estate in Bucks, was a leading English borough magnate who influenced the return of six MPs.[1] His three brothers, George, John, and Samuel Smith, sat for his boroughs but were generally too radical to be classified as Grenvillites. Carrington also, after 1806, cordially and generously opened his various boroughs to the Grenvillites. George Henry Fitzroy, Earl of Euston (1760–1844), son of the third Duke of Grafton, was a Cambridge friend of William Pitt and his co-member for that University. Euston was one of the friends of Pitt who most desired a broadbottom Government in 1804; and when that endeavor failed, he made no secret of his disappointment in the weakness of Pitt's second Administration.[2] Euston wrote Grenville in February, 1806, expressing a good opinion of his Ministry, and he followed him into opposition in 1807.[3]

---

1. Thomas Hinton Burley Oldfield, *The Representative History of Great Britain and Ireland* (London, 1816), VI, 288.

2. Bury St. Edmunds, Bury St. Edmunds and West Suffolk RO, Grafton Papers: 423/365, Grafton to Euston, March 4, 1804; 423/367, Euston to Camden, April 14, 1805 (extract); 423/375, Grafton to Euston, n.d.

3. Ibid., 423/374, Lord Grenville to Euston, Feb. 19, 1806.

Other supporters of Pitt's second Administration, though not necessarily intimate friends of that Prime Minister, also aided Lord Grenville. George Capel Coningsby, fifth Earl of Essex (1757–1839), a Northite and Portland Whig, was Carrington's closest friend and like that Baron gave an early and permanent support to the Grenvillites.[4] Following the dissolution of Grenville's Ministry, Essex was one of the most dependable, if silent, supporters of the opposition, as his name appears on nearly every important minority division list during the 1807 Parliament. Essex was apparently instrumental in securing for Lord Grenville the occasional support of his nephew, John George, fourth Baron Monson.[5]

John Somers Cocks (1760–1841), who succeeded his father as the second Baron Somers in January, 1806, had been a critical supporter of Shelburne and Pitt in the Commons since 1782. He was listed by Government whips as a "doubtful" Pittite in the summer of 1805.[6] He followed Grenville upon his elevation to the Lords in 1806 and had a high voting record in person or by proxy on opposition motions following March, 1807. Somers considered himself "politically connected" with Lord Grenville, though Grenville, in keeping with his low stance as a party leader, once wrote of Somers that "tho' favourably disposed to my opinions [he] acts entirely on his own impressions."[7]

Philip Yorke, third Earl of Hardwicke (1757–1834), was a follower of Fox until the French war and an Addingtonian after 1801. While serving as Addington's Lord Lieutenant of Ireland he was converted to the necessity of Catholic emancipation and thus came gradually to support Lord Grenville (not Sidmouth) after 1806. Indeed, by January, 1807, Hardwicke and Grenville had commenced a friendly correspondence, which they kept up for years.[8] During the ministerial crisis of March, 1807, Hardwicke told the King outright that his anti-Catholic actions might lead to a replay of the Gordon riots, not to speak of the possible repercussions in Ireland.[9] Hardwicke's Grenvillite political

4. Great Britain, Parliament, Historical Manuscripts Commission, J. J. Cartwright, ed., *Report on the Manuscripts of the Earl of Lonsdale* (London, 1893), Essex to Lowther, March 10, 1806, pp. 175–76; BM, Fox Papers, Add. MSS. 47569, Fox to Bedford, June 16, 1806.

5. BM, Holland House Papers, Add. MSS. 51661, Bedford to Holland, n.d., list of peers.

6. Joshua Wilson, *A Biographical Index to the Present House of Commons* (London, 1806), pp. 131–32; BM, Liverpool Papers, Add. MSS. 38359, list of Commons members, 1805.

7. BM, Liverpool Papers, Add. MSS. 38280, Somers to Liverpool, Sept. 25, 1819; BRO, Fremantle Papers, 47, Lord Grenville to Fremantle, Feb. 23, 1809.

8. BM, Hardwicke Papers, Add. MSS. 35646, Lord Grenville to Hardwicke, Jan. 13, 1807.

9. Ibid., Hardwicke to his wife, March 28, 1807.

stance was not followed by other members of the Yorke family. Both
his brothers, Sir Joseph and Charles Philip, the latter a close friend
of Spencer Perceval, continued to support post-1807 "Tory" Governments.[10] During and áfter 1807, Grenville came to rely heavily
upon the political advice of Hardwicke, consulted closely with him on
party strategy, and invited the Yorke family frequently to Dropmore.[11]

Other peers were also definitely attracted by Grenville to support the
Talents. Among these was Frederick William Hervey, fifth Earl of
Bristol (1769–1859), who in 1805 was considered a Pittite.[12] Bristol
does not seem to have had any close personal relationship with Grenville, though he followed him faithfully for years.[13] Four other peers
who may have been drawn into support of the Talents or (after March,
1807) of the combined opposition by Grenville's role as party leader
were Robert Grosvenor, second Earl Grosvenor; George Ferdinand
Fitzroy, second Baron Southampton; Anthony Ashley Cooper, fifth Earl
of Shaftesbury; and Richard Lumley, sixth Earl of Scarborough, upon
his entry into the Lords six months after the fall of the Talents.
Grosvenor, Southampton, and Shaftesbury, like Bristol, were considered in 1805 to be followers of Pitt,[14] and all three supported the
Grenville-led opposition to the Pittites after 1807. That Southampton
and Scarborough had attended Eton with William Grenville (and
Southampton had had the same tutor) may have created a tie.[15] Henry
Edward, nineteenth Baron Grey de Ruthyn, a young peer, was alleged
by the Duke of Bedford to be possibly susceptible to Grenville's
political influence, and he occasionally supported the opposition in
1809 and 1810.[16]

Grenville's personal following among the Bishops was slight, owing to his advanced views on the Catholic question.[17] The Bishop of
Bangor, William Cleaver, who had followed him in 1805, during the

10. *Dropmore,* Auckland to Lord Grenville, Feb. 27, 1810, X, 15–16; BM, Hardwicke Papers, Add. MSS. 35394, Hardwicke to Yorke, March 8, 1810.

11. BM, Hardwicke Papers, Add. MSS.: 35324, Lord Grenville to Hardwicke,
April 2, 1807; 35647, Lord Grenville to Hardwicke, June 28, 1809.

12. BM, Liverpool Papers, Add. MSS. 38359, list of peers, 1805.

13. Duke, Grenville-Hamilton Papers, Box 158, Bristol to Lord Grenville, Nov.
17, 1820 (transcript).

14. BM, Liverpool Papers, Add. MSS. 38359, list of peers, 1805.

15. Richard Arthur Austen-Leigh, ed., *The Eton College Register, 1753–1790* (Eton,
1921).

16. BM, Holland House Papers, Add. MSS. 51661, Bedford to Holland, list of
peers.

17. Fox remarked in June, 1806, on the lack of support for the Ministry from the
Bishops' bench—always an ill omen. BM, Fox Papers, Add. MSS. 47569, Fox to
Bedford, June 16, 1806.

Talents' Ministry was translated to St. Asaph, where he remained until his death in 1815. In the divisions immediately subsequent to the fall of the Talents, Cleaver's support of Grenville was quite selective.[18] Only with the obvious weakness of the Portland-Perceval Government in 1809 and 1810 did Cleaver return to a more decided support of his benefactor. Charles Moss (1763–1811), a college friend of Grenville, who was appointed Bishop of Oxford two months before the fall of the Talents, gave much more vigorous assistance to the opposition after 1807.[19] Pitt's old friend and tutor, George Pretyman Tomline (1750–1827), Bishop of Lincoln, told George Rose in 1808 that he considered himself a follower of Grenville, whom he supported on occasion during 1807. Like Cleaver, perhaps sniffing a new Grenville Administration, Tomline was much more active in his support in 1809 and 1810.[20]

The activities of Edward Venables Vernon (1757–1847), Bishop of Carlisle, illustrate the problems facing an ambitious prelate with a Grenville orientation. Vernon was the brother-in-law of the Earl of Carlisle and the Marquis of Stafford, both firm Grenvillites by 1805. Vernon, however, refused to desert Pitt, who was promising to give him the see of Lincoln when vacant.[21] The day after Pitt's death, Vernon announced his support for the Grenvillites.[22] When the Talents fell, he affirmed his support for Grenville on all non-Catholic issues; but on Stafford's motion regarding the change of Ministers, he declined to vote at all. Grenville, according to Carlisle, was furious at what he considered to be time-serving, and Carlisle made it clear to his brother-in-law that his options with the opposition were forever closed. Vernon then supported Portland and received his reward several months later through translation to the archiepiscopal see of York.[23]

Grenville lost the support of at least one powerful peer through

18. *Parl. Debates,* IX: (April 13, 1807), 422; (June 26, 1807), 607.
19. Henry Richard Vassall Fox, Third Baron Holland, *Memoirs of the Whig Party during My Time,* ed. Henry Edward Vassall Fox, Fourth Baron Holland (2 vols.; London, 1852–54), II, 91; Duke, Charles Moss Papers, Lord Grenville to Moss, Oct. 8, 1806.
20. BM, Rose Papers, Add. MSS. 42773, Lincoln to Rose, Nov. 14, 1808.
21. Castle Howard Papers: Bishop of Carlisle to Bangor, April 6, 1807; Bishop of Carlisle to Lord Carlisle, June 12, 1807.
22. SRO, Sutherland Papers, D686/11/37, Bishop of Carlisle to Stafford, Jan. 24, 1806. Stafford was less than overwhelmed by this hasty conversion. Dunrobin Castle Papers, HeP6b/2/2/10, Lady Stafford to Gower, Feb. 18, 1806.
23. Castle Howard Papers: Bishop of Carlisle to Bangor, April 6, 1807; Lord Carlisle to Bishop of Carlisle, May 25, 1807 (copy); Bishop of Carlisle to Lord Carlisle, June 12 and 15, 1807. SRO, Sutherland Papers, D686/11/58, Bishop of Carlisle to Stafford, n.d.

lackadaisical conduct and bad party management, that of his distant cousin, the second Duke of Northumberland, who influenced the return of between five and seven members of Parliament.[24] Northumberland had long been a follower first of Fox and then of the Prince of Wales; but he was not consulted by them during the formation of the Talents' Ministry and allegedly received the intelligence of that transaction from his porter.[25] He consequently followed an ambiguous line during the spring months of 1806, now supporting, now opposing the new Ministry.[26] In July, however, the Marquis of Buckingham brought in Northumberland's eldest son, Lord Percy, for Buckingham, thus, in the words of Palmerston, "proclaiming in the most public way the Duke's union with the Grenvilles." But, when Fox died on September 13, Northumberland, to the embarrassment of all concerned, set up Percy for Fox's expensive seat at Westminster. Sheridan, who coveted the seat himself, stepped down as a candidate and Percy was elected.[27] A few weeks later, however, to Northumberland's dismay, Parliament was dissolved. At the ensuing election, Northumberland apparently declined to spend any more money at Westminster, and Percy came in for one of his father's boroughs, while Sheridan, with the support of Grenville, was returned for Westminster. The Duke, who, perhaps not unjustly, considered that he had done Grenville a great favor by returning a member in his interest for such an important London constituency, remarked concerning Grenville: "He has been, & will be pretty well punished for the adoption of this measure. After all that has happen[ed] they have no possible claim to my countenance & support, & they may rest assured that such measure as they meet unto me such measure will I meet unto them in return."[28]

Thus, during 1806 and 1807, at least ten (and possibly sixteen) members of the House of Lords gave allegiance to Lord Grenville's section of the Grenville-Foxite alliance. The factors leading to such junctions can be analyzed in some instances: (1) in terms of personal friendship with Grenville, as was certainly the case with Bulkeley, Carrington, and the Bishop of Oxford; (2) family loyalty, as was the case with Braybrooke and Glastonbury; and (3) ideological consideration, as

24. Oldfield, *Representative History*, VI, 286; Sir Henry Lytton Bulwer, *The Life of Henry John Temple, Viscount Palmerston, with Selections from his Diaries and Correspondence* (London, 1871), I, 39.

25. Bulwer, *Life of Palmerston*, I, 38.

26. BRO, Fremantle Papers, 44, Thomas Fremantle to William Fremantle, April 6, 1806.

27. Bulwer, *Life of Palmerston*, I, 38-40.

28. *Correspondence of Prince of Wales*, Northumberland to McMahon, Dec. 5, 1806.

was the case with Hardwicke. For all ten individuals the recognition
that Grenville was Pitt's logical heir in terms of ability, gravitas, and
even lineage must have played a major role in the decision to follow
him. At that time the Duke of Portland, Pitt's heir in fact in 1807, had
barely risen from his deathbed and would soon return to it, and was
hardly an inviting national totem about which to gather. When Grenville left office in March, 1807, forty-eight years old, in good health,
and by far the most experienced national politician in the empire, few
would have dreamed that his ministerial career was at an end.

During the Parliament of 1806, at least three members of the
Commons besides Sir Robert Williams and Lord Euston—John Anstruther, William Conyngham Plunket, and Thomas Knox—adhered
directly to the Grenvillites. Anstruther (1753–1811) had been a firm
pre-war supporter of Fox and had established himself as an expert on
Indian and judicial affairs.[29] As a Portland Whig, he served from 1797
to 1806 as Chief Justice of Bengal, during which period he formed a
close working relationship with Wellesley. Upon his return to England
and Parliament in 1806, Grenville, perhaps as a favor to Wellesley,
made him a Privy Councillor and, before the dismissal of the Ministry,
was considering him for the Board of Control.[30] Anstruther formally
separated himself from Wellesley's politics and adhered to the Grenvillites at this time, and he remained loyal to that connection despite
attempts made by Portland in 1809 to attach him to the Government.[31]
During the period of their political association, which was cut short by
Sir John's death in 1811, Grenville appears to have valued his opinion
highly.[32]

W. C. Plunket (1764–1854), the eloquent Irish patriot, was appointed Solicitor General for Ireland in 1803 and Attorney General in
1805. The Talents continued him in office. The impetus for the
introduction of Plunket into the Commons appears to have come from
Grenville's friend, William Wickham, late Chief Secretary of Ireland,
who, aware that Plunket's anti-Union speeches during the 1800 debates
in the Irish Commons had deeply impressed his political antagonists,
surmised that he would be a great help to the Talents on Irish business
in the new Parliament. Grenville thus insisted that Plunket stand on

29. Namier and Brooke, II, 25–26.
30. Julian R. McQuiston, "Rose and Canning in Opposition, 1806–1807," *Historical Journal*, XIV, No. 3 (1971), p. 524.
31. *Court and Cabinets of George III*, Dardis to Buckingham, April 25, 1810, IV,
437–38; *Later Correspondence of George III:* Portland to George III, June 18, 1809, V,
299–300; George III to Portland, June 19, 1809, V, 300–301.
32. BM, Thomas Grenville Papers, Add. MSS. 41853, Lord Grenville to Thomas
Grenville, Jan. 12, 1809.

Carrington's interest for Midhurst; but Plunket, who felt that the Irish
Attorney General should remain on the west side of the Irish sea, looked
upon such a move as distasteful.[33] Once at Westminster, however, he
did earn high marks for his abilities. Yet, in his own opinion and
despite urgings from the Portland Administration to the contrary, this
foray disqualified him from continuing to hold his Attorney Generalship upon the change of Ministers, and he resigned.[34] He returned to
his Dublin law practice and remained out of Parliament until 1812,
when he was returned for Trinity College.

Thomas Knox (1754–1840), son of the first Viscount Northland in
the Irish peerage, attended Christ Church, Oxford, with Lord Grenville's two brothers. He entered Westminster in 1806 as a member for
county Tyrone, serving there until 1812, when he was succeeded by
his son and namesake. Though no particular intimacy seems to have
prevailed between either of the Knoxes and the Grenville family, in
1817 and 1818 they aided the Grenvillites in their attempt to establish
a third party in the Commons. At that time, the senior Knox distinctly
told Thomas Grenville that "his original attachment" was to Lord
Grenville and "that he had never varied from it though he had incurred
in his own person and in his son's a good deal of hostility from the
Government."[35] Lord Grenville seems to have accepted this statement,
and throughout the 1820s he endeavored to obtain Northland (as Knox
became upon his father's death) a British peerage.[36]

2. The Grenvillites and the Catholics, 1792–1812

For nearly thirty years Lord Grenville was among the foremost English
advocates of Catholic emancipation. Such support was unquestionably made more difficult by the Stowe-Catholic ménage, which
included his sister-in-law Lady Buckingham, who had been a Roman
Catholic convert since 1772, her daughter Lady Arundel, and certain of
their dependents. The role played by Mary Elizabeth Nugent, Mar-

33. NLI, Plunket Papers: PC921, Plunket to Wickham, Dec. 13, 1806; PC921,
Lord Grenville to Plunket, Dec. 20, 1806; PC922, Wickham to Plunket, Dec. 26,
1806.
34. Ibid., PC922, Redesdale to Plunket, April 9 and 13, 1807; HRO, Wickham
Papers, 38M49/6/11, Plunket to Wickham, May 5, 1807.
35. *Later Correspondence of George III*, V, 598; *Dropmore*, Thomas Grenville to Lord
Grenville, April 15, 1817, X, 423–24.
36. BM, Liverpool Papers, Add. MSS. 38301, Lord Grenville to Liverpool, June
19, 1826 (copy).

chioness of Buckingham, in determining the generally pro-Catholic line of her brother-in-law was certainly not decisive, and there is no evidence that she unduly influenced her husband. However, many of her contemporaries did not take that perspective.

From all indications, the Grenville-Nugent marriage was a successful one. Buckingham was still writing love letters to his wife decades after their marriage.[37] From most accounts, the Marchioness was an amiable woman. Her sister-in-law, Lady Carysfort, found her "a creature endowed with such superior powers and . . . energy of mind and spirit" that she was "the life of every society in which she found herself."[38] But the religious issue was ever present in the background, causing personal and political problems for both her family and the Whig party. Common gossip quite unfairly saw her as a force behind Mrs. Fitzherbert, the Roman Catholic "wife" of the Prince of Wales, or somehow behind the events leading up to Pitt's resignation in 1801.[39]

Buckingham did all he could to keep his wife's religious proclivities as quiet as possible; it was a situation, Lady Carysfort wrote, "over which my dear Brother always tried to throw a veil."[40] Buckingham even saw to it that his wife was buried publicly with Anglican rites, though privately with the rites of her own faith.[41] Such subterfuge, however, was of little consequence.

The Pittite press attacked Lady Buckingham, especially before and during the 1807 no-popery election, as part of a cabal formed to influence the Grenvilles in favor of the Catholics. Press references circulated concerning the popish chapel at Stowe, and there were absurd suggestions that her husband, his two brothers, or her eldest son, Lord Temple, were closet Papists.[42] Lord Grenville, on one such occasion when the *Morning Herald* announced his apostasy from the Established

37. HEH-STG, Box 9. For an account of Lady Buckingham's conversion to Catholicism, her husband's attempts to forbid her the practice of her religion, and her eventual triumph, see the memoir of Lady **Arundel** in *The Rambler*, n.s., III: Part XIII (January, 1855), pp. 44–59; Part XIV (February, 1855), pp. 117–26.

38. Elton Hall Papers, Lady Carysfort to her daughter, March, 1812 (copy).

39. Great Britain, Parliament, Historical Manuscripts Commission, H. C. Maxwell Lyte, ed., *Report on the Manuscripts of His Grace the Duke of Rutland Preserved at Belvoir Castle* (4 vols.; London, 1888–1905), Hobart to Rutland, Dec. 28, 1785, III, 271–72.

40. Elton Hall Papers, Lady Carysfort to her daughter, March, 1812 (copy).

41. *Sun* (London), March 27, 1812; Lady Francis Dillon Jerningham, *The Jerningham Letters, 1780–1843*, ed. Egerton Castle (London, 1896), Lady Jerningham to Lady Bedingfeld, March 23, 1812, II, 18.

42. *Courier* (London), March 30, April 8 and 24, 1807; *Dropmore*, Thomas Grenville to Lord Grenville, Dec. 23, 1809, IX, 433.

Church, contemplated prosecuting the editor.[43] In 1812, when Lady Buckingham died, her niece heard it remarked that "many people exult extremely . . . calling it the salvation of England."[44]

To label the Grenville family (or the Grenvillite party in general) as "liberals" on the Irish question is to invite condemnation for naïveté. One might as well say that Edmund Burke and Charles James Fox, because they favored the impeachment of Warren Hastings and shed tears over the Begums of Oudh, desired to redress the economic wrongs done by the British to the Indian masses. There were, indeed, few redeeming political features involved in the relationship between English politicians and the Irish Catholic peasantry from the time of the Battle of the Boyne in 1690 until the Great Famine in the 1840s. However, within the confines of a ruling caste, the Grenvillites were among the politicians most sympathetic to Irish grievances, although a jaundiced observer might be pardoned for remarking that sympathy is cheap.

Whether he was prodded by his wife or not, the Marquis of Buckingham had, by at least 1791, apparently concluded that the English policy of uniting the Irish Protestants (Anglicans and Presbyterians) by excluding Roman Catholics from the franchise and Parliament was bankrupt.[45] His brother, Lord Grenville, however, was far less enlightened and only grudgingly accepted the semiemancipatory Acts of 1792 and 1793 (which terminated the most obnoxious anti-Catholic legislation and admitted qualified Irish Catholics to the franchise while still refusing them entry to Parliament or the higher ranks of the military).[46] The violent Irish Rebellion of 1798 horrified both of the Grenville brothers and confirmed their views of the efficacy of a union between Great Britain and Ireland. But Buckingham understood—and Lord Grenville did not—that the removal of the remaining Catholic disabilities was almost a sine qua non for the success of such a governmental system.[47] However, Grenville gradually came to accept the logic of Buckingham's arguments over the next few years, and by 1800 he was a firm emancipationist.[48]

43. *Sun* (London), March 18, 1812; Elton Hall Papers, Charlotte Proby to ?, July 1, 1812 (draft copy); *Dropmore*, Grey to Lord Grenville, n.d., X, 187.

44. Elton Hall Papers, Charlotte Proby to ?, July 1, 1812 (draft copy).

45. *Court and Cabinets of George III*, Hobart to Buckingham, n.d., II, 184.

46. Ibid., Lord Grenville to Buckingham, Oct. 11, 1792, II, 220.

47. BM, Thomas Grenville Papers, Add. MSS. 48152: Buckingham to Thomas Grenville, March 11, 1798; Lord Grenville to Thomas Grenville, Aug. 7, 1798. *Dropmore*, Buckingham to Lord Grenville, Nov. 17, 1799, VI, 27; *Court and Cabinets of George III*, Lord Grenville to Buckingham, Nov. 5, 1798, II, 411.

48. BM, Auckland Papers, Add. MSS. 34457, Lord Grenville to Hodson, Nov. 2, 1809 (copy).

In February, 1801, Grenville was not unsympathetic to the dilemma of his sovereign with regard to the coronation oath.[49] Yet, after the resignation of Pitt's first Ministry, he, like other leading politicians, faced his own quandary as to the future of the Catholic question during George's reign. Should he, like Pitt, simply shelve the issue in the face of the King's known sentiments, or should he continue to press it in some form or another? At certain times (for example, November, 1802, and April, 1804, when he was prepared to join Pitt in a new Government; or January, 1806, when he became Prime Minister) he seemed to have adopted the former solution; at other times (for example, May, 1805, and May, 1808, when he introduced the Catholic petition in the House of Lords), the latter. In other words, while he was in office or when office appeared to beckon, he seemed quite prepared to waive the issue; and when out of favor with the King, he was equally prepared to debate it. This is not to suggest that Grenville did not favor emancipation, but only to point out a problem that disturbed many politicians during the decade before the Regency.

All those who were committed to the Catholic cause, including Grenville, Canning, Pitt, Castlereagh, Fox, Holland, Grey, and Moira, as well as its opponents, including Sidmouth, Perceval, Hawkesbury, and Portland, knew the King would never accept it, and, indeed, that to agitate the question might well drive him mad. Consequently, the options open to Catholic supporters remained necessarily limited. They knew that a Ministry could not be sustained if they brought in a full measure of emancipation, although they might play at the edges, as Grenville and Howick attempted unsuccessfully in 1807. The choice, then, was between power, with the possibility of ameliorating some of the minor Catholic disabilities while providing as just governance as possible for the Irish Catholics, and the abandonment of Ireland to the anti-Catholic Redesdales and Wellesley Poles—a choice that was not particularly enviable.

During the formation of the Talents' Ministry, Grenville, as he admitted himself in 1807, made no attempt to raise the Catholic question with George III; indeed, not one word passed between them on the matter.[50] And Lord Sidmouth, the great opponent of Catholic concessions, in accepting office in the Ministry, "distinctly stated" his well known views on any further Catholic appeasement.[51] The basic

49. *Court and Cabinets of George III,* Lord Grenville to Buckingham, Feb. 2, 1801, III, 129.

50. *Dropmore,* Lord Grenville to Elliot, Feb. 13, 1807, IX, 38; BM, Holland House Papers, Add. MSS. 51661, Bedford to Holland, Feb. 8, 1807.

51. *Parl. Debates,* IX (March 26, 1807), 246.

aggravation that could, of course, turn a ministerial benign neglect of Catholic grievances into a forced espousal involved the likelihood or not of the parliamentary introduction of a Catholic petition; and, needless to say, the Government wanted no such thing. Howick, writing in December, 1806, mentioned an implied understanding with the King that the Ministry would not promote it.[52] Grenville himself, having introduced a Catholic petition in 1805, was perfectly aware that if the Irish Catholics were to again petition for relief, such a move would greatly embarrass him and lead others to question his political consistency. But, in a statement remarkable for its honesty, Grenville remarked that he had "long accustomed myself to look at my duties in a higher point of view than that of consistency alone, which as often means perseverance in what is wrong as adherence to what is right. And I am fully satisfied that I should be deeply criminal, and even that I should be considered so, if I were to urge this question to the effect of breaking up the Government." Should the petition be brought forward, he was prepared to express his agreement with it but to "condemn without reserve the conduct and motives of those who have now pressed it forward."[53]

To Fox fell the task of persuading the Dublin Roman Catholics not to petition for relief during 1806. The Catholics themselves were divided by personal rivalries and differing strategical viewpoints, and Fox—not envisioning a general election as early as November, 1806—advised them to await a new Parliament before taking action. In return for that concession, he promised that the new Irish Administration would give the Catholics favors compatible with the 1792 and 1793 Acts, including tithe reform and the opening of corporations and army commissions to them.[54]

The history of the fall of the Talents' Ministry has already been dealt with in depth,[55] so here one need only deal with this question as it affected Grenville's personal attitude toward Catholic emancipation and as it caused divisions both within the Grenvillite party and between the Grenvillites and the Foxites.

It is somewhat questionable whether the Irish record of the Talents was as bad as it has been portrayed.[56] The Administration was in office for only thirteen months, hardly time to redress the accumulated

52. Durham Papers, Howick to Ponsonby, Dec. 31, 1806.

53. *Dropmore,* Lord Grenville to Elliot, Feb. 13, 1807, IX, 38.

54. BM, Fox Papers, Add. MSS. 47569, Fox to Hay, Feb. 20, 1806; BM, Holland House Papers, Add. MSS.: 51468, Ryan to Fox, Feb. 24, 1806; 51469, Ryan to Fox, March 3, 1806; 51572, Parnell to King, Sept. 8, 1806; 51572, King to Holland, n.d.

55. Michael Roberts, *The Whig Party, 1807–1812* (2d ed.; London, 1965).

56. Ibid., pp. 7–34.

grievances of centuries. By early 1807, an allegedly thorough reform of the tithe system was in contemplation for the first session of 1808.[57] The heads of the Irish Government, as judged by their correspondence, were men of good will who sincerely desired to ameliorate Catholic distress. Whatever their initial failure to stipulate for the Irish Catholics in 1806, taking into consideration the long view, one is dealing here with individuals who, despite hedging at various times, were out of office most of their active lives after 1801 or 1807 because of their advocacy of Catholic emancipation. Still, George Ponsonby, the Lord Chancellor, was suspected by the Catholics of more concern for electoral politics than for the redress of Catholic grievances; and William Elliot, the Chief Secretary, was equally unpopular. Little attempt was made to reform the Castle system or the magistracy in a direction approved of by the Catholics;[58] and, as has been shown elsewhere, the fall of the Talents created hardly a ripple in Irish Catholic circles.[59]

Between December, 1806, and February, 1807, with a new Parliament elected and sitting, Ministers on both sides of the Irish sea attempted to prevent a Catholic petition—an action that Howick felt would, if taken, lead to a dissolution of the Government.[60] A number of immediate options to appease the Catholics short of actual emancipation were discussed. In England both Howick and Grenville leaned toward a tithe modification; but in Ireland Ponsonby, backed by Bedford, Elliot, and Plunket, while agreeing with the general idea, impressed upon the English Government the necessity of a thorough preparation for so delicate a subject.[61] Bedford wanted a provision introduced to pay the Catholic clergy, but he had grave doubts as to the utility of a scheme of Grenville's to raise Catholic regiments.[62] Ponsonby broached the subject of allowing Catholics to serve as sheriffs, but Howick felt this was too minute a point upon which to risk a parliamentary discussion of the general Catholic topic. However, Howick came to sympathize with Grenville's plan for improvement of the situation of

57. *Dropmore,* Lord Grenville to Bedford, March 11, 1807, IX, 68–69.

58. The Catholics were especially irate when Orange yeomen burnt a Catholic house during the 1806 "Orange Days" and were let off by the Protestant magistracy. BM, Holland House Papers, Add. MSS. 51572, King to Holland, Nov. 4, 1806.

59. Roberts, *The Whig Party,* p. 31.

60. BM, Holland House Papers, Add. MSS. 51544, Howick to Holland, Dec. 22, 1806.

61. Durham Papers: Howick to Ponsonby, Dec. 31, 1806; Ponsonby to Howick, Jan. 4 and 19, 1807. BM, Holland House Papers, Add. MSS. 51661, Bedford to Holland, Dec. 31, 1806, and Feb. 8, 1807.

62. BM, Holland House Papers, Add. MSS. 51661, Bedford to Holland, Dec. 31, 1806.

Roman Catholics in the military with regard to rank and the open practice of their religion in Britain as well as in Ireland.[63] At this late hour, Bedford began pressing Ponsonby to recognize the necessity of a thorough reform of the magistracy, especially a reevaluation of the position of "those furious Orange Magistrates, who are a disgrace not only to the Commission of the Peace, but to the Country in which they live."[64] To make matters worse, the timetable for a Catholic petition was subjected to unforgivable failures in communication between officials in Dublin and London.[65] In short, the Government was caught totally unprepared to respond in the face of a petition it should have known was coming sooner or later. If as much energy had been expended during all of 1806 as in the three months before the crisis of March, 1807, perhaps the Catholic perception of the Government's good will might have prevented, or at least postponed, the necessity of an immediate petition.

The plan eventually decided upon as the Talents' short-term appeasement was the ill-fated Roman Catholic Army and Navy Service Bill, which was seemingly approved by the Cabinet and the King between February 9 and 12, 1807.[66] It is probably true, as argued elsewhere: (1) that the King, Sidmouth, and Ellenborough misunderstood the Catholic concessions within the Bill; (2) that, therefore, they did not countenance admission of Roman Catholics to the staff positions from which they had been expressly excluded by the 1793 Act of the Irish Parliament, but were simply prepared, albeit reluctantly, to grant to the Irish Catholic military the same footing within England as they had obtained in Ireland fourteen years earlier; and (3) that Grenville and Howick "allowed Sidmouth and Ellenborough, as they later allowed the King, to misinterpret the meaning of the concession."[67] The correctness of this final thesis is certainly supported by the various missives, from the Cabinet and personally from Grenville, to the King on the Catholic Bill,[68] which are models of ambiguity.[69]

63. Durham Papers: Ponsonby to Howick, Jan. 4, 1807; Howick to Ponsonby, Jan. 10, 1807 (copy).

64. BM, Holland House Papers, Add. MSS. 51661, Bedford to Holland, Jan. 18, 1807.

65. BM, Holland House Papers, Add. MSS. 51661: Bedford to Holland, Dec. 18 and 31, 1806, and Jan. 18, 1807; 51544, Holland to Howick, n.d., and Feb. 20, 1807.

66. The full details are in Roberts, *The Whig Party*, pp. 13–14.

67. Ibid., p. 20. See also William B. Hamilton, "Constitutional and Political Reflections on the Dismissal of Lord Grenville's Ministry," *Canadian Historical Association Report* (1964), pp. 89–104.

68. *Dropmore:* Cabinet minute, Feb. 10, 1807, IX, 109–10; Lord Grenville to George III, Feb. 11, 1807, IX, 108.

69. Elliot and Windham, as well as Sidmouth and the King, were not quite sure if

Grenville's private correspondence, however, between February 12, when the King approved the Bill, and the Cabinet of March 1, when Sidmouth expressed surprise at Grenville's interpretation of the concessions, seems to indicate that he was not in the least concerned about the progress of the Bill and that he was, in fact, convinced it would pass.[70] Howick, likewise, seemed to feel that the Catholic Bill per se was a closed issue.[71] The truth is that the Bill, which, in retrospect, was to take on such important connotations in the fall of the Talents, was not considered as a particularly important question after February 12, as it was becoming abundantly clear that such a measure would in no way prevent the presentation of a Catholic petition.

Although Howick desired to stop the progress of the petition, he doubted, if that failed, whether he could remain a Minister. Bedford seemed to agree. Grenville was equally adamant that the Government should not break up.[72] Various maneuvers were considered to defer the petition. Influential Catholic leaders in England were approached. A letter from the Prince of Wales to the Irish Catholics, advising extreme caution, was considered. Howick sent Lord Ponsonby to Ireland to use his influence with the Dublin Catholic leaders, and he also conceived the idea (which Grenville adopted in 1810) of allowing the petition to remain unmoved on the table.[73]

The ambiguity, whatever its cause, was concluded on March 11 by the King's open disavowal of the Bill; and, after four days of frantic discussion and attempted compromise, the Talents agreed, at a March 15 Cabinet, to withdraw the Bill, to which agreement they added the famous caveat that they might feel the necessity of advising future legislation upon Ireland "as the course of circumstances shall appear to require."[74] Present at this Cabinet were Lord Grenville, Thomas Grenville, Holland, Howick, Moira, Petty, and Windham.

As a consequence of the King's action, the Foxites favored immediate resignation, but they were deterred momentarily by Lord Grenville and his brother. However, another prominent Grenvillite, Lord Spencer, who was ill at Althorp, not only opposed the Government's decision to

the staff was included in the new concessions. *Dropmore,* **Bedford** to Spencer, Feb. 17, 1807, IX, 113–14; Durham Papers, Windham to Howick, March 2, 1807.

70. *Dropmore,* Lord Grenville to Elliot, Feb. 13, 1807, IX, 37.

71. Durham Papers, Howick to Ponsonby, Feb. 18, 1807.

72. Ibid.; BM, Holland House Papers, Add. MSS. 51661, Bedford to Holland, Feb. 28, 1807.

73. BM, Holland House Papers, Add. MSS. 51544, Holland to Howick, n.d. and Feb. 20, 1807; Durham Papers, Howick to Ponsonby, Feb. 18, 1807; Althorp Papers, 67, Elliot to Spencer, March 3, 1807.

74. *Dropmore,* Cabinet minute, March 15, 1807, IX, 116–18.

116]   THE GRENVILLITES, 1801–29

remain in office but announced his intention of returning to London to resign. This factor shook his closest friend, Thomas Grenville, who told Buckingham on March 16 that, had he known of Spencer's intentions at the time of the March 15 Cabinet, "nothing should have led me to concur in the measure" of yielding to the King.[75] Elliot and Bedford in Ireland and Fitzwilliam, a member of the Cabinet without portfolio, in England, announced their intentions to resign.[76] Thus, the King's action, in requesting the pledge from the Talents never again to submit legislation on the Irish question, probably saved the Ministry from internal dissolution and, without foresight on George's part, allowed it to go with a dignity and unity that might not have been present had George declined to make an issue of their one term for remaining in (or clinging to) office.

True to form, once Lord Grenville had departed from office, his opinion concerning the necessity of a solution to the Catholic question was invigorated. Both in Parliament, where he moved the Catholic petition in May, 1808, and in his private correspondence, he dwelt upon the great dangers the country faced from the possibility of French landings in Ireland and the "hostile neutrality" Britain could expect in such an event from the Irish masses. Not so naïve as to consider that the addition of a few dozen Catholics to Parliament would materially effect this tragic situation, Grenville envisioned emancipation as but a first step in the great process of Anglo-Irish conciliation, including a tithe reform that would bring satisfaction "to the feelings & potatoe gardens of every petty farmer & peasant in Ireland."[77]

Although the rejection by Irish Catholic leaders in 1808 of any plan for a Veto by the King on the nomination of Catholic Bishops had soured Grenville's relationship with them and materially affected his opinion of their good sense, his commitment to the general cause remained unshaken.[78] The failure of the opposition negotiations of both September, 1809, with Perceval, and February, 1812, with the Regent, hinged to a great extent upon the emancipation issue. In 1809,

75. Sheffield Papers, F64/a33–1, Howick to Fitzwilliam, March 17, 1807; *Court and Cabinets of George III*, Thomas Grenville to Buckingham: March 14, 1807, IV, 135–37; March 16, 1807, IV, 139–40. BM, Thomas Grenville Papers, Add. MSS. 41854, Spencer to Thomas Grenville, March 14, 1807.

76. BM, Holland House Papers, Add. MSS. 51661, Bedford to Holland, March 18, 1807; *Dropmore:* Elliot to Lord Grenville, March 17, 1807, IX, 97–98; Fitzwilliam to Lord Grenville, March 18, 1807, IX, 100.

77. *Parl. Debates,* IX (May 27, 1808), 643–65; BM, Auckland Papers, Add. MSS. 34457, Lord Grenville to Auckland, July 26, 1807; BM, Thomas Grenville Papers, Add. MSS. 41852, Lord Grenville to Thomas Grenville, Nov. 26, 1807.

78. For a discussion of the Veto question, see Roberts, *The Whig Party,* pp. 34–58.

with the breakup of the Duke of Portland's Ministry through illness and
political intrigue, Spencer Perceval seemed genuinely to desire inclusion of the opposition leaders in an extended Government. Both in his
correspondence with Perceval and in private letters to friends, Grenville
maintained that the principal objection to his entering the Government
concerned his attachment to the Catholic cause. He told Auckland that
to have remained silent on Catholic emancipation in his answers to
Perceval's overtures would have occasioned "a breach of . . . plain
dealing" and a deception of friends, enemies, and the public.[79] His
colleague Lord Grey doubted that Grenville had acted wisely in raising
the Catholic question prematurely; yet had serious negotiations commenced, Grey left little question as to his persuasion: permission from
the King would be required to prepare legislation involving "complete
emancipation" that would be subject to the Veto and substantial
guarantees for the established Church.[80] Grey thought both he and
Grenville were in agreement on these points.[81]

Whether Grenville was prepared to go quite that far is another
question. The issue is complicated by the fact that Grenville was
canvassing for the office of Chancellor of Oxford University, that citadel
of no-popery, even before the death of the Duke of Portland, the
incumbent, on October 30, 1809. In this pursuit, he had the support of
ten Bishops and was, thus, hardly desirous of fanning the flames of
Catholic agitation at that precise moment. Indeed, Grenville's friend
Auckland thought that he desired to adjourn the question during the
King's lifetime.[82] However, when Sidmouth (in anger at Perceval's
wish to exclude him from his new Administration but to admit two
Addingtonians, Bragge Bathurst and Benjamin Hobhouse) asked
Grenville in late October to set the King's mind at ease on the Catholic
question, his answer was ambiguous. He certainly refused to accept any
pledge not to raise the Catholic question. However, he ducked the main
point of Sidmouth's query on the grounds that since the King had never
negotiated with him, he did not know what would be required to set his
mind at ease.[83]

79. *Later Correspondence of George III*, George III to Perceval, Sept. 30, 1809, V, 376;
BM, Auckland Papers, Add. MSS. 34457, Lord Grenville to Auckland, Oct. 13, 1809;
Roberts, *The Whig Party*, pp. 351–53.

80. HRO, Tierney Papers, Grey to Tierney: 31M70/33m, Oct. 2, 1809;
31M70/33n, Oct. 3, 1809; 31M70/33q, Nov. 17, 1809.

81. *Dropmore*, Grey to Grenville, Nov. 3, 1809, IX, 370.

82. Ibid., Auckland to Grenville, Oct. 20, 1809, IX, 343.

83. Durham Papers, Grenville to Grey, Oct. 27, 1809. He was equally vague in a
letter to the principal of Brasenose College. *Dropmore,* Grenville to Hodson, Nov. 2,
1809, IX, 359–62.

During the Oxford election, Grenville told William Wickham, his chief electoral agent, to spread the word that should a petition be introduced in the upcoming session of Parliament, he would not be responsible for its contents, and he lamented the step "as much as anyone can."[84] However, at the same time, Grenville was highly displeased by a letter from Lord Buckingham to the conservative Catholic leader, Lord Fingall, which was made known at Oxford, in which the Marquis stated that he would actually oppose the petition in the Lords unless the Veto were conceded.[85] Grenville did present the Catholic petition to the Lords in March, 1810; but, unlike his conduct in 1805 and 1808, he moved nothing on it.[86]

Taking three factors into consideration—Grenville's disappointment over the failure of the Veto, his refusal to enter into a coalition with Perceval on the grounds of emancipation, and his ultimately successful Oxford aspirations—a pattern emerges. Taking a hard stand, Grenville would refuse to enter the Administration without some Catholic concessions from the King; but, on a softer note, his legitimate dissatisfaction with the Catholic leadership over the Veto question enabled him to forego acting as their champion in 1810, thus maintaining both his honor and his Oxford chances. The strategy was successful. Despite the Court's effort to further the claims of Lord Eldon (who, along with the Duke of Beaufort, stood against him), ten Bishops supported Grenville, which help Holland partially attributed to a persuasion that he might soon be at the Treasury.[87] The final vote was 406, Grenville; 393, Eldon; and 238, Beaufort. The opposition was jubilant. Francis Horner saw the "high Church . . . pulled down from its most ancient and formerly impregnable height; taken by storm in its strongest hold."[88] Henry Brougham thought it better than a majority in Parliament, giving no-popery a "death blow."[89] The *Morning Chronicle* viewed it as "epocha in our domestic history."[90] Such hyperbole,

84. HRO, Wickham Papers, 38M49/1/19, Grenville to Wickham, Nov. 27, 1809.
85. BM, Thomas Grenville Papers, Add. MSS. 48153, Grenville to Thomas Grenville, Nov. 29, 1809.
86. *Parl. Debates,* XVI (March 8, 1810), 11**
87. Durham Papers, Thomas Grenville to Grey, n.d.; Henry Richard Vassall Fox, Third Baron Holland, *Further Memoirs of the Whig Party, 1807–1821,* ed. Giles Stephen Holland Fox-Strangeways, Baron Stavordale (London, 1905), pp. 41–42.
88. *Memoirs and Correspondence of Francis Horner, M.P.,* ed. Leonard Horner (2d ed.; Boston, 1853), Horner to Murray, Dec. 15, 1809, I, 506.
89. Henry Peter Brougham, First Baron Brougham and Vaux, *The Life and Times of Henry Lord Brougham: Written by Himself* (3 vols.; New York, 1871–72), Brougham to Grey, Dec., 1809, I, 339–40.
90. *Morning Chronicle* (London), Dec. 18, 1809.

however, merely masked a personal triumph for Grenville, having no meaning at all for Catholic emancipation.

The problem involving George III's conscience was never really solved. In 1811, with the King's final illness and the advent of a Regency, Grenville was enabled to take a more decided and emphatic course on emancipation without experiencing qualms concerning his sovereign's health. He had no sympathy with the argument that since the King was still alive it would be "indelicate" to act on Catholic concessions.[91] During the negotiations of February, 1812, there were no qualifications in the reply of Grenville and Grey to the Duke of York, who was acting as the Regent's intermediary. The "immediate repeal of those civil disabilities under which so large a portion of his Majesty's subjects still labour, on account of their religious opinions" was a sine qua non of the "total change" which played a role in the failure of the overture.[92]

There were divisions on the Catholic question even within Grenville's own family circle. In 1801, Grenville doubted whether his brother-in-law, Lord Carysfort, an Irish landowner, supported the Catholics, but Carysfort gave him assurances. However, in 1803, after Emmet's rebellion, Carysfort changed his mind.[93] Not until 1812 did he again give his approbation to the question.[94] Another brother-in-law, Lord Fortescue, who nearly always followed Grenville's politics, failed to support the Catholic petition in 1805, though he voted for it in 1808.[95] At times even Thomas Grenville thought Lord Grenville went too far in his espousal of the Catholic cause, though he loyally supported him in public.[96] Lord Spencer, on the other hand, was even more attached to emancipation than Lord Grenville and felt that any temporizing (such as Grenville's refusal to press the Catholic claims in 1810) could be fatal to the party.[97]

The wider Grenvillite group was also divided on the Catholic issue. Although Lord Bulkeley endorsed Catholic emancipation after his reunion with the Grenvillites in 1806, he sincerely wished that "the Catholic question was at the bottom of the sea, for it hangs like a

91. *Memoirs of the Regency*, Grenville to Buckingham, Jan. 6, 1812, I, 178–79.

92. Ibid., Grenville and Grey to York, Feb. 15, 1812, I, 233.

93. *Dropmore:* Grenville to Carysfort, Feb. 6, 1801, VI, 436; Carysfort to Grenville, Feb. 28, 1801, VI, 456–58; Carysfort to Grenville, Nov. 7, 1803, VII, 196.

94. *Parl. Debates*, XXI (Jan. 31, 1812), 477–78.

95. *Later Correspondence of George III*, Hawkesbury to George III, May 28, 1808, V, 81.

96. BM, Thomas Grenville Papers, Add. MSS. 41852, Grenville to Thomas Grenville, Nov. 26, 1807.

97. Ibid., 41854, Spencer to Thomas Grenville, Jan. 11, 1810.

millstone round the necks of those who have attached themselves to Lord Grenville, more especially as he adheres to it with a pertinacity and obstinacy which can be agreeable to none but his opponents."[98] Lord Auckland, whom Grenville closely consulted on all subjects after 1806, had opposed emancipation during the crisis of 1801, and nothing happened during the next decade to change his mind. Only toward the end of his life, in 1812, did he adopt a more favorable viewpoint.[99] Other members of the Lords who generally followed Grenville's lead in 1808 but failed to support the Catholic petition either in person or by proxy included Bristol, Carnarvon, and the Bishops of Oxford and St. Asaph. Unfortunately, the division lists for the petitions of 1810 and 1811 in the Lords seem not to have survived. By 1812, Bristol at least was supporting the cause (Carnarvon and Oxford were dead).[100]

In the Commons, where division lists are more numerous, the number of Grenvillites who failed to support either the petition of 1808 or of 1811 included: Auckland's sons, William and George Eden; Bulkeley's half-brother, Sir Robert Williams; Thomas Knox, an Irish Grenvillite; and Carnarvon's son, Lord Porchester. By 1812, George Eden (whose brother William was dead by then), Knox, and Porchester (who was then in the Lords, where he had succeeded his father in 1811) had come round. Williams, however, who had been a Grenvillite since the 1790s, never voted in favor of a Catholic petition during the five-year duration of the 1807 Parliament and in 1812 supported the die-hard Protestants in their parliamentary struggle against mere consideration of the question.[101]

98. *Auckland,* Bulkeley to Auckland, Jan. 2, 1813, IV, 386.
99. PRO, Dacres Adams Papers, 30/58/4, Auckland to Pitt, Jan. 31, 1801; *Parl. Debates:* XI (May 27, 1808), 692–93; XXI (Jan. 31, 1812), 477–78.
100. *Parl. Debates,* XXII (April 21, 1812), 703–4.
101. Ibid.: XXI (Feb. 4, 1812), 670; XXIII (June 22, 1812), 710–11.

[CHAPTER VI]

The Grenville-Foxite Coalition: Part Three

1. *Grenville-Foxite Political and Social*
Relations, 1804–17

The Grenvillite group with which the Foxites acted in politics was
loosely composed of two sections corresponding to the differences in
political perspective and personality emanating from Stowe and Dropmore. The first Marquis of Buckingham (and his son in later years) was
the de jure chief of the foremost faction, replete with its patronage
network and traditional family orientation, within the English governing class. Yet, the first-rate importance of the Grenvillites during the
years between Amiens and Waterloo was not due to such a customary
political circumstance but to the more ideologically routed body of men
around Lord Grenville. The Stowe Grenville political type was already
becoming passé by the 1780s and seemed—almost, but not quite—on
the road to extinction as a serious model for practical politics.

The political instability after Pitt's resignation in 1801, as ministerial construction again became fluid and frequent, may well have resur-
rected such factionalism in one form or another; but whatever his eldest
brother's stance, Lord Grenville was not leading a party of place-hunters
bent chiefly on office and its emoluments. By 1807 Grenville's own
followers included Portland Whigs, pre-1804 and pre-1806 Pittites,
and a few rising young men of talent. When the split between the
Grenvillites and the Whigs took place in 1817, the majority of the
Grenvillites who were still active, except, significantly, those connected with the Stowe Grenvilles through patronage ties, adhered not
to the second Marquis of Buckingham in his attempt to form a third
party but to the Whig opposition. In assigning the reasons for such a
political juxtaposition—the course of which will be traced in this and a
subsequent chapter—it is necessary to examine both the specific nature
of the Grenvillite party and the social and personal relationships between the Grenvillites and the Foxites.

The exact position occupied by Lord Grenville in party politics between 1804 and 1817 is elusive and dependent upon one's views of the essence of party configurations in the early nineteenth century. The concept of party, incorporating such terms as Whig, Foxite, Pittite, Grenvillite, Addingtonian, Canningite, and so forth, involved more than the parliamentary division of members into Government or opposition supporters. Eventually, especially during and after the 1820s, the various smaller connections did tend to be grafted onto the larger designations. England may, indeed, have long been tending toward something approximating the mid-nineteenth century two-party system of Conservative and Liberal, the one in Government, the other in opposition; but the ultimate victory of such a system was neither preordained nor without temporary falterings. Certainly the political nation leaned more toward two parties in 1788 than in 1808 or even 1828.

In the somewhat rarefied sphere of self-identity or self-consciousness, the years between the defeat of Burgoyne at Saratoga and the triumph of Earl Grey over the victor of Waterloo saw a one-party system. For, despite some qualifications, there was a degree to which the Whigs of 1778 were the direct and lineal ancestors of the Whigs of 1830; and the succession of Rockingham, Fox, and Grey provided a political compass by which other groups (whether or not approvingly or even always consciously) could chart their own course. Whatever their faults or virtues, the Foxite-Whigs generally thought of themselves in party terms as party men in a sense that Addington, Grenville, Canning, Wellesley, and even Pitt hardly approved. That such considerations would prevail in the future must not blind us to the fact that at the beginning of the nineteenth century only one party generally held them. Thus it was the Whigs who gloried in their heritage, approved of party, made consistent use of clubs, and claimed to provide an alternative government. Also, while personal loyalties were certainly important within the opposition leadership, there was always a degree to which Fox or Grey were more than mere Foxites, i.e., they were part of something larger as members of a Whig party.

The term *Whig* was a badge of honor and denoted something quite different from the party name of a personal follower of any one man. *Whig* was a term that nearly every politician of the period, even Ministers in 1812,[1] employed at one time or another to describe his own

1. Archibald Foord, *His Majesty's Opposition, 1714–1830* (Oxford, 1964), p. 443. Lord Grenville regarded the Pittites in 1812 as "the party of the Tories, & the old Court, & high Church." BM, Thomas Grenville Papers, Add. MSS. 41853, Lord Grenville to Thomas Grenville, May 17, 1812.

ideological position. Since few laid specific claim to the mantle of toryism at least until the 1820s, Lord Grenville was, of course, a Whig; but whether, after 1804 or 1806, he was a member of what was generally recognized as an entity called the Whig party is yet another question.

Certainly it is legitimate to make some distinction between Whig and Foxite in the first decade of the nineteenth century and to not necessarily insist upon the use of these terms as synonyms.[2] Divisions within the so-called Whig party were always common, and those existing after 1793 and 1801 are generally recognizable. Even during the middle 1780s, long before the flight of the Portland Whigs, a qualified differentiation could be observed between the followers of Fox and the Prince of Wales (and of Burke), with some individuals, such as Sheridan, occupying strategic positions in both camps.[3]

Unquestionably the mantle of whiggery, as Fox and Holland envisioned it, was broad enough to cover the former Portland Whigs after 1804; and, indeed, within a decade and a half of the formation of the Grenville-Foxite coalition, the ancient fissure was largely healed and forgotten, as the Spencers, Mintos, Carlisles, and Fitzwilliams resumed their rightful places in the Whig pantheon. But the split of 1793 and 1794 had been a bitter one, and some time was needed to heal the wounds.[4] The role of the Grenvillite party was a critical one during the period of convalescence, in that it provided a temporary port of safety for many who might otherwise have hesitated to renew old connections.

One contemporary wrote years later that he had no doubt as to the position occupied in party terms by the Grenvillite group. Lord Holland, in his memoirs, was always careful to distinguish between "the followers of Mr. Fox" and the Whigs in general. However, there is no question that he saw the Foxites and the Grenvillites, despite disagreements on various issues, as members of one party in which both groups were "branches" of whiggery.[5] Yet Lord Brougham, who is not always

2. Though here one is asking more than one is likely to get in return. When Althorp went up to Cambridge in 1800, his mother told him to "beware of all whigs." Sir Ivor Jennings, *Party Politics* (Cambridge, England, 1961), II, 65. Since the Spencers, despite their approbation of Pitt's war, certainly considered themselves as representatives of the true Whig tradition, what Lady Spencer no doubt meant was a warning against Foxites or, even more specifically, against French principles. But this illustrates the difficulty present in party terminology.

3. Foord, *His Majesty's Opposition*, p. 409.

4. Carlisle, in 1806, debating with Morpeth as to the possibility of his attending Fox's funeral, asked him to "manage with Holland that I am not confounded with the mob of the Whig Club . . . but dont let him suppose I have mentioned the subject to you." Castle Howard Papers, Carlisle to Morpeth, n.d.

5. Henry Richard Vassall Fox, Third Baron Holland: *Memoirs of the Whig Party*

the most consistent authority, had his doubts. In a passage of his *Historical Sketches* concerning the 1804 coalition, Brougham makes the assertion that "Lord Grenville joined the Whig Party."[6] But in his preface to the *Life of Plunket,* he denied that Plunket, whom he identified correctly as a follower of Lord Grenville, had "ever belonged to the Whig party," leaving the reader with the impression that he excluded Grenville from that situation as well.[7]

Most historians, both pre- and post-Namier, who have contemplated the problem of the party position of the nineteenth century Grenvillites, have concurred with Holland that Grenville was indeed a Whig, though not of course a Foxite.[8] Only one major historian, George Macaulay Trevelyan, whose family had close ties with the old Whig leadership, has questioned this prevailing assumption; he more than once describes the Grenvillites as a "Tory group."[9]

Some historians have been discriminating concerning the nature of the Grenvillites' whiggery. Although Arthur Aspinall, writing in the 1920s, divided the general post-1807 Whig party into the three groups of Grenvillite, Foxite, and Mountain, he further divided the first group into the two subgroups of Tories led by Buckingham and former Portland Whigs.[10] Aspinall is followed by Ivor Jennings in this assessment.[11] Sir Spencer Walpole, while calling the Grenvillites Whigs, saw the content of that commitment as representative of the "old Whigs," which Michael Roberts refined still further (unfairly, perhaps, as far as Lord Grenville is concerned) as pre-Rockingham

---

during My Time, ed. Henry Edward Vassall Fox, Fourth Baron Holland (2 vols.; London, 1852–54), I, 187; *Further Memoirs of the Whig Party, 1807–1821,* ed. Giles Stephen Holland Fox-Strangeways, Baron Stavordale (London, 1905), pp. 216–18.

6. Henry Peter Brougham, First Baron Brougham and Vaux, *Historical Sketches of Statesmen Who Flourished in the Time of George III* (2 vols.; London, 1856–58), I, 330.

7. David Plunket, *The Life, Letters, and Speeches of Lord Plunket* (London, 1867), I, 23.

8. Harriet Martineau thought the new opposition was "Whig in its principles." *History of the Peace: Being a History of England from 1816 to 1854, with an Introduction, 1800 to 1815* (4 vols.; Boston, 1865–66), I, 169. See also the following: Sir Spencer Walpole, *A History of England* (New York, 1913), I, 298; Arthur Aspinall, *Brougham and the Whig Party* (Manchester, 1927), p. 38; H. W. Carless Davis, *The Age of Grey and Peel* (New York, 1964), p. 47; A. Bryant, *The Age of Elegance, 1812–1822* (New York, 1950), p. 371; Jennings, *Party Politics,* II, 65; Michael Roberts, *The Whig Party, 1807–12* (2d ed.; London, 1965), pp. 175–76; Austin Mitchell, *The Whigs in Opposition, 1815–1830* (Oxford, 1967), p. 76; Patrick C. Lipscomb, "Party Politics, 1801–2: George Canning and the Trinidad Question," *Historical Journal,* XII, No. 3 (1969), p. 445n.

9. *British History in the Nineteenth Century* (London, 1922), pp. 115, 194.

10. Aspinall, *Brougham,* p. 38.

11. Jennings, *Party Politics,* II, 65.

whiggism comparable to the Bloomsbury Gang that surrounded the fourth Duke of Bedford.[12]

But an attempt to categorize the Grenvillites into a party notch, presupposes that they saw themselves in such a light. That Grenville considered himself connected in some special manner with a Whig party after 1804 is doubtful. Neither he nor Buckingham seem ever to have called themselves Whigs or to have given any sign that they regarded their ideological positions as altered by the coalition with the Foxites. Nor is there any evidence that they identified with the galaxy of Whig heroes from the seventeenth or eighteenth centuries.[13] Probably, unlike Fox or Holland, neither of the Grenville brothers had an especially well-defined sense of party and, thus, never stopped to consider all the intricate practical or philosophical ramifications of his precise relationship with the Whig party, much less whether he himself was a Whig.

From certain external evidence it is at least apparent that the senior Grenvilles meant to keep their distance from Whigs and Foxites. Neither Lord Grenville nor Buckingham ever joined the two great social and political associations of English whiggery, the Whig Club or Brooks's. Such reserve in the face of the grand paraphernalia of whiggery had certainly not been apparent with regard to the person or followers of Lord North, who entered a long-lasting coalition with Fox and Portland in 1783. North joined Brooks's and even appeared in public during the 1780s wearing the blue and buff colors of Charles James Fox and General Washington! North's biographer, in fact, describes him, perhaps a trifle unfairly, as a "Fox Whig."[14]

Among the early members of the Whig Club, which was instituted in May, 1784, were such later associates of the Grenvillites as Fitzwilliam, Windham, Laurence, and Thomas Grenville.[15] During the early nineteenth century, meetings were held once a month during the parliamentary session. One important ritual at such gatherings were toasts to quick and dead Whig heroes. Neither before, during, nor after the Talents' Ministry did these toasts ever include any made to Lord Grenville or, indeed, to any other member of the Grenvillite party.[16]

At other Whig-sponsored dinners, however, the record varied. In

---

12. Walpole, *History of England,* I, 298; Roberts, *The Whig Party,* pp. 175–76.

13. Both the Grenvilles and the Wynns, of course, had immediate forebears who were prominent Tories long after that creed had become unfashionable.

14. Alan Valentine, *Lord North* (Norman, Oklahoma, 1967), II, 420–22, 429.

15. *Whig Club, Instituted in May, 1784; Members, Rules & Toasts in 1786.*

16. See the *Morning Chronicle* (London) account of various Whig Club meetings: March 7, 1804; March 11, 1806; June 4, 1806; April 6, 1808; June 8, 1808; April 12, 1809; and April 4, 1810. The *Courier* (London), Feb. 4, 1807, also wondered about Grenville's relations with the Whig Club.

February, 1806, at a gathering to celebrate Fox's reelection for Westminster, Alderman Combe toasted Grenville, but he did so in such an
apologetic manner that he somewhat tactlessly recalled a long-held
desire that Fox form an exclusive Foxite Ministry.[17] When Sheridan
succeeded Fox at Westminster later in the year, Grenville's health was
drunk at a victory celebration.[18] During his short Ministry, Grenville
had worked to achieve a reform of the Scottish judiciary; and in
remembrance of that action the Scottish Whig clubs and Fox birthday
dinners occasionally toasted him.[19] Despite these few exceptions,[20]
Lord Holland's memoirs notwithstanding, it is doubtful, when the
standard toast of "Norfolk (or Holland or Grey) and the Whigs of
England" was proposed, that the members of London or provincial
Whig clubs were dwelling upon Lord Grenville or the Marquis of
Buckingham.

The Fox Club was instituted in 1790 as a sort of appendage to the
Whig Club. A list of its members around 1815 or 1816 included no
definitive Grenvillites, although two members, Morpeth and Francis
Horner, had a tenuous link with the Grenvilles in 1815.[21]

While William Grenville, along with almost all of his friends and
relatives, did hold a membership in White's Club, the chief Government social center, during the pre-1801 period,[22] neither he nor the
first Marquis of Buckingham ever joined Brooks's Club, which occupied an even more important social role for the Whig opposition than
did White's for the Pittites. Thomas Grenville had joined Brooks's in
1779 but probably resigned after the Whig schism of 1794 (as did his
friend Earl Spencer), as there is no evidence of his activities in the
association after that date. Lord Grenville's decision not to join
Brooks's, however, had no influence on the younger members of his set
(or, after a decent interval, on the older members) who rushed to join

17. *Morning Chronicle* (London), Feb. 14, 1806.

18. *Courier* (London), Oct. 23, 1806.

19. See accounts in the *Morning Chronicle* (London) of a provincial Whig Club
meeting at Dunfermline, May 27, 1807, and a Fox birthday dinner at Edinburgh,
Jan. 31, 1809.

20. At the Fox birthday dinner held at Glasgow in Jan., 1811, when it appeared
that Grenville would momentarily be First Lord of the Treasury, no toast was made to
him, though a wide variety of individuals were remembered, including: George III, the
Prince of Wales, Princess Charlotte, Holland, Grey, Whitbread, Lord Archibald
Hamilton, Norfolk, Ponsonby, Erskine, Lauderdale, Sheridan, Romilly, Burdett, and,
of course, the memories of Wallace, Hampden, Sydney, and Washington, *Morning
Chronicle* (London), Jan. 31, 1811.

21. BM, Holland House Papers, Add. MSS. 51561.

22. Algernon Bourke, ed., *The History of White's with the Betting Books from 1743 to
1878 and a List of Members from 1736 to 1892* (1892).

(or, in the case of the Portland Whigs, to rejoin) the Club only a few months after the formation of the Grenville-Foxite coalition.

Folkestone, Charles Wynn, Althorp, and Laurence were members of Brooks's Club by July, 1804; Ebrington by 1805; Stafford by 1806; Richard Neville, William Shipley (Charles Wynn's brother-in-law), Pascoe Grenfell, Henry Wynn, and Essex by 1807; William Fremantle and Carrington by 1808; Bulkeley by 1809; Hereford by 1811; Cawdor, Spencer, Grafton (formerly Lord Euston) and Newport by 1812; and Plunket by 1813. In May and June, 1816, a large number of Grenvillites joined: the second Marquis of Buckingham, Lord Carysfort and his son Granville Proby, Lord Fortescue and his son George Fortescue, Sir George Nugent, Scrope Bernard Morland, and Sir Robert Williams.[23] When the first Duke of Buckingham gave his support to Liverpool in 1822, he, along with his faction, withdrew from Brooks's and the delighted Whigs held a celebration.[24]

Lord Grenville and the first Marquis of Buckingham were likewise cut off from another chief center of London whiggery, though for a reason that caused a painful personal problem within opposition ranks. Elizabeth Vassall, Lady Holland, was divorced from her first husband and had cohabited with the third Baron Holland for several years prior to their marriage in 1797. In 1800, Lady Carysfort, Lord Grenville's sister, while wife of the British Ambassador in Berlin, had snubbed the visiting Lady Holland.[25] When Lord and Lady Grenville visited Whig country houses, Lady Grenville refused to associate with or even appear at the same place as Lady Holland, causing an awkward situation within an aristocratic party that enjoyed mixing business and pleasure at its country homes.[26] Needless to say, when Grenville invited Holland to Dropmore, his wife was not included in the invitation.[27] Naturally, Lady Holland was among the Whig personages who most disliked the Grenville connection, as also was her intimate, John Allen, the librarian and a sort of philosopher-in-residence at Holland House.[28]

Throughout four decades, Holland House occupied a position of

23. *Memorials of Brooks's from the Foundation of the Club in 1764 to the Close of the Nineteenth Century* (London, 1907).

24. John Cam Hobhouse, First Baron Broughton, *Recollections of a Long Life,* ed. Charlotte (Hobhouse) Carleton, Baroness Dorchester (6 vols.; New York, 1909–11), II, 179.

25. E. Tangye Lean, *The Napoleonists: A Study in Political Disaffection, 1760–1960* (London, 1970), p. 130.

26. Durham Papers, Tierney to Grey, Dec. 6, 1815.

27. BM, Holland House Papers, Add. MSS. 51530, Lord Grenville to Holland, Oct. 10, 1809.

28. John Gore, ed., *The Creevey Papers* (rev. ed.; New York, 1963), p. 89; BM,

prime importance in London—and hence national—society. Its political role in the formation of party strategy and the crystallization of
intellectual topics can scarcely be exaggerated; and, in addition, it
provided for rising young politicians and intellectuals an environment
in which to be impressed and to impress.

Lord Grenville only dined at Holland House on four occasions during
his life, on two of which Lady Holland's dinner book indicates that she
was not present at the table. The first Marquis of Buckingham never
dined there. Thomas Grenville, who as a bachelor was less prone to
petticoat politics, dined there frequently from the commencement of
the Grenville-Foxite coalition through the middle 1830s. Others
among those associated at one time or another with Lord Grenville's
politics who frequented the dinners at Holland House included Windham, Minto, Charles Wynn, Spencer, Elliot, Lord and Lady Stafford,
Essex, Newport, Ebrington, Morpeth, and Francis Horner (who often
lived there). Temple (later first Duke of Buckingham) and William
Fremantle dined there less frequently, and Carysfort only once. With
the exception of Thomas Grenville, those Grenvillites who dined most
often at Holland House during the years after 1812—for example,
Spencer, Essex, Ebrington, and Newport—were precisely the individuals who were moving farthest away from Lord Grenville's position on
sensitive issues.[29]

Since Grenville and Buckingham provided no equivalent social setting to Brooks's, the Whig Club, or Holland House, it was only natural
that both generations of their followers should find social sustenance
with those with whom they had coalesced. The daily conversation at
Brooks's or Holland House, however, was hardly the milieu in which to
encounter ideas in line with Lord Grenville's conservative position on
such issues as parliamentary reform or civil liberties. This factor,
perhaps, explains in part why so few Grenvillites adhered to Grenville's
neutral political line at the time of the 1817 schism. Even the extraordinarily loyal nephew of Lord Grenville, Charles Wynn, was suspected
of not wishing a union with Liverpool in 1819 because it would
necessitate a break with Brooks's.[30]

Grenville's interaction with his chief Foxite colleagues in the

---

Holland House Papers, Add. MSS. 52204A, Allen's Journal, Sept. 19, 1806; *The
Journal of Elizabeth Lady Holland, 1791–1811*, ed. Giles Stephen Holland Fox-
Strangeways, Sixth Earl of Ilchester (London, 1908), II, 182–83.

29. BM, Holland House Papers, Add. MSS.: 51950, 51951, 51952, Lady Holland's
dinner books.

30. *Memoirs of the Regency*, William Fremantle to Buckingham, Feb. 16, 1819, II,
308.

Lords—Grey (who succeeded his father as the second Earl Grey in November, 1807), Holland, and Lansdowne—was cordial. He established close personal relations with Lansdowne, the most conservative member of the Foxite trio, and to a lesser extent with Holland, with whom he shared a mutual love for classical scholarship. With Grey the links were less personal. By 1816, when little remained to be said politically, Grey's friends noticed that he and Grenville had almost ceased writing to one another; and after the final split in 1817, they seldom communicated again.[31]

Among the other Foxites with whom Grenville maintained friendly relations were the Dukes of Gloucester and Bedford; Peter, Baron King, who married Earl Fortescue's daughter in 1804; the economist Francis Horner; the noted historian Sir James Mackintosh; and George Ponsonby.[32] In his relationship with Richard Brinsley Sheridan, however, Grenville created problems not dissimilar to those he found with Lady Holland. According to Lord Holland, Grenville considered Sheridan immoral and a profligate, and refused to invite him to the political dinners held at his home.[33]

The political cooperation and generally good feelings that existed between the Grenvillites and the Foxite leadership during this period can be observed in the Whig canvass for Grenville at the election for the Chancellorship of Oxford University in November and December, 1809. Cowper, Derby, Fitzwilliam, Grey, Holland, Norfolk, Thanet, and Windham were particularly helpful in promoting his cause.[34]

But relatively good personal relationships between Grenville and some of the parliamentary Whig chieftains hardly guaranteed wider acceptability for the Grenvillites within the Whig party at large. In 1815, a Government poet wrote of the supporters of Grenville and Grey, "Unable their rancour a moment to smother/The followers of

---

31. Durham Papers: Howick to Ponsonby, Aug. 26, 1806; Grey to Holland, Oct. 29, 1811; Holland to Grey, Feb. 12, 1816. Holland: *Memoirs of the Whig Party*, II, 50–52; *Further Memoirs of the Whig Party*, pp. 271–72.

32. BM, Mackintosh Papers, Add. MSS. 52442, Mackintosh's Journal, July 28, 1817; BM, Liverpool Papers, Add. MSS. 38271, Liverpool to Lord Grenville, April 12, 1818 (draft); Hugh Fortescue, Second Earl Fortescue, ed., *A Selection from the Speeches of the late Lord King with a Short Introductory Memoir by Earl Fortescue* (London, 1844), pp. 6–7; *Memoirs and Correspondence of Francis Horner, M.P.*, ed. Leonard Horner (2d ed.; Boston, 1853), Horner to Holland, Oct. 19, 1812, II, 118–19; NLW, Coedymaen Papers, V/310, Lord Grenville to Charles Wynn, July 2, 1817; Bedford, Bedford RO, Whitbread Papers, WI/2467, Bedford to Whitbread, April 13, 1809.

33. Holland, *Memoirs of the Whig Party*, II, 64–65, 239.

34. See the numerous letters in *Dropmore*, IX, 341–426; and BM, Holland House Papers, Add. MSS. 51824, Cowper to Holland, Nov. 2, 1809. See also the papers of Charles Moss, Bishop of Oxford, at the Perkins Library at Duke University.

neither will trust in the other."[35] The charge was not as true on Grenville's side as it was on Grey's. Francis Horner, a Whig lawyer and no enemy to the Grenville connection, remarked in 1809 that every time he went on circuit he had to satisfy people "who never mention Mr. Fox's name, but with reverence" on the score of the unpopular Grenvilles.[36]

The Grenvillites were disliked by the Radicals and, of course, by the followers of Samuel Whitbread in the Commons. They nicknamed Lord Grenville "the Bogey," and wrote and spoke against his family sinecures in the press and in the Commons. Thomas Creevey, a Whitbread lieutenant who was also close to Lady Holland, was particularly active in propagating anti-Grenvillian views. The animus of the Radicals against the Grenvillites spilled over, with some justification, into a feeling that Grey deferred too often to Grenville's opinions, causing a definite though not permanent split within the opposition by the spring of 1809.[37]

The Duke of Bedford, among others, sought unsuccessfully to promote conciliation between Grey and Whitbread and between the Grenvillites and the Mountain. Whereas Whitbread felt that the Grenvillites and Foxites ought not to be identified as composing the same party or as "amalgamated in one Body," Bedford, who disagreed, told him that:

> as those two Parties approached one another, and made some sacrifices for purposes of publick advantage, tho' certainly none of *Principle* were made on our side—You and I however may think that Fox in some instances went too far—perhaps Lord Grenville's Friends think that in some he went too far—be that as it may, the Parties having united, and acted together fairly & honourably for the general weal, I think we ought to remain together as one firm consolidated Party—The Grenvillites did not require of us to give up the Whig Club, nor did we require of them to become members of it, but in every sentiment I have heard utered in publick by Ld Grenville for the last 3 years, I do not recollect one of which a Whig would be ashamed.[38]

Such urgings as Bedford's did little good, however, and by 1811 Grey wrote that he knew it was impossible to restrain "our friends . . . who

35. *The New Whig Guide* (London, 1819).

36. LSE, Horner Papers, Vol. IV, Horner to Allen, Sept. 28, 1809.

37. *Parl. Debates,* XXIII (May 7, 1812), 73–88; Gore, ed., *Creevey Papers,* Bennet to Creevey, April 3, 1815, p. 102; Bedford, Bedford RO, Whitbread Papers, WI/2427, Creevey to Whitbread, Dec. 11, 1808.

38. Bedford, Bedford RO, Whitbread Papers, WI/2467, Bedford to Whitbread, April 13, 1809.

compose our wing of the Army" from abusing the Grenvillites.[39] Even
Tierney, despite pressure from Grey and Holland, refused to accept an
offer from the first Marquis of Buckingham to sit for St. Mawes and
owned that he did not choose to appear "personally connected with and
under obligation to the Grenvilles."[40]

2. The Disintegration of the Grenvillite Party, 1807–12

The Grenvillites by 1807 were far from encompassing a monolithic
political group. They had no important newspaper,[41] no social club,
and held few political meetings as a group. Unlike the situation
between 1801 and 1806, when a strong Grenvillite party indubitably
existed, it is tempting to view them as a mere adjunct (and not a
particularly important one at that) of a much larger Whig party. That,
however, would be a mistake. For at least a few years after the fall of the
Talents' Ministry, the Grenvillites were a relatively large group of men
who, were it not for the presence of Lord Grenville at the head of the
opposition, would in most cases probably not have supported opposition at all; and in this fact lay an abundant portion of their strength.

By 1811 or 1812, that situation had altered entirely, and lasting
political and social ties had formed between many leading members of
Grenville's group and the main body of the Whig opposition, ties
which long survived the Grenville-Foxite schism of 1817. An examination of the Grenvillites during the 1807 Parliament shows the disintegration, similar to that of the Northites during the 1784 Parliament, of
what had been one of the strongest Westminster political groups. But,
whatever happened later, between 1783 and 1785 the Northites were
important in numerous ways to the Foxite Whigs' perception of their
own strength; so, too, the importance exerted by the Grenvillites in
1805 and 1806 continued for the six years or so after 1804.

Certainly by 1811 and 1812, it becomes obvious that many if not
most of Lord Grenville's (though not Buckingham's) followers could no
longer regard themselves in any positive way as Grenvillites in the sense
that that term had been used since 1801. This may have been the result
of the nonchalance and political divisions among their potential leaders.

39. Durham Papers, Grey to Holland, Oct. 29, 1811.
40. Ibid.: Tierney to Grey, Sept. 6 and Oct. 8, 1812; Grey to Holland, Oct. 2,
1812.
41. The Grenvilles seem to have controlled a London daily, the *Morning Star*,
during 1805 and 1806, only a few copies of which appear to survive at the British
Museum. Arthur Aspinall, *Politics and the Press, 1780–1850* (London, 1949), p. 284.

It is even difficult to perceive a strictly Grenvillite policy to be im-
plemented during much of the 1807 Parliament or, considering voting
patterns, to describe the Grenvillites as the conservative wing of the
opposition. On most issues the so-called Grenvillites, even those who
sat for Buckingham's boroughs and who might best be termed a
connection or faction, were as divided in their political views as were the
Foxites; and neither in the Lords nor in the Commons did any of the
Grenville brothers attempt to keep together those members who had, at
least in 1807, appeared to place themselves under their banner.

The very looseness of Grenville's hold over his political group makes
it difficult to ascertain its exact numerical strength, and any final
evaluation must, thus, be somewhat haphazard. One historian of the
early nineteenth century Whig party thought that after 1807 the
recognizable Grenvillites in the House of Lords numbered only about
five.[42] Actually, the number of those who could be described as
Grenvillites around 1808 included some twenty-four to twenty-six
peers. Six of these—Braybrooke, Buckingham, Carysfort, Fortescue,
Grenville, and Glastonbury—were members of the Grenville family
itself; one—Bulkeley—was directly attached to Buckingham; four
—Carlisle, Carnarvon, Minto (who went to India in 1807), and
Spencer—remained connected with Grenville from the days of the
struggles against the peace of Amiens; eight—Auckland, Bute, Cawdor, Hereford, Stafford, the Bishop of St. Asaph, and two tentative
Grenvillites, Lucan and Yarborough—had joined the Grenvillites between 1803 and the time of Pitt's death in 1806; and seven
—Carrington, Bristol, Essex, Hardwicke, Somers, and the Bishops of
Lincoln and Oxford—chiefly former Pittites, adhered to Grenville
during or shortly after 1806.[43] Taking four important division lists that
have survived from the 1807 Parliament, Stafford's motion relative to
the change of administrations in 1807, the minorities on the addresses
in 1807 and 1810, and Grenville's motion on the Orders in Council in
1809, the percentage of Grenvillites in relation to the entire opposition
in the Lords varied from 31 to 34 percent.[44]

If the exact situation of the Grenvillites in the Lords is sometimes
doubtful (and it becomes increasingly so in the years after 1809), the
problem of determining the exact number of Grenvillites in the Commons is doubly so. Michael Roberts thought there were twelve during

42. Roberts, The Whig Party, p. 333.

43. There is some, though by no means conclusive, evidence that Lords Grey de
Ruthyn, Grosvenor, Monson, Scarborough, Shaftesbury, and Southampton acted with
Grenville.

44. Parl. Debates: IX (April 13, 1807), 422, and (June 26, 1807), 607; X (Feb. 18,
1808), 642; XV (Jan. 23, 1810), 37.

the Parliament of 1807: Sir John Anstruther, William Fremantle, Thomas Grenville, Francis Horner, John Dashwood King, Sir John Newport, William Conyngham Plunket, Sir Watkin and Charles Wynn, and Lords Althorp, Kensington, and Temple.[45] Of this list, Plunket was not in Parliament during these years, Kensington was acting with Whitbread,[46] and I have found no evidence that King ever followed the political line of Buckingham or Grenville.

When the Parliament of 1807 was elected, and considering here the arrangements that usually followed a general election, at least twenty-two members of the Commons can be classified as definite Grenvillites. Among these are: the Marquis of Buckingham's six members—Scrope Bernard, Thomas Grenville, Richard Neville, Sir George Nugent, and Lords Ebrington and Temple; the Welsh contingent of the party, comprised of Sir Watkin and Charles Wynn, their brother-in-law William Shipley, and Lord Bulkeley's representative Sir Robert Williams; two sons of Lord Carlisle—Lord Morpeth and William Howard; Lady Buckingham's half-brother Sir George Cranfield Berkeley; Lord Auckland's son William Eden; Lord Carnarvon's son Lord Porchester; Buckingham's protégé William Fremantle; and six friends of Lord Grenville—Sir John Anstruther, William Elliot, Lord Euston, Pascoe Grenfell, Thomas Knox, and Sir John Newport. During the course of the Parliament, other definite additions were made to the Grenvillite party: in 1808, Stafford's son Lord Gower; and in 1810, Buckingham's second son Lord George Grenville (later Baron Nugent of Ireland) and Auckland's son George Eden.

Other MPs were also associated with Grenvillite peers, either by blood or through parliamentary influence (or both), though not all of them by any means supported their relative's or patron's political views. Thus Lords Stafford and Hardwicke each returned members who seldom if ever supported the opposition after 1807.[47] Earl Spencer's son Viscount Althorp, who had certainly entered public life in 1804 as a follower of Lord Grenville, by 1808 and 1809 was far to the left of many Foxites and whatever relationship the senior Grenvilles maintained with him was purely avuncular. Bulkeley returned a supporter of Whitbread for his pocket borough of Beaumaris for Welsh electoral reasons.[48] Of Lord Carrington's six members, only Francis Horner might conceivably be described as a Grenvillite (at least after 1811), as

45. Roberts, *The Whig Party*, p. 333.

46. Bedford, Bedford RO, Whitbread Papers, WI/2489, Creevey to Whitbread, Nov. 8, 1809 (copy).

47. Stafford returned Lord Granville Leveson Gower and Edward Bootle Wilbraham; Hardwicke, Charles Philip Yorke.

48. BM, Thomas Grenville Papers, Add. MSS. 42058, Shipley to Thomas Grenville, Oct. 12, 1811.

134] THE GRENVILLITES, 1801-29

the three Smith brothers were frequent supporters of Whitbread. Of
Stafford's six members in 1808, only William Fremantle could be
definitely called a Grenvillite, though ties may possibly have existed
with another member, George Granville Venables Vernon, son of the
Archbishop of York.[49] Lord Yarborough returned four members, yet
his own ties to Grenville were so nebulous that to classify those MPs as
Grenvillites would be unhelpful and probably misleading. There is
little indication that most of the MPs returned by Carrington, Stafford,
and other Grenvillite peers considered themselves as in any way separate
from other members of the general opposition. The Grenvillites in the
Commons certainly had no recognizable leader whose line they could
follow. Thus, the percentage of Grenvillites in the Commons in relation
to the over-all opposition must remain somewhat obscure. But taking
the 1807 and 1810 minorities on the amendment to the address, a
provisional figure of around 14 percent seems to be the best estimate.[50]

The House of Commons between 1807 and 1812 was not the
Grenvillites' best arena. Thomas Grenville, the obvious choice for a
leader, resigned his seat in 1810 and is listed in the *Parliamentary
Debates* as having voted only three times between 1807 and 1809.
Charles Wynn, who did emerge as his uncle's spokesman in the Commons around 1812, was earlier often absent on crucial opposition
motions, along with the entire Grenvillite Welsh group.[51] Insofar as
anyone spoke the sentiments of Lord Grenville in the Commons during
this period, it was his nephew, Lord Temple. But Temple, who
frequently sulked, was never one to spend an inordinate amount of time
in Parliament, and he was not respected by his fellows. As early as May,
1808, the "non attendance of Lord Temple & others of his family and
connection in the House of Commons" was frequently remarked
upon.[52] In May, 1810, upset by the fragmentation of part of the
left-leaning section of the opposition into followers of Burdett and
Whitbread, Temple resolved upon a semisecession from Parliament.[53]
He did not greatly care what people thought of his absence and felt that
attendance "cannot be of any use until a party is formed united in itself
and acting upon defined, ascertained and fixed principles."[54] Certain
other former Grenvillite MPs and efficient men of business, such as

49. HRO, Wickham Papers, 38M49/1/18, Grenville to Wickham, Jan. 23, 1811.
50. *Parl. Debates:* IX (June 26, 1807), 658; XIV (Jan. 23, 1810), 105.
51. BRO, Fremantle Papers, 46, Buckingham to Fremantle, Jan. 23, 1808.
52. BM, Holland House Papers, Add. MSS. 51593, Albermarle to Holland, May
18, 1808.
53. BM, Thomas Grenville Papers, Add. MSS. 41854, Temple to Thomas Grenville, May 28, 1810.
54. BRO, Fremantle Papers, 55, Temple to Fremantle, May 27, 1810.

William Wickham, John King, and W. C. Plunket, were not in
Parliament; and Windham, who was certainly an effective leader of the
new opposition from 1801 to 1806, had quarreled with Lord Grenville.
Adding further to the Grenvillite weakness, the rate of attrition among
that group during the Parliament of 1807 was inordinately high: In
1809, Ebrington resigned; in 1810, William Eden died, and Berkeley
and Thomas Grenville resigned; in 1811, Anstruther died, Sir George
Nugent went to India, and Euston and Porchester went to the Lords.

Lord Althorp is a good reflection of the disintegration of Grenvillite
influence in the Commons. His father, Earl Spencer, was the closest
nonfamily supporter of both Lord Grenville and Thomas Grenville, and
the latter asserted that his fondness for the young Viscount equaled that
for his own nephews. But by the spring of 1809, Althorp, to the
Grenvilles' horror, was lending support to Whitbread and Folkestone
(and indirectly, Thomas suspected, to Burdett and Horne Tooke) and
dividing in small minorities on radical proposals of the more advanced
Whigs.[55] In this he was hardly alone.[56] Some of the more responsible
Grenvillite peers were quite cognizant of the problem, and Auckland
for one literally begged Lord Grenville to attempt to exert his opinions
and influence in the Commons, to rally his forces, and thus to not leave
the "wild horses" in control.[57] In short, a chaotic situation in the
Commons calls into question almost the existence of any autonomous
Grenvillite party there in the years after 1808 or 1809.

The attempts of Grenville to create an order out of this anarchy
proved disappointing. When Lord Howick, the opposition leader in the
Commons, went to the Lords as the second Earl Grey in November,
1807, at least five MPs, none of them Grenvillites, had some claim to
succeed him: Lord Henry Petty, R. B. Sheridan, George Tierney,
Samuel Whitbread, and William Windham. Of the five, Grenville
preferred Petty while doubting his industry, and he absolutely vetoed
Sheridan, Whitbread, and Windham. Then the Grenvillites, with no
particular hope or enthusiasm, helped to push forward as a noncontroversial candidate George Ponsonby, late Chancellor of Ireland, the
uncle of Lady Grey.[58] Ponsonby proved a miserable choice, however,

55. Althorp Papers, 78, Thomas Grenville to Spencer, March 30 and April 1, 1809;
Dropmore, Thomas Grenville to Lord Grenville: March 29, 1809, IX, 285–86, and April
1, 1809, 288.

56. For example, William Howard. *Parl. Debates,* X (Jan. 28, 1808), 182.

57. *Dropmore,* Auckland to Grenville, Dec. 28, 1808, IX, 251.

58. BM, Thomas Grenville Papers, Add. MSS.: 41852, Lord Grenville to Thomas
Grenville, Nov. 22, 1807; 41854, Spencer to Thomas Grenville, Dec. 13, 1807; 41857,
Stafford to Thomas Grenville, Dec. 14, 1807; 41857, Holland to Thomas Grenville,
Dec. 15, 1807.

and failed to stop or to even temporarily halt the tides of party disunity. By March, 1809, Grey, Lord Grenville, and Thomas Grenville were attempting to persuade him to step down in favor of Petty. Such a transferral could only have been effected had the opposition leaders in the Lords unhesitatingly demanded it—which they never did—and Ponsonby remained at his station until his death in 1817.[59] The Grenvilles were hardly overjoyed with this situation; but by 1810 Thomas Grenville, at least, had decided that the opposition (with Petty now in the Lords as the Marquis of Lansdowne) would find itself in more difficulty without Ponsonby than with him "and a choice of evils is all that is left."[60]

Lord Grenville saw only one real hope of combating the radical predominance in the Commons—his old policy of uniting George Canning with his branch of the opposition. Canning and Grenville were closely connected from at least 1796, when the younger man became Under Secretary at the Foreign Office, and Canning in 1806 described their relationship to Perceval and Castlereagh as one "of constant and intimate private friendship, and (with the exception of . . . 1804) of uninterrupted concurrence in political opinion and conduct."[61] It was a misfortune that, with both of his closest confidants—Wellesley and Canning—among the "Tories," Lord Grenville was unable after 1807 to keep on cordial terms. The break with Wellesley was probably the fault of neither man, but the split between Canning and Grenville was certainly subject to the whims of irascible temperament. Henry Wynn, Grenville's nephew, an unemployed diplomat, desired to make a tour of war-torn Spain. Canning, then Foreign Secretary in the Duke of Portland's Ministry, refused the request on the grounds that the Spanish might consider Wynn the King's accredited envoy. The Grenville brothers were furious at what they considered to be inane reasoning, and parties on both sides in the quarrel made remarks about the other that may have caused regret upon later reflection.[62] In spite of this, how-

59. Ibid., 41853, Lord Grenville to Thomas Grenville, March 28, 1809; *Dropmore*, Thomas Grenville to Lord Grenville, March, 1809, IX, 282–83; Roberts, *The Whig Party*, pp. 314–15.

60. HEH-STG, Box 176, Grenville to Buckingham, Dec. 17, 1809; *Court and Cabinets of George III*, Thomas Grenville to Buckingham, Jan. 10, 1810, IV, 418.

61. *The Diaries and Correspondence of the Right Hon. George Rose*, ed. Leveson Vernon Harcourt (London, 1860), II, 312–13.

62. NLW, Henry Wynn Papers, 2/2790D: Thomas Grenville to Henry Wynn, Sept. 5, 1808; Henry Wynn to Canning, n.d. (draft). Great Britain, Historical Manuscripts Commission, Francis Bickley, ed., *Report on the Manuscripts of Earl Bathurst, Preserved at Cirencester Park* (London, 1923): Grenville to Bathurst, Sept. 7, 1808, p. 75; Canning to Bathurst, Oct. 30, 1808, pp. 77–78.

ever, Grenville's opinion of Canning's talents and his desire for a coalition with the younger man remained steady; but any personal intimacy between them was halted until the middle 1820s.

The resignation of the Canningites at the time of the dissolution of Portland's Ministry in September, 1809, left them as floating, non-committed members of the House of Commons. Inevitably, given the state of the opposition, this led to discussions as to the advisability of their joining Grenville. A number of persons who were generally well informed considered this option likely.[63] Lord Grey, however, put a decided negative on any negotiations with Canning and totally refused to countenance cooperation with him, either in or out of office, on the grounds of his constant intrigues and bad manners since 1807. He told Holland that "in politics especially, time, & a change of circumstances render resolutions of this nature seldom very permanent," but, he added, "I foresee nothing that is likely to produce any alteration in this."[64] Grey, true to his word and despite the action of other Whigs in 1827, remained secure in his decision on this matter until Canning's death. Grey's prohibition against Canning had the complete support of two leading members of the Grenville family in the Commons, Temple and Charles Wynn; and Canning at this stage denied any desire to coalesce with Grenville and Grey.[65]

During the opposition's aborted attempt to form a Ministry in January, 1811, the question of Canning's role in any projected Government rivaled the Grenville-Foxite quarrels over Lord Grenville's Auditorship. A number of important politicians, including the Prince of Wales, Buckingham, and Lord Lansdowne, agreed with Grenville that Canning should enter the Ministry. Grey, however, stated that he would sooner retire from public life than connect himself with George Canning, and the main body of the old Whig leadership concurred.[66] In the face of such hostility, Grenville was forced to yield. Buckingham's son, Lord Temple, who had always been a cynic, suspected that the Whig opposition to Canning was motivated by a desire to keep

63. HRO, Tierney Papers, 31M70/30b, Gordon to Tierney, Sept. 29, 1809; DRO, Sidmouth Papers, 152M, Buckinghamshire to Sidmouth, Oct. 4, 1809.

64. Durham Papers, Grey to Holland, Oct. 5, 1809; *Dropmore,* Grey to Grenville, Oct. 5, 1809, IX, 334.

65. NLW: Coedymaen Papers, Temple to Wynn, Oct. 9, 1809; Charles Wynn Papers, 1084D, Wynn to Temple, Oct. 18, 1809. BM, Canning-Wilbraham Papers, Add. MSS. 46841, Canning to Wilbraham, Dec. 19, 1809.

66. Holland, *Further Memoirs of the Whig Party,* pp. 80–83; BM, Holland House Papers, Add. MSS. 52004B, Allen's Journal, Jan. 13 and 14, 1811; LSE, Horner Papers, Vol. V: Allen to Horner, Jan. 15, 1811; Horner to Allen, Jan. 16, 1811. *Dropmore,* Thomas Grenville to Lord Grenville, Jan. 11, 1811, X, 104.

Grenville's party weak in the Commons.[67] But the conservative Whigs who opposed Canning at this juncture seemed to believe sincerely that a strong Government could be formed without his aid as long as they had the support of the future Regent. They were probably correct in this assumption, considering how the two previous weak Governments had, with George III's support, weathered the political storms of 1809 and 1810. Grey felt that Grenville's insistence upon Canning was based not so much upon a desire to strengthen numbers in the Commons as to prevent the Grenvillites from having to be represented there by Whitbread or Tierney.[68]

In the autumn of 1812, Lord Grenville made one final attempt to connect Canning with the opposition. Lord Liverpool (formerly Lord Hawkesbury), who was now Prime Minister, in July, 1812, had offered Canning the Foreign Ministry; but Canning had refused, because he was not simultaneously to be leader of the House of Commons.[69] Such reticence impressed Grey not a whit and no overture was made.[70]

If the natural leaders of the Grenvillites in the Commons failed to display any particular parliamentary talents or fortitude, their leader in the Lords had little justification to reproach them. Between 1807 and the effective end of his political career as a party leader in 1817, Grenville, in conjunction with Grey, constantly expressed his dislike for active opposition and his preference for country life. Even before giving up his seals of office in 1807, Grenville wrote Howick: "I feel great repugnance to any course of very active opposition—having been most unaffectedly disinclined to take upon me the task in which I have been engaged, & feeling no small pleasure in an honourable release, I could not easily bring myself to struggle much to get my chains on again."[71] He had little motivation to change his mind during the next decade.

He told Buckingham at the same time, in regard to the opposition, that "the error of doing too much is far more dangerous than that of doing too little; and let it also be remembered, that if my friends and near connexions should feel themselves bound to go much beyond my line, that very circumstance will impose on me the necessity of keeping still more within it, than I should otherwise do."[72] Both Bucking-

67. HEH-STG, ST. 96, Temple's Diary, Jan., 1811.

68. BM, Holland House Papers, Add. MSS. 52004B, Allen's Journal, Jan. 14 and 17, 1811.

69. BM, Morley Papers, Add. MSS. 48220, Canning to Boringdon, July 28, 1812; Durham Papers, Grenville to Grey, Nov. 10, 1812.

70. Durham Papers, Grey to Holland, Nov. 14, 1812.

71. Ibid., Grenville to Howick, March 20, 1807.

72. Court and Cabinets of George III, Grenville to Buckingham, March 27, 1807, IV, 149.

ham and Temple were aghast at this attitude, and the Marquis prophesied—correctly as it turned out—that if such a policy were kept up "it can not be long a question whether we shall retain a party much larger than that which disapproved the peace of Amiens."[73] By December, 1807, Grenville was writing such pessimistic accounts of the efficacy of a vigorous opposition that Lauderdale wondered if he meant to secede from Parliament altogether.[74]

Unfortunately for the opposition, Lord Grey, Grenville's chief colleague on the Foxite side, was only too open to such pessimism and in 1808 even suggested his own withdrawal from Parliament, leaving Grenville to carry on the leadership of the opposition alone—"a project," Grenville remarked to his brother, "which you may well suppose is not quite to my taste."[75] Grey spent critical political periods ministering to his usually pregnant wife or ill children at Howick, and Grenville tended his rhododendrons in Cornwall. In January, 1809, Grenville fairly told his troops that he contemplated an irregular parliamentary attendance during the upcoming session, and during much of the 1810 session he was seriously ill at Dropmore.[76] He frequently wrote letters to supporters, as in the case of Newport in 1811, in the following vein: "It is very evident to me that no situation is likely to arise that will tempt me to embark again in any public situation—probably none in which my assistance will be desired, but certainly none in which the hope of doing any good will be such as to counter-balance all the innumerable pains & difficulties of the attempt." He therefore expressed a wish to spend the rest of his life in "peace & quiet."[77] The demoralizing effects such letters must have had upon his ambitious colleagues cannot be overlooked in any discussion of the decline of the Grenvillites after 1807. Few, after all, desire to attach themselves to a sinking ship.

Michael Roberts held that as leaders of the opposition Grey and Grenville were an "ill-assorted pair—the one an early advocate of Parliamentary Reform, the other a consenting party to Pitt's repressive legislation," their alliance held together only by "mutual forbearance upon subjects of controversy, and zealous cooperation for Catholic Emancipation." J. E. Cookson, the historian of the middle years of the Liverpool Ministry, reflecting on the Grenville-Foxite alliance, wrote

73. Ibid., Temple to Buckingham, n.d., 147; BM, Thomas Grenville Papers, Add. MSS. 41851, Buckingham to Thomas Grenville, April, 1807.

74. BM, Holland House Papers, Add. MSS. 51691, Lauderdale to Holland, Dec. 28, 1807.

75. BM, Thomas Grenville Papers, Add. MSS. 41852, Grenville to Thomas Grenville, Jan. 7, 1808.

76. Ibid., 41853, Grenville to Thomas Grenville, Jan. 12, 1809.

77. Bodleian, Grenville-Newport Papers, Grenville to Newport, Dec. 17, 1811.

that they had "never run well in harness, each being hopelessly out of step with the other over the war, parliamentary reform and domestic disorder."[78] Such viewpoints presuppose more political argumentation and even decisiveness than may indeed be correct.

A revival of popular reform agitation, such as had seldom characterized the opening decade of the nineteenth century, occurred in 1809. Within opposition ranks, this crisis concluded in the temporary departure of Samuel Whitbread from the Whig party and the confirmation of George Ponsonby as leader of the opposition in the Commons. Roberts interpreted such events as a Grenvillite victory over the Foxites.[79] In these observations, he appears to assume that Grenville and Grey were separated by decided and important policy differences and that in 1809 a definite Grenvillite policy emerged victorious. Both of these premises are doubtful. While there certainly were important disagreements within the opposition during these years on any number of issues, such as economical and parliamentary reform, Copenhagen, the Spanish war, and Ireland, whether these differences should be seen in terms of Grenvillite versus Foxite is questionable. Perhaps a more accurate appraisal would view the division as occurring between progressives and conservatives, with the latter category including most of the Grenvillites and the Whig leadership.

The political relationship between Grenville and Grey was quite close, and whatever radicalism may have existed in Charles Grey's youth was certainly a distant echo by 1807. Grey attributed Grenville's good humor and lack of resentment over Whitbread's activities in 1808 to the fact that he and Grenville were "as perfectly agreed as we are."[80] By the spring of 1809, when the activism of Whitbread was giving the staid opposition leaders serious trouble, Whitbread discussed with the Foxite leadership the matter of his separation from the party. At that time Thomas Grenville told Spencer that Grey agreed so heartily with him on the necessity of separating from Whitbread, that "I almost thought I overheard myself in a soliloquy."[81] In June, 1809, when the Portland Ministry was gravely weakened by internal dissension and Tierney heard rumors about the commencement of talks to include some Whigs in the Government, Grey told him to avoid any communication with the Ministry so as to nip "at once & decisively" any hint or idea of a separation between himself and Lord Grenville.[82]

78. Roberts, *The Whig Party*, p. 2; J. E. Cookson, *Lord Liverpool's Administration: The Crucial Years, 1815–1822* (Edinburgh, 1975), p. 133.

79. Roberts, *The Whig Party*, p. 135.

80. Lieutenant General C. Grey, *Some Account of the Life and Opinions of Charles, Second Earl Grey* (London, 1861), Grey to ?, Jan. 27, 1808, p. 180.

81. Althorp Papers, 78, Thomas Grenville to Spencer, March 24 and 28, 1809.

82. HRO, Tierney Papers, 31M70/33h, Grey to Tierney, June 27, 1809.

Grey was as trusted by the more conservative Grenvillites as he was by Lord Grenville and Thomas Grenville. Lord Glastonbury, who had been active in politics since the Duke of Grafton's Administration, observed that the ties which bound Grey and Grenville were among the strongest of his long political lifetime.[83] William Fremantle came out of a conference with Grey in 1810 observing that Grey was more enraged against the progressives among his friends than even Buckingham's son Temple was.[84] Some of the more advanced Whigs, such as Brougham and the precocious Lord John Russell—not to speak of Whitbread and his immediate followers—were hurt and upset at Grey's increasing conservatism and, indeed, partially attributed it to Grenville's pernicious influence.[85] But none doubted that during these years the harmony between the two opposition leaders proceeded from a general unity of belief, however regretable, rather than from an artificial desire to conciliate Grenvillites and Foxites.

The unfortunate lack of adequate and complete parliamentary division lists during much of the early nineteenth century prevents the emergence of any exact synthesis of the overall voting pattern of any particular group. While one usually knows the identity of individuals who voted against the Government on an important national issue, one seldom knows (except from correspondence) who voted in support of the Government. An additional problem, of course, concerns parliamentary absentees. Still, from the information available, it is clear that throughout the decade after 1807, little consistency emerges on key policy questions among members of the Grenvillite party, especially (though not exclusively) in the House of Commons. Even among the first Marquis of Buckingham's six members, much less among followers of more distant Grenvillite peers, a considerable division of opinion occurred on national issues ranging from parliamentary reform to the Peninsular war.

The general lack of unity is attributable both to the absence of a strong or respected Grenvillite leader in the House of Commons and the failure of Grenville and Buckingham to exert themselves in providing some control over their potential Commons followers. The situation was further complicated by the fact that Buckingham and Lord Gren-

83. BM, Thomas Grenville Papers, Add. MSS. 41857, Glastonbury to Thomas Grenville, Sept. 30, 1809.

84. *Court and Cabinets of George III*, Fremantle to Temple, May 26, 1810, IV, 444–45.

85. Henry Peter Brougham, First Baron Brougham and Vaux, *The Life and Times of Henry Lord Brougham: Written by Himself* (3 vols.; New York, 1871–72), Brougham to Rosslyn, Dec. 1, 1807, I, 273; HRO, Tierney Papers, 31M70/72c, Whitbread to Tierney, Dec. 25, 1807; BM, Holland House Papers, Add. MSS. 51677, Russell to Holland, Aug. 7, 1810.

ville themselves were often at odds on important questions. They disagreed on such crucial issues as the Duke of York affair, aspects of the Regency Bill, the Peninsular war, and (probably) on the reversion Bills. The Foxite leaders in both Houses were in a similar state of disarray on any number of questions. Therefore, in spite of one's views on the state of the opposition during the course of the 1807 Parliament, taking into account the important national issues, one would be hard pressed to find many on which either a Grenville-Foxite dichotomy is emergent or a specific Grenvillite policy is ascertainable.

On foreign policy, which was so divisive within the coalition before 1806, the Grenvillites and Foxites were coming more and more into general agreement. By 1807, Grenville had adopted a position on the French war perilously close to that viewpoint he had so vigorously opposed in 1801 and 1802: "I should most cordially rejoice in the conclusion of a truce . . . that would give us a little breathing time, & the chance of events to improve a state of things that hardly could be made worse."[86]

In February, 1808, the radically inclined Samuel Whitbread and his friends submitted peace resolutions to the House of Commons that were at least partially meant to impose an *"experimentum crusis"* on the Grenvillites. However, probably to Whitbread's surprise, Grenville aided him in drafting, or at least correcting, the peace resolutions; and while no prominent Grenvillite (or such conservative Whigs as Tierney, Ponsonby, or Petty) voted for the resolutions, neither did they speak against them in the Commons.[87]

On the question of the utility and morality of the 1807 British expedition to Copenhagen, there was a minor split among the Grenvillites. Thomas Grenville, Spencer, and Stafford were in favor of the expedition and the resulting bombardment; Lord Grenville was decidedly adverse to it and compared it in Parliament to France's attack upon Naples.[88]

From the very beginning, in 1808, Grenville was extremely dubious about the Peninsular war, though he highly approved the patriotic sentiments that induced his nephews to participate in the struggle.[89]

86. BM, Thomas Grenville Papers, Add. MSS. 41852, Grenville to Thomas Grenville, Nov. 18, 1807.

87. *Parl. Debates,* X (Feb. 29, 1808), 856–70; Bedford, Bedford RO, Whitbread Papers: WI/4183, Belsham to Whitbread, Feb. 21, 1808; WI/4184, draft of the peace motion of Feb., 1808.

88. HRO, Tierney Papers, 31M70/33i, Tierney to Grey, Nov. 26, 1807 (copy); Bedford, Bedford RO, Whitbread Papers, WI/2483, Creevey to Whitbread, Jan. 8, 1808; *Parl. Debates,* X (Jan. 21, 1808), 19.

89. *Court and Cabinets of George III,* Grenville to Buckingham, Aug. 10, 1808, IV, 239–40.

At the earliest possible moment of the parliamentary session of 1809, he denounced Ministers for sending an army into the interior of Spain, observing that Britain should have been content with naval forays on the Iberian coast.[90] Grey agreed with him, though he placed more emphasis upon the lack of information and planning on the part of Ministers than upon the basic strategical decision to send troops to Spain.[91]

Lord Grenville, who regarded the Peninsular war as a wasteful expenditure of blood and money, felt no qualms in calling for complete withdrawal of the British army, and his speeches on the subject were oddly reminiscent of Whig criticism of Pitt's war strategy of the 1790s.[92] The opposition was as divided on the conduct of the Peninsular war as it was on other issues, but hardly on a Grenville-Foxite line. For example, the Marquis of Buckingham's perspective was quite different than his brother's. Buckingham was in frequent communication with at least three well-placed individuals who imparted to him a favorable view of the proceedings: Lord Wellington himself, who during the 1780s, as Arthur Wellesley, had acted as his aide-de-camp in Ireland; Admiral George Cranfield Berkeley, a Grenvillite MP who had the chief naval command off the coast of Portugal; and Admiral Thomas Fremantle, who had twice sought election to the House of Commons as a Grenvillite and held an important naval command in the Mediterranean.[93] By early 1810, Buckingham wanted to fight the French in Portugal rather than in Ireland, and he mildly scolded his brother for failing to do justice to Wellington's military conduct. The disagreement between the brothers continued until Buckingham's death in 1813.[94]

There were always significant Whigs, such as Holland, Lord John Russell, and Francis Horner, who approved the war, while deprecating certain aspects of its conduct, on the old grounds that it was a struggle for national independence.[95] However, Grey and most of his Whig colleagues sustained Grenville's anti-Peninsular policy at least until the spring of 1811, when Grey rose in the Lords to praise Wellington for

90. *Parl. Debates,* XII (Jan. 19, 1809), 12–13.
91. Ibid., XIV (April 21, 1809), 123–25.
92. Ibid.: XV (Feb. 22, 1810), 511–25; XIX (March 21, 1811), 450–57.
93. *Court and Cabinets of George III,* Wellington to Buckingham: Nov. 16, 1809, IV, 387; July 17, 1810, 449–50. *Memoirs of the Regency,* I: Berkeley to Buckingham, May 4, 1811, 80–81; Berkeley to Buckingham, May 12, 1811, 83–86; Thomas Fremantle to Buckingham, n.d., 89–90.
94. *Dropmore,* X, Buckingham to Grenville: Feb. 15, 1810, 11; Oct. 27, 1810, 59; May 24, 1812, 272–73.
95. BM, Holland House Papers, Add. MSS. 51530, Grenville to Holland, June 6, 1809; John Russell, First Earl Russell, *Recollections and Suggestions, 1813–1873* (Boston, 1875), pp. 5–6; LSE, Horner Papers, Vol. V, Horner to Jeffrey, Jan. 8, 1811.

the deliverance of Portugal and to acknowledge his own past errors of judgment.[96] Yet Grey's doubts still persisted, and in May, 1812, he joined Grenville in expressing serious reservations to Wellington's brother, Lord Wellesley, about the practicality of continuing the Peninsular war in light of the perilous state of finances—a position both Holland and Buckingham found distasteful.[97] But, if Grey proved indecisive, Grenville never veered from his position. He told Holland in 1813 that Britain would have been in a far better position to aid the currently successful European coalition against Napoleon if previous resources had not been wasted in the Peninsula, and during the 1820s he was still attempting to persuade friends that Napoleon had been conquered in Russia and not in Spain.[98]

On questions concerning offices in reversion and general sinecurial reform, while the Grenvillites were hardly among the more forward groups pressing for a cleansing of the Augean stables, they also were not necessarily among the reactionaries. Attempts made between 1807 and 1812 to investigate, regulate, and abolish sinecures or reversions drew support from two Grenville nephews, Richard Neville and Charles Wynn; three MPs who sat for a borough under Buckingham's control, Scrope Bernard, Lord Gower, and (again) Richard Neville; and numerous other Grenvillite parliamentarians, including Lord Grenville.[99] Just as obviously, some of the more conservative members of the party, such as the Lords Auckland and Carlisle, and especially the patronage-laden Marquis of Buckingham, opposed such measures.[100]

The Grenvillites were, in general, as divided on the great domestic scandal of 1809—the accusation against the Duke of York's mistress, Mrs. Clarke, for selling army commissions—and the resultant clamor for reform as they were on economical reform issues. Buckingham, who was decidedly against the Duke, worried that the illness-induced absence of two of his members, Thomas Grenville and General Nugent, from the Commons would be interpreted as evidence of Grenvillian softness toward corruption. When William Fremantle informed his mentor Buckingham that out of gratitude for past favors he could not in

96. *Parl. Debates*, XIX (April 26, 1811), 766–68.

97. *Memoirs of the Regency*, memorandum of Grenville and Grey to Wellesley, May 24, 1812, I, 314–15; Holland, *Further Memoirs of the Whig Party*, p. 118; *Dropmore*, Buckingham to Grenville, May 24, 1812, X, 272–73.

98. NLW, Coedymaen Papers, Grenville to Wynn: VI/297, Oct. 6, 1813; VI/387, Jan. 21, 1823.

99. *Parl. Debates:* IX (July 7, 1807), 739*–40*; XXI (Feb. 7, 1812), 701; XXII (March 24, 1812), 164; XXII (May 4, 1812), 1178–80. Roberts, *The Whig Party*, p. 186; *The Times* (London), March 1, 1810.

100. *Parl. Debates*, X: (March 1, 1808), 870; (March 10, 1808), 1047–53.

conscience vote on any motion disapproving the Duke's conduct, the Marquis only very reluctantly accepted the excuse.[101]

In the large if unsuccessful minorities on motions or addresses (to the King) that accused the Duke of foreknowledge of the corruption, the number of Grenvillites who followed Buckingham's lead in opposing York included two of his MPs, his nephew Richard Neville and Lord Gower; two other Grenville nephews, Sir Watkin and Charles Wynn; and four members of the Grenvillite party, Pascoe Grenfell, William Howard, Sir John Newport, and William Shipley.[102] While Buckingham's son, Lord Temple, supported nothing quite so extreme, he had some hand in drawing up a motion which, while it absolved the Duke of personal corruption, suggested to the King that he remove his son from office. Temple also made two extremely anti-York speeches in the Commons, after the first of which Admiral Fremantle, who like his brother William supported the Duke, wrote that "Temple has no more feeling than a calf."[103]

On the other hand, Lord Grenville was totally averse to any anti-York activity and generally thought Spencer Perceval was correct in his view that the House of Commons had no reason to charge the Duke with connivance at corruption. Grenville also attempted to ease Fremantle's embarrassing position with Buckingham.[104]

Likewise, on other reform questions of 1809, no definite Grenvillite policy is clearly discernible; rather, what emerged was, at best, an ad hoc antiradical alliance of Grenvillites and conservative Whigs and, at worst, a moderate confusion. The announced—if only temporary—separation in March, 1809, between the conservative members of the opposition and Samuel Whitbread was an event as much desired by the Whig leadership as by the Grenvillites. As a sort of follow-up to that event, a radical motion on April 17 for a committee to inquire into general national abuses drew no support from among the recognizable followers of the Grenvillites, and both leading Grenvillites and Whigs verbally opposed it.[105]

The extraparliamentary agitation in 1809 for some measure of parliamentary reform showed the divisions between both the conservatives

101. *Dropmore*, Buckingham to Grenville, March 14, 1809, IX, 280–81.

102. *Parl. Debates*, XII: (March 15, 1809), 639–40; (March 17, 1809), 670.

103. *Court and Cabinets of George III*, Temple to Buckingham, n.d., IV, 330; *Parl. Debates*, XII: (March 15, 1809), 569–77; (March 20, 1809), 730–33. BRO, Fremantle Papers, 45, Thomas Fremantle to William Fremantle, March 20, 1809.

104. *Court and Cabinets of George III*, Grenville to Buckingham, March 16, 1809, IV, 333; *Dropmore*, Buckingham to Grenville, March 14, 1809, IX, 280–81.

105. *Parl. Debates*, XIV (April 17, 1809), 53.

and radicals and the Burdettites and Whitbread.[106] However, there was generally no real Grenville-Foxite split. William Grenville had never supported Pitt's moderate parliamentary reform proposals during the 1780s, though his brother-in-law, Lord Carysfort, and one of his closest advisors, Lord Carrington, were then keen reformers.[107] By 1809, as Grenville himself admitted, his views on reform were "a little whimsical." He regarded reform per se as a more desirable object than he had in past times; but, in general agreement with the conservative Whigs, he feared appeasing the radicals with a small dose of it.[108]

On April 21, in the House of Lords, during the debate on the Peninsular war, and perhaps as a sop to those of his followers upset by the break with Whitbread, Grey avowed that both he and Grenville were friendly toward a "temperate, intelligible, and definite reform."[109] However, in the Commons, during the May debate on Curwen's moderate parliamentary reform measure that would have merely disallowed the procuring of seats by corrupt practices, Temple, who as Buckingham's son may have been more conservative than Lord Grenville, supported the bill only because "it took away one of the greatest arguments in favor of Parliamentary Reform." His uncle, Lord Grenville, on the other hand, exhibited a more positive approbation of it than did even such Whigs as Lauderdale.[110] During the same month, in the debate on Madocks' resolution charging two Ministers, Perceval and Castlereagh, with procuring the election of MPs through corrupt and criminal practices, the most prominent Whigs and Grenvillites tended to leave the House before the vote or simply failed to appear at all.[111]

On Brand's motion for the moderate reform of Parliament (defeated 115 to 234) in May, 1810, which, among other things, would have abolished—with compensation—rotten and pocket boroughs, reestablished triennial Parliaments, and slightly extended the franchise, a qualified break does occur between many Grenvillites and the Foxite leadership. Tierney and Ponsonby, at least, supported the measure,

106. Roberts, The Whig Party, pp. 239–50.

107. John Ehrman, The Younger Pitt: The Years of Acclaim (London, 1969), pp. 224–28; John Proby, Second Baron Carysfort, Thoughts on the Constitution with a view to the proposed Reform in the Representation of the People, and Duration of Parliaments (London, 1783).

108. BM, Thomas Grenville Papers, Add. MSS. 41853, Grenville to Thomas Grenville, March 28, 1809.

109. Parl. Debates, XIV (April 21, 1809), 149.

110. Ibid., XIV (May 4, 1809), 378; Duke, Grenville-Hamilton Papers, Box 149, Grenville to Lauderdale, June 20, 1809 (copy).

111. Parl. Debates, XIV (May 11, 1809), 509–18, 527; Later Correspondence of George III, Dundas to Richmond, May 12, 1809, V, 278.

while the Grenvillites failed to attend or (for one of the only times during this period) actually voted with Ministers. Still, illustrative of some lack of unity within the Grenvillite group, one of Buckingham's MPs and several of Lord Grenville's friends supported the measure.[112]

The opposition weathered the debates surrounding the institution of the Regency in December, 1810, and January, 1811, despite the fact that Lord Grenville and a few of his personal followers felt obliged to remain loyal to the principles they had espoused during the first Regency crisis in 1788 and 1789. Thus the projected Prime Minister in any future predominately Whig Ministry opposed a Whig motion that would have requested the Prince of Wales to take upon himself the exercise and authority of the Crown during the King's illness. But Grenville so heartily condemned the Government's general conduct, speaking of "accumulated criminality," that he softened incipient Whig criticism of his action.[113] Opposing him, from among his following in the Lords, were Carlisle, Essex, Hereford, Lucan, Spencer, Stafford, and even his brother-in-law Carysfort.[114] During the debate on Regency limitations in January, 1811, Grenville approved of the peerage restrictions on the Regent's power—as he had over twenty years before—which Holland thought a "prudish and pedantic notion of nominal rather than real consistency."[115] The Marquis of Buckingham, however, wrote to the Prince of Wales, apologizing that because of illness he could not come to London to uphold him and acknowledging his disagreement with his brother.[116]

In January, 1811, when for the last time in his life Lord Grenville was seriously involved in the process of forming a Ministry, he displayed the essential weakness and instability of his party, especially in comparison with similar negotiations in 1806. Spencer, Home Secretary in 1806, had insisted for years that he would never accept office again. He retained this sentiment in January, 1811, and refused to join in the negotiations or even to come to London. Thomas Grenville wrote Spencer, his closest friend, that this stand on his part left him feeling "maimed & crippled."[117] Thomas, however, after having served as first

112. *Parl. Debates,* XVII (May 21, 1810), 162–64; NLW, Coedymaen Papers, VIII/505, Wynn to Grenville, May 22, 1810; *Later Correspondence of George III,* Fremantle to Grenville, May 22, 1810, V, 295.

113. *Parl. Debates,* XVII (Dec. 27, 1810), 447–59; BM, Holland House Papers, Add. MSS. 51544, Holland to Grey, Dec. 31, 1810.

114. *Parl. Debates,* XVIII (Dec. 27, 1810), 466.

115. Ibid., XVIII (Jan. 4, 1811), 738–45; Holland, *Further Memoirs of the Whig Party,* pp. 77–78.

116. HEH-STG, ST. 96, Temple's Diary, Jan., 1811.

117. *Dropmore,* Spencer to Grenville: Sept. 28, 1809, IX, 326–27; Jan. 9, 1811, X, 99. Althorp Papers, 86, Thomas Grenville to Spencer, Jan. 11, 1811.

Lord of the Admiralty in 1806 and having been out of Parliament since 1810, was himself now reluctant to accept the Admiralty or, indeed, any office. When he learned that Grey wished the Admiralty for Holland, he found the situation only too congenial for his predilections.[118] Despite strong pressure from his youngest brother, the Marquis of Buckingham categorically refused to again travel to Ireland as Lord Lieutenant on account of his health and out of disgust at the recent conduct of the Roman Catholics.[119] William Elliot, the Irish Chief Secretary in 1806, and Lord Morpeth, formerly at the Board of Control, both refused office.[120] Lord Carlisle, who had held no official position in the 1806 Ministry, was deeply hurt in January, 1811, by Grenville's failure to consult him, though he maintained that he would never have accepted office. This careless attitude toward a powerful supporter over the past decade certainly illustrates Grenville's weakness as a party leader. Carlisle himself admitted that this failure of communication might be considered by some as "a mere form"; yet, he said, "by Forms the World is humanized & govern'd."[121]

Considering the refusal of the vast majority of his important adherents even to consider serving in a new Administration, the Foxite attitude toward Grenville's desire to include Auckland in the Cabinet as Lord President appears petty. Apparently, the Foxites refused this request because of Auckland's reputation as an intriguer, which he earned a quarter of a century earlier when he deserted Fox. Grenville finally prevailed upon his colleagues to accept Auckland as President of the Board of Control, without the Cabinet.[122] A few other followers of Grenville were scheduled to receive non-Cabinet posts: Temple, Secretary at War; Charles Wynn, Judge Advocate; Sir John Newport, (possibly) Chancellor of the Irish Exchequer; William Wickham and William Fremantle, to serve at the Treasury under Grenville.[123] Unlike

118. Althorp Papers, 86, Thomas Grenville to Spencer, Jan. 11, 1811; BM, Thomas Grenville Papers, Add. MSS. 41854, Spencer to Thomas Grenville, Jan. 13, 1811; BM, Holland House Papers, Add. MSS. 52004B, Allen's Journal, Jan. 14 and 17, 1811; Durham Papers, Thomas Grenville to Grey, Jan. 15, 1811.

119. HEH-STG, ST. 96, Temple's Diary, Jan. 7, 1811.

120. Durham Papers, Grenville to Grey, Jan. 28, 1811; Castle Howard Papers, Thomas Grenville to Morpeth, n.d.

121. BM, Thomas Grenville Papers, Add. MSS. 41854, Carlisle to Thomas Grenville, Jan. 24, 1811.

122. BM, Holland House Papers, Add. MSS. 52204B, Allen's Journal, Jan. 14, 1811; NLW, Henry Wynn Papers, 3/2791D, Charles Wynn to Henry Wynn, Feb. 13, 1811.

123. *Dropmore:* Thomas Grenville to Grenville, Jan. 11, 1811, X, 104; Grey to Grenville, Jan. 14, 1811, X, 106; Newport to Grenville, Jan. 16, 1811, X, 107–8. HRO, Wickham Papers, 38M49/1/18, Grenville to Wickham, Jan. 23, 1811; NLW, Henry Wynn Papers, 3/2791D, Charles Wynn to Henry Wynn, Feb. 13, 1811.

the 1806 arrangements, the projected new Cabinet was top-heavy with Foxites. The only Grenvillite definitely scheduled for the Cabinet was the leader himself at the Treasury, with Lord Hardwicke a possibility to serve as Privy Seal.[124]

At a time when Buckingham incorrectly thought both Auckland and Hardwicke were to be included in the new Cabinet, he bemoaned the fact that only three Cabinet offices were given to Grenvillites.[125] Temple felt that his uncle "would lose much consideration in the Country from the whole surrender of himself to the Foxite Party," and he was in favor of "throwing up the game and dissolving the Party."[126] Indeed, dissolving the party was the only alternative to what transpired. It was hardly the fault of the Foxites that Grenville's family and friends, for whatever reason, declined office. The contrast with 1806 was so glaring that it must have been obvious to all concerned, especially in light of Grenville's known disinclination to act the part of a truly effective party leader, that from henceforth the Grenville-Foxite coalition would be a quite different entity from that known to Fox and Grey in 1804 and 1806.

The most serious quarrel to affect Grenville-Foxite relations between the formation of the coalition in 1804 and the Hundred Days in 1815 erupted during the 1811 negotiations. The cause was Lord Grenville's sinecure, the Auditorship of the Exchequer. During the Talents' Ministry, Grenville had been authorized by a special Act of Parliament, introduced by Fox, to have a deputy exercise the duties of his Auditorship while he retained the £4,000 per annum salary.

After the fall of the Talents' Ministry, however, the Whigs made a concerted effort to deny such cozy deals to their opponents. Thus, in 1807, Spencer Perceval was unable to hold simultaneously the Chancellorship of the Exchequer and the salary for the Chancellorship of the Duchy of Lancaster.[127] In 1809, he was unable to hold the sums from the salaries of both the Treasury and the Chancellorship of the Exchequer. Likewise, when Charles Philip Yorke became First Lord of the Admiralty in 1810, he was not allowed to keep the salary of his Tellership of the Exchequer.[128]

In light of this resistance, Grenville and Grey had reached an agreement in 1809 that if the former should be returned to the Treasury, he would give up the Auditorship. But in January, 1811, when Grey came

124. NLW, Henry Wynn Papers, 3/2791D, Charles Wynn to Henry Wynn, Feb. 13, 1811.
125. *Dropmore,* Buckingham to Grenville, Jan. 9, 1811, X, 98.
126. HEH-STG, ST. 96, Temple's Diary, Jan., 1811.
127. *Parl. Debates,* IX (March 25, 1807), 197–200, 219–20.
128. Durham Papers, Whitbread to Grey, Jan. 19, 1811.

to London, Grenville informed him that the 1809 agreement was off, because he could not afford the financial sacrifice. Aghast, Grey bluntly told Grenville that such a stance was unacceptable.[129]

Grenville's position, however, was rather odd. On January 10, he was prepared to relinquish the Treasury to Grey, to take the Home Office, and to give up the emoluments of his sinecure as he had from 1794 to 1801 while Foreign Secretary. Yet he refused to give up the emoluments should he go to the Treasury, because he had not been required to do so in 1806.[130] For the moment, both sides were implacable, despite an attempt by Thomas Grenville to perform his old role as mediator. Even if Grenville was prepared to give up his emoluments while at the Treasury, Grey, who had no relish for the first place himself, was fully prepared to refuse that compromise on the grounds that the question was one of principle and not of economy. On January 17, Grenville proposed first Ponsonby, a ludicrous choice, and then Lansdowne for the Treasury, but there was a hitch in both of these proposals. Grenville himself intended to be the Prime Minister, though at the Home Office, and thus to be in control of the traditional prerogatives of the premier position, with continuing access to the sovereign and control over "the general Patronage of Church & State."[131] Indeed, Grenville sent Grey a fifteen-page manifesto to this effect. Then, possibly on the advice of Stafford and Carrington, he thought better of such an epistle; and on January 17, he twice sent Auckland to retrieve the damaging document. Grey refused to return it unless one of the Grenville brothers distinctly asked for it—which Thomas did.[132]

In his response to this extraordinary manifesto, Grey fairly acknowledged Grenville as the leader of the party, though he intimated that "Lord Grey's personal strength & influence is at least equal to his." He insisted that he had always desired Grenville to have the Treasury; but he promised Grenville that, if that proved impossible, he should have a share of power equal to himself in whatever position they found themselves. Grey, who was equally willing to see a Grenvillite like Lord Spencer at the Treasury, offered to give Grenville the Foreign Office,

129. BM, Holland House Papers, Add. MSS. 52204B, Allen's Journal, Jan. 13, 1811.

130. *Dropmore*, Grenville to Thomas Grenville, Jan. 10, 1811, X, 101.

131. Grey, *Account of Grey*, Grey to ?, Jan. 18, 1811, pp. 271–72; BM, Holland House Papers, Add. MSS. 52204B, Allen's Journal, Jan. 13 and 14, 1811; Durham Papers: Thomas Grenville to Grey, Jan. 15, 1811; Grenville to Grey, Jan. 17, 1811.

132. BM, Holland House Papers, Add. MSS. 52204B, Allen's Journal, Jan. 16 and 17, 1811; Durham Papers, Grenville to Grey, Jan. 17, 1811.

and proposed for himself only the Lord Presidency of the Council. But, obviously deeply hurt, he chided his colleague for insisting on a much more than equal share of the patronage of Government, and he wondered whether Grenville would have dared propose such an arrangement to Fox. Grey also doubted that Spencer, should he go to the Treasury, would ever allow the general patronage of his office to reside, for whatever reason, in another department.[133] Holland thought Grenville's "evil genius" got the better of him at this time and that his conduct more became a merchant than a statesman.[134]

Cordiality was restored between the opposition leaders by January 18, and Grenville came up with a new proposal. He agreed to accept the Treasury, to abandon all Government offices to the Foxites except the Secretaryship at War for Temple and the Board of Control for Auckland, and then to revert in essence to the 1806 precedent for his Auditorship, placing it in trust in Stafford's hands although keeping the salary. He also insisted on Whitbread's acquiescence in such an arrangement and a firm commitment on his part to defend him in the Commons if necessary. Both Grey and Holland urged Whitbread to accept. Whitbread, however, stood his ground. He had no objection to Grenville's putting the Auditorship in trust, but he would not allow him to draw his salary as Auditor while at the Treasury.[135]

Grenville thought the matter over for several days; then, on January 22, he acquiesced in the Whig demands and announced that he would give up the Auditorship salary, unlike his conduct in 1806.[136] Such a concession was, of course, unnecessary. On January 21, Grey and Grenville had advised the Prince of Wales that, while they were prepared to undertake the Government, he should not change his Ministers if it was believed the King might soon recover. On January 25, the Prince sent Lord Hutchinson and William Adam to Camelford House to tell the opposition peers that he had resolved, upon consultation with the King's physicians, not to remove Perceval and his colleagues.[137]

133. Durham Papers, Grey to Grenville, Jan., 1811 (draft).
134. Holland, *Further Memoirs of the Whig Party*, p. 87.
135. BM, Holland House Papers, Add. MSS. 52204B, Allen's Journal, Jan. 18 and 19, 1811; Gore, ed., *Creevey Papers*, Creevey to his wife, Jan. 19, 1811, p. 74.
136. Durham Papers, Grenville to Grey, Jan. 22, 1811.
137. *Dropmore*, Grey and Grenville to the Prince of Wales, Jan. 21, 1811, X, 108–9; Holland, *Further Memoirs of the Whig Party*, pp. 90–91.

[CHAPTER VII]

The Grenville-Foxite Coalition: Part Four

1. The Grenvillite Party, 1811–16

After the Prince made his decision in January, 1811, to retain his father's Ministers pending the King's possible recovery, the opposition endured a seventeen-month bout of political uncertainty cushioned by the increasing likelihood that, though the reign of George III was effectively over, Spencer Perceval would remain Prime Minister. Superficially, however, the first six months of 1812 seemed to promise as great a departure in domestic politics as the last six months of the same year were to produce in international affairs. Yet, in reality, the Regent's assumption of full royal power in February and the assassination of the Prime Minister in May, made little difference to the governmental structure. The various postassassination negotiations in 1812, involving Wellesley and Moira as the Regent's agents, hardly divided the opposition. In the doubtful event that Wellesley and Canning should form a ministry based on Catholic emancipation, the termination of the Spanish war, and the resumption of cash payments by the Bank of England, Grenville admitted a fluttering of interest; yet, if Grey should refuse to join such a government, Grenville too was prepared to decline his assistance.[1] Both opposition chiefs, using the old war cry of "measures not men," were totally unsympathetic to Wellesley's offer of four or five Cabinet seats.[2] When they likewise refused to concede the Household officials to the Regent, thus ensuring the failure of Moira's attempt to form a ministry in June, 1812, it was disapproved by the Foxite Whitbread and the Grenvillite Hardwicke, but the other opposition leaders generally concurred.[3]

1. *Dropmore,* Lord Grenville to Thomas Grenville, May 12, 1812, X, 246.
2. *Memoirs of the Regency,* Grenville and Grey to Wellesley: May 24, 1812, I, 315; June 3, 1812, I, 341–42. BM, Wellesley Papers, Add. MSS. 37297, Wellesley to Grey, June 1, 1812.
3. BM, Holland House Papers, Add. MSS.: 52204C, Allen's Journal, June 6,

Although the Regent was probably satisfied that the outcome of the protracted negotiations retained the essence of his former Ministry now under the lead of the Earl of Liverpool (formerly Lord Hawkesbury), if the opposition leaders had so desired, they could certainly have entered office on fairly generous terms. But stripping a month of complicated talks to their most basic consideration, neither Grey nor Grenville would ultimately approve a coalition in which Moira, Canning, and Wellesley would inevitably occupy the highest stations as regards both access to the Regent and efficient offices. Both men felt little attraction for office, and there certainly is no reason to doubt the sincerity of Grenville's remark to Wickham, after the failure of the whole business, that he returned "with infinite joy to . . . Rhododendrons."[4] It seems doubtful that after June, 1812, Grenville again seriously contemplated entering office. By November, after the general election, he was beseeching Grey without success to allow him to resign the leadership of the opposition and telling Buckingham that he was "sick of the whole concern." As to the leadership of the party, he wrote: "The thing must find its own level; for I cannot do what I used, and am disposed to do even less than I could. Nothing restrains me but the resolution, that, as far as in me lays, there shall be no breakup of a party such as the country requires, to control such a court."[5]

Grenville's lack of interest in entering office except upon the most advantageous terms drained whatever vitality may have remained in the Grenvillite section of the opposition.[6] As far as any Grenvillite cohesion was concerned, the course of the 1812 Parliament merely accelerated the trend set by its 1807 predecessor. Although the leading political figures in the nation might continue to write in terms of a Grenvillite party, its inner core was soft and its outer layer fast decomposing. For example, when the first Marquis of Buckingham died in February, 1813, elevating Temple to the Lords, the retired Thomas Grenville was persuaded with some difficulty to come forward as Temple's successor for Bucks. Yet he declined any regular parliamentary attendance, would

---

1812; 51544, Holland to Grey, June 7, 1812. BM, Hardwicke Papers, Add. MSS. 35650, Hardwicke to Moira, June 7, 1812; Durham Papers, Grey to Holland, June 7, 1812.

4. HRO, Wickham Papers, 38M49/1/18, Grenville to Wickham, June, 1812.

5. Durham Papers, Grenville to Grey, Nov. 10, 1812; *Memoirs of the Regency,* Grenville to Buckingham, Nov. 25, 1812, I, 415.

6. See, for example, the congratulatory statement of Grey in Northumberland to Grenville in Cornwall during the general election of 1812. They were "completely disengaged from the bustle of the new elections" and "whatever the result may be, therefore, it cannot be ascribed to any management of ours." *Dropmore,* Nov. 1, 1812, X, 298–99.

only go to the House on extremely important questions, and even sat in the gallery until the division.[7]

Insofar as anyone led the Grenvillites in the Commons between 1812 and 1825, it was Lord Grenville's nephew, Charles Watkin Williams Wynn (1775-1850), MP for Montgomeryshire. Charles, the very opposite of his gadabout brother Sir Watkin, was a sober, diligent, scholarly, and somewhat vulnerable individual—in personality and interests (if not always in ability) the son his two Grenville uncles never had. He was a leading parliamentary expert on the precedents and privileges of the House of Commons and one observer saw him as a "personification of *Hatsell's*.[8] Wynn's lifelong desire, actively pursued from 1812 to 1835, was to become Speaker of the House of Commons.

Wynn, unfortunately, had one major and ultimately insurmountable obstacle to the attainment of that post—his highpitched voice. Popularly known as "squeaker Wynn" and for forty years the object of innumerable jokes, he was among the long-suffering group picked out by that exquisite wit, George Canning, for special ridicule. One MP in 1817 wondered how he could vote for Wynn as Speaker when any culprit kneeling at the bar of the House "must laugh."[9] Wynn's speech problem was a misfortune for the Grenvillites; for, as Lord Grenville retired more and more from an active political role, the two leading members of his group, his nephews Buckingham and Wynn, each became associated with a personal characteristic—the former with his bulk and the latter with his voice—that marked them for a political hilarity hitherto reserved for Henry and Hiley Addington.

As one of the last political acts of his life, the first Marquis of Buckingham chose an advanced Whig, Francis Horner (1778-1817), as an MP for St. Mawes. Horner, the son of an Edinburgh merchant, had long since received the foundation for the advanced opinions on economics and law that drew him into the circles of Bentham and (though they disagreed on certain issues) Malthus.[10] The fact that this cofounder of the *Edinburgh Review* came to sit for a Grenville-controlled borough certainly both tempers any evaluation of the family as extreme conservatives and calls into question the extent to which Buckingham always expected his MPs to reflect his own political disposition.

7. Ibid., Thomas Grenville to Lord Grenville, Feb. 14, 1813, X, 330.

8. Thomas Barnes, *Parliamentary Portraits or Sketches of Some of the Most Distinguished Speakers of the House of Commons* (London, 1815), p. 47.

9. BM, Mackintosh Papers, Add. MSS. 52442, Mackintosh's Journal, May 15, 1817.

10. *Memoirs and Correspondence of Francis Horner, M.P.*, ed. Leonard Horner (2d ed.; Boston, 1853): Horner to Murray, Oct. 27, 1808, I, 464; Horner to Malthus, Sept. 15, 1810, II, 35.

For some years prior to making Horner's acquaintance, Lord Grenville had been moving toward an avant-garde position on various economic questions. From his youth he had been a disciple of Adam Smith,[11] and after his resignation as Foreign Secretary in 1801, he began a thirty-year odyssey that ultimately led him to emerge as one of the foremost parliamentary opponents of the Orders-in-Council, the Bank of England, the East India Company, the Corn Laws, the Navigation Acts, and the Sinking Fund. Most of the leaders of the Foxite wing of the opposition did not exhibit very much interest in such matters or, if they did, were often found on what Richard Cobden would have seen as the nonprogressive side. Lauderdale was an out-and-out protectionist, Tierney an effective advocate (in 1813) of the East India Company's monopoly, and Grey favorable to the Corn Laws. Only a few weeks before his death, Fox spoke of his lack of faith in Adam Smith,[12] and Holland admitted that he hardly understood the Navigation Acts or the Corn Laws.[13] Grenville, on the other hand, once described himself as "an ardent & youthful lover" of political economy.[14] This fact goes far to explain the increasingly close personal and political proximity of Grenville to such young reformers as Lord King and Francis Horner.

Even before the commencement of the Grenville-Foxite coalition, Lord Grenville was associating himself publicly with those who, like Lord King, the husband of his niece Hester Fortescue, were crusading for an examination of the necessity for a continuation of the Bank restriction on cash payments. And young Horner, fresh from Scotland, marveled in 1804 at the degree to which the Foxite King influenced Grenville's economic opinions.[15] The chief reason for the change in Grenville's attitude toward the war, strongly marked after 1807, centered, of course, around what he perceived as Britain's precarious economic position and the necessity for a defensive war with no costly expeditions.[16] There is little indication that Horner and Grenville were in any way closely connected until 1810. Before 1806, Horner shared

11. *Court and Cabinets of George III*, Grenville to Buckingham, March 6, 1788, I, 359.

12. *The Diary and Correspondence of Charles Abbot, Lord Colchester, Speaker of the House of Commons, 1802–1817*, ed. Charles Abbot, Second Baron Colchester (London, 1861), II, 70–71.

13. BM, Holland House Papers, Add. MSS. 51547, Holland to Grey, Sept. 2, 1825, and March 9, 1827.

14. Ibid., 51531, Grenville to Holland, n.d.

15. LSE, Horner Papers, Vol. II, Horner to Leonard Horner, April, 1804.

16. BM, Auckland Papers, Add. MSS. 34457, Grenville to Auckland, July 28, 1807; *Court and Cabinets of George III*, Thomas Grenville to Buckingham, Oct. 9, 1807, IV, 206.

the natural prejudices of his social and ideological acquaintances against the Grenvilles, feeling they mixed "but ill with Fox's principles."[17] Only during the Ministry of 1806–7, when he observed the Grenville-Foxite coalition from the perspective of a minor parliamentary commissionership, did he come to admire it.[18]

The first intimate contact between Grenville and Horner occurred, apparently, in 1810, when Horner was appointed chairman of a committee in the Commons to investigate the state of the currency. His conduct of the committee, despite the ultimate failure of its recommendation to return to cash payments within two years, earned him nearly universal praise and marked him out as one of the up and coming young men in the House.[19] Therefore, in January, 1811, Grenville asked Horner to become one of the Secretaries of the Treasury in the event of a Grenville-Grey Ministry.[20] As an example of the ever-growing ties between the two men, Horner went out of his way in the Commons to defend the Marquis of Buckingham's sinecure when it was under attack by Whitbread and Creevey in May, 1812.[21] When Lord Carrington was unable to return Horner to the Commons for Wendover in 1812, Grenville, who was not taking an active part in the general election, took steps to secure his friend a seat. St. Mawes was finally pounced upon, though not before a nervous Lord Temple made inquiries to Horner's friends as to his sentiments on parliamentary reform.[22]

Horner died in Italy in early 1817 of a disease—probably tuberculosis—that had long prevented him from taking that part in the Commons which his talents and reputation suggested. Had he lived, he would probably have emerged as the greatly needed opposition leader in the Commons. Grey frankly expressed that wish;[23] Holland implied consent;[24] Tierney thought he bade "fair, at any rate more fairly than any of his contemporaries, to acquire great distinction."[25] Thus Horner

17. LSE, Horner Papers, Vol. II, Horner to his father, May 14, 1804.

18. *Memoirs of Horner,* Horner to Jeffrey, Sept. 15, 1806, I, 397–99.

19. Ibid., II: Horner to Grenville, Feb. 11, 1810, 5–6; Grenville to Horner, Feb. 12, 1810, 6–7.

20. Ibid., Grenville to Horner, Jan. 22, 1811, 54–55.

21. *Parl. Debates,* XXII (May 7, 1812), 84–85.

22. *Memoirs of Horner,* Horner to Smith, Oct. 11, 1812, II, 115–16; BM, Holland House Papers, Add. MSS.: 51530, Grenville to Holland, Oct. 14, 1812; 51597, miscellaneous political material, marked "1813."

23. BM, Holland House Papers, Add. MSS. 51553, Grey to Lady Holland, Oct. 22, 1815 (copy).

24. Henry Richard Vassall Fox, Third Baron Holland, *Further Memoirs of the Whig Party, 1807–1821,* ed. Giles Stephen Holland Fox-Strangeways, Baron Stavordale (London, 1905), pp. 45–46.

25. BM, Holland House Papers, Add. MSS. 51584, Tierney to Holland, n.d.

might have served as the needed link between the Grenvillites and Foxites and so might have prevented the 1817 schism.

The extent to which Grenville was moving to the left on financial and economic issues is repeatedly illustrated by his conduct during and after 1811. He was very much involved in the decision-making process that led to Lord King's determination to refuse to accept paper currency from his Irish tenants; and Grenville directly advised King, against the opinions even of Horner, to take legal action against one of his tenants, a Bank director. Holland, too, had his doubts about the wisdom of King's actions, but Grenville defended King's policy and character in the Lords and deeply regretted in public the considerations that had led him after 1797 to support the periodic extensions of the Bank Restriction Bill.[26]

While Grenville's negative attitude toward embarking on any effective ministerial negotiations in 1812 no doubt partially reflected desires for rhododendrons and retirement, the terms he laid down to Grey as the only price upon which he would accept office also reflected his growing economic radicalism. In line with these terms, he would have: compelled the Bank to resume cash payments within six months; completely revamped the financial system so as to diminish "almost to nothing the advances of the Bank to Government"; immediately repealed the Orders-in-Council; effected a thorough economical reform for the army, navy, and ordnance; and broken up the monopoly of the East India Company. These reforms, coupled, of course, with Catholic emancipation and a thoroughly defensive war, were certainly a definite governmental program unlike anything Grenville had developed before 1806, and in that sense mirrored a form of opposition leading to an alternative government not generally seen in the Hanoverian period. However, in relating these programs to a perhaps startled Grey, Grenville added, in what must rank as one of his more pixilating understatements, "I do not believe that either the P[rince] R[egent] or the Public are yet prepared to let us serve them in the only way in which they can be served."[27]

Grenville, of course, in 1813, approved of ending the East India Company's monopoly in the subcontinent. He certainly deprecated the efforts of those within the opposition, who, like Tierney, wished to support the monopolistic claims of the Company either from conviction

---

26. Ibid., 51534, Thomas Grenville to Lady Holland, July 2, 1811; LSE, Horner Papers, Vol. V: Horner to King, n.d.; Horner to Lord ?, Nov. 19, 1811. *Parl. Debates,* XX (July 2, 1811), 821–24.

27. Durham Papers, Grenville to Grey, Jan. 28 and May 17, 1812.

or as a means of opposing a Government bill.[28] Still, the final Charter Bill did far too little in Grenville's opinion to break up the hated monopoly. In a speech in the Lords, later printed, Grenville criticized the Company's continued China monopoly and, anticipating Derby and Disraeli, advocated a public declaration of the sovereignty of Crown and Parliament over Indian affairs and hence the complete separation of the Indian Government from the Company.[29]

Over the Corn Law question in March, 1815, Grenville led an ineffectual opposition to the agricultural interest, which group included many of his closest friends and connections, as well as—at least in the Lords—most of the opposition. Grenville told the legislators outright that they had no right to relieve one class of the community at the expense of another. However, Lord Hardwicke, a Grenvillite, spoke in favor of protection; and Lord Grey, who favored the Corn Bill, voted with Grenville only on procedural grounds.[30] Ultimately only six of Grenville's relatives or friends—Buckingham, Bulkeley, Carlisle, Essex, Fortescue, and Spencer—followed him on the meager minority Corn divisions.[31] In the Commons, six members associated with Grenville by blood or friendship spoke in favor of the Corn Bill: William Elliot, Pascoe Grenfell, Frankland Lewis (Bulkeley's MP for Beaumaris), Sir John Newport, Lord Proby, and Sir Watkin Wynn. And only six Grenvillite members voted to delay the third reading of the Corn Bill for six months: William Fremantle, Francis Horner, Scrope Bernard Morland, Lord Nugent, Sir Robert Williams, and Charles Wynn.[32]

The turn in the fortunes of war during 1813 led to another political juxtaposition on the part of the opposition leaders. Just as many prominent Whigs, such as Holland, had supported the Peninsular war out of sympathy for a people struggling for national independence, so too did these same men begin to regard an increasingly beleaguered France as likewise fighting for her freedom, as in 1793 and 1794,

28. *Memoirs of the Regency*, Grenville to Temple, Jan. 10, 1813, II, 15–16; Holland, *Further Memoirs of the Whig Party*, pp. 173–74.

29. William Wyndham Grenville, Baron Grenville, "Substance of the Speech of Lord Grenville on the Motion made by the Marquis Wellesley in the House of Lords on the 9th of April, 1813, for the Production of Certain Papers on Indian Affairs," *Pamphlets on India Question* (London, 1813), pp. 4–41.

30. *Parl. Debates*, XXX: (March 13, 1815), 126, 139; (March 15, 1815), 187–202. Holland, *Further Memoirs of the Whig Party*, p. 215.

31. *Parl. Debates*, XXX: (March 13, 1815), 149; (March 15, 1815), 305; (March 20, 1815), 262–63.

32. Ibid.: XXIX (Feb. 23, 1815), 1010–30; XXIX (March 1, 1815), 1123; XXIX (March 3, 1815), 1228; XXX (March 6, 1815), 23, 59; XXX (March 10, 1815), 124.

against the forces of reaction. Grenville, who had unalterably opposed the Peninsular war as a wasteful expenditure of British money and lives, came in 1813 to favor an all-out effort to crush Bonaparte's power once and for all. Holland, in October, 1813, even before Leipzig, saw no reason to continue the conflict, and an animated series of letters passed between him and Grenville reflecting their profound disagreement. Grey tended to concur more with Holland than with Grenville, who at this time lamented one of the first disagreements of substance during their long association.[33]

For the first time since 1805, problems began to develop between the Grenvillites and Foxites over the origin of the 1793 war. Grey received reports at Howick that Grenville, in responding to the address on the first day of the session, November 4, 1813, had alluded in an unfavorable manner to the conduct of the Foxites in 1793. Grenville heatedly denied the charge; but he took the occasion to remind his colleague that a profound cleavage did exist between them on that question and added, "My original opinions in favor of the necessity & wisdom of the measures of 1792 & 3 have been confirmed by every succeeding event."[34]

Holland then felt it incumbent to speak in the Lords to avow his joy over the on going liberation of Europe, and he compared his current feelings of elation with those experienced in 1792 at the retreat of the Duke of Brunswick! He also expressed strong disapproval of the policy of previous Ministers who "went about knocking at every door in Europe, to ask who would accept money to fight against France," referring specifically he said, to 1805, though few could have missed an allusion to the Pittite-Grenvillite system of the 1790s.[35] The speedy conclusion of the war in April, 1814, thus may have prevented any deeper fissure from opening in the opposition coalition.

The treaty with France and the initial stages of the Congress of Vienna caused little friction between Grenvillites and Foxites, as Grenville's parliamentary condemnation of a continued large military expenditure was popular and the 1814 restoration of the Bourbons was not nearly as burning an issue to many Whigs as the 1815 one would be.[36] The news of Napoleon's return from Elba, however, filled both

33. BM, Holland House Papers, Add. MSS.: 51826, Grenville to Holland, Oct. 16, 1813; 51545, Holland to Grey, Oct. 19 and 30, 1813. Durham Papers, Grenville to Grey, Oct. 21 and Nov. 1, 1813.

34. Durham Papers, Grenville to Grey, Nov. 24, 1813.

35. *Parl. Debates,* XXVII (Dec. 20, 1813), 290–92; BM, Holland House Papers, Add. MSS. 51545, Holland to Grey, Dec. 18, 1813.

36. *Parl. Debates:* XXVIII (June 28, 1814), 364–69; XXIX (Nov. 8, 1814), 14–21.

Grenville and Buckingham with dismay and caused problems both between Grenvillites and Foxites and within the Grenville group itself. Lord Grenville felt that the French Emperor, despite protestations of peaceful intentions, could not be trusted and only wanted time to rebuild his military forces;[37] he told Newport that peace was "impossible either for this country or for the rest of Europe as long as Bonaparte continues on the Throne of France."[38]

Important Whig leaders, even Lansdowne, who often agreed with Grenville on foreign policy, refused to support renewal of a war to restore the Bourbon family.[39] Grenville, in a search for allies outside of his own immediate group, found only the conservative Whig, Lord Fitzwilliam, prepared to countenance his anti-Bonaparte leanings. Even the usually loyal Grenvillian, Lord Spencer, had grave doubts as to the propriety of a renewed war.[40] But the most immediate internal problem among the Grenvillites involved Buckingham's borough occupant, Francis Horner, Grenville's ablest lieutenant during the recent Corn debate.

Horner was in total sympathy with the pacific views of Holland and Grey. On April 7, he voted in the minority of thirty-seven in favor of Whitbread's peace amendment.[41] A sensitive and discriminating individual, he realized immediately the discomfort to which such views would subject his parliamentary patron, the Marquis of Buckingham. In such a touchy situation, the amity of all involved served both as a tribute to Horner's undoubted worth and as a model of a conciliatory political relationship between patron and member. Horner met with Grenville to discuss their mutual difficulties; then, in a letter to Buckingham, he offered to resign his seat at St. Mawes. The Marquis replied that he hoped no separation would occur over a single issue, and he urged him to keep his seat. He fairly warned Horner, however, that if radical and prolonged discord eventually resulted, this perception might well change.[42] The matter was, of course, settled by the relative swiftness of Wellington's victory over Bonaparte at Waterloo.

37. HEH-STG, Box 176, Grenville to Buckingham, April 1, 1815.
38. Duke, Newport Papers, Grenville to Newport, March 28, 1815.
39. Durham Papers, Lansdowne to Grey, April, 1815.
40. Sheffield Papers: F32f72, Grenville to Fitzwilliam, March 30, 1815; F32f73, Cavendish to Fitzwilliam, March 31, 1815; F32f74, Elliot to Fitzwilliam, April 1, 1815.
41. Durham Papers, Horner to Grey, April 2, 1815; *Parl. Debates,* XXX (April 7, 1815), 463.
42. *Memoirs of Horner,* Horner to his father, April 18, 1815, II, 251–53; HEH-STG, Box 158, Horner to Buckingham, April 28, 1815; *Memoirs of the Regency,* Buckingham to Horner, April 29, 1815, II, 116–17.

A number of Grenvillites or former Grenvillites, including Grafton (formerly Euston), Carnarvon, Essex, and Spencer, voted against Grenville on the war division in the House of Lords; while Buckingham, Bulkeley, Carrington, Fortescue, Stafford, and Somers supported Grenville and the Government.[43] In the Commons, likewise, the Grenvillites were split. The anti-war force included Francis Horner, Lord Morpeth, Sir John Newport, and (the only Grenville family member to desert, Lord Braybrooke's son) Richard Neville; whereas William Elliot, William Fremantle, Thomas Knox, Frankland Lewis, W. C. Plunket, Sir Robert Williams, and both Wynn brothers remained loyal to Grenville and Buckingham.[44]

These divisions in May, 1815, showed the weakness of the Grenvillites as a major element of the opposition. The question at hand was a momentous one, and the fact that so many important Grenvillites defected, especially in the Lords, signified for all to see not only a split between Grenvillites and Foxites but also the schism within the Grenvillite party itself.

The defection of Spencer—and he remained convinced of the righteousness of his stand even after Waterloo—was particularly remarked upon at the time,[45] though the question of the permanence of his independence was not entirely settled until 1817. It would certainly be difficult to regard the Carlisle connection as any longer united with the Grenvilles after this date. The Earl was ill at Castle Howard during most of the period, and Morpeth was definitely acting with the Foxites. The Staffords voted on the same side as Lord Grenville during the 1815 crisis, though as open supporters of Ministers and not as Grenvillites. Five months earlier, Stafford's odd conduct had led Grenville to assume that trouble was in the offing, though he wrote his brother that "after a connection of so many years it would have been more seemly not to part company without a few words of explanation & civility." Thomas Grenville scoffed at his brother's fears, but he was in error.[46]

Other Grenvillite peers had either died (as had the first Marquis of

43. *Parl. Debates,* XXXI (May 23, 1815), 371; NLW, Henry Wynn Papers, 18/2806D, Carrington to Mrs. Wynn, May 24, 1815; BM, Hardwicke Papers, Add. MSS. 35652, Somers to Hardwicke, March 25, 1816.

44. *Parl. Debates,* XXXI (May 25, 1815), 447–48; John Gore, ed., *The Creevey Papers* (rev. ed.; New York, 1963), Bennet to Creevey, May 31, 1815, pp. 117–18; *Courier* (London), May 27, 1815.

45. BM, Holland House Papers, Add. MSS. 51742, Spencer to Holland, Aug. 13, 1815; BM, Liverpool Papers, Add. MSS. 38193, Canning to Liverpool, June 29, 1815; Durham Papers, Tierney to Grey, Nov. 1, 1815.

46. BM, Thomas Grenville Papers, Add. MSS. 41853, Lord Grenville to Thomas Grenville, Dec. 30, 1814, and Jan. 3, 1815.

Buckingham, Auckland, Bute, Carnarvon, and Minto) or were so infirm or aged (as were Carysfort and Glastonbury) as to have lost nearly all political worth. The two surviving Grenvillite Bishops, Lincoln and St. Asaph, seem to have had no connection with Lord Grenville after 1811. Indeed, Tierney felt that one reason why no permanent Grenvillite split from the Foxites occurred in 1815 was the group was so weak—"reduced to almost their own Family Strength"—that he remarked, "I do not see what other game they can play with any advantage."[47] The political events of the following two years were to show that even the bond of "Family Strength" was weakened.

The anti-Grenvillite, left-wing "Mountain" section of the opposition had hopes that the schism of 1815 would be lasting.[48] This, however, was not the wish of either Grey or Grenville. Grey, indeed, was less aggressively anti-war than he might have been, solely from a desire to conciliate the Grenvilles and thus, ultimately, to reunite the opposition.[49] On his side, Grenville did not favor separation from Grey; and he told Wickham that, despite their differences, he would far sooner see a renewed war in Grey's hands than in Castlereagh's.[50]

Yet, during the prorogation of Parliament after Waterloo, Grenville was angry at the tolerance of the opposition, especially of the opposition press, toward prominent French Bonapartists, and during these months he ceased his subscription to the *Morning Chronicle*.[51] He was also extraordinarily touchy on the subject of his now-beloved Bourbons and the origins of the war against the French revolutionaries.[52] But on most substantive measures contained in the revised peace treaty his sentiments were close enough to those of the general Whig leadership to preclude a severance. Grenville totally opposed the Government's policy of keeping French-paid British troops on French territory both on the grounds of their exposure to "debauchery & vice" and because of the unconstitutional aspect of removing Parliament's check on the Army's purse.[53]

Tierney especially desired to introduce a strong amendment to the address at the opening of the parliamentary session in February, 1816.

47. Durham Papers, Tierney to Grey, Nov. 1, 1815.
48. Gore, ed., *Creevey Papers*, Bennet to Creevey, May 31, 1815, pp. 117–18.
49. Durham Papers, Grey to Holland, June 26, 1815.
50. HRO, Wickham Papers, 38M49/1/18, Grenville to Wickham, April 19, 1815.
51. HEH-STG, Box 176, Grenville to Buckingham, Oct. 19, 1815; BM, Thomas Grenville Papers, Add. MSS. 41853, Lord Grenville to Thomas Grenville, Dec. 19, 1815; NLW, Coedymaen Papers, V/303, Grenville to Wynn, Jan. 24, 1816.
52. BM, Holland House Papers, Add. MSS. 51585, Tierney to Lady Holland, Jan. 7, 1816; Durham Papers, Grey to Holland, Jan. 14, 1816.
53. HEH-STG, Box 176, Grenville to Buckingham, Oct. 19, 1815.

He met Thomas Grenville in London and at Althorp during December and early January to discuss the matter and found an "eager desire to oppose Ministers" as long as there was no condemnation of either the 1815 war or the restoration of the Bourbons.[54] Grey did not come to London during 1816, and Lord Grenville was irritated when, in the absence also of George Ponsonby, titular leader of the opposition in the Commons, Tierney and Abercromby called a meeting at Brooks's on the Wednesday before the commencement of the session to draw up the amendment. The three major points decided upon—a condemnation of the long prorogation, a pledge of retrenchment, and a reference to the general distress—were innocuous enough. Yet Lord Grenville refused to concur in it and, indeed, threatened to vote against it for fear that during the debate "more than half of the principles & opinions urged in its support would probably be much more repugnant to mine than anything said by its adversaries."[55] At this point, Tierney thought the end of the Grenville-Foxite alliance was at hand.[56] But Grenville was partially appeased when no amendment was moved in the Lords.

2. *The Grenville-Foxite Schism of 1817*

The remainder of the 1816 session produced no major tension between the Grenvillites and the rest of the opposition; but in 1817, the by then recurrent dispute over an amendment to the address once again fanned separatist flames. Also, during 1816 and early 1817, a relatively new source of contention aggravated the relationship between the two groups—the national distress which was leading to the revival of parliamentary reform agitation and extraparliamentary activity on the part of the Spenceans and the Hampden Clubs. These factors, especially the Spa Fields riots in December, 1816, and the attack upon the Regent following his return from opening Parliament on January 28, 1817, necessarily led to a renewal of the debate on the proper scope for the civil liberties of Englishmen. The Grenvilles had usually favored a repressive interpretation on the limits of those liberties, while the Foxites had traditionally taken a more libertarian approach.

54. Durham Papers, Tierney to Grey, Oct. 21, 1815; BM, Holland House Papers, Add. MSS.: 51584, Tierney to Holland, Dec. 8, 1815; 51585, Tierney to Lady Holland, Jan. 7, 1816.

55. Austin Mitchell, *The Whigs in Opposition, 1815–1830* (Oxford, 1967), p. 89; NLW, Coedymaen Papers, V/303, Grenville to Wynn, Jan. 24, 1816; BM, Holland House Papers, Add. MSS. 51531, Grenville to Holland, Jan. 28, 1816.

56. Durham Papers, Tierney to Grey, Jan. 14, 1816.

Grey held to the principle he had adopted in 1810, when, with Grenville's consent, he had approved a moderate parliamentary reform; though he did not regard that question as a sine qua non of Whig political activity on a par with retrenchment, Catholic emancipation, or a change in foreign policy. He candidly told Fitzwilliam, who was more conservative on parliamentary reform than were the Grenvilles, that he preferred the current system to anything smacking of annual parliaments or universal suffrage.[57] Though Holland had pledged loyalty to Grey, he was even less enthusiastic about any effective parliamentary reform, admitting that the closer he looked at it, "the less I own I like it & even when I saw it at a distance I was none of its most fervent admirer."[58] Holland was, as usual, more concerned with tyranny in other countries than with distress in his own; he felt that continuation of British support for the Bourbons and British troops in France should form a mainstay for opposition attack in the upcoming session.[59]

The Grenvillites, on the other hand, with, of course, no desire to seize as their own either the issues of parliamentary reform or anti-Bourbonism, much preferred to concentrate upon retrenchment.[60] But Holland, much less conciliatory than the year before, told Grey that while retrenchment and economy were certainly desirable goals in themselves, "they are really too indefinite not to say too contemptible objects to bind together a large body of Men without any stronger tie."[61] When Holland wrote Grenville to ascertain his views, the reply was disconcerting. Grenville remarked that he was tired of Parliament, had no desire to influence the conduct of others, and doubted that he could agree to any amendment.[62] He was so bitter against the Mountain at this time that he told his brother the very idea of dividing on the same side of the aisle with them was more distasteful to him than supporting Ministers.[63]

Grey did not quite concur with Holland on the importance of the French issue in deciding future strategy. He saw the question of continued British support for the Legitimists as a dishonorable one on

57. Ibid., Grey to Holland, Nov. 23 and Dec. 8, 1816; NRO, Fitzwilliam Papers, 85, Grey to Fitzwilliam, Dec. 13, 1816.
58. Durham Papers, Holland to Grey, Dec. 2, 1816.
59. Ibid., Holland to Grey, Dec. 4, 1816.
60. NLW, Wynn-Southey Papers, 4/4814D, Wynn to Southey, Dec. 1, 1816; BM, Holland House Papers, Add. MSS. 51828, Buckingham to Holland, Jan. 2, 1817.
61. Durham Papers, Holland to Grey, Jan. 13, 1817.
62. BM, Holland House Papers, Add. MSS. 51531, Grenville to Holland, Jan. 14, 1817.
63. BM, Thomas Grenville Papers, Add. MSS. 41853, Lord Grenville to Thomas Grenville, Jan. 15, 1817.

which to break the coalition, because it was too closely tied to those
original circumstances of the 1793 war, on which the Grenvillites and
Foxites had previously agreed to disagree.[64] Thus, it was finally decided
on Grey's initiative to move only a watered-down amendment, merely
calling for stark retrenchment and containing no mention of parliamentary reform or the Bourbons.[65]

But the weak amendment and the Grenvillite acquiescence in it
fooled few as to the permanence of the by then battered Grenville-Foxite
alliance. In early February, 1817, a parliamentary committee (whose
members included Lord Grenville and William Elliot) was elected to
examine in secret the evidence of alleged treasonable and seditious
activities on the part of various and sundry revolutionaries.[66] It was by
then common knowledge both that the Government desired to suspend
Habeas Corpus and that the Grenvilles contemplated a departure from
the main body of the opposition. Indeed, when the Grenville brothers
visited Sir James Mackintosh, the conservative Whig historian, on
January 30, he surmised that they intended to canvass him in preparation for the expected party realignment. Some of the Whigs
—Mackintosh, who sat on Lord Cawdor's interest; James MacDonald, who had once sat on Stafford's interest; and James Abercromby,
once MP for a Carrington borough—made ineffectual attempts at
a reconciliation.[67]

Grenville was as concerned as Grey that the separation be conducted
in a dignified manner and appear as the result of overriding and
differing conceptions of public duty.[68] He thought the condition of the
country was more alarming than it had been in 1795, but he refused to
be pushed precipitously into abandoning allies of thirteen years, at least
until the report of the secret committee was made public and the Foxites
openly censured it.[69] On February 18 in the Lords and on February 19
in the Commons, the committee made its report accusing the Hampden
Clubs of desiring a revolution, condemning the Spenceans for the Spa
Fields riots and insurrectionary agitation, and inviting the Government
to introduce legislation suspending Habeas Corpus.[70] There was never

64. Durham Papers, Grey to Holland, Jan. 17, 1817.
65. BM, Mackintosh Papers, Add. MSS. 52442, Mackintosh's Journal, Jan.
23, 1817.
66. *Parl. Debates,* XXXV (Feb. 5, 1817), 215–20.
67. John William Ward, First Earl of Dudley, *Letters of the Earl of Dudley to the
Bishop of Llandaff* (London, 1840), Dudley to Llandaff, Feb. 1, 1817, p. 159; BM,
Mackintosh Papers, Add. MSS. 52442, Mackintosh's Journal, Feb. 4 and 6, 1817.
68. HEH-STG, Box 186, Grenville to Buckingham, Feb. 11, 1817.
69. Ibid., Box 164, Fremantle to Buckingham, Feb. 11, 1817.
70. *Parl. Debates,* XXXV: (Feb. 18, 1817), 411–19; (Feb. 19, 1817), 438–47.

a definite announcement in Parliament or a definite communication between Grenville and Grey as to the schism. The clearest statement Grenville made about his future party particulars occurred on February 23 in a friendly but firm letter to Grey.

> Nothing can be more just & natural than that you should be *seen* where on every account you must *stand,* at the head of those who have the good fortune to agree with you, on this most important question. . . . I am sure you believe that these differences in the view which we have taken of this most difficult & alarming crisis of the Country, are as painful to me as I am confident they are to you. How far they may extend themselves in their effects on the details of our respective Parliamentary conduct I do not know. To me there remains but a very short period of service there, and a call, I trust, for very limited exertions. To more indeed I am utterly unequal. But while we act there at all we must act as we think the Public Interest requires. Whenever I may be so happy as to agree with you, your cooperation cannot fail to be to me, as it has always hitherto been, a matter of the highest pride & satisfaction.[71]

In the Lords, most of the remaining Grenvillite peers followed Grenville's lead on the suspension, though only momentarily; among them: family members Braybrooke, Buckingham, Carysfort, Fortescue, and Glastonbury; and Grenville's friends Bristol, Bulkeley, (probably) Carrington, Hardwicke, Somers, and Spencer (though Essex supported the Whigs).[72] Many more Grenvillites defected in the Commons. Of Buckingham's six members, two—his brother Lord Nugent and his cousin Lord Ebrington—voted against suspension and separated themselves from any continuing ideological connection with the Grenvillites. Braybrooke's son Richard Neville and Lord Grenville's old friend Sir John Newport did likewise. William Elliot, William Fremantle, Pascoe Grenfell, (Bulkeley's MP) Frankland Lewis, Scrope Bernard Morland, and (Carysfort's son) Granville Proby voted for suspension.[73]

Six months later, the final and definitive political separation between Grenville and Spencer occurred. Grenville, who approved the Government's continuation of the suspension, said so in the Lords; and, immediately following his statement, Spencer, who had approved of the February proceedings, rose to dissent, expressing "great pain in differ-

71. Durham Papers, Grenville to Grey, Feb. 23, 1817.
72. NLW, Coedymaen Papers, 12, Charles Wynn to his wife, Feb. 22, 1817; NLW, Henry Wynn Papers, 18/2806D, Carrington to Mrs. Wynn, July 1, 1817; *Parl. Debates,* XXXV (Feb. 24, 1817), 588.
73. *Parl. Debates,* XXXV: (Feb. 25, 1817), 651; (Feb. 26, 1817), 718, 734, 758–59; (Feb. 27, 1817), 766. NLW, Coedymaen Papers, 12, Charles Wynn to his wife, Feb. 27, 1817.

ing from the noble baron, for whose opinions and character he had entertained for many years such high respect." Several other former Grenvillite peers who had either failed to vote in February or had supported the Government—the evidence is not clear—including the Duke of Grafton and Lords Carnarvon, Cawdor, and Hereford, stood forth against continued suspension.[74]

During these debates, Grenville in effect announced his retirement from normal everyday political affairs.[75] He continued to attend Parliament on important occasions, speaking out on such issues as Peterloo, Queen Caroline's divorce proceedings, and the Catholic question; but he never again played the role of a party leader beyond giving advice to his nephews. His semiretirement ended the Grenvillite party in the House of Lords. The second Marquis of Buckingham had neither the talent nor the charisma to attract the support of other members of his family or of his uncle's friends; and by this time most of the remaining Grenvillite peers were too old to play an active role in politics. Insofar as they acted at all, most of the important ones continued to support the Whig opposition, even when the rump of Grenvillites joined Liverpool's Tory Administration after December, 1821.

All of Lord Grenville's family connections in the Lords had followed him in voting for the suspension of Habeas Corpus in February, 1817. But for his brothers-in-law, Fortescue and Carysfort, this did not lead to any permanent separation from the Whigs.[76] Fortescue continued to aid the Whig party both on the local level (in Devon) and on the national level. Because of the Whig politics of Fortescue's son, Lord Ebrington, and his son-in-law, Lord King, an estrangement grew up between that family and the Stowe Grenvilles.[77] Carysfort, too, supported the Whigs insofar as Hunts electoral aid went, though he was frequently too ill to attend Parliament. Lord Grenville still held his proxy, but only for the Catholic question; and Carysfort told Fitzwilliam: "You do not know how much I have suffered by finding upon so many Questions Opposition between the Friends with whom I had so long invariably acted, by which I mean yourself & Lord Grenville, for I care in Politics, for nobody else. Even with Lord Grenville I cannot agree."[78]

74. *Parl. Debates*, XXXVI (June 16, 1817), 1013–16.
75. Ibid., 1013–14.
76. Ibid., N.S.: III (Nov. 10, 1820), 1744–46; VIII (April 24, 1823), 1253; VIII (June 19, 1823), 1072.
77. *Correspondence of Charlotte Grenville, Lady Williams Wynn,* ed. Rachel Leighton (London, 1920), Lady Wynn to Henry Wynn: June 1, 1824, p. 316; June 22, 1824, pp. 317–18.
78. NRO, Fitzwilliam Papers: 100, Carysfort to Milton, Feb., 1820; 104, Carysfort to Fitzwilliam, March 19 and 21, 1821.

Neither Grenville's brother-in-law, Lord Braybrooke, nor his cousin, Lord Glastonbury, seems to have taken any further partisan political line after 1817. Of Lord Grenville's nephews in the House of Commons, Fortescue's son Viscount Ebrington, Braybrooke's son Richard Neville, Carysfort's son Granville Proby, and Buckingham's brother Lord Nugent continued to adhere to the Whig party. Thus, of the Grenville family, only the Marquis of Buckingham, Watkin Wynn, and Charles Wynn embarked upon a new course of political activity in 1817.

Lord Spencer was by this time firmly separated from the Grenvillites and following the Whig line of his son Althorp. An increasingly conservative Thomas Grenville ceased to write to Spencer on political subjects, but he understood his closest friend's predicament and told him in 1820, "I should be more distressed than gratified by finding that you agreed in opinion with me . . . for you could not agree with me without strongly differing from those who are nearest to you in blood & affection."[79] Other peers who had once been politically united with Grenville, such as the Duke of Grafton and Lords Cawdor and Essex, had long before 1817 become virtually indistinguishable from the main body of the Whig opposition, whom they continued to support. Lord Carrington supported Grenville's stand upon Peterloo and Queen Caroline's divorce, but his sons and brothers in the Commons were firm Whigs long before 1817, and Carrington never in any way associated with the Stowe branch of the Grenvillites.[80] The evidence concerning the political line after 1817 of Lord Hardwicke, who had been one of Grenville's closest counselors after 1807, is not clear, though his support of the Whigs in 1820 in the initial stages of the Queen's affair presupposes a continuing alliance with that group.[81]

Three surviving Grenvillite peers—Bristol,[82] Hereford,[83] and Somers—seem to have used the occasion of the 1817 schism to adhere directly to the Tory Administration of Lord Liverpool. In reward, Bristol received a Marquisate in 1826 and Somers the Lord Lieutenancy of Hereford in 1817 and an Earldom in 1821.[84] The only Grenvillite peer who pledged support to a continuing Grenvillite group minus Lord Grenville was Lord Bulkeley, the old friend and early supporter of the

79. Althorp Papers, 123, Thomas Grenville to Spencer, May 2, 1820.

80. NLW, Henry Wynn Papers, 18/2806D, Carrington to Hester Wynn, Dec. 5, 1819; Parl. Debates, N.S., III (Nov. 10, 1820), 1744–46.

81. Parl. Debates, N.S., II: (June 27, 1820), 49; (July 14, 1820), 472.

82. Ibid., XIX (June 13, 1828), 1346.

83. Leeds Papers, 78A, Wynn to Canning, April 21, 1827.

84. BM, Liverpool Papers, Add. MSS.: 38573, Somers to Liverpool, April 21, 1817; 38268, Somers to Liverpool, Aug. 29, 1817.

first Marquis of Buckingham. He was not, however, able to carry with him his own half-brother, Sir Robert Williams, who remained aligned with the Whigs.[85]

The end of any Grenvillite party in the Lords transformed what remained of the party in the Commons into what, judging from Buckingham's political conduct from 1817 to 1829, can only be termed a faction—indeed, Lord Grenville called it such[86]—a faction in the worst sense of the contemporary meaning of the term. Henceforth the Grenvillites were of little national political importance save as a small group jockeying for power. But the importance of the Grenvillite party from 1801 to 1817 had been of a quite different nature: Lord Grenville had been the main force uniting many prominent families, both Portland Whig and Pittite, into what was to become the great national post-1830 governing party of Britain. And, while the Grenville family's participation in a coalition with Grey, Holland, and Lansdowne had lasted a mere thirteen years, the ties that bound the Aucklands, Carlisles, Fortescues, Mintos, Spencers, and Staffords (who had returned to the Whig fold by 1830) to the Whig and Liberal parties proved to be of a more significant duration.

85. NLW, Harpton Court Papers, c/375, Bulkeley to Lewis, June 19, 1817; HEH-STG, Box 156, Bulkeley to Buckingham, July 13, 1817.
86. *Memoirs of George IV*, Grenville to Buckingham, Dec. 5, 1821, I, 245–46.

[CHAPTER VIII]

The Grenvillite Faction, 1813–22

1. The Stowe Grenville Connection, 1813–16

The breach in Grenvillite ranks caused by Lord Grenville's semiretirement from political concerns in 1817 was filled only in the physical sense by his nephew, Lord Buckingham, who was called by his detractors the *gros Marquis*. In terms of numbers, prestige, and quality, the post-1817 Grenvillites were a sorry lot. Richard Temple Nugent Brydges Chandos Grenville (1776–1839), second Marquis of Buckingham, afforded three decades of entertainment to an audience that viewed his escapades alternately with undisguised disgust and intense humor. And, insofar as the Grenvillites have received a generally bad name from historians as a set of power-hungry, grabbing, unprincipled individuals, they owe that reputation chiefly to the two Marquises of Buckingham, especially to the second.

The second Marquis of Buckingham held three efficient offices of state during his lifetime: a short period at the Board of Control from 1800 to 1801 and a joint Paymastership and the Vice Presidency of the Board of Trade from 1806 to 1807. During the general election of 1806, his inept handling of Hampshire electoral affairs was a major embarrassment to his uncle's Administration.[1] When Lord Temple (as he was then styled) left the Paymastership in March, 1807, the Pittite press, capitalizing on his rather bumbling presence, began a long attack on him for taking the official stationery, pens, and ink with him,[2] and a poem circulated in London society:

> Says Grenville, to our Church at home
> I still prefer the Church of Rome.
> But prethee Temple why this Vapour
> About your ninety Reams of paper?

1. *Parl. Debates*, VIII (Feb. 13, 1807), 747.
2. See, for example, the *Courier* (London), April 24, 1807, and Jan. 9, 1811.

No matter what the people deem us,
I'm *Romulus* and you are *Remus*.[3]

The second Marquis of Buckingham was an inordinately proud man, conscious of his rank in society and always expectant that others recognize what he deemed to be his worth. Such was his estimation of his worth that within fifteen years of his father's death, he had managed to alienate and destroy any meaningful relationship with his wife (Anne Eliza Brydges, daughter of the last Duke of Chandos), his only son, his two Grenville uncles, his cousins (even the faithful Charles Wynn), the Whigs, the Tories, and the Canningites. By 1830, Lord Grey believed that Buckingham had become the most unpopular man in England.[4] Under his leadership the Grenvillite connection became the *"odium Grenvillium,"* perhaps the most universally despised political group in post-1714 Britain.

In 1817 the general political trend promised by the Grenvillite separation from the Whigs elated Buckingham. He had long worked toward that goal; so also had Lord Liverpool, the Prime Minister. Liverpool had always desired to unite to his conservative Administration the numerous connections, factions, or parties that had formed the mainstay of the younger Pitt's long domination of British politics. A Pittite reunion of sorts had already taken place, with both Lord Castlereagh and Lord Sidmouth serving in the Ministry, but during the summer of 1812 George Canning refused a generous Cabinet offer. In 1813, however, Canning repented his refusal, dissolved his party, and adhered to the Ministry; then, after finding places for his followers, he took the Lisbon embassy.

The Grenvillites were to prove more difficult to sway, and in making this attempt Liverpool chose as his avenue of approach the weakest section of the party. Five days after the death of the first Marquis of Buckingham in 1813, in an obvious gesture of good will, he had the new Marquis appointed Lord Lieutenant of Bucks.[5] Buckingham had, of course, distinctly marked his disapproval of opposition politics when as Lord Temple he had refused to participate in general House of Commons business after 1810, and he still retained suitable anti-Whitbread sentiments in 1813.[6] Still, he made no public move to separate from the Whig coalition, and the Prime Minister had no

3. BRO, Fremantle Papers, 50.

4. Guy Le Strange, ed. and trans., *Correspondence of Princess Lieven and Earl Grey* (London, 1890), Grey to Princess Lieven, June 17, 1830, II, 9.

5. NLW, Coedymaen Papers, 12, Charles Wynn to his wife, Feb. 24, 1817; *Memoirs of the Regency,* Liverpool to Buckingham, Feb. 16, 1813, II, 22.

6. BRO, Fremantle Papers, 55, Buckingham to Fremantle, May 13, 1813.

intention of giving him a great deal for nothing. Thus, when in 1814, as greedy as his late father was, he requested additional Bucks patronage, he received a polite refusal.[7]

Left to himself Buckingham would no doubt have made a quick deal with Liverpool, received a minor office or embassy, and emerged a normal (if pro-Catholic) supporter of the long late-Georgian political peace. Yet he was not a free agent. He was bound by ties of affection and family tradition to his Grenville uncles and, however much he might dislike it, to the Whig party. Perhaps even more important, he was astute enough to realize that his romance with Liverpool would yield greater fruit should he embrace the Ministry along with his uncles rather than alone.

Since in 1814 or 1815 Lord Grenville had no intention of joining Liverpool, Buckingham was forced to adopt a policy of somewhat shady secret dealings with Ministers that reflects little credit on his reputation and only too clearly reminds one of the antics of his great-uncle Temple. In December, 1814, Buckingham was drafting a memorandum with Sir John Francis Cradock, a friend of the Regent, affirming his support for both Catholic emancipation and his two uncles; but, without the slightest consultation with anyone, he gave as his opinion that not only the Grenvilles but Grey as well might adhere to the Regent.[8] A few months later, during the Hundred Days, again in indirect secret communication with the Regent, he embarrassed his Buckingham MP, William Fremantle, who was forced at one point to inform the Regent's startled Private Secretary that the conversations in question had been launched without Lord Grenville's knowledge. Fremantle himself, in a breach of political etiquette, actually read to the Secretary extracts from Grenville's private letters to himself expressing anti-Bonapartist opinions.[9]

Immediately after Waterloo, Buckingham accelerated his secret dealings. Through the medium of Lord Buckinghamshire, President of the Board of Control and an old friend of his father's, he contacted the Prime Minister, requesting the French embassy in return for his support. Liverpool's response was hardly encouraging, as he wondered chiefly about the views of Buckingham's "connections," specifically Lord Grenville.[10] The Marquis gingerly and indirectly sounded out his

7. BM, Liverpool Papers, Add. MSS.: 38259, Buckingham to Liverpool, Oct. 15, 1814; 38260, Liverpool to Buckingham, Oct. 29, 1814 (draft).

8. HEH-STG.: Box 156, copy of memorandum, Dec. 27, 1814; ST. 96, comments by Buckingham on the memorandum.

9. Ibid., Box 164, Fremantle to Buckingham, March 31 and n.d., 1815.

10. Ibid.: ST. 96, Buckingham to Buckinghamshire, June 26 and 28, 1815; Box 158, Buckinghamshire to Buckingham, June 27 and July 1, 1815.

uncles, though without giving the slightest hint of the extent of his contact with the Government. His uncles advised him that while he was, of course, free to take his own line, the rest of the Grenvillites (Wynns, Fortescues, Nevilles, etc.) would not follow.[11] Buckingham went to Paris in the autumn of 1815, and before leaving England made some type of new overture to Buckinghamshire that apparently involved an idle threat to return to disapprove the peace unless he were given the French embassy.[12]

The Grenville-Foxite schism of 1817 and the virtual extinction of the wider Grenvillite party in the House of Lords transformed all of Buckingham's political prospects, and he attempted to forge his few remaining followers into a more solid entity. By 1816, three of his six MPs—Francis Horner, Lord Ebrington, and Lord Nugent—were in no real sense Grenvillites. By this time Horner was quite ill, and the cautious way in which the usually exuberant Marquis had treated Horner's antiwar stance a year earlier perhaps reflected a certain sympathy for his physical deterioration. Also, during the winter after Waterloo, Horner and Buckingham disagreed on the treatment of certain French Bonapartists (especially on the execution of Marshal Ney), causing Thomas Grenville to worry—needlessly as it turned out—that Buckingham's reputation would suffer greatly if he threw Horner out of Parliament.[13] The Marquis probably realized this as well as anyone else; and in all his private correspondence with William Fremantle, his chief political confidant, despite fulminations against Holland House, the Mountain, and indeed the entire Whig party, he never mentioned an intention to force Horner to give up his seat before the conclusion of Parliament. In any event, Horner's death in February, 1817, ended the problem.

Lord Ebrington, who was enjoying excellent health, was another matter. Hugh Fortescue (1783–1861), Viscount Ebrington and (after 1841) second Earl Fortescue, first cousin to the second Marquis of Buckingham and a member for Buckingham borough, had long caused political problems for his uncles. He was returned for Buckingham borough at the general election of 1812 and a few weeks later casually informed his family that from forgetfulness he had neglected to tell them that should the motion for reducing the first Marquis of Buckingham's Tellership come forward in Parliament (and it did not),

11. Ibid., Box 168, Buckingham to Grenville, July 16, 1815; BRO, Fremantle Papers, 55: Buckingham to Fremantle, July 2, 1815; memorandum of a conversation between Fremantle and Grenville, July 17, 1815.

12. BRO, Fremantle Papers, 55, Buckingham to Fremantle, Dec. 11, 1815.

13. *Dropmore,* Thomas Grenville to Lord Grenville, Jan. 1, 1816, X, 410.

he would not vote against it. Thomas Grenville, flushed with anger, suspected quite rightly that the *"democrates"* had gotten hold of Ebrington.[14] When the Viscount opposed the suspension of Habeas Corpus in February, 1817, and supported Burdett's parliamentary reform motion in May, the second Marquis of Buckingham not unnaturally desired to be rid of his cousin.[15] Ebrington resigned, and when Buckingham, perhaps to show good will toward the Fortescue family, offered the vacant seat to Ebrington's younger brother George, while making it clear that he would be expected to follow the line of his patron, the offer was declined.[16]

The first Marquis of Buckingham's second son, Lord George Grenville (1789–1850), second Baron Nugent of Ireland after 1812, inherited his father's girth, his grandfather Nugent's literary predilections, and his Uncle Tom's disposition. Like such other sons of Grenvillite peers as Althorp, Morpeth, Ebrington, and Richard Neville, he was a liberal in politics, no doubt astounding his family when on the occasion of the third reading of the Habeas Corpus Bill in June, 1817, he remarked to loud cheers from the opposition that he preferred seeing England revolutionized to enslaved.[17] In April, 1817, Nugent, stating his approval of triennial Parliaments, offered to resign his Aylesbury seat, but Buckingham refused in respect to their father's memory.[18]

Horner's death and Ebrington's resignation gave Buckingham two seats to fill. St. Mawes went to a close school friend of Charles Wynn, Joseph Phillimore (1775–1855), Regius Professor of Civil Law at Oxford. Phillimore, via Wynn and another close friend, Francis Horner, had long established a cordial relationship with the Grenvillites, for example, aiding Lord Grenville in his campaign against the Orders-in-Council.[19] He was thus a natural choice to succeed Horner at St. Mawes, though it soon became uncomfortably obvious to the Marquis that Phillimore considered himself more a political follower of Wynn than of Buckingham.

Ebrington's seat at Buckingham was filled by the Marquis's distant cousin, James Hamilton Stanhope (1788–1825), a distinguished soldier during the late Spanish war and a son of the third Earl Stanhope.

14. Ibid., Thomas Grenville to Lord Grenville: Nov. 1, 1812, X, 300–301; Nov. 12, 1812, X, 308.

15. HEH-STG: Box 168, Buckingham to Ebrington, May 27, 1817; Box 176, Grenville to Buckingham, May 13, 1817.

16. DRO, Fortescue Papers: 1262M/FC38, Buckingham to George Fortescue, May 25, 1817; 1262M/FC32, Nugent to Ebrington, n.d.

17. *Parl. Debates*, XXXVI (June 27, 1817), 1219–25.

18. HEH-STG, Box 8, Nugent to Buckingham, April 25, 1817.

19. *Dropmore*, Auckland to Grenville, Jan. 31, 1811, X, 115.

This was Buckingham's first attempt to fill one of his seats with a personal friend, and it was an ill-considered choice. In June, 1817, Stanhope sent Buckingham a statement of his political philosophy, denying a party bias and admitting an attachment to Pitt's principles and Catholic emancipation. He also promised to follow Ebrington's example if differences should arise between them.[20] Eleven months later Stanhope, a stranger to parliamentary and party practices, accepted an invitation from Liverpool to call upon him at Fife House. When he arrived he was surprised to discover a large gathering of ministerial supporters met to discuss the marital and monetary status of the royal Dukes. Despite his protestations of innocence, Buckingham flew into a rage at Stanhope's attendance at the meeting and hotly informed him to look elsewhere at the next general election for a seat in Parliament.[21]

At the general election of 1818, General Sir George Nugent, Buckingham's maternal first cousin and often before a Grenvillite MP, was returned for Buckingham. The absentee Thomas Grenville was not returned again for Bucks at the general election of 1818. Buckingham's only child, Lord Temple, succeeded his great-uncle. In early 1818, Buckingham gained control of one seat at Winchester, where Lady Buckingham's uncle, J. H. Leigh, sat until 1823.

Only one House of Commons man of the first rank (unless one considers Charles Wynn as such), William Conyngham Plunket, MP for Trinity College and a Grenvillite since 1806, continued in allegiance to Buckingham after 1817. When the Marquis heard, just prior to the general election of 1818, that Plunket's continuation in his seat was in jeopardy due to the electoral activities of J. W. Croker, he offered him St. Mawes. Phillimore was under engagement to resign his seat, but Plunket narrowly won reelection.[22] Thomas Frankland Lewis (1780–1855), from a prominent Radnorshire family and Lord Bulkeley's MP for Beaumaris borough from 1812 to 1826, likewise adhered to the Grenville line after the schism. Bulkeley's support for the Grenville-Foxite coalition was especially unpopular in anti-Catholic Wales, and both he and Lewis looked with favor upon its termination.[23] One other Grenvillite in the Commons who supported Buckingham

20. HEH-STG, Box 160, Stanhope to Buckingham, June 7, 1817.

21. *Memoirs of the Regency,* Stanhope to Buckingham, n.d., II, 254–55; HEH-STG, ST. 97, Buckingham to Stanhope, April 14, 1818.

22. NLI, Plunket Papers, PC920, Buckingham to Plunket, May 16 and June 10, 1818; *Memoirs of the Regency,* Plunket to Buckingham, June 20, 1818, II, 261–62.

23. NLW, Harpton Court Papers: c/374, Bulkeley to Lewis, Jan. 12, 1814; c/375, Bulkeley to Lewis, June 19, 1817.

following 1817 was Thomas Knox, son of that Thomas Knox who had followed Lord Grenville during the 1806 and 1807 Parliaments.[24]

Thus, when the second Marquis of Buckingham began his political career at the head of the Grenvillite faction, he had by early 1818 eleven definite followers in the Commons—six of his own borough or county members (at Aylesbury, Nugent followed the Whigs), plus the two Wynns, Plunket, Lewis, and Knox.

2. The Third Party, 1817–19

Buckingham had three options in 1817: (1) to enter into immediate support of Lord Liverpool's Administration, assuming, of course, the procurement of advantageous terms; (2) to re-form some type of Grenville-Whig coalition; (3) to attempt to form a third or center party in the House of Commons. There is little question that he would have preferred, on correct terms, the first option. It was only when his 1817 plans for such an event collapsed that in some desperation and with few illusions he attempted the third option. The second option was never expressly pursued as such, though the possibility remained tantalizingly in the background as a means to lull the opposition or disturb the Government.

Party compositions during the first six months of 1817 seemed as fluid to most observers as they had been during the first six months of 1812 or the last six months of 1809. An upheaval was obviously occurring within the opposition coalition as the Grenvilles and Whigs parted company; yet the finished contour of the political scene was not clear to ministerial supporters, oppositionists, or Grenvillites. Lord Liverpool on several occasions during those months cast out his net in an attempt to pull in Lord Grenville. The overtures were always unofficial—usually in a thirdhand manner from George Harrison, Assistant Secretary of the Treasury—or were at least never straightforward enough to risk an embarrassment to the Ministry by a public Grenvillian rejection.[25] The semioverture was sweetened by intimations that Liverpool had some disposition to see Grenville's nephew, Charles Wynn, as Charles Abbot's successor as Speaker of the House of Commons.[26] Grenville, however, was totally unenthusiastic about any such dalliance with Ministers.[27]

24. *Dropmore*, Thomas Grenville to Lord Grenville, April 15, 1817, X, 423-24,
25. HEH-STG, Box 164, Fremantle to Buckingham, Feb. 8 and April 23 (two letters), 1817; BRO, Fremantle Papers, 55, Buckingham to Fremantle, April 21, 1817.
26. BRO, Fremantle Papers, 55, Buckingham to Fremantle, April 21, 1817.
27. HEH-STG, Box 176, Grenville to Buckingham, Feb. 8, 1817.

Liverpool quickly came to the realization that, rather than Pitt's colleague, he might be stuck with the *gros Marquis;* for only Lord Buckingham snapped greedily and repeatedly at the bait. He foolishly believed that a two-hour conversation on financial matters between Lord Grenville and George Harrison constituted on his uncle's part "an indirect communication to the Govt, and I consider this first step as so important to me, that I . . . am very anxious to follow it up."[28] He seized as his own the faint prospect of Wynn's Speakership and instructed his confidant, William Fremantle, to subordinate every other activity to concluding such an agreement.[29] Yet in 1817 Lord Grenville had no more intention of granting Buckingham's whim than he had had in 1815, and he finally told the Marquis what should have been obvious to him: that Wynn would be dishonored in the eyes of the Commons if members ever suspected that he became Speaker due to a family bargain with the Government.[30]

Upon Abbot's resignation, the support for Charles Wynn's succession came not from the Government, which successfully put up Manners Sutton, but from the opposition. Such Whig luminaries as Duncannon, MacDonald, Mackintosh, Brougham, and Grey pledged assistance, and the division of 150 to 312 was not mean,[31] though one observer acknowledged that "many were with difficulty brought into the field, so violent was the *odium Grenvillium.*"[32]

Some political and press observers interpreted the Whig rally to Wynn's cause as a guarantee either that there was no imminent danger of a Grenville-ministerial juncture or that the Grenville-Foxite coalition might yet be patched up.[33] This positive view was encouraged when, during the spring of 1817, some of Buckingham's friends in the House of Commons rather liberally supported Whig-inspired motions on retrenchment and economical reform.[34] But Charles Wynn viewed

28. BRO, Fremantle Papers, 55, Buckingham to Fremantle, Feb. 9, 1817.

29. Ibid., April 21, 1817.

30. HEH-STG, Box 181, Grenville to Buckingham, May 4, 1817.

31. NLW, Coedymaen Papers, VIII, Wynn to Grenville, April 24 and May 30, 1817; BM, Holland House Papers, Add. MSS. 51654, Mackintosh to Lady Holland, n.d.

32. Josceline Bagot, ed., *George Canning and His Friends* (London, 1909), Lyttelton to Bagot, June 4, 1817, II, 52.

33. John William Ward, First Earl of Dudley, *Letters of the Earl of Dudley to the Bishop of Llandaff* (London, 1840), Dudley to Llandaff, June 3, 1817, pp. 167–68; *Morning Chronicle* (London), June 4, 1817.

34. See the division lists in the *Parl. Debates* on: Calcraft's motion for a committee on salt duties, XXXV (April 25, 1817), 1352; Tierney's motion on the office of a third Secretary of State, XXXVI (April 29, 1817), 82; Calcraft's motion for a further reduction in the army, XXXVI (May 12, 1817), 559.

the collapse and death on July 1, 1817, of George Ponsonby, whom ten years earlier the Grenvillites had helped foist on the party as opposition leader in the Commons, as taking away "the only remaining link which connected the Vale and the Mountain" and therefore tending to increase the chances and the strength of a projected Grenvillite third party in the 1818 session of Parliament.[35] Ponsonby's death, however, raised the interesting possibility in the mind of some conservative Whigs that a Grenvillite, William Conyngham Plunket, might take the lead of the entire opposition in the Commons and thus reunite the two groups. The Duke of Gloucester, who was in communication with Plunket, knew that he did not desire the post due to family and professional commitments, but he doubted that Plunket would refuse a personal request from his old chief.[36] However, Lord Grenville declined to make such a request.[37]

Buckingham gave no direct sign that he favored a Plunket-led, reunited opposition; but, following the rejection of his spring overtures to Liverpool, he did appear more cordial to the Whigs. Bennet thought the Grenvilles were not only "nibbling but biting at us once more";[38] Sir James Mackintosh, during a visit to Stowe in late July, found "some disposition to return to the Old Station";[39] and in September, friendly letters were exchanged between Buckingham and Lansdowne.[40] Buckingham probably meant no more than to recruit, if possible, Mackintosh and probably Lansdowne, who was known to have severe doubts about Whig foreign policy, to his progressing plans for a third party. Yet Buckingham was an individual who kept his options open; and during the ensuing years, whenever his relations with the Government soured, he made observable lurches in the Whig direction.

It was Thomas Grenville who in February, 1817, first threw out the notion of Buckingham forming a thoroughly independent political party. Both Fremantle and Buckingham, who at that precise moment had other concerns, thought the proposal absurd; and the Marquis prophesied correctly that insufficient Commons talent could ever be found to participate in such an attempt.[41]

35. HEH-STG, Box 181, Wynn to Buckingham, July 1, 1817.

36. Ibid., Box 162, Gloucester to Buckingham, July 11, 1817.

37. Ibid., Box 176, Grenville to Buckingham, July 4, 1817.

38. John Gore, ed., *The Creevey Papers* (rev. ed.; New York, 1963), Bennet to Creevey, July 20, 1817, p. 149.

39. BM, Mackintosh Papers, Add. MSS. 52442, Mackintosh's Journal, July 28, 1817.

40. BM, Holland House Papers, Add. MSS. 51654, Mackintosh to Lady Holland, Sept. 19, 1817.

41. HEH-STG, Box 164, Fremantle to Buckingham, Feb. 11, 1817; BRO, Fremantle Papers, 55, Buckingham to Fremantle, Feb. 16, 1817.

Thomas continued to press the object on his nephew throughout the spring of 1817, though he admitted to his brother his grave doubts as to Buckingham's emotional capacity to organize and lead such an ambitious undertaking. While Lord Grenville did not exactly endorse the project, he worried that the Marquis might break into ministerial ranks as a single individual and therefore, in effect, encouraged the move by suggesting that Buckingham consult such relatives and old friends as Charles Wynn, William Elliot, W. C. Plunket, Lord Lansdowne, and Lord Carnarvon.[42]

Lansdowne and Carnarvon were both in Italy, yet the rapidity with which they returned their proxies to vote against the continued suspension of Habeas Corpus must have shown the Grenvilles that they were unlikely allies.[43] William Elliot, who had followed Lord Grenville's politics since 1802 and the peace of Amiens, also refused to separate from the Whigs. The hesitation on Elliot's part prevented any effective action on the Grenvilles' side during the parliamentary session of 1817.[44] When the third party did emerge during the 1818 session, Elliot never joined it; and in July, 1818, a few weeks before his death, he fully concurred in the selection of George Tierney as Ponsonby's successor in the Commons.[45]

With Elliot's noncooperation and Lord Grenville's refusal of Buckingham's request that he ask W. C. Plunket to lead the venture, the role of party leader fell upon the less than capable shoulders of Charles Wynn. Lord Grenville, who was always uncommonly fond of his Welsh nephew, had a moment's trepidation over Wynn's squeaky voice; but he rationalized that Wynn's "talents, knowledge, & insight of character" would carry him through, though he urged Buckingham to cultivate Frankland Lewis just in case.[46]

This move placed Wynn, who had no overriding belief in his own qualifications, in a difficult position. During the spring of 1817, Buckingham had thought the whole concept of a third party absurd; now, however, he began to bombard his cousin with suggestions for the individual makeup of the group and the political strategy that ought to be pursued. Wynn, who was more wary than Buckingham, saw quite

42. HEH-STG, Box 164, Fremantle to Buckingham, April 23, 1817; *Dropmore,* Thomas Grenville to Lord Grenville, April 18, 1817, X, 425–26; BM, Thomas Grenville Papers, Add. MSS. 41853, Lord Grenville to Thomas Grenville, April 16, 1817.

43. BM, Holland House Papers, Add. MSS. 51686, Lansdowne to Holland, May 18, 1817; HEH-STG, Box 172, Thomas Grenville to Buckingham, July 12, 1817.

44. HEH-STG, Box 181, Wynn to Buckingham, July 12, 1817; NLW, Coedymaen Papers, 20, Buckingham to Wynn, Sept. 15, 1817.

45. HRO, Tierney Papers, 31M70/25, Elliot to Tierney, July 19, 1818.

46. HEH-STG, Box 176, Grenville to Buckingham, July 4, 1817.

clearly that Buckingham's repeatedly used analogy with the 1801
Grenvillite party—"that little bench [which] turned out the Gov't"[47]
—was inapplicable without a bond of union comparable to the anti-
Amiens standard. When Buckingham urged his cousin to start
recruiting MPs, Wynn wondered just what the Marquis desired him to
ask them, "when there is no one prominent measure upon which a
decided line can . . . be adopted." As far as Wynn was concerned, one
great hope existed for the formation of an effective and numerically
significant group. If the Whigs should put up a radical such as Romilly
or Brougham as their new opposition leader in the Commons—which
they did not—"that would in itself supply us with a Standard &
gathering point of dissent."[48] Yet he agreed to accept the position and
to "go strait forward, do my best & leave the event to Providence."[49] In
private, he was more sarcastic, however. To his close friend, the poet
Robert Southey, he referred to the Grenvillites as "a little like the Army
of the Republic of Sn Marino which takes the field consisting of a
General five men & a Drummer of great experience."[50]

The problem during the following sessions of Parliament was that
Wynn, once persuaded of the necessity to act, did just that to the
utmost of his somewhat limited vigor. But Buckingham, who had
insisted that Wynn play such a role and probably viewed the third party
merely as a device to make him appear more desirable to Liverpool, soon
lost interest in the whole proceeding and began to condemn Wynn for
carrying out precisely the role that he had suggested earlier.

Liverpool, perhaps getting wind of the third party prospect, sent
George Harrison to Buckingham on January 24, 1818, to discuss the
upcoming speech from the throne and no doubt to renew the seduction.
The Marquis intimated a strong possibility that the Administration
might receive his support, and upon request of Harrison agreed to
transmit the outline of the speech to his uncle.[51] Lord Grenville and
Thomas Grenville, who had been informing all their former Whig allies
of an intention to retire totally from partisan politics, and Charles
Wynn, who was bending every effort to form an effective third party,
were greatly agitated by this indiscretion.[52] Against the advice of
Wynn, Lord Grenville wrote his nephew a reproachful letter and

47. NLW, Coedymaen Papers, 20, Buckingham to Wynn, Sept. 15, 1817.
48. HEH-STG, Box 181, Wynn to Buckingham, Oct. 26, 1817.
49. NLW, Coedymaen Papers, VIII/547, Wynn to Grenville, Nov. 19, 1817.
50. NLW, Wynn-Southey Papers, 4/4814D, Wynn to Southey, n.d.   ·
51. BM, Liverpool Papers, Add. MSS. 38367, memorandum of a conversation with
the Marquis of Buckingham, Jan. 24, 1818.
52. HEH-STG, ST. 97, Buckingham to Grenville, Jan. 26, 1818; *Dropmore*,
Thomas Grenville to Lord Grenville, Jan. 26, 1818, X, 432–33.

reiterated to Harrison his intention to retire.[53] Buckingham, who had enough sense to realize that the Government's attraction to him was predicated to a great extent upon his uncle's prestige, felt betrayed; and he therefore disavowed any further interest in the third party.[54] He told Fremantle that Lord Grenville had destroyed the political greatness of their family for a generation, and he maintained that he too would depart from the parliamentary scene.[55] It was altogether an inauspicious start for a major Grenvillite political attempt.

The session opened on January 27, 1818, and none of the Grenvillites spoke during the debate on the address. However, Wynn and three Grenville-borough MPs—Joseph Phillimore, Scrope Bernard Morland, and James Stanhope—took their seats below Bankes' bench, between the opposition benches and the door. Significantly Fremantle did not at the moment join them, probably a reflection of Buckingham's current irritation.[56] Within a few hours of assuming their seats, Thomas Knox joined them. Others flirted with the Grenvillites without actually sitting on their bench: Pascoe Grenfell, an old member of the group; two independent-minded members, J. H. Tremayne and Sir Thomas Dyke Acland; and some connections of Lord Somers. By March, Fremantle had arrived on the bench,[57] though he had not abandoned his long-held opinions on the absurdity of the entire attempt or his desire for a juncture with Ministers. Buckingham thoroughly agreed with Fremantle's negative attitude and threw back to a now enthusiastic Wynn some of Charles's own doubts of the previous autumn: "I think," he wrote, "that Fremantle is not more impatient than he ought to be for a junction. But I see that he, as I do, distrusts very much the formation of a third party, a thing which never existed yet, to any good purpose, vide journals, registers, history, newspapers & precedents."[58] But, despite these views, Buckingham was politically astute enough to realize the advantages that a strong neutral party could give him in negotiations with Ministers. Therefore, during the spring and summer of 1818, he made an unsuccessful attempt to recruit two power-

53. *Memoirs of the Regency,* Grenville to Buckingham, Jan. 27, 1818, II, 204–8; NLW, Coedymaen Papers, V/316, Grenville to Wynn, Jan. 28, 1818.

54. NLW, Coedymaen Papers, 20, Buckingham to Wynn, Feb. 1, 1818.

55. BRO, Fremantle Papers, 55, Buckingham to Fremantle, Feb. 15, 1818.

56. Durham Papers, Tierney to Grey, Jan. 28, 1818; BM, Mackintosh Papers, Add. MSS. 52443, Mackintosh's Journal, n.d.

57. *Memoirs of the Regency:* Phillimore to Buckingham, Jan. 31, 1818, II, 211–13; Wynn to Buckingham, March 6, 1818, II, 236–37.

58. Ibid.: Fremantle to Buckingham, April 4, 1818, II, 243; Wynn to Buckingham, April 4, 1818, II, 244. NLW, Coedymaen Papers, 20, Buckingham to Wynn, April 5, 1818.

ful political figures, the Marquis Wellesley and Charles Philip Yorke, to his side.[59]

With regard to the Whigs, the Grenville-Foxite schism, which was never enunciated in a public manner in Parliament, was becoming a general fact of life. Tierney thought, after a conversation with Lord Grenville in December, 1817, that some prospect of a reunion yet remained. But, from a letter written by Grenville to Holland a month later, Grey surmised that "the separation was complete"; and aside from the loss of Grenville himself, he found little to regret in the departure of the rest of the faction.[60] By March, 1818, the *Morning Chronicle* was referring to the "rats" of Stowe.[61]

. Buckingham took some pains, however, not to close the door totally on the possibility of future cooperation with the Whigs. He took Tierney for a cruise on his yacht during August, 1818; and, as the new opposition leader told Lady Holland, he was "very kind & civil to me, and, with certain exceptions, speakes in very courteous terms of the opposition generally. He seems to think that if we play our cards properly we shall soon turn out the Ministers with whom he takes some pains to let me know he has no connection. Whether he has any desire to come back again to our ranks I cannot tell, but I am sure he will acquit me of having used any flattering or encouraging words to entice him to do so."[62] Though neither Buckingham nor Fremantle had any desire in 1818 to return to former moorings, their correspondence makes clear that at times they reluctantly considered the possibility.[63]

Looking at the division lists of the parliamentary session of 1818, the ostensible dozen or so members of the third party exhibited little consistency of opinion with regard to voting patterns. James Stanhope and J. H. Leigh never supported the opposition; William Fremantle did so seldom; whereas, on the other hand, Charles Wynn and Joseph Phillimore gave relatively frequent votes to their old allies.[64] Thus,

59. *Memoirs of the Regency*, Wellesley to Burroughs, May 8, 1818, II, 257–60; BM, Hardwicke Papers, Add. MSS. 45046, Yorke to Buckingham, Aug. 26, 1818 (draft).

60. NLW, Coedymaen Papers, 20, Buckingham to Wynn, Dec. 17, 1817; BM, Holland House Papers, Add. MSS. 51545, Grey to Holland, Jan. 28, 1818.

61. Reading, Berks RO, Braybrooke-Glastonbury Papers, D/EZ6/2, Braybrooke to Bulkeley, March 11, 1818.

62. BM, Holland House Papers, Add. MSS. 51585, Tierney to Lady Holland, Aug. 26, 1818.

63. *Memoirs of the Regency*, Fremantle to Buckingham, Oct. 18, 1818, II, 280–81.

64. See the division lists in *Parl. Debates*, XXXVII, (Feb. 10, 1818) 329; XXXVIII(1818): (April 15) 114, (April 21) 264, (May 1) 708, (May 14) 723, (May 15) 734, (May 18) 783, (May 22) 898. BRO, Fremantle Papers, 55, Buckingham to Fremantle, March 4, 1818.

even within the third party a rough liberal-conservative split emerged, posing those loyal to Charles Wynn and those loyal to Buckingham somewhat at odds.

During the 1819 session, this liberal-conservative dichotomy caused no little trouble. On Calcraft's motion to add Brougham's name to the committee investigating the Bank, Lord Temple, Scrope Bernard Morland, Frankland Lewis, and William Fremantle refused to vote, Fremantle considering it a party question. Charles Wynn and Joseph Phillimore supported Calcraft.[65] Buckingham, who disliked Brougham, rebuked Wynn and used this as another excuse to disclaim all interest in the third party.[66] The Marquis, in a letter to Fremantle, observed that Wynn "cannot resist hearing himself speak & seeing himself vote"; and he flayed his cousin for failing to communicate with him and for pretending "to be the mouth piece of the Grenville Party."[67]

A similar pattern emerged on the question of the King's Windsor establishment and the increased allowance projected to be paid to the Duke of York as his father's guardian upon the death of the Queen, his mother. Both Charles Wynn and Lord Grenville opposed the grant. Buckingham and the Duke's old friend, William Fremantle, attempted to rally the party in York's favor. Lord Temple, Fremantle, Sir George Nugent, and Bernard Morland voted for the grant; Charles Wynn against it; Frankland Lewis, Thomas Knox, and Joseph Phillimore (rejecting a personal request from the Marquis) failed to vote at all.[68]

The membership of the third party remained relatively static. Neither W. C. Plunket in Ireland nor Sir Watkin Wynn in Wales was steady in parliamentary attendance. Pascoe Grenfell was voting decidedly within Whig ranks, except on the Peterloo question, but Lord Blandford and Lord Charles Spencer-Churchill from the Marlborough connection kept up a mild flirtation with the third party.[69] It is unclear how many members per se sat on the Grenvillite bench by 1819. As Phillimore wrote early in the session to tell Buckingham of the "respectable appearance" the bench had assumed, there apparently was an

65. *Memoirs of the Regency,* Fremantle to Buckingham: Feb. 9, 1819, II, 300–301; Feb. 12, 1819, II, 305–6.

66. NLW, Coedymaen Papers, 20, Buckingham to Wynn, Feb. 10, 1819.

67. BRO, Fremantle Papers, 46, Buckingham to Fremantle, Feb. 10, 1819.

68. *Memoirs of the Regency:* Fremantle to Buckingham, Feb. 16, 1819, II, 307–8; Wynn to Buckingham, n.d., II, 323; Phillimore to Buckingham, Feb. 22, 1819, II, 316–17.

69. Ibid.: Wynn to Buckingham, March 20, 1819, II, 332; Wynn to Buckingham, n.d., II, 323; Fremantle to Buckingham, Feb. 9, 1819, II, 300–301.

increase over 1818. But Plunket, who was certainly considered a Grenvillite by the Whigs,[70] did not sit on the bench, and other sympathisers may have remained in their old places as well.

3. The Pittite Reunion

On the two major issues of 1819 and 1820, the Peterloo massacre (when British troops fired upon a Manchester crowd) and the divorce proceedings against Queen Caroline, the Grenvillites, unlike their former Whig allies, supported the Administration. Buckingham, of course, wanted to join the Government in the troubled circumstances growing out of the Manchester affair, but he received no encouragement.[71] Charles Wynn was undoubtedly correct in his assumption that in early 1820 the Ministry did not need the Grenvillites in a formal union because, as he said, they knew that "our own principles & the extreme hostility of Opposition will oblige us to support them gratis & will therefore content themselves with administering to us plenty of Compliments."[72] The small compliments were forthcoming: no Government candidate stood against W. C. Plunket at Trinity College during the general election of 1820;[73] Lord Grenville's close friend, Doctor Hodson, received a Divinity Professorship at Oxford;[74] Buckingham obtained the Garter and some minor patronage for his rotten borough of St. Mawes.[75]

The relatively strong parliamentary position of the Ministers after the Manchester disturbances quickly faded as the primary question of the day switched from radical agitation to the rights of a temporarily popular Queen Consort. Although Lord Grenville felt that George IV had acted unwisely in removing his wife's name from the liturgy,[76] both he and Buckingham gave consistent parliamentary support to the Ministers and their sovereign on the divorce issue. When Lord Gren-

70. Ibid.: Phillimore to Buckingham, Feb. 22, 1819, II, 316–17; Fremantle to Buckingham, Nov. 18, 1819, II, 374.

71. HEH-STG, ST. 97, Buckingham to Wellesley, Aug. 1, 1819; Edmund Phipps, Memoirs of the Political and Literary Life of Robert Plumer Ward, Esq. (London, 1850), II, 47.

72. NLW, Coedymaen Papers, 29, Wynn to Phillimore, n.d.

73. NLI, Plunket Papers, PC921, Grenville to Plunket, Dec. 23, 1819; The Croker Papers: The Correspondence and Diaries of the late Right Honourable John Wilson Croker, 1809 to 1830, ed. Louis J. Jennings, (London, 1885), I, 157.

74. Memoirs of George IV, Grenville to Buckingham, July 24, 1820, I, 55.

75. BM, Liverpool Papers, Add. MSS. 38285, Buckingham to Liverpool, May 29, 1820; HEH-STG, Box 248, Morland to Napton, May 3, 1820.

76. BM, Thomas Grenville Papers, Add. MSS. 41853, Lord Grenville to Thomas Grenville, June 20, 1820.

ville accused the Queen of undoubted adultery, the Secretary to the
Treasury thought his accompanying oration stamped Caroline's guilt
"beyond redemption."[77] The whole thrust of the divorce crisis,
Canning's resignation from the Cabinet, George IV's dissatisfaction
with his Ministers—Liverpool especially—over what he considered
their timidity, the unquestioned popularity of the Queen in the country
and in Parliament, the eventual abandonment of the entire proceedings against her, all led, as early as June, 1820, to a revival of Buckingham's hopes for inclusion either in the current Administration or
in a future one.[78]

When the Bill of Pains and Penalties against Queen Caroline was
abandoned by the weakened Government on November 10, the Marquis was so certain that a royal summons would be forthcoming that
he called Wynn to Stowe to discuss their response.[79] But when the
overture came, it was made not to Buckingham but to Lord Grenville.
On November 25, the King summoned Grenville for talks, which
ultimately lasted five hours, at the Cottage in Windsor Park. Two
days before the meeting, the King had sent Liverpool notice that he
wished to consult Grenville concerning further proceedings against the
Queen. At the meeting the King abused his Ministers, alluded to
Canning's adultery with the Queen when she was Princess of Wales,
and directly asked Grenville to form a Government. Grenville categorically refused.[80]

Although the Cabinet sought without avail to acquire the talents of
Robert Peel, it had no intention, during that period, of applying to
Buckingham or Wynn.[81] Yet the Marquis retained the somewhat
pathetic hope that the King would call upon him to form a Government
either by himself or in conjunction with Wellesley, Lauderdale, and
Wellington. He even asked Fremantle, who always had a social entrée
to the royal family, to inform George IV of his availability to serve as a
channel of communication to those peers.[82]

77. *Parl. Debates*, N.S., III (Nov. 6, 1820), 1681–89; *The Correspondence of Charles Arbuthnot*, ed. Arthur Aspinall, Royal Historical Society, Camden Third Series, LXV (London, 1941), Arbuthnot to Mrs. Arbuthnot, Nov. 6, 1820, p. 20.
78. HEH-STG, ST. 97, Buckingham's private diary, June 10 and 11, 1820.
79. NLW, Coedymaen Papers: 20, Buckingham to Wynn, Nov. 25, 1820; VIII/594, Wynn to Grenville, Nov. 12, 1820.
80. HEH-STG, ST. 97, Buckingham's private diary, Nov. 25, 1820; Leeds Papers, 26, Canning to his wife, Nov. 28, 1820; *Memoirs of George IV*, Thomas Grenville to Buckingham, Nov. 26, 1820, I, 80–81.
81. Great Britain, Historical Manuscripts Commission, Francis Bickley, ed., *Report on the Manuscripts of Earl Bathurst, Preserved at Cirencester Park* (London, 1923), Arbuthnot to Bathurst, Dec. 19, 1820, p. 491.
82. BRO, Fremantle Papers, 46, Buckingham to Fremantle, Dec. 24, 1820, and Jan. 14, 1821; NLW, Coedymaen Papers, 29, Wynn to Phillimore, Dec. 30, 1820.

The desire of Liverpool to avoid any immediate overture to Charles Wynn may have been directed in part by Wynn's known predilection for certain opposition measures, often expressed by parliamentary votes between 1817 and 1820. Actually, Wynn was not so pro-Whig as he was anti-Government, though he admitted in December, 1820, that if forced to choose between the Whigs and the Ministry he would pick the former. When the parliamentary session of 1821 began, William Fremantle complained that Wynn and his friend, Joseph Phillimore, were so decidedly disposed to the Opposition that "their minds are at all times on the alert to catch an opportunity of attacking the Government."[83] Buckingham, too, complained of Wynn's "half-Whig" principles.[84] But, like all Grenvilles, Charles Wynn was susceptible to the lure of governmental patronage, and the fact that he seldom voted for Whig-inspired motions during the 1821 parliamentary session may have had much to do with the suddenly improved prospects of his brother Henry, who desired to resume a diplomatic career interrupted after the battle of Jena in 1806. Both Liverpool and the Foreign Secretary, Lord Castlereagh, promised Buckingham and Henry Wynn that a diplomatic post would be found soon.[85]

The Liverpool Ministry was weakened after the fiasco of the Queen's affair. Powerful members of the Cabinet, like the Duke of Wellington, were anxious to receive the open approbation of Lord Buckingham and his connection.[86] The Prime Minister himself was fully conscious of the need to strengthen the Administration, but he leaned more toward a general and thorough ministerial overhaul than to a mere Grenvillite adherence. During the first six months of 1821, Liverpool courted W. C. Plunket with the Irish Attorney Generalship;[87] also, Frankland Lewis, a Welsh Grenvillite MP, accepted at £1,500 per annum the appointment of a parliamentary commissionership to inquire into the collection of the Irish revenue.[88] But still, despite Wellington's urgings, no overture was made to the senior members of the Grenvillite faction.

83. NLW, Coedymaen Papers, 29, Wynn to Phillimore, Dec. 21, 1820; *Memoirs of George IV,* Fremantle to Buckingham, Jan. 31, 1821, I, 115.

84. BRO, Fremantle Papers, 46, Buckingham to Fremantle, June 12, 1821.

85. BM, Liverpool Papers, Add. MSS. 38259: Buckingham to Liverpool, Feb. 27, 1821; Liverpool to Buckingham, Feb. 27, 1821 (copy). NLW, Henry Wynn Papers, 5/2793D, Buckingham to Henry Wynn, March 18 and 29, 1821.

86. *Memoirs of George IV,* Wellington to Buckingham: March 27, 1821, I, 144; April 2, 1821, I, 150. HEH-STG, ST. 97, Buckingham to Wellington, April 1 and 25, 1821.

87. *Memoirs of George IV:* Plunket to Buckingham, Dec. 3, 1821, I, 241–42; Wynn to Buckingham, n.d., I, 135–36.

88. BRO, Fremantle Papers, 51, Buckingham to Fremantle, June 1, 1821.

Finally, by June, 1821, Liverpool finalized his plans. On June 10 he wrote the King, telling him of his desire to retire Sidmouth from the Home Office with a £3,000 per annum pension and—if the King wished—a continued Cabinet position without office, and to then "connect with the Government those Individuals & Interests which form at present no part of it, but between which & the Government, there exists a general Coincidence of opinion on the great Principles of Domestic and Foreign Policy." His original plan envisioned George Canning (out of office since the previous autumn) at the Admiralty, Lord Melville at the Home Office, Wynn ("as the Representative of the Grenville connexion in the House of Commons") at the Board of Control, and Robert Peel (out of office since 1818) in some presently undefined situation.[89] The King demurred, ostensibly on the grounds of Sidmouth's demotion, but actually, as Londonderry (formerly Lord Castlereagh) pointed out, because of his distaste at including Queen Caroline's friend, George Canning, in his councils.[90] By June 15, however, Liverpool had resolved that the King must accept either the substance of his proposals or his resignation.[91] Indeed, the Cabinet had decided that the "touchstone" of the King's sincerity to his Ministry involved not his acceptance or rejection of Canning but of the Grenvilles. This reasoning, as reported by Charles Arbuthnot, Secretary to the Treasury, gives a good notion of ministerial estimates of the general importance of the faction. It was felt that a refusal to admit the Grenvilles would indicate a desire to keep a weak Ministry by prohibiting union with one of the necessarily chief sections of any alternative government. Thus, George could destroy his Ministry at will.[92] The only objection to a Grenvillite juncture, one observer reported, rested on the knowledge that the overture would involve giving Buckingham some inkling of the bad relations between King and Ministers, thus enabling him, if the offer were rejected, to injure the Government. However, it was felt with good reason that the "well-known avidity of the Grenvilles for power and office" made such a rejection highly unlikely.[93]

Liverpool, in deference to the King's desire to have Sidmouth accompany him as Home Secretary on his upcoming Irish tour, agreed in July to suspend temporarily the entire ministerial reshuffle until George's

89. BM, Liverpool Papers, Add. MSS. 38289, Liverpool to George IV, June 10, 1821 (copy).

90. Ibid.: 38190, George IV to Liverpool, June 11, 1821; 38289, Londonderry to Liverpool, n.d. (c. June 11, 1821).

91. Ibid., 38289, Liverpool to Arbuthnot, June 15, 1821.

92. *Correspondence of Arbuthnot,* Arbuthnot to Willimott, June 17, 1821, p. 24.

93. *The Diary of Henry Hobhouse, 1820–1827,* ed. Arthur Aspinall (London, 1947), p. 66.

return.[94] Liverpool informed Canning of the entire state of the affair, but Wellington gave William Fremantle only a hazy sketch of the problem. This failure in communication led Fremantle to advise Buckingham to hold himself "liberated from all connexions with the Government," and led Charles Wynn, according to Fremantle, to desire a junction with the Whigs.[95]

By October, with the Irish journey extended to Hanover, Liverpool felt that in all probability George would refuse to accept Canning and would then change his Ministers.[96] Canning himself discovered a way out of that impasse. Since rumors about London led Canning to believe that Lord Hastings (formerly Moira) intended to resign his Governor Generalship in India, he implied to the Prime Minister that his own appointment in India might prove an "escape" both for himself and for the King. Liverpool opened up discussions on the matter with Londonderry in Hanover and discovered the King not at all averse to that appointment. Thus, during the first week of November, Londonderry was able to give Liverpool assurances that George would not break up the Ministry.[97] Buckingham, who knew nothing of these decisions, was mortified by the long ministerial silence and contemplated connecting himself with either Canning or Lansdowne.[98]

On November 21, Wellington requested William Fremantle's presence in London at an interview with the Prime Minister and informed him that Liverpool was finally prepared to strengthen his Ministry. Sometime between November 25 and 28, Fremantle called upon Liverpool and received the general outline of the arrangement: India for Canning; Sidmouth's retirement; (probably) the Home Department for Peel; either the Board of Control or the Secretaryship at War with a Cabinet seat for Charles Wynn; the Attorney Generalship of Ireland for Plunket; a Board seat for another Grenvillite; the Swiss mission for Henry Wynn; and a Dukedom for Buckingham. Fremantle balked at the arrangement's failure to gratify Buckingham's desire for Ireland or the Admiralty.[99] On November 30, however, Buckingham met Liver-

94. BM, Liverpool Papers, Add. MSS. 38289, Liverpool to George IV, June 29, 1821 (copy).

95. Leeds Papers, 70, Liverpool to Canning, July 2, 1821; *Memoirs of George IV*, Fremantle to Buckingham, July 4, 1821, I, 172–75.

96. DRO, Sidmouth Papers, 152M, Liverpool to Sidmouth, Oct. 4, 1821.

97. Leeds Papers, 70: Canning to Liverpool, Oct. 8, 1821 (copy); Liverpool to Canning, Nov. 7 and 10, 1821.

98. BRO, Fremantle Papers, 46, Buckingham to Fremantle, Nov. 15 and 23, 1821.

99. *Memoirs of George IV:* Wellington to Fremantle, Nov. 21, 1821, I, 231; Fremantle's memorandum of his conversation with Liverpool, I, 232–35. NLW, Coedymaen Papers, 21, Buckingham to Wynn, Nov. 28, 1821.

pool, and the Marquis's lack of office proved no barrier. Before agreeing to the arrangement, however, Buckingham told the Prime Minister that he must consult Plunket and Wynn.[100]

Plunket's approbation presented no problem for Buckingham, but Charles Wynn's did. As part of the new Irish order, Liverpool intended the Chief Secretaryship for the extremely anti-Catholic Henry Goulburn, no doubt as a counterbalance to two pro-Catholics, the Marquis Wellesley as Lord Lieutenant and Plunket as Attorney General, and as part of his long and successful attempt to keep a balance within the Government on the Catholic question.[101] There was also a necessity to appease the right wing of his supporters, as Sidmouth wanted not Wellesley but Wellington sent to Ireland and, always the firm Protestant, was tormented by the thought that the Irish Government would soon be in the hands of pro-Catholics.[102] Yet, the presence of Goulburn as Chief Secretary taking orders from another anti-Catholic, Robert Peel, at the Home Office, coupled with Sidmouth's continuing Cabinet position without portfolio, formed the basis of the opposition of Charles Wynn and Lord Grenville to the junction.

Buckingham, desirous of his Dukedom, was only mildly perturbed at Sidmouth's intended status, which did, indeed, tilt the Cabinet balance toward the Protestants. He urged Wellesley to visit Dropmore to attempt to settle Lord Grenville's mind without, however, letting his uncle know his own responsibility for the visit.[103] Before Wellesley's visit, Londonderry met Buckingham and Wynn in London and was able to assure them that Sidmouth's remaining in the Cabinet was desired by his colleagues, as well as by the King, as a mark of respect.[104]

Lord Grenville's hesitations were not assuaged by these assurances; and, obviously looking for an excuse to prejudice his nephews, he took it as a gross insult to Charles Wynn that Liverpool took this moment to travel to Bath. He set out his views in a letter to Wynn that naturally vexed Buckingham and nearly caused Charles to break off the negotia-

100. HEH-STG, Box 168, memorandum of a conversation between Buckingham and Liverpool, Nov. 30, 1821.

101. BM, Liverpool Papers, Add. MSS. 38290, Goulburn to Liverpool, Nov. 26, 1821.

102. DRO, Sidmouth Papers, 152M: Sidmouth to Liverpool, Nov. 22, 1821; Sidmouth to Bathurst, Dec. 11, 1821.

103. BM, Liverpool Papers, Add. MSS. 38390, Arbuthnot to Liverpool, Dec. 5, 1821; BM, Wellesley Papers, Add. MSS. 37310, Buckingham to Wellesley, Dec. 3, 1821.

104. Charles Duke Yonge, *The Life and Administration of Robert Bankes, Second Earl of Liverpool, K.G., late First Lord of the Treasury* (London, 1868), Londonderry to Liverpool, Dec. 5, 1821, III, 159–60.

tions. The major point against acceptance of the overture was the Catholic question, Grenville argued, in light of Sidmouth's balance-upsetting position and the King's increasing anti-Catholicism, which made the passage of emancipation unlikely. As for Liverpool's absence in Bath, Grenville wondered how Wynn could go "alone" into a Cabinet without even meeting the Prime Minister, as that would involve "such a degradation of your situation, & claim to attention & respect as no man ever submitted to." If Buckingham wanted a Dukedom, let him take it, but this need not involve Wynn's acceptance of office.[105]

Wellesley arrived at Dropmore on December 8, and saw Grenville, Buckingham, and Wynn in separate interviews. His arguments evidently affected Wynn in a positive way, for on the following day Wynn again conversed with Londonderry and informally accepted the office, provided he would be free to allude in his acceptance letter to the Prime Minister to their policy differences.[106] In what was, after all, a rather unusual missive, which Londonderry urged Liverpool to accept with equanimity, Wynn criticized the appointment of Goulburn, avowed his freedom to resign on the Catholic question, and affirmed his option both to originate any Irish legislation and to announce publicly that his main reason for accepting office was to ameliorate the condition of the Irish Catholics.[107] Simultaneously, Buckingham also wrote Liverpool, notifying him that his cousin had accepted the offer made "to him, through me" and reminding the Prime Minister that Fremantle was to receive a seat at one of the Boards—preferably under Liverpool at the Treasury. He then requested, as the first of an ultimately long list of favors, that Fremantle likewise be admitted to the Privy Council.[108]

The patronage ambitions of the other Grenvillites remained. Plunket, of course, became the Attorney General of Ireland. Phillimore actually desired that the Government either turn out the Judge Advocate General in favor of himself or appoint him Judge of the Admiralty, of which neither position was forthcoming.[109] Wynn wrote the Prime Minister that he would be "mortified" if the individual

105. *Memoirs of George IV*, Grenville to Buckingham, Dec. 5, 1821, I, 245–46; NLW, Coedymaen Papers: 21, Buckingham to Wynn, Dec. 8, 1821; VI/350, Grenville to Wynn, Dec. 7, 1821.

106. BM, Liverpool Papers, Add. MSS. 38290, Sidmouth to Liverpool, Dec. 9, 1821; Yonge, *Life of Liverpool*, Londonderry to Liverpool, Dec. 9, 1821, III, 163–64.

107. *Memoirs of George IV:* Wynn to Buckingham, Dec. 13, 1821, I, 247–48; copy of Wynn's letter to Liverpool and the reply, I, 249–53.

108. BM, Liverpool Papers, Add. MSS. 38290, Buckingham to Liverpool, Dec. 14, 1821.

109. *Memoirs of George IV*, Phillimore to Buckingham, Dec. 13, 1821, I, 253–54.

"more closely connected with me in public life as well as private friendship than any other Member of the House of Commons" were not included in the arrangement. In late January, Joseph Phillimore was granted a seat at the Board of Control under Wynn.[110] Fremantle received an appointment to the Privy Council and, like Phillimore, went to the Board of Control rather than to the position he desired at the Treasury. Like the man in the parable who had worked for one day and received the same wages as the man who had worked for one hour, Fremantle was disappointed at finding himself getting equal treatment with Phillimore; and he told Buckingham, "I own I thought I was entitled to a little better berth than he was."[111]

Lord Grenville, in what Wynn told Liverpool was "the only point which he considers himself personally interested to obtain," wanted a United Kingdom peerage for Viscount Northland of Ireland, who, as Thomas Knox, had supported him since 1806. Liverpool promised Wynn that he would recommend Northland whenever he advised an advancement in the peerage on grounds of favor as opposed to public service. This promise, which was not to be fulfilled for five years, was not enough for Grenville, who continued throughout January, 1822, to press upon Wynn in the strongest terms his obligation to satisfy Northland's ambitions.[112] Perhaps Liverpool's negative attitude toward Grenville's sole request was considered by him a fit punishment for the Baron's sustained equivocal attitude toward the entire transaction; for Grenville had little justification for requesting anything, directly or indirectly, from Ministers.

As late as December 10, Liverpool assumed that Grenville's scruples would be overcome, especially if Plunket went to Ireland, and one of the chief inducements for the Grenvillite union in the first place was to effect a Pittite reunion topped with Government approbation by that prominent elder statesman.[113] On about December 9, after Wellesley had visited Dropmore, Wynn described his uncle as "deprived of sleep & . . . perfectly overcome this Morning by his anxiety on the subject." And Buckingham, whom Wynn described as an

110. BM, Liverpool Papers, Add. MSS. 38290, Wynn to Liverpool, Dec. 17 and 23, 1821.

111. *Memoirs of George IV:* Liverpool to Buckingham, Dec. 16, 1821, I, 255–56; Fremantle to Buckingham, Jan. 30, 1822, I, 281–82.

112. BM, Liverpool Papers, Add. MSS. 38290: Wynn to Liverpool, Dec. 17, 1821; Liverpool to Wynn, Dec. 18, 1821 (copy). NLW, Henry Wynn Papers, 6/2794D, Grenville to Wynn, Jan. 20, 1822; NLW, Coedymaen Papers, IX/618, Wynn to Grenville, Jan. 23, 1822.

113. DRO, Sidmouth Papers, 152M, Liverpool to Sidmouth, Dec. 10, 1821; BM, Huskisson Papers, Add. MSS. 38743, Binning to Huskisson, Dec. 10, 1821.

eager child of two about to receive a bauble, wrote "in such terms to one Uncle & spoke in such to the other that it required all their temper to prevent a breach."[114]

The acceptance of the overture by Wynn and Buckingham appears not in the least to have affected either uncle's negative view. But what was no doubt unforgivable from the standpoint of both the new Duke and the Ministers was the way in which the news leaked out that all was not easy within the Grenvillite ranks. Thomas Grenville wrote Lord Morpeth on December 22, informing him that he found Goulburn's appointment "detestable" and that "the two old uncles of Dropmore & Cleveland Square having retired from all publick business, have desired to decline any advise or interference whatever in these discussions, & have insisted with their nephews that they should absolutely decide for themselves in a matter where it is as difficult to advise as in a matrimonial connection . . . there is such a total want of vigour & foresight in the Ministers as to make one tremble to see one's friends in participation of their responsibility."[115] Within two days, whether from Morpeth or from another source, such as Sir John Newport, with whom Lord Grenville was in communication, Holland House received this exquisite piece of information regarding the elder Grenvilles; and, inevitably, during the first week of January the opposition press, both in London and in Buckinghamshire, was gleefully printing the outline of the dissatisfaction.[116]

In January, Lord Grenville urged Joseph Phillimore not to accept a seat at any of the Boards. Then, for the coup de grace, when Liverpool proposed to Grenville his desire to visit Dropmore, no doubt to receive the blessing of Pitt's old colleague, he received the somewhat chilling response that Grenville had retired from politics and that the Prime Minister's visit might be misconstrued by some.[117] That Grenville's attitude hurt Charles Wynn deeply is evident from his correspondence,[118] and it must have played a major role in the increasingly bad relationship between the Grenvillites and the Ministers once the juncture was effected. Liverpool had purchased, at not ungenerous and what some thought scandalous terms, the support of what he had

114. NLW, Coedymaen Papers, 12, Wynn to his wife, n.d.

115. Castle Howard Papers, Thomas Grenville to Morpeth, Dec. 22, 1821.

116. Leeds Papers, 65, Granville to Canning, Dec. 24, 1821; *Morning Chronicle* (London), Jan. 8, 1822; *Traveller* (London), Jan. 7, 1822; NLW, Coedymaen Papers, IX/625, Wynn to Grenville, n.d.

117. NLW, Coedymaen Papers, Grenville to Wynn: VI/355, Jan. 16, 1822; VI/356, Jan. 16, 1822.

118. NLW, Henry Wynn Papers, 6/4816D, Charles Wynn to Henry Wynn, May 6, 1822.

conceived to be the Grenville family; he must have suffered acute embarrassment to discover that the most noted elder statesman in England was not included in the package.

Opinions concerning the strength, importance, and desirability of the Grenvillite connection varied within governmental circles. Liverpool was conscious always of "reuniting with the Government the Grenville part of Mr. Pitt's original connection";[119] Londonderry, the Government leader in the Commons, worried about a neutral party running loose in the House;[120] the Canningites, Wellington, and even Sidmouth emphasized the secure votes and the impression of renewed strength that the Grenvillites would give the Ministry.[121] But while in general the leading Government politicians approved the juncture, a certain amount of resentment was inevitable over such a high-priced alliance. Two members of the Cabinet expressed disapproval: Lord Harrowby, the Lord President, on the grounds that Wynn was unqualified for his office and that Buckingham's elevation in the peerage would upset other ambitious Marquises, and Eldon, the Lord Chancellor, who hated coalitions.[122] In February, 1822, Lord Granville observed, "Everybody I meet, both adherents to, & opponents of, Ministers exclaim against the inordinate price paid for their junction."[123]

The Whig response was predictable. Lord Grey's opinion that it created in him "a disgust which it is impossible to express" was fairly typical.[124] A "great party" was held at Brooks's to celebrate the resignation of Buckingham and his cohorts from the Club.[125] Buckingham and the Duke of Bedford fought a duel when Bedford publicly adverted to a ministerial purchase of the faction.[126] On a less serious

119. Lewis Melville [Lewis Saul Benjamin], ed., *The Huskisson Papers* (London, 1931), Liverpool to Huskisson, Jan. 8, 1822, p. 132.

120. Yonge, *Life of Liverpool*, Dec. 6, 1821, III, 160–62; *The Journal of Mrs. Arbuthnot, 1820–1832*, ed. Francis Bamford and Gerald Wellesley, Seventh Duke of Wellington (London, 1950), I, 132–34.

121. PRO, Granville Papers, 30/29/8/6/284, Canning to Granville, Jan. 21, 1822; BM, Huskisson Papers, Add. MSS. 38743, Binning to Huskisson, Dec. 10, 1821; DRO, Sidmouth Papers, 152M, Sidmouth to Manners, Dec. 12, 1821; Leeds Papers, 65, Granville to Canning, Dec. 18, 1821.

122. Bickley, ed., H.M.C. *Bathurst*, Harrowby to Bathurst, Dec. 22, 1821, p. 525; Horace Twiss, *The Public and Private Life of Lord Chancellor Eldon, with Selections from His Correspondence* (London, 1844), Eldon to Lady F. J. Bankes, Jan. 14, 1822, II, 446.

123. Leeds Papers, 65, Granville to Canning, Feb. 7, 1822.

124. Durham Papers, Grey to Holland, Jan. 18, 1822.

125. John Cam Hobhouse, First Baron Broughton, *Recollections of a Long Life,* ed. Charlotte (Hobhouse) Carleton, Baroness Dorchester (6 vols,; New York, 1909–11), II, 179.

126. HEH-STG, Box 160, Bedford to Buckingham, April 25 and 29, 1822.

level, jokes about Buckingham's weight, Wynn's voice, and the dear-
ness of the juncture made the rounds of London society.[127] Lord
Darnley actually prepared a collection of English and Latin poems,
called "Buckinghamiana," of which the following stanzas about the
Duke of Buckingham and Chandos are illustrative.

> Two Dukes at once, and both in one!
>   Where has our Sovereign found such Merit?
> Is the new Duke then greater grown
>   Than old ones who the rank inherit?
> Unworthy of his high estate
>   The Devil still must have his due
> For though he is any thing but *great*
>   At least he's *big* enough for *Two*.[128]

The Whigs also coordinated a parliamentary attack upon the Grenvillite predominance at the Board of Control and Henry Wynn's salary
as Minister to the Swiss Cantons. Thomas Creevey, an ancient enemy of
all Grenvilles, in a speech which Sir James Mackintosh labeled as "full
of injustice & malignity but irresistibly droll & very sarcastic," labeled
"notorious" the fact that the Board was now in effect the preserve of one
particular family interest. To the great hilarity of the entire House (and
Mackintosh reported the ministerialists as "convulsed with Laugh-
ter"), Creevey wondered what would happen when Charles Wynn,
Joseph Phillimore, and William Fremantle got together to discuss a
Mahratta war or to send instructions to George Canning.[129] Henry
Wynn's position, scheduled at a yearly rate of £4,000, up 1,600 percent since 1791, raised numerous eyebrows among the economically
reform-minded.[130]

Thus, with poetry, jokes, duels, resignations from clubs, and parliamentary attacks, the social relationship of the Grenvillites and the
Whigs came to an end, or nearly so. Only one constant remained
virtually unchanged. Lady Holland worried that Thomas Grenville, a
still beloved figure in spite of his ducal nephew, might cease his
welcome attendance at her table. He assured her that she need not

127. Mackintosh, for example, heard that "the Grenvilles are bought by Weight"
and that in taking Charles Wynn, Ministers showed "they were resolved to have a
Squeak for it." BM, Mackintosh Papers, Add. MSS. 52445, Mackintosh's Journal, Feb.
4 and 20, 1822.
128. BM, Holland House Papers, Add. MSS. 51572, Darnley to Holland, Jan. 16
and Feb. 17, 1822.
129. *Parl. Debates*, N.S., VI (March 14, 1822), 1120–30; BM, Mackintosh Papers,
Add. MSS. 52445, Mackintosh's Journal, March 14, 1822.
130. *Parl. Debates*, N.S., VI (March 26, 1822), 1279–1309; VII: (May 15, 1822)
652–53, (May 16, 1822) 669–70.

concern herself; though he poignantly added, "perhaps I cannot see without some regret that the unbridled license of the party-language of these days should break in upon the harmony of private society, even for those who have long quitted publick life: but I . . . am most certainly always happy to meet such kind friends as you & Ld Holland."[131]

131. BM, Holland House Papers, Add. MSS. 51534, Thomas Grenville to Lady Holland, June 1, 1822.

[CHAPTER IX]

The End of the Grenvillite Faction, 1822–29

THE saga of Grenvillite politics after 1822 was one of rapid decline. Buckingham added eleven certain votes to Government strength in the House of Commons in 1822: Lord Chandos, William Fremantle, Thomas Knox, J. H. Leigh, Thomas Frankland Lewis, Scrope Bernard Morland, General Sir George Nugent, Joseph Phillimore, William Conyngham Plunket, Sir Watkin Wynn, and Charles Wynn. As was probably inevitable under the circumstances, Knox, Lewis, and especially Plunket, who was now carving out an independent position for himself as Attorney General of Ireland, all of whom were politically closer to Lord Grenville than to Buckingham, amalgamated quickly into the general body of "Tory" ministerial supporters, and there seems no reason to regard them any longer as connected in a special way with the Duke of Buckingham. A similar situation had occurred in the Grenvillite party after 1808, when many individuals who were originally attracted to opposition by the personality or politics of Lord Grenville found themselves drawn more and more into the Foxite Whig party. The Wynns were in a different position as first cousins to the Duke and intimately connected with him throughout a quarter century of past political activity. However, Buckingham quarreled and broke with the Wynns in 1825 and thereafter that family followed its own political line. Joseph Phillimore, always more oriented toward the Wynns than the Grenvilles, was not retained for his Grenville borough at the general election of 1826. William Fremantle, too, the Duke's oldest and closest friend, broke politically with him in 1827 and resigned as an MP. The Marquis of Chandos, the Duke's only child, opposed his father on the central political issue of the day—Catholic emancipation—and, indeed, after 1826 strove to raise the county and borough of Buckingham against his father's emancipationist politics. Of those Grenvillites who remained superficially attached to the Duke,

Bernard Morland was aged, ill, and ineffective both in politics and in his banking concerns; General Nugent rarely attended Parliament; and there was always some question whether in the last analysis the MPs for Winchester (J. H. Leigh and his successor Sir Edward Hyde East) followed the Duke or Chandos.

After January, 1822, relations between the Stowe Grenvilles and the Government were such that Lord Liverpool, the Prime Minister, must frequently have questioned his initial sagacity in courting the faction. Buckingham manifested the same conduct toward Liverpool that his father had exhibited toward Pitt thirty and forty years earlier—a steady flow of petty intrigues coupled with threats to withdraw support. Only a matter of days after Buckingham's adherence to Liverpool, the Duke of Wellington and his confidant Mrs. Arbuthnot speculated that an odd communication from him desiring a "confidential connexion" with the Wellesleys presaged treason to other Ministers.[1] Between the end of March and the middle of August, 1822, Buckingham on three occasions discussed the prospect of leaving Administration ranks. The first dissatisfaction arose out of a supposed slight he received from the King;[2] the second out of a failure to obtain Treasury patronage for his borough of St. Mawes;[3] and the third out of a desire to insure that a Catholic sympathizer succeeded Londonderry as leader of the Commons.[4] A year later he was complaining of ministerial neglect and accusing Liverpool of rudeness to his Buckingham borough member, General Nugent.[5] He was also angry at Lord Melville, the First Lord of the Admiralty, for refusing to grant a patronage request; and this event, coupled with dislike for Canning's Spanish policy, led to renewed talk of withdrawal of support and to a ducal refusal to attend Liverpool's dinner at the conclusion of the 1823 parliamentary session.[6] These actions, along with Lord Grenville's known lack of enthusiasm for the Administra-

1. *Despatches, Correspondence, and Memoranda of Field Marshal Arthur, Duke of Wellington, K.G.,* ed. Arthur Richard Wellesley, Second Duke of Wellington (8 vols.; London, 1867–80), Buckingham to Wellington, Dec. 19, 1821, I, 210; *The Journal of Mrs. Arbuthnot, 1820–1832,* ed. Francis Bamford and Gerald Wellesley, Seventh Duke of Wellington (London, 1950), I, 132–33.

2. BRO, Fremantle Papers, 46, Buckingham to Fremantle, March 31, 1822.

3. NLW, Coedymaen Papers, 22, Buckingham to Wynn, June 2, 1822; *Journal of Mrs. Arbuthnot,* I, 167.

4. *Memoirs of George IV,* Wynn to Buckingham, Aug. 20, 1822, I, 366; *The Diary of Henry Hobhouse, 1820–1827,* ed. Arthur Aspinall (London, 1947), pp. 94–95.

5. HEH-STG: ST. 95, Buckingham's Private Diary, Jan. 5 and 18, 1823; Box 182, Wynn to Buckingham, Jan. 28, 1823.

6. NLW, Coedymaen Papers, 23, Buckingham to Wynn, April 4 and 17, 1823; BRO, Fremantle Papers, 46, Buckingham to Fremantle, June 25, 1823.

tion, go far to explain the coolness and reserve that Charles Wynn, the new President of the Board of Control, found directed against him by Cabinet colleagues.[7]

The suicide of Lord Londonderry (the former Lord Castlereagh) in August, 1822, on the eve of George Canning's departure for India, provided the occasion for substantial embarrassment to Ministers from their Grenvillite allies. Despite the initial reluctance of George IV, Canning, who had yet to charm the King with his attentions, was the logical choice to succeed Londonderry as Foreign Minister and as leader of the House of Commons.[8] Should he remain in England, however, Canning not unnaturally desired to provide further for his closest political adherent, William Huskisson, a member of the Board of Trade and a Commissioner of Woods and Forests. Huskisson had long coveted Wynn's office. To accomplish such a goal, in September and October, 1822, Ministers divined plans either to send Wynn as Canning's successor to India[9] or to make him Speaker of the House of Commons.[10]

Buckingham's reaction to this was immediate and violent. He made clear to all concerned that if his cousin were to leave the Cabinet, unless he himself were granted the Admiralty or Ireland, he would withdraw support from the Government and would force his borough members, Joseph Phillimore and William Fremantle, to resign their posts at the Board of Control.[11] While the Prime Minister had no intention of giving Buckingham an efficient office, he briefly considered admitting him to the Cabinet without portfolio. The King, however, took the line that the Cabinet was already overcrowded and that nothing would ever satisfy the vanity of a man left unassuaged by the Garter and a Dukedom.[12]

When Wynn discovered that his close friend Phillimore might be forced from office, he was naturally reluctant to leave the Cabinet.[13] This, coupled with Buckingham's outburst, led to Wynn's increased

7. *Memoirs of George IV,* Wynn to Buckingham, July 15, 1822, I, 350–51.

8. Buckingham's first thought on hearing of Londonderry's tragedy was to canvass for Canning as his successor. *Despatches of Wellington,* Buckingham to Wellington, Aug. 20, 1822, I, 261–62.

9. NLW, Charles Wynn Papers, 6/4816D, Charles Wynn to Henry Wynn, n.d.; Leeds Papers, 67, Canning to Huskisson, Sept. 21, 1822 (copy).

10. Leeds Papers, 70, Canning to Liverpool, Sept. 14, 1822 (copy); *Memoirs of George IV,* Wynn to Buckingham, Sept. 23, 1822, I, 381–82.

11. NLW, Coedymaen Papers, 22, Buckingham to Wynn, Sept. 22 and Oct. 3, 1822; Leeds Papers, 70, Canning to Liverpool, Sept. 28, 1822; BRO, Fremantle Papers, 46, Buckingham to Fremantle, Sept. 16, 1822.

12. BM, Liverpool Papers, Add. MSS. 38411, fol. 83, Liverpool to George IV, n.d. (draft); *Journal of Mrs. Arbuthnot,* I, 194.

13. NLW, Coedymaen Papers, II/182, Wynn to Thomas Grenville, Oct. 4, 1822.

isolation among the Ministers.[14] He was not asked to normal Cabinet dinners; Canning was rude to him in the House of Commons; and Peel communicated with him only to the extent of avoiding a public break—though, as a result of a ministerial reshuffle in 1823, Huskisson was finally admitted to the Cabinet.[15]

While relations between Stowe and Downing Street were far from cordial after 1821, Lord Grenville, who had originally opposed the alliance with Liverpool, was coming to a more positive view of the Administration. After a fifteen-year personal estrangement, there was a rapprochement between Grenville and his old friend George Canning. Lord Grenville, unlike his ducal nephew, expressed a general approbation of the Foreign Secretary's controversial foreign policy.[16] In early 1823, Grenville was left a semiinvalid by a stroke; and in 1824 he sold his London home, with the result that his visits to the capital were less frequent.[17]

He continued to hold court at Dropmore, however, and one observer saw him acting the part of a ministerial oracle.[18] In December, 1823, the long delayed visit of the Prime Minister to Dropmore, the absence of which had caused such a furor two years earlier, finally took place.[19] Grenville's change in attitude toward the Ministry in part reflected its growing economic liberalism—though enough of his frequent patronage requests were requited to keep him in a good mood.[20] He encouraged Huskisson, now President of the Board of Trade, in his efforts to liberalize the Navigation Acts—only regretting that the restrictive system was not abolished altogether.[21] When his Whig nephew, Lord

14. Leeds Papers: 78A, Canning to Wynn, Oct. 6, 1822 (copy); 67, Huskisson to Canning, Oct. 8, 1822.

15. *Memoirs of George IV,* Wynn to Buckingham: n.d., I, 398; Oct. 27, 1823, II, 11–12. *Despatches of Wellington,* Buckingham to Wellington, May 28, 1823, II, 98–99.

16. Leeds Papers, 63: Grenville to Canning, April 6 and Aug. 23, 1822, July 24, 1823, and Dec. 27, 1826; Canning to Grenville, Sept. 20, 1822, and Jan. 29, 1825.

17. NLW, Charles Wynn Papers, 6/4816D, Charles Wynn to Henry Wynn, Feb. 24, 1823; *Correspondence of Charlotte Grenville, Lady Williams Wynn,* ed. Rachel Leighton (London, 1920), Lady Wynn to Henry Wynn, Jan. 14, 1824, pp. 304–5.

18. Josceline Bagot, ed., *George Canning and His Friends* (London, 1909), Lyttelton to Bagot, Oct. 18, 1822, II, 135–36.

19. Durham Papers, Essex to Grey, Dec. 25, 1823.

20. BM, Liverpool Papers, see for example, Add. MSS.: 38575, Grenville to Liverpool, Jan. 21, 1823; 38299, Grenville to Liverpool, Sept. 2, 1824; 38299, Liverpool to Grenville, Sept. 6, 1824 (copy); 38301, Grenville to Liverpool, June 16, 1826; 38301, Liverpool to Grenville, June 19, 1826 (copy).

21. BM, Huskisson Papers, Add. MSS.: 38745, Grenville to Wynn, March 8, 1824, and Wynn to Huskisson, March 8, 1824; 38746, Grenville to Huskisson, April 27, 1825.

Ebrington, asked his aid in an electoral contest in 1824, Grenville refused on the grounds that the Administration, "as *now* conducting itself, has on most points, (certainly not on all,) my concurrence, & good opinion."[22]

Buckingham's relations with the two most important members of his connection, his cousin Charles Wynn and his son the Marquis of Chandos, displayed the same increasing irritability as did his relations with Ministers. The Duke's confidence in Wynn's judgment was always marginal after 1817, when Charles took a decidedly more whiggish attitude in Parliament than Buckingham. This disenchantment took on increasingly personal overtones after 1822. The Duke's constant complaint involved Wynn's failure to communicate with him frequently enough, for, like his father vis-à-vis Lord Grenville, Buckingham expected almost daily letters full of confidential information from one whom he considered his representative in the Cabinet.[23] Buckingham was also occasionally angered by Wynn's failure to provide Indian patronage for his favorites.[24]

His relationship with the Marquis of Chandos was more complicated. Richard Plantagenet Temple Nugent Brydges Chandos Grenville (1797–1861), after 1839 second Duke of Buckingham and Chandos, emerged during the 1830s and 1840s as one of the leaders of the Tory right. To the more liberal members of his family he was a somewhat unsavory figure, the defender of game laws and slavery; and Lord Grenville once observed that he caricatured the faults of his father as his father had caricatured those of the first Marquis of Buckingham.[25] His upbringing evidently left much to be desired, as his great-uncle Thomas Grenville spoke of the low and debauched company he kept as a youth, and his cousin Charles Wynn remarked on his self-conceit and adolescent lack of moral control.[26] He entered Parliament for Bucks at the general election of 1818, and in 1819 married the Lady Mary Campbell, youngest daughter of the Earl of Breadalbane.

22. DRO, Fortescue Papers, 1262M/FC81, Grenville to Ebrington, Dec. 27, 1824.

23. BRO, Fremantle Papers, Buckingham to Fremantle: 46, March 12 and Sept. 16, 1822; 48, June 27, 1825.

24. NLW, Coedymaen Papers, 23, Buckingham to Wynn, Feb. 11, 1823; HEH-STG, Box 182, Wynn to Buckingham, Feb. 13, 1823.

25. NLW, Henry Wynn Papers, 12/2800D, Charles Wynn to Henry Wynn, May 18, 1846; *Parl. Debates, N.S.,* VIII (April 28, 1823), 1297. For the best current account of the career of the second Duke of Buckingham and Chandos, see David Spring, "Lord Chandos and the Farmers, 1818–1846," *Huntington Library Quarterly,* XXXIII, No. 3 (1970), pp. 257–81.

26. *Dropmore,* Thomas Grenville to Lord Grenville, Dec. 10, 1816, X, 416; NLW, Henry Wynn Papers, 12/2800D, Charles Wynn to Henry Wynn, May 18, 1846.

There was precious little domestic harmony at Stowe or the Chandos estate of Avington during the decades following the death of the first Marquis of Buckingham. The Duke and Duchess were on far from good terms, a resentment no doubt aggravated by the possibility that Buckingham may have committed adultery with his cousin, Louisa Hardy.[27] In 1829, when Buckingham returned from nearly three years in Italy, the Duchess denied him her bed.[28] Neither the Duke nor the Duchess liked their daughter-in-law, Lady Chandos.[29] Chandos himself was not a faithful husband; and he and his wife, whose marital problems were already in progress in 1821, were divorced in 1850.[30] Some of the tension between the Duke and Duchess of Buckingham arose from differing viewpoints on the Catholic question. Both individuals had had Roman Catholic mothers, a factor that appears to have strengthened the Duke's commitment to emancipation but to have developed in the Duchess a literal horror of papists.[31] The Duchess passed her aversion to Catholicism on to her only child; and during the late 1820s Chandos emerged, to the chagrin of the Grenvilles and especially of his father, as an ultra-Protestant.

The years between 1823 and 1826 brought a general revamping of the Grenvillite faction toward a more Stowe-oriented position. J. H. Leigh, the Duchess of Buckingham's uncle, resigned his Winchester seat in February, 1823, and was succeeded by Sir Edward Hyde East (1764–1847), a Jamaican landlord, an old Indian hand, a lifelong friend of the Duchess of Buckingham, and an individual without any of the Foxite-whiggish connections possessed by so many of the former Grenvillites.[32] Until 1831 East sat at Winchester, suspected by some to be a "creature" of the Duchess and Chandos; while in reality, as one of the terms of his acceptance of the borough, he had agreed to vote in favor of Catholic emancipation.[33] To East's unhappy lot during the late 1820s fell the attempt to mediate the frequent arguments between the Duke, the Duchess, and Chandos. Buckingham's relations with one of his MPs for St. Mawes, Joseph Phillimore, had long been sour; and long

27. San Marino, California, Henry E. Huntington Library, Stowe-O'Conor Papers, 63, Lady Arundel to O'Conor, Oct. 1, 1815 (hereinafter referred to as HEH-STO).

28. HEH-STG, Box 11, Buckingham to his wife, May 4, 1832.

29. Ibid.: ST. 95, Buckingham's Private Diary, June 10, 1823; Box 340, Lady Chandos to the Duchess, n.d.

30. Ibid., Box 325, Temple to Lady Temple, thirty-seven letters, 1821.

31. *The Journal of the Hon. Henry Edward Fox, 1818–1830*, ed. Giles Stephen Holland Fox-Strangeways, Sixth Earl of Ilchester (London, 1923), pp. 309–11.

32. *The Assembled Commons, 1836: An Account of Each Member of Parliament* (London, 1836).

33. BRO, Fremantle Papers, 46, Buckingham to Fremantle, Feb. 18, 1823.

before his break in 1825 with Phillimore's friend, Charles Wynn, he had determined not to return him at a subsequent general election.[34] Thus, in 1826, Phillimore came in for Yarmouth instead; and in his place Buckingham brought in his Buckinghamshire neighbor, Sir Codrington Edmund Carrington (1769–1849), a former law officer in India and a conservative on issues involving civil liberties.[35] As a condition of his acceptance, Carrington agreed to support Catholic emancipation and to resign over any political difference with his patron.[36]

The chief event responsible for the effective breakup of the Grenvillite faction as it had existed in one form or another since the 1780s was the dispute between Buckingham and the Government over the Duke's desire to replace Lord Amherst as Governor General of India. The initial misfortunes surrounding the Burmese war in 1824 and 1825 and the mutiny of Bengal sepoys at Barrackpore in 1824 served to lower Amherst's reputation at home with the Court of Directors, the Board of Control, and Ministers in general. Buckingham, writing to Wynn in March, 1825, confided that only *"one vigorous mind"* was wanting in India, though he did not reveal to his cousin the identity of the remarkable individual he proposed.[37] It was thus with a sense of shock that Wynn received a preposterous communication from the Duke on July 8, 1825, in which he proposed himself for the situation, that he might "settle your frontiers in Peace." Several weeks later Wynn was horrified to discover that the Duke's son, Lord Chandos, had actually approached Amherst's friend, the Foreign Secretary, George Canning, who could barely conceal his disgust at Buckingham's general conduct, to canvass for his support. Canning made polite small talk; and the Duke, as usual, transformed his expressions of good will into definite commitments and conceived without reason that Canning had "hinted at no competition" and had "distinctly *promised me his support* whenever a vacancy should take place."[38] Liverpool, too, was informed of the intrigue in early August and refused to commit herself beyond affable and meaningless pleasantries.[39]

Liverpool must have wondered what was afoot, as Charles Wynn had made no secret to him of his intense dislike of his cousin's application,

34. Ibid., 51, Buckingham to Fremantle, March 27, 1823.

35. JRL, Carrington Papers, 1/2, Buckingham to Carrington, Dec. 22, 1819.

36. Ibid., 1/6a, Buckingham to Carrington, Sept. 20, 1825.

37. NLW, Coedymaen Papers, 25A, Buckingham to Wynn, March 30, 1825.

38. Ibid., 25B: Buckingham to Wynn, July 8 and 31, 1825; Wynn to Buckingham, Aug. 1, 1825 (copy). Leeds Papers, 99B, Canning to Buckingham, Aug. 4, 1825.

39. NLW, Coedymaen Papers, 25B, Liverpool to Buckingham, Aug. 7, 1825 (copy).

ostensibly because the Indian climate posed a potential health hazard for the overweight peer, and had asked to be excluded from the decision-making process that surrounded the appointment of a new Governor General.[40] Although by the end of September the Prime Minister was persuaded of the necessity to recall Amherst, he thought Sir Thomas Munro, an old hand at Indian affairs, would be a far more suitable successor than the "fat Duke."[41]

By this stage the Duke was declaiming in all directions his distrust of Wynn's vigor on the matter and his intention to withdraw support from Ministers if the Governor Generalship were not forthcoming.[42] Inevitably, the press got wind of the situation. On September 30, with Liverpool spending a month at Walmer Castle, both Canning and Wynn, in that order, were scheduled for a Windsor audience with the King. Apparently neither man had any intention to bring up the subject of Amherst's recall or Buckingham's succession to the post, but at the first meeting George IV himself mentioned to Canning a newspaper report of a ship being readied at Portsmouth to carry Buckingham to India. At Wynn's audience, too, the subject was raised. The King expressed acquiescence, or certainly raised no objections, at seeing the Duke succeed Amherst.[43]

Since at this point Amherst's recall appeared inevitable, Canning and Wynn seem to have decided upon a plan according to which Wynn, in the presence of Canning, would informally propose Buckingham as Amherst's successor at the upcoming meeting of the "chairs" (the Chairmen of the East India Company) on Monday, October 3.[44] Wynn later maintained that he thought Canning had received the approval of Lord Liverpool for this course of action; and, indeed, Canning (if he was himself aware) may well have failed to enlighten him as to the exact stance of the Prime Minister.[45] Still, it is difficult to sympathize overly with Wynn's predicament, as he was employing a type of intrigue that begs to be discovered. He was under no illusion that the "chairs" would accept Buckingham, but he intended to propose him anyway and then fall back upon Sir Thomas Munro when the inevitable veto occurred. That course of action would at least satisfy the Duke as to his own motives.[46] After his Windsor audience, Wynn penned Buckingham a

40. BM, Liverpool Papers, Add. MSS. 38412, Wynn to Liverpool, Aug. 7, 1825.

41. Leeds Papers, 99B, Liverpool to Canning, Sept. 29, 1825.

42. BRO, Fremantle Papers, 46, Buckingham to Fremantle, Sept. 20, 1825.

43. *Journal of Mrs. Arbuthnot,* I, 433–34; NLW, Coedymaen Papers, 34, 1826 memorandum of Canning on the Indian affair (copy).

44. Leeds Papers, 99B, Canning to Liverpool, Oct. 1, 1825.

45. NLW, Coedymaen Papers, 26, Wynn to Liverpool, Oct. 9, 1825 (copy).

46. Ibid., 12, Wynn to his wife, n.d.

quick note that was a model of dissimulation and that he probably regretted sending for the remainder of his life.

> I trust that it will gratify you to know that it is determined to do all that the Government can, to give effect to your wishes and that you will therefore be proposed on Monday to the Chairman & Deputy Chairmen by Canning & myself—Ld. Liverpool having to day left town—to this the King has fully assented though he expressed much surprise at your determination. May God preserve you to dispose the Event of this whatever it may be to your health, honor, & comfort—I am most anxious to see you either tomorrow or on Sunday, to talk of the best means of success & of the course to be adopted in different events. [47]

Had events taken place as Wynn foresaw, all might have been well, at least with regard to his own position in Buckingham's affections. However, on October 2, the day before the proposed soundings on the nomination, Wellington, who had a more favorable perspective on the Burmese war than his contemporaries, arrived in London and put a quick stop to any Government-sponsored activity to recall Amherst. Therefore, when Wynn and Canning met the "chairs" on October 3, it was with the successful intention of persuading them to temporarily suspend recall proceedings. [48] Wynn was then put in the uncomfortable position of having to own up to the indiscretion contained in his letter of September 30 to the Duke of Buckingham. [49]

In this action he had no allies; Canning, of course, who may have been playing Wynn false—the evidence is not entirely clear—blamed Wynn entirely for the fiasco, [50] as also did Liverpool. The Prime Minister was adamant in his denial that he had ever authorized Buckingham's name to be brought forward in the matter. [51] Buckingham, of course, thought he had been betrayed. [52] Strangely, the only support received by Wynn during this trying time was from William Fremantle, his old bête noire within the Grenvillite group, who not only fully sympathized with his predicament and wrote to tell him so, but also agreed with him that the best way to end Buckingham's foolish pretensions was to have them rejected by the "chairs." Fre-

47. Ibid., 34, Wynn to Buckingham, Sept. 30, 1825 (copy).

48. Leeds Papers, 99B, Canning to Wynn, Oct. 2, 1825 (copy); BM, Liverpool Papers, Add. MSS. 38193, Canning to Liverpool, Oct. 3, 1825.

49. BM, Liverpool Papers, Add. MSS. 38412, Wynn to Liverpool, Oct. 4, 1825.

50. Leeds Papers, 99B, Canning to Liverpool, Oct. 6 and 14, 1825 (copies); BRO, Fremantle Papers, 46, Buckingham to Fremantle, Oct. 30, 1825.

51. *Despatches of Wellington*, Liverpool to Wellington: Oct. 6, 1825, II, 514–15; Oct. 17, 1825, II, 544.

52. BRO, Fremantle Papers, 46, Buckingham to Fremantle, Oct. 30, 1825.

mantle also told Chandos outright that Canning was attempting to drive a wedge between Buckingham and Wynn "to get rid of the Grenvilles altogether."[53]

To make matters worse, Liverpool, under Wellington's proddings, was forced to tell the Duke of Buckingham that, even if Amherst were recalled, Sir Thomas Munro and not he was the designated successor.[54] Persevering as ever, Buckingham took this to mean that such a bar was only operative while the war continued. Thus, Liverpool was forced to again write the Duke that, even if India were "in a state of Profound Peace," if his nomination had taken place as scheduled and the "chairs" had raised no objections, these circumstances still would not commit the Government to acceptance.[55]

Throughout late October and November, 1825, the Court of Directors frequently expressed its lack of confidence in Amherst.[56] Finally, at a Cabinet meeting in early December, after the Court had unanimously proposed Munro as Amherst's successor, a firm agreement was reached to continue the Governor General in his post and to force the Court, if it disagreed, to exercise its legal right to recall him.[57] The Directors had no intention of doing this in the face of governmental displeasure, and the matter was dropped, leaving Buckingham no other option but to retire gracefully from the scene. That, however, was not his way.

In December, the Duke demanded of Wynn that he make the issue of his Indian designs a "Vital Question" in the Cabinet and threatened, if he should refuse, to inform the King and Liverpool that the Grenville-Wynn alliance was at an end, leaving the Duke free to form fresh connections.[58] By this point, the Duke, nearly insane with dark suspicions and unfounded optimism, believed Wynn was intriguing with Lord Wellesley against his Indian objects[59] and, simultaneously, that he was about to be offered a Cabinet seat or the Lord Lieutenancy of

53. Ibid., memorandum of a conversation between Chandos and Fremantle, Nov. 1, 1825. The Duke of Wellington and Mrs. Arbuthnot likewise distrusted Canning's motives. *Journal of Mrs. Arbuthnot,* II, 9–10.

54. NLW, Coedymaen Papers, 26: Wellington to Liverpool, Oct. 10, 1825 (copy); Liverpool to Buckingham, Oct. 13, 1825 (copy).

55. NLW, Coedymaen Papers, 25B: Buckingham to Wynn, Oct. 19, 1825; Liverpool to Buckingham, Oct. 24, 1825 (copy).

56. Ibid., 12, Wynn to his wife, n.d., and Nov. 17, 1825; BM, Liverpool Papers, Add. MSS. 38412, Wynn to Liverpool, Nov. 21, 1825.

57. NLW, Charles Wynn Papers, 6/4816D, Charles Wynn to Henry Wynn, Dec. 13, 1825.

58. Ibid., IX/706, Wynn to Grenville, Dec. 19, 1825.

59. Actually, Wynn was hoping that if Wellesley went to India, Buckingham would succeed him in Ireland. BM, Liverpool Papers, Add. MSS. 38756, Liverpool to Wynn, Jan. 2, 1826.

Ireland.[60] Unrequited in his desire, on December 27 the Duke sent George IV all those documents on the Indian question that reflected well upon him; but he omitted, as Liverpool quickly pointed out to the King, those papers that showed him in a less favorable light.[61] In reaction, both Wynn and Canning, after reading the Duke's account, wrote long self-serving versions of their own and presented them to the King.[62] George's decided judgment denied any ducal complaint against the Ministers and also slapped Wynn's wrist for disclosing the transactions of a royal audience to a person not in the Cabinet.[63]

For the next three years, Buckingham's conduct exhibited little political or personal stability and by 1829 had led most of his contemporaries to disregard the Grenvillites as a political force. In early January, 1826, he struck out again in all directions, asking Plunket to cease communicating with him on the Irish question through Wynn[64] and hinting that Fremantle should resign from the Board of Control.[65] Then, in his normal fashion, he made a volte-face in February and March, telling Fremantle he had decided not to withdraw support from Ministers and even achieving a short-lived personal reconciliation, promoted by his uncles and brother, with Charles Wynn.[66] Buckingham remarked to Wynn: "Let us then row our separate boats, assisting each other if we can, whilst we ore in Company, but not necessarily engaged to steer the same course, in the same track, or to carry the same sail."[67] To Fremantle, however, Buckingham was quite clear; he wrote: "I consider the engagement of 1821 as at an end, and the connexion between the Government and myself as over, *through Wynn*. Whether it is to continue under any other shape will depend upon the conduct of Government towards me."[68] Indeed, the sores of the past year burned too hotly for Buckingham to forget—especially with Chandos continuing to inflame him against the entire Wynn family.[69] By November,

60. BRO, Fremantle Papers, 46, Buckingham to Fremantle, Dec. 27, 1825.

61. NLW, Coedymaen Papers, 34, Buckingham to the King, Dec. 27, 1825 (copy); *The Letters of King George IV, 1812–1830*, ed. Arthur Aspinall (Cambridge, 1938), Liverpool to the King, Dec. 28, 1825, III, 132–33.

62. Grenville saw no material difference between the accounts of Wynn and Canning. NLW, Coedymaen Papers, 34, Grenville to Wynn, Feb. 9, 1826.

63. NLW, Coedymaen Papers, 34, George IV to Liverpool, March 9, 1826 (copy).

64. NLI, Plunket Papers, PC920, Buckingham to Plunket, Jan. 1, 1826.

65. BRO, Fremantle Papers, 46, Fremantle to Buckingham, Jan. 12, 1826 (copy).

66. Ibid.: 46, Buckingham to Fremantle, Feb. 5, 1826; NLW, Coedymaen Papers, 27: Nugent to Buckingham, March 14, 1826 (copy); Buckingham to Wynn, March 24, 1826.

67. NLW, Coedymaen Papers, 27, Buckingham to Wynn, April 2, 1826.

68. BRO, Fremantle Papers, 46, Buckingham to Fremantle, April 5, 1826.

69. HEH-STG, Box 330, Chandos to Buckingham, May 24, 1826.

1826, the two cousins were again quarreling over an alleged debt of honor, which the Duke supposed Wynn owed to him, to restore good will with Liverpool. Wynn denied any such obligation, and the cousins did not communicate again for a number of years.[70]

The attempts of William Fremantle to maintain neutrality between Wynn and Buckingham occasioned his first major disagreement with the Duke in over forty years of personal and political association. During October, 1825, when the Duke and Chandos were busy canvassing the Court of Directors, Fremantle was in Brighton. On October 20, Buckingham coolly ordered him to attend the London canvass and informed him that he must make a political choice between Charles Wynn, his chief at the Board of Control, and himself, his parliamentary patron.[71] Five days later, Fremantle was still in Brighton, denying any personal influence over the Court of Directors, and reminding the Duke of his long years of devotion to the Grenville family.[72] At a meeting with Chandos on November 1, Fremantle was adamant both in his approbation of Wynn's conduct and in his refusal to canvass, an activity against Amherst that he regarded dishonorable while sitting at the Board of Control. Perhaps realizing their need for allies, both the Duke and his son accepted Fremantle's position for the moment.[73]

Fremantle continued to press Wynn's innocence on the Duke, and by the spring of 1826 Chandos was abusing Fremantle to his father for disloyalty to the Stowe Grenvilles and maintaining that the Fremantles "have to serve *their own interests,* without considering the objects or the policy of *their friends.*"[74] When Liverpool offered Fremantle the Treasurership of the Household on May 1, he accepted and resigned his office at the Board of Control; but he had no desire to relinquish Buckingham borough. Chandos and Buckingham at least toyed with the idea of not returning him at the general election later that May; they agreed to do so only after Fremantle made a definite promise to yield the seat if the Duke should separate completely from the Government.[75]

70. NLW, Coedymaen Papers, 27: Buckingham to Wynn, Nov. 12, 1826; Buckingham to Mrs. Wynn, Nov. 19, 1826.

71. Ibid., 18, Fremantle to Wynn, Oct. 11, 1825; BRO, Fremantle Papers, 46, Buckingham to Fremantle, Oct. 20, 1825.

72. BRO, Fremantle Papers, 46, Fremantle to Buckingham, Oct. 25, 1825.

73. Ibid., memorandum of a conversation between Chandos and Fremantle, Nov. 1, 1825; NLW, Coedymaen Papers, 18, Fremantle to Wynn, Nov. 8, 1825.

74. *Memoirs of George IV,* Fremantle to Buckingham, Dec. 17, 1825, II, 288; HEH-STG, Box 330, Chandos to Buckingham, n.d., and May 5, 1826.

75. BRO, Fremantle Papers: 48, Liverpool to Fremantle, May 1, 1826; 46, Fremantle to Buckingham, May 27, 1826. HEH-STG, Box 330, Chandos to Buckingham, May 24, 1826.

When Buckingham opposed Canning's Administration in 1827, Fremantle fulfilled his promise. With his stacks of sinecures and offices, Fremantle was one of the canniest courtiers of the period; his long years of friendship with sovereigns, from George III to Victoria, and with politicians, from Lord Grenville to Sir Robert Peel, bespeaks an ability to survive, prosper, and accommodate to changing situations. His refusal to espouse Buckingham's line from 1825 to 1827 is as good an indication as any of the Duke's slipping prestige.

Throughout the Indian crisis, Buckingham remained convinced that a majority of the Court of Directors—sixteen out of twenty-four, Chandos told him—were favorably disposed to his appointment as Amherst's successor.[76] Others concerned with the issue, who were by no means out of touch with the sentiments of the Court—Liverpool, Wynn, Wellington, and Fremantle—were equally certain that the Court would never accept him.[77] The Duke was certainly mistaken on some of his information regarding the Court. He thought that Campbell Majorbanks, the Chairman of the East India Company in 1825, was on intimate terms with Fremantle and often dined with him. In reality, Fremantle had never held private communication with Majorbanks.[78] When in December, 1825, the Court of Directors unanimously recommended Munro to succeed Amherst, Charles Wynn was rather amused at the Duke's fancy that "he had so large a party in the Court that he could carry his nomination agst. the Govt."[79] Some of the Directors who legitimately desired Amherst's recall possibly envisioned that the more hostility was raised against him and the more his successor was discussed the better. Yet, it seems obvious also that a number of Buckingham's friends, as well as his son, saw it in their interest throughout 1826 to encourage his Indian hopes long after they held any rational prospect of success.[80]

The purity of Chandos's motives is certainly suspect with regard to

76. NLW, Coedymaen Papers, 25B, Buckingham to Wynn, Oct. 7, 1825.

77. Ibid.: Coedymaen Papers, 26, Liverpool to Wynn, Oct. 13, 1825; Charles Wynn Papers, 6/4816D, Charles Wynn to Henry Wynn, Dec. 13, 1825. *Journal of Mrs. Arbuthnot*, I, 418; BRO, Fremantle Papers, 46, Fremantle to Buckingham, Dec. 15, 1825 (copy).

78. BRO, Fremantle Papers, 46: Buckingham to Fremantle, Oct. 20, 1825; Fremantle to Buckingham, Oct. 25, 1825.

79. NLW, Charles Wynn Papers, 6/4816D, Charles Wynn to Henry Wynn, Dec. 13, 1825.

80. *Memoirs of George IV*, Ward to Buckingham, Jan. 7, 1826, II, 196; HEH-STG: Box 330, Chandos to Buckingham, April 28, May 12 and 15, 1826; Box 157, East to Buckingham, May 13 and 16, 1826.

the Indian affair, and the Duke himself was privately questioning them by April, 1827.[81] His object appears to have been, if possible, to send his father off to India or, in lieu of that, to destroy his relationships with the pro-Catholic members of his circle, so that he might then push his own anti-Catholic line. Chandos poisoned the Duke's susceptible mind not only against Phillimore, Wynn, and Fremantle but also against Lord Grenville, who he charged had directed Wynn's conduct and had received accolades from the Government as the *real* leader of the Grenvillites.[82]

By June, 1826, Buckingham no longer had any representatives in office. Fremantle had resigned from the Board of Control and all ducal connection with Wynn and Phillimore was ended. In November, Buckingham received no invitation from Liverpool for the annual dinner for ministerial supporters.[83] The Duke, who evidently had no realization that his political power was slipping away, in late 1826 indulged in the pathetic daydream that Canning would soon attempt an alliance with him; and in early 1827 he actually opened unsuccessful communications with Frederick Robinson, Chancellor of the Exchequer, to engage him to replace Wynn as his "especial link of connection" with the Administration.[84] When Buckingham heard well-founded rumors that Amherst intended to return to England in 1828, he wrote Liverpool for the last time on February 8, 1827, requesting the Indian succession. Two days later he received the chilling response that "it is not in my power to be in any way instrumental towards forwarding your Grace's wishes with respect to the Govt. of India."[85]

Liverpool's stroke on February 17, 1827, which resulted in his political eclipse (and his death a year later), precipitated a chaotic political period that lasted for at least a year and opened a power vacuum at the center of politics which Buckingham intended to use to his full advantage. For nearly half a century, the Grenvilles had turned similar situations to their benefit. Buckingham initially urged Wellington to rally the Tory party, to settle the Catholic question, and to send him to Ireland or India. When such a prospect proved unfruitful, the Duke

81. HEH-STG, ST. 98, Buckingham's Private Diary, April 4, 1827.

82. Ibid., Box 330, Chandos to Buckingham, May 6 and 8, 1826.

83. NLW, Coedymaen Papers, 18; Fremantle to Wynn, Nov. 7, 1826.

84. BRO, Fremantle Papers, 46, Buckingham to Fremantle, Dec. 28, 1826; BM, Hardwicke Papers, Add. MSS. 45038, East to Yorke, Feb. 7 and 27, 1827.

85. Leeds Papers, 78A, Wynn to Canning, Feb. 3, 1827; HEH-STG, Box 168, Buckingham to Grace, Feb. 8, 1827; BRO, Fremantle Papers, 46, Liverpool to Buckingham, Feb. 10, 1827 (copy).

wrote Bathurst, who he incorrectly surmised would soon be at the Treasury, requesting India and promising, without a trace of irony, the "same connexion of mutual support . . . which united me with the late Government."[86] In March, Buckingham was again writing Wellington and urging him to form a mixed Government excluding Canning; at about the same time, he approached Lord Lauderdale to discuss the possibility of his entering into an opposition.[87]

When Canning was asked by the King on April 10 to form a Ministry and Eldon, Wellington, Peel, Melville, Westmoreland, Bathurst, and Bexley resigned their offices, Buckingham believed his hour had finally come. He pathetically thought: "Canning *cannot afford* to cast me off and to lose the strength which I can give him. I therefore may make my own terms. If he refuses, then I can fall back upon Melville & Londonderry, and aid an Opposition which without me will be very strong, and with me will be so powerful that he cannot stand against it."[88] When the Duke contacted the new Prime Minister, however, Canning had what must have been enormous pleasure in refusing categorically any of his Indian aspirations, in denying that his appointment would be of *"immense public advantage"* as the Duke believed, and in maintaining: "I hope I will not give offense to your Grace . . . when I say . . . I am of opinion that your Grace is not the 'fittest' Choice for the Government of India that might be made at the present moment."[89]

Buckingham, stung to the quick, immediately vowed to enter an opposition, requested Fremantle's resignation from Buckingham borough, and told his brother, Lord Nugent, that any member of the Grenville family who maintained a friendly relationship with Charles Wynn, whom Canning retained at the Board of Control, was no longer his friend. Fremantle, at least, felt sorrow at the Duke's humiliation; he remarked: "The real truth is that he has so destroyed his Interest & Power, by all the detestable Intrigues he has been working thro' Underling's, and is so misinformed & prejudiced by the rash and absurd conduct of Lord Chandos, that he is now left without an Union, political or Personal: He has to fall back on four Votes in Parliament, for

86. Arthur Aspinall, ed., *The Formation of Canning's Ministry, February to August, 1827*, Royal Historical Society, Camden Third Series, Vol. LIX (London, 1937): Buckingham to Wellington, Feb. 21, 1827, pp. 10–11; Wellington to Buckingham, Feb. 22, 1827, p. 12; Buckingham to Bathurst, Feb. 26, 1827, p. 27.

87. *Despatches of Wellington*, Buckingham to Wellington, March 20, 1827, III, 611–12; Aspinall, ed., *Canning's Ministry*, Tierney to Bagot, May 1, 1827, pp. 205–6.

88. HEH-STG, ST. 98, Buckingham's Private Diary, April 11, 1827.

89. Aspinall, ed., *Canning's Ministry*, Canning to Buckingham, April 13, 1827, pp. 71–72.

Sir Edwd East belongs to the Dss & Ld. Chandos who take care to let him know this. I really & sincerely pity the Duke."[90]

During May, 1827, without consulting his father, Chandos joined Peel, and during this season the Duchess was likewise urging her husband to join the Tories. The Duke claimed that Peel's anti-Catholic principles forbade a union.[91] Probably the real reason for Buckingham's reluctance to join Peel stemmed not from principles but from the notion, incredible in the light of his past relationship with the new Prime Minister, that he would shortly be offered Ireland. While in April he had insisted on opposition, in May he informed his Commons members to hold off from voting and, above all, not to sit with Chandos in the House. He likewise told his two uncles, both of whom were on excellent terms with Canning, that he "was very desirous out of respect for their feelings to join the Govt."[92] Nothing, of course, came of the Irish plans, and by the middle of June the Duke, principles or no principles, was considering an alliance with Peel.[93]

But time and his debts were closing this aspect of Buckingham's political career. As early as May, 1826, he had conceived the idea of going abroad on account of his precarious economic condition, and his plans were finalized during the early summer of 1827.[94] He sought an audience of the King, gave him his proxy to deliver unconditionally into the hands of Frederick Robinson, (since April) Viscount Goderich, Secretary for War and the Colonies, and departed on his yacht for Italy, with no member of his family accompanying him, leaving behind him the wreck of the Grenvillite faction.[95]

The role of Chandos in establishing his father's unenviable political position was, after the Duke's own irascibility, paramount. Besides poisoning his father's mind against his lifelong political associates and close relatives, he was concerned with developing an anti-Catholic

90. HEH-STG, ST. 98, Buckingham's Private Diary, April 14 and 15, 1827; BRO, Fremantle Papers, 138, Fremantle to Thomas Fremantle, April 19, 1827.

91. BRO, Fremantle Papers, 46, Buckingham to Fremantle, May 15, 1827; Richard Plantagenet Temple Nugent Brydges Chandos Grenville, Second Duke of Buckingham and Chandos, ed., *The Private Diary of Richard, Duke of Buckingham and Chandos, K.G.* (London, 1862), I, 19.

92. BRO, Fremantle Papers, 138, memorandum of a conversation between Fremantle and Buckingham, May 22, 1827; HEH-STG, ST. 98, Buckingham's Private Diary, May 15 and 19, 1827.

93. HEH-STG, ST. 98, Buckingham's Private Diary, June 17, 1827.

94. NLW, Coedymaen Papers, 34, Buckingham to Wynn, May 9, 1826.

95. NLW, Charles Wynn Papers, 6/4816D, Charles Wynn to Henry Wynn, July 20, 1827; HEH-STO, Buckingham to O'Conor: 527, Oct. 27, 1826; 535, Dec. 26, 1826.

opposition to the Duke's interest in both the county and borough of Buckingham. Probably Chandos's chief reason for opposing the Fremantle family was their support for the traditional Grenville policy on the Catholic question; and when, against his wishes, Thomas Fremantle, William's nephew, succeeded his uncle at Non-Conformist Buckingham in 1827, Chandos let it be known in advance that he would neither propose Fremantle to the electors nor personally attend the election as a burgess.[96]

When young Fremantle canvassed at Buckingham it swiftly became obvious to him that in a pocket borough of the Duke of Buckingham, containing only twelve electors, trouble was afoot. Some burgesses were absent; Fremantle thought on purpose. Others told him outright they would never vote for a supporter of Catholic emancipation, and he assumed he would have but a "bare majority." The Duke was worried enough to advise Fremantle against avowing open support for emancipation, rather voicing vague generalities should the subject come up.[97]

With his son openly acting with Peel, Buckingham demanded and received the resignation of three burgesses, including Chandos, and replaced them with pro-Catholic friends.[98] At the same time, upon hearing that at the Magistrates' Chamber at Aylesbury a Chandos-sponsored anti-Catholic address to Robert Peel had been introduced, he expressed his disgust at the proceedings in a strong letter addressed to the Magistrates in petty session. He was so angry at Chandos that he at least summoned up the courage to tell his diary he "broke off political connexion with him."[99]

After July, 1827, with the Duke conveniently in Italy, Chandos proceeded apace with his plans to organize Buckinghamshire against emancipation. In late 1827, amid addresses and militia reviews, Chandos received the then anti-Catholic Tory champions, Wellington and Peel, at Buckingham, Wotton, and Stowe. Both Chandos's uncle, Lord Nugent, and William Fremantle regarded this affair as a no-popery rally.[100] Then, during the autumn of 1828, to the furor of both Lord Grenville and the absent Buckingham, Chandos inaugurated a Protestant Buckinghamshire Brunswick Club to agitate against emancipa-

96. BRO, Fremantle Papers, 49, Thomas Fremantle to William Fremantle, April 26, 1827.

97. Ibid., May 17, 1827.

98. HEH-STG, ST. 98, Buckingham's Private Diary, June 11, 1827; *Bucks Chronicle* (Aylesbury), June 23, 1827.

99. HEH-STG, ST. 98, Buckingham's Private Diary, May 21, 22, and 23, 1827.

100. *Bucks Chronicle* (Aylesbury), Dec. 15, 1827; BRO, Fremantle Papers, 138: Nugent to Thomas Fremantle, Dec. 9, 1827; William Fremantle to Thomas Fremantle, Dec. 18, 1827.

tion, and over 400 of the local farmers and the lower gentry attended several meetings—though Buckingham gloated from afar that few of the upper gentry or the "leading men of the County" came.[101] When Wellington and Peel finally agreed to support a Catholic emancipation Bill early in 1829, Chandos presented 97 anti-Catholic petitions to the House of Commons, signed by 7,000 Bucks inhabitants. On February 21, escorted by 300 mounted gentlemen and farmers, while a crowd estimated at 3,000 pulled his carriage through Buckingham, Chandos presided over a Protestant meeting involving the hundreds of Buckingham, Ashendon, and Cottesloe. Upon learning of this, the Duke of Buckingham accused his son of vilifying both his and his grandfather's character, and he wrote a public letter to the hundreds condemning the action.[102] But the Protestant meeting was a last futile gesture; and, with the passage of emancipation assured, Buckingham was able to rejoice that he had lived to see the day and Lord Grenville to see that his life's work had not been in vain.[103]

Grenville, insofar as he acted in politics at all after 1826, might well be called a Canningite, as he was certainly no longer in agreement with the rump of the Grenvillites around the Duke of Buckingham. He did not support Buckingham and Chandos in 1826 and 1827 in their opposition to ministerial attempts to modify the Corn Laws; and Chandos told his father, surely incorrectly, that Canning received support from Lord Grenville in his opinion not to send the Duke to India.[104] In 1827 both Grenville brothers were forward in urging the union between the successive Canning and Goderich Administrations and the Whigs; and they made known, by more than one channel, their desire that their old colleagues Lansdowne and Holland accept office.[105] The very reason that Canning retained Charles Wynn, for whom he had no love, at the Board of Control was probably due to the cordial relations prevailing between Dropmore and Downing Street and the knowledge

101. *Standard* (London), Sept. 22 and 27, 1828; *Bucks Chronicle* (Aylesbury), Oct. 25, 1828; BRO, Fremantle Papers, 49, Buckingham to Fremantle, Oct. 27, 1828.

102. *Bucks Gazette* (Aylesbury), Feb. 28, March 21, and April 11, 1829; *Diary of Buckingham*, III, 104.

103. *Diary of Buckingham*, III, 87; Great Britain, Historical Manuscripts Commission, Francis Bickley, ed., *Report on the Manuscripts of Earl Bathurst, Preserved at Cirencester Park* (London, 1923), Grenville to Bathurst, May 10, 1829, p. 659.

104. NLW, Coedymaen Papers, 27, Buckingham to Wynn, May 6, 1826; HEH-STG, Box 330, Chandos to Buckingham, n.d.

105. NLW, Charles Wynn Papers, B.1/71, Thomas Grenville to Wynn, April 18, 1827; BM, Holland House Papers, Add. MSS. 51687, Rogers to Lansdowne, April 23, 1827 (copy); HRO, Tierney Papers, 31M70/37d, Holland to Tierney, n.d.; BRO, Goderich Papers: .50, Thomas Grenville to Rogers, Aug. 9, 1827; .07, Lansdowne to Goderich, Aug. 13, 1827.

on Canning's part of the pain that Wynn's dismissal would occasion his fond uncle. In April, 1827, Canning even offered to send Wynn to India as Governor General in succession to Amherst. Wynn apparently expressed no interest in such an appointment, though Canning might well have been perversely delighted in the outcry such an advancement would have elicited from the Duke of Buckingham.[106] Canning's successor, Lord Goderich, appointed Frankland Lewis, an old Welsh Grenvillite, as Secretary to the Treasury, partially to please Lord Grenville.[107] When Goderich resigned, however, and Wellington became Prime Minister in January, 1828, Grenville found himself out of sympathy with an Administration for the first time in six years. Perhaps it had to do with Charles Wynn's dismissal from office; but whatever the cause, he saw the advent of Wellington as the "triumph of bigotry, & anti-liberalism."[108]

Buckingham watched from abroad the dramatic political events from the end of Canning's Ministry in 1827 to the adoption of Catholic emancipation by Wellington and Peel in 1829. He was at Gibraltar when news of Canning's death reached him; and, pronouncing himself "ready to start for England at a moment's warning," he wrote William Fremantle to relay an offer of his services. But no response was forthcoming from Goderich.[109]

The chief reason for Buckingham's long sojourn in Italy was his declining financial situation. The Duke was not an imaginative man of business; and he seems to have had few investments outside of land, which, although heavily encumbered with mortgages and debts, produced £64,000 yearly in rents during the early 1820s. He was, likewise, afflicted with a generally incompetent set of bankers, estate agents, and solicitors.[110] The senior Tellership of the Exchequer, a valuable source of income for the Stowe Grenvilles, worth well over £20,000 per annum during the period of the Peninsular war, lapsed in 1813 on the death of the first Marquis of Buckingham, and his successor had no sinecure to make up for the loss. The first Duke of Buckingham was conscious of his need to economize, and in 1823 he made largely unkept promises to reduce an expensive life style.[111] Buckingham's

106. Leeds Papers, 78A, Canning to Wynn, April 15 and 25, 1827 (copies).

107. NLW, Coedymaen Papers: VI/436, Grenville to Wynn, Aug. 9, 1827; IX/731, Wynn to Grenville, n.d.

108. NLW, Harpton Court Papers, C/418, Grenville to Lewis, Jan. 25, 1828.

109. HEH-STG, ST. 98, Buckingham's Private Diary, Aug. 22, 1827; BRO, Fremantle Papers, 46, Buckingham to Fremantle, Aug. 23, 1827.

110. HEH-STG: Box 284, Morland to Ledbrooke, Sept. 14, 1824; Box 12, Thomas Grenville to the Duchess, Dec. 28, 1827.

111. NLW, Coedymaen Papers, 23, Buckingham to Wynn, Feb. 16, 1823.

idea of economy, however, seemed to involve spending Christmas at Avington rather than at Stowe; and in 1826, despite protestations of increasing poverty, Lady Wynn heard that her nephew was spending sums of £1,200 and £2,000 for additions to the Stowe library. A Buckinghamshire newspaper estimated that the new yacht built by the Duke to take him to Italy had cost over £16,000.[112] When in 1827 the Duchess of Buckingham requested a loan of £10,000 from Thomas Grenville, who had inherited the estates of his cousin, Lord Glastonbury, he rather coolly refused and expressed his wonder that the Duke could afford to keep up a great yacht if he were indeed so distressed.[113]

The Duchess was worried enough about the Grenville financial situation that after her husband's departure for the Continent she took steps to ensure that her marriage settlement, involving control of the Chandos estates, was overturned and came into her own hands and those of Lord Chandos, thus eliminating the Duke's hold upon them. Buckingham acquiesced in this desire.[114]

All of the Grenvilles entertained grave doubts about the competence of the Duke's solicitors, the Robsons; and after 1827, the Duke increasingly placed his financial concerns in the more capable hands of Sir Edward Hyde East, MP for Winchester.[115] East discovered that the Duke owed personal debts of around £33,000, including yacht bills, solicitors' expenses, bond debts, and county expenses, in addition to owing Coutt's House £60,000. Chandos had personal debts of £9,200 and claimed that his father owed him £58,000. East insisted upon both strict retrenchment in Italy (about £3,000 per annum) and definite plans for debt repayment in England through the sale or mortgage of unsettled property and by the accumulation of savings out of annual income.[116] The Duke agreed to sell certain properties, among them the Warwickshire estate, which sold for £120,000; to pay most of his son's debts; and to settle all of his unsettled estates upon Chandos, though reserving a joint power to sell or mortgage them.[117]

In 1833, the Duke put his own estates, though not his wife's, in

112. Ibid., Dec. 19, 1823; *Correspondence of Lady Wynn,* Lady Wynn to Henry Wynn, Feb. 3, 1826, p. 343; *Bucks Chronicle* (Aylesbury), Aug. 18, 1827.

113. HEH-STG: Box 146, Duchess to Thomas Grenville, Dec. 20, 1827; Box 12, Thomas Grenville to the Duchess, Dec. 28, 1827.

114. Ibid.: Box 4, East to the Duchess, Dec. 31, 1827, Jan. 8 and Feb. 27, 1828; Box 145, Buckingham to East, Feb. 4, 1828.

115. Ibid.: Box 12, Thomas Grenville to the Duchess, Dec. 28, 1827, and April 27, 1828; Box 145, Buckingham to East, Feb. 4, 1828.

116. Ibid., Box 4, East to the Duchess, March 15 and 21, 1828.

117. Ibid.: Box 145, Buckingham to East, May 3, 1828; Box 4, East to the Duchess, May 17, 1828.

trust.[118] But he still envisioned for himself a surplus of £20,000 yearly after payment of all annual charges out of rents, which were then estimated at only £52,247 per annum. East was aghast at such extravagance, and he attempted without success to persuade the Duke to cease residence at Stowe and to attempt to live on less than £8,000 per year.[119] The second Duke of Buckingham and Chandos, whose lack of business sense was as profound as his father's and who by 1844 had amassed debts of £1,000,000, was, of course, left to reap the whirlwind.[120]

While in Italy, Buckingham sent his representative for St. Mawes, Sir Scrope Bernard Morland, whom William Fremantle described with some but not much exaggeration as "the only remnant of the Grenville party in Parlt.," instructions on voting procedures in the Commons and ordered him to inform his other members that they were not to follow the voting line of Chandos.[121] After Morland became gravely ill in November, 1828, Buckingham, in the reductio ad absurdum of Grenvillite politics, appointed seventy-one-year-old General Sir George Nugent, who rarely even attended the Commons, as leader of the Grenvillite connection in that House.[122]

When Lord Anglesey was recalled as Lord Lieutenant of Ireland in January, 1829, an intrigue was initiated by Chandos and East to obtain the succession for Buckingham. Chandos told Wellington that he offered the Duke's name in accord with his father's "frequently expressed" desire to receive the post.[123] Buckingham, in Rome, claimed that the whole proceedings took place without his knowledge or consent. Whatever the rights or wrongs of that transaction, Wellington refused Chandos's request. The words used by William Fremantle in communicating with his nephew when he heard of the affair might well serve as the last lament of the traditional Grenvillite connection: "It is of a piece with all he [Buckingham] has done for the last ten years, never fixing on any one point, deceiving every part, & every

118. HRO, Shelley Rolls Papers, 18M51/287, Settlement of the Grenville estates, Aug. 2, 1833 (copy).
119. HEH-STG: Box 4, East to the Duchess, May 11 and June 16, 1832; Box 153, East to the Duchess, May 30, 1833.
120. David Spring, "The Fall of the Grenvilles, 1844–1848," *Huntington Library Quarterly*, XIX, No. 2 (1956), p. 166.
121. BRO, Fremantle Papers, 139, William Fremantle to Thomas Fremantle, Nov. 23 and 30, 1828.
122. HEH-STG: Box 150, Nugent to the Duchess, Feb. 21, 1828; Box 330, Chandos to Buckingham, May 5, 1826.
123. *Despatches of Wellington*, V: Chandos to Wellington, Jan. 13, 1829, 440; Wellington to Williams, Jan. 18, 1829, 453.

friend he deals with, and having no scruples of writing right hand &
left, imagining that People would not shew and compare his letters.
. . . No Party will have him. . . . I am really so hurt at all the
Duke has done (not as regarding myself) but as affecting the great
influence & power the Grenvilles possessed that I never think of it,
without putting myself in a passion."[124]

124. *Diary of Buckingham*, III, 68; BRO, Fremantle Papers, 139, William Fremantle to Thomas Fremantle, Jan. 20, 1829.

[CHAPTER X]

Conclusion

IN their post-1829 careers, Buckingham, Charles Wynn, Lord Chandos, Lord Grenville, and Thomas Grenville seldom attempted to act together as a unit, though they agreed at least in disapproving the Reform Bill. When Buckingham returned from Italy in November, 1829, he supported Wellington's Ministry in a futile hope for the Irish Lord Lieutenancy.[1] He received the Lord Stewardship instead, in July, 1830, from which he resigned when Grey formed a Whig Administration in November, 1830. His role during the 1831–32 reform crisis was essentially that of a firm supporter of Wellington; and, had that Duke formed a Ministry in May, 1832, Buckingham would probably have received the Admiralty.[2] During his seven remaining years, generally under Whig ministries, Buckingham often acted with Lord Londonderry and the Duke of Cumberland on the extreme right wing of the political spectrum.[3]

Chandos, who had done so much after 1825 to insure that the Grenvillite faction would be increasingly ineffective, had a more successful career during the 1830s than any other member of his family. One of the leading protectionist advocates in England, he built up a strong political machine in Buckinghamshire (as "the Farmer's friend") and at the general election of 1835 was able to rout the Whigs in the county.[4] During Peel's second Ministry, in 1841, the new Duke of

1. *Despatches, Correspondence, and Memoranda of Field Marshal Arthur, Duke of Wellington, K.G.*, ed. Arthur Richard Wellesley, Second Duke of Wellington (8 vols.; London, 1867–80), Wellington to Peel, Dec. 10, 1829, VI, 320.
2. HEH-STG, Box 162, memorandum of Buckingham on the Reform Bill, May 11, 1832; Arthur Aspinall, ed., *Three Early Nineteenth Century Diaries* (London, 1952), pp. 249–51.
3. George Kitson Clark, *Peel and the Conservative Party* (London, 1929), pp. 124–26.
4. David Spring, "Lord Chandos and the Farmers, 1818–46," *Huntington Library Quarterly*, XXXIII, No. 3 (1970), pp. 257–81; *Bucks Gazette* (Aylesbury), Jan. 17, 1835.

Buckingham and Chandos entered the Cabinet as Lord Privy Seal, but he resigned in February, 1842, in a dispute over protection.

Charles Wynn's political path after leaving the Board of Control in January, 1828, was somewhat erratic, as perhaps befitted the former leader of the Grenvillite connection in the House of Commons. He opposed Wellington's Administration; accepted the Secretaryship at War from his old colleague Earl Grey in 1830; resigned his office in disgust at the scope of the Reform Bill in 1831;[5] and served Peel during his first Ministry, in 1834–35, as Chancellor of the Duchy. He ended his long parliamentary career in 1850 as a Peelite, when, as Father of the House and "seperated from all my old Connections & friends," he took sustenance that in his free trade views he "could call up the spirit of Lord Grenville" and "have the satisfaction of his support & approbation."[6]

Lord Grenville died in 1834 at the age of seventy-five. His last years were clouded, as the popular agitation surrounding the reform issue caused the old social conservative to experience great qualms. By 1832, he thought the kingdom was in its worst state since 1648.[7] Thomas Grenville, too, ended his long life "with a horror of organick changes."[8] By the mid-1830s, he had ceased to frequent the company of his old, whiggish friends, Holland and Lansdowne.[9] During the 1840s, Thomas regaled London society with talk of Horace Walpole and the elder Pitt, though he declined to dine and sleep at Windsor upon invitation of the Queen, during the reign of whose great-great-grandfather he had been born. When Greville heard of Thomas Grenville's death at ninety-one, in December, 1846, he described him as "a philosopher, a gentleman, and a Christian," and recounted: "He dined and went to sleep in his chair, and from that sleep he never awoke."[10]

The two-party system, at least in the early embryonic form it was developing during the 1830s, made a party like the Grenvillites increasingly anachronistic. Just as the two-party system insured that the

5. NLW: Coedymaen Papers, 29, Wynn to Phillimore, Feb. 6, 1830; Charles Wynn Papers, 7/4817D, Charles Wynn to Henry Wynn, March 25, 1831.

6. NLW, Charles Wynn Papers, 8/4818D, Charles Wynn to Henry Wynn, Jan. 1 and Aug. 2, 1847, and Jan. 3, 1850.

7. BRO, Grenville Papers, 632, Lord Grenville to Thomas Grenville, May 22, 1832.

8. Charles Cavendish Fulke Greville, *The Greville Memoirs*, ed. Lytton Strachey and Roger Fulford (London, 1938), V, 44–45.

9. BM, Holland House Papers, Add. MSS. 51534, Thomas Grenville to Lord Holland, Jan. 1, 1837; Alexander Llewellyn, *The Decade of Reform* (Newton Abbot, 1972), p. 75.

10. Greville, *Memoirs*, V, 366–68.

sovereign had less option in the determination of his first minister, so also it necessarily limited the role that traditional factions like the Grenvillites were able to play on the political stage. Lord Grenville and the first Marquis of Buckingham intrigued and maneuvered from 1801 to 1806, first playing with one group, then another, to achieve certain results. The second Marquis of Buckingham did the same from 1817 to 1821. That similar tactics from 1825 to 1829 got him nowhere reflects, certainly, his own temper and the decline of his particular faction's power, but also the changing of a political structure. The Grenvillites had no real successors. This is not to suggest that any pure two-party system had become the absolute norm. Rather, groups such as the Peelites after 1846 or the followers of Lord Hartington after 1886 were committed, unlike the later Grenvillites, to a known stand on certain issues. It was no longer in fashion simply to bid for high station regardless of commitment, as Buckingham found to his surprise in 1827.

Much analysis, of course, remains to be done on the precise membership, organizational structure, and party discipline of most of the early nineteenth-century political groupings; and until that endeavor is completed, one can only make tentative judgments on the nature of political parties and political factionalism during that period. Yet, it appears that, long before 1829, factions, connections, and small parties were ceasing to be the ordinary political phenomena. As Austin Mitchell has perceptively pointed out, the hue and cry which accompanied the political transfigurations from 1827 to 1829 suggest the "exceptional nature of that period."[11] In a sense the Grenvillites stand out as much for their longevity as for their obvious decline in those years. The Wellesleyites, a small group, seldom of decisive importance, had vanished from the political scene by the early 1820s. For all practical purposes, both the followers of Sidmouth and the Prince of Wales had disappeared as united groups in 1812, when Sidmouth joined the Government and Moira departed for India. The exact position of the Canningites is more elusive: they first crop up in 1801, in a hazy sense, as a group dedicated to Pitt's return to office, then in 1809 as a more distinct party after Canning's retirement from the Ministry, and finally, in the years after Canning's death in 1827, as a body that included Huskisson and Palmerston. But considering Canning's disbanding of his own party in 1813 and his generally excellent relations with Liverpool thereafter, one does not quite get the feeling that the Canningites were comparable to the Grenvillites: that is, a definite group acting together for over a generation.

11. Austin Mitchell, *The Whigs in Opposition, 1815-1830* (Oxford, 1967), p. 4.

The Grenvillites, indeed, seem to be distinguished by their continuity over three decades; but, in fact, they varied considerably in composition and numbers over those years. When the party first emerged in the autumn of 1801, it consisted of the traditional Grenvillite faction or connection—individuals long associated through kinship, friendship, and patronage ties with the first Marquis of Buckingham or to a much lesser extent with Lord Grenville. It also encompassed a number of former Portland Whigs who were discouraged by the peace treaty and the generally anti-Catholic tone of Addington's Ministry and were thus prepared to follow Grenville's political line. In 1804, the Grenville-Foxite alliance enabled these former Portland Whigs to renew both political and social ties with those whom they had abandoned in the antirevolutionary fervor of 1793 and 1794. Then a number of followers of the late William Pitt adhered to Grenville's own wing of the Grenville-Foxite establishment in 1806 and 1807. Thus, the Grenvillites by 1808 included at least two distinct groups: the Grenvillite connection or faction, which included members of the Grenville family, who had generally acted together since the early 1780s, as well as a number of individuals who were in the main attached to the first Marquis of Buckingham through patronage ties; and the more ideologically oriented Grenvillite party, which was composed of both former Portland Whigs and Pittites.

In 1808, at the height of its numerical strength, the Grenvillite group in Parliament consisted of approximately twenty-four peers and twenty-two commoners. In the Lords, seven peers[12] may be viewed as members of the traditional Grenvillite connection and seventeen peers[13] as part of a larger Grenvillite party. In the Commons, twelve MPs[14] were connected to the senior Grenvilles by either family or patronage ties and ten[15] either by more ideological considerations or through connections with Grenvillite peers.

Between 1808 and 1815, there was an attrition of Grenvillite strength in both Houses, especially in the Commons, as more and more

12. Buckingham, Grenville, Braybooke, Bulkeley, Carysfort, Fortescue, and Glastonbury.

13. Auckland, Bristol, Bute, Carlisle, Carnarvon, Carrington, Cawdor, Essex, Hardwicke, Hereford, the Bishop of Lincoln, Minto, the Bishop of Oxford, the Bishop of St. Asaph, Somers, Spencer, and Stafford. In addition, some (by 1808) nebulous ties existed with Grosvenor and Lucan and, even more tentatively, with Grey de Ruthyn, Monson, Scarborough, Shaftesbury, Southampton, and Yarborough.

14. Sir George C. Berkeley, Scrope Bernard, Lord Ebrington, William Fremantle, Thomas Grenville, Richard Neville, Sir George Nugent, William Shipley, Lord Temple, Sir Robert Williams, Sir Watkin Wynn, and Charles Wynn.

15. Sir John Anstruther, William Eden, William Elliot, Lord Euston, Pascoe Grenfell, William Howard, Thomas Knox, Lord Morpeth, Sir John Newport, and Lord Porchester.

individuals drew closer to the main branch of the Whig party. Numerous political and social circumstances account for this gradual shift of
commitment: the lack of any effective leadership role on the part of Lord
Grenville; the absence of a strong Grenvillite leader in the Commons;
the growing attraction toward a more liberal ideology on reform questions among younger members of the Grenvillite group (who then often
pulled their somewhat more conservative fathers in the Lords with
them); the attractive social milieu offered by Holland House and
Brooks's to the Grenvillites that was in no way countered by any leading
members of the Grenville family. In 1815, when Lord Grenville attempted to drum up support for two policies upon which he felt deeply,
opposition to the Corn Laws and to Bonaparte, he found that few of his
old adherents followed him on either question. Two years later the
Grenville-Foxite coalition ended, and Grenville's semiretirement from
active public life began. Then Grenville's former followers gave ample
evidence of the pull of the two major parties: a majority of them
continued to support the Whigs, while a small minority adhered
directly to Liverpool's "Tory" Ministry, with only a sad rump left to
carry on an independent Grenvillite line.

In 1817, the year of the Grenville-Foxite schism, of the forty-six
individuals labeled as definite Grenvillites for the year 1808, thirty-two
survived as parliamentarians (excluding Thomas Grenville, who was in
the Commons until 1818 but never attended). Of these, seventeen[16]
continued in support of the Whig opposition (though many of that
number were almost indistinguishable from the Foxites as early as
1809), including all six of the surviving Portland Whigs.[17] On the
other hand, five Grenvillites,[18] four of them former Pittites, either in
1817 per se or several years earlier, attached themselves directly to
Liverpool's "Tory" Ministry. Of the remaining ten 1808 Grenvillites,
three[19] seem to have adopted no definite political line; one (Lord

16. In the Lords: Carlisle, Carnarvon (Porchester in the Commons in 1808),
Carysfort, Cawdor, Essex, Fortescue, Grafton (Euston in the Commons in 1808),
Hardwicke, and Spencer. In the Commons: Lord Ebrington, William Elliot, Pascoe
Grenfell, William Howard, Lord Morpeth, Richard Neville, Sir John Newport, and Sir
Robert Williams. Also, the sons of three deceased Grenvillite peers, Lord Nugent, son
of the first Marquis of Buckingham, and the sons of Auckland and Minto, who had
inherited their titles, remained attached to the Whig party. None were in the Commons
in 1808.

17. In the Lords: Carlisle, Cawdor, Essex, Hardwicke, and Spencer. In the Commons: William Elliot.

18. Bristol, Hereford, the Bishop of Lincoln, Somers, and Stafford.

19. Braybrooke, Carrington, and Glastonbury.

Grenville) claimed to have retired from partisan politics; and only six,[20] under the leadership of the second Marquis of Buckingham and Charles Wynn, embarked upon an ambitious and independent political line of their own. Looking at these political transactions from the perspective of the narrow Grenvillite connection or faction as opposed to the wider Grenvillite party, of the fourteen surviving members of the 1808 Grenvillite connection,[21] only six[22] joined the second Marquis of Buckingham in the third party. None of the eighteen surviving members of the broader Grenvillite party joined Buckingham.[23]

Looking more specifically at the inner Grenvillite connection, one can see the decline of the group in terms not only of a changing political structure but also of the dissolution of those attributes that had made them traditionally strong. The kinship ties were weakened not only by the pull of opposing ideological forces, which made the first Duke of Buckingham's brother adhere to the Whigs or his son to the Tories, but also by a declining family birthrate. Neither Lord Grenville nor Thomas Grenville had children. The first Marquis of Buckingham had three offspring, who among them gave him only one grandchild, the Marquis of Chandos. Therefore, by the 1820s, a once strong family group had generally failed to perpetuate itself. Then, too, the first Duke of Buckingham, no doubt from personal character deficiencies, was unable to retain his friends. One by one, J. H. Stanhope, Lord Ebrington, Charles Wynn, and William Fremantle found themselves in his bad graces. This failure of the Grenville family to retain ties linking family and friends was reinforced by the decline of the family's patronage powers. The loss of control over parliamentary boroughs after passage of the Reform Bill, coupled with the various sinecurial and economical

20. In the Lords: Bulkeley and Buckingham. In the Commons: Scrope Bernard Morland, William Fremantle, Sir Watkin Wynn, and Charles Wynn.

21. In the Lords: Braybrooke, Bulkeley, Buckingham (Lord Temple in 1808), Carysfort, Fortescue, Glastonbury, and Grenville. In the Commons: Scrope Bernard Morland, Lord Ebrington, William Fremantle, Richard Neville, Sir Robert Williams, Sir Watkin Wynn, and Charles Wynn.

22. Same as footnote 20.

23. Although the Grenvillites were in decline after 1808, between that date and 1816, eight MPs adhered to a general Grenvillite line: Lord Gower; Francis Horner; Thomas Knox; Thomas Frankland Lewis; Lord Nugent; Granville Proby; John, Lord Proby; and W. C. Plunket. By 1817, Nugent and Granville Proby were associated with the Whigs; Gower supported Liverpool; Thomas Knox, T. F. Lewis, and W. C. Plunket were associated with the Grenvillites in a third party attempt; and the death of Francis Horner and the illness of Lord Proby prevented the necessity of a choice on their parts.

reform legislation, left a substantial gap in Buckingham's ability to reward his partisans.

When Buckingham entered into a coalition with Liverpool's Ministry in December, 1821, eleven members of the Commons[24] and only one peer (Lord Bulkeley, who died in 1822) followed his line. By 1825, to further illustrate the pull exercised by the Ministry over the Grenvillite faction, only eight MPs[25] and no peers were associated with Buckingham. In 1826 Buckingham controlled only six members of Commons[26] and, after 1827, with his own son opposing his politics, only five.[27]

The 1832 Reform Bill merely ratified in a formal sense what the political events from 1825 to 1829 had already made abundantly clear—the Grenvillite connection in its traditional sense was finished. St. Mawes borough was abolished completely, and supporters of the Reform Ministry were returned at the general election of 1832 from the former Grenville strongholds at Winchester and from one seat at Buckingham. At that general election, only two members were returned to the House of Commons who boasted any special tie with the Duke of Buckingham: Lord Chandos (who had been politically reunited with his father after Catholic emancipation ceased to be an issue) for Buckinghamshire; and Thomas Francis Fremantle for Buckingham borough. However, as R. W. Davis has persuasively argued in an article on Buckingham borough after 1832, the Reform Bill subtly changed the nature of the borough to such an extent that one can legitimately question whether it was any longer a nomination borough or whether Fremantle ought to be viewed as a Grenville nominee in the pre-1832 sense.[28]

24. William Fremantle, Thomas Knox, J. H. Leigh, T. F. Lewis, Scrope Bernard Morland, Sir George Nugent, Joseph Phillimore, W. C. Plunket, Lord Temple, Sir Watkin Wynn, and Charles Wynn.

25. Lord Chandos, Sir Edward H. East, William Fremantle, Scrope Bernard Morland, Sir George Nugent, Joseph Phillimore, Sir Watkin Wynn, and Charles Wynn.

26. Sir Codrington E. Carrington, Lord Chandos, Sir Edward H. East, William Fremantle, Scrope Bernard Morland, and Sir George Nugent.

27. Sir Codrington E. Carrington, Sir Edward H. East, Thomas F. Fremantle, Scrope Bernard Morland, and Sir George Nugent.

28. R. W. Davis, "Buckingham, 1832–1846: A Study of a 'Pocket Borough'," *Huntington Library Quarterly*, XXXIV, No. 2 (1971), p. 180.

[BIBLIOGRAPHY]

UNPUBLISHED MANUSCRIPT SOURCES

Aberyswyth, Wales; National Library of Wales:
  Aston Hall Papers
  Charles Wynn Papers
  Charles Wynn-Robert Southey Papers
  Coedymaen (Wynn) Papers
  Harpton Court Papers
  Henry Wynn Papers

Althorp, Northamptonshire, England:
  Spencer Papers

Ann Arbor, Michigan, U.S.A.; William L. Clements
  Library:
  Canning Papers

Aylesbury, England; Buckinghamshire Record Office:
  Fremantle (Cottesloe) Papers
  Goderich (Ripon) Papers
  Grenville Papers

Bangor, Wales; University College of North Wales:
  Baron Hill Papers
  Plas Newydd Papers

Bedford, England; Bedfordshire Record Office:
  Whitbread Papers

Bury St. Edmunds, England; Suffolk Record Office:
  Grafton Papers

Castle Howard, Yorkshire, England:
  Carlisle Papers

Chelmsford, England; Essex Record Office:
  Braybrooke Papers

Dublin, Ireland; National Library of Ireland:
   Plunket Papers

Dunrobin Castle, Sutherland, Scotland:
   Sutherland Papers

Durham, England; University of Durham:
   Grey of Howick Papers

Durham, North Carolina, U.S.A.; William R. Perkins
   Library:
      Grenville Papers, W. B. Hamilton collection
      Moss Papers
      Newport Papers

Elton Hall, Huntingdonshire, England:
   Proby Papers

Exeter, England; Devon Record Office:
   Fortescue Papers
   Sidmouth Papers

Leeds, England; Sheepscar Library:
   Canning (Harewood) Papers

London, England; British Museum:
   Auckland Papers
   Buckingham Letter Books
   Canning-Frere Papers
   Canning-Wilbraham Papers
   Fox Papers
   Grenville (Thomas) Papers
   Hardwicke Papers
   Holland House Papers
   Huskisson Papers
   Liverpool Papers
   Mackintosh Papers
   Melville Papers
   Morley Papers
   Peel Papers
   Rose Papers
   Wellesley Papers
   Windham Papers

London, England; British Library of Political and
   Economic Science, London School of Economics:
      Horner Papers

London, England; National Army Museum:
   Nugent Papers

London, England; Public Record Office:
 Chatham Papers
 Dacres Adams Papers
 Granville Papers

Manchester, England; John Rylands University Library:
 Carrington Papers

Nether Winchendon, Buckinghamshire, England:
 Spencer Bernard Papers

Northampton, England; Northamptonshire Record
 Office:
  Fitzwilliam (Milton) Papers

Oxford, England; Bodleian Library:
 Grenville-Newport Papers

Reading, England; Berkshire Record Office:
 Braybrooke-Glastonbury Papers

San Marino, California, U.S.A.; Henry E. Huntington
 Library:
  Stowe-Grenville Papers
  Stowe-O'Conor Papers

Sandon Hall, Staffordshire, England:
 Harrowby Papers

Sheffield, England; Central Library:
 Wentworth Woodhouse Muniments
 (Fitzwilliam Papers)

Stafford, England; Staffordshire Record Office:
 Sutherland Papers

Winchester, England; Hampshire Record Office:
 Political Lampoons
 Shelley Rolls
 Tierney Papers
 Wickham Papers

[INDEX]

Kirkwall, Thomas John Hamilton
Fitzmaurice, Viscount (4th Earl of Orkney),
26
Knox, Thomas (1st Earl of Ranfurly), 120, 133,
221n; as Grenvillite, 107–8, 176; and
Grenville-Liverpool junction, 191
Knox, Thomas (2d Earl of Ranfurly), 223n,
224n; and Third party, 108, 181, 183;
pro-war view (1815), 161; as Grenvillite,
175–76; as Tory, 196
Lake, (General) Gerard (1st Viscount Lake), 24
Lansdowne, Henry Petty Fitzmaurice, 3d
Marquis of, 87, 90, 96n, 98, 115, 142, 169,
178, 179, 188, 213; and Whig leadership,
105; relations with Lord Grenville, 128–29;
on Canning-Grenville alliance (1811), 137;
and ministerial negotiations (1811), 150;
anti-war view (1815), 160; relations with
Thomas Grenville, 219
Lauderdale, James Maitland, 8th Earl of, 36,
74, 82, 90, 91, 96, 126n, 146, 185, 210; and
French negotiations, 72; anti-Grenvillite
views of, 77; on Lord Grenville's inactivity,
139; economic views of, 155
Laurence, French, 61, 62, 69, 73, 79, 87, 89, 93,
94, 95, 125; as Fitzwilliamite, 53; and
Cobbett, 60; anti-Pittite views, 66; and
ministerial negotiations (1806), 86; and
Brooks's, 127
Lawley, Robert (1st Baron Wenlock), 69
Leeds, Francis Osborne, 5th Duke of, 14
Leigh, Chandos, 29–30
Leigh, James Henry, 201, 224n; as Winchester
MP, 29–30; as Grenvillite, 175, 196; and
Third party, 182
Leipzig, battle of, 159
Lennox, Charles (4th Duke of Richmond), 63
Lewis, Thomas Frankland, 166, 179, 214,
223n, 224n; for Corn Laws, 158; pro-war
view (1815), 161; as Grenvillite, 175, 196;
and Third party, 183; relations with
Liverpool, 186
Lille, peace negotiations (1796), 54, 56–57
Lincoln, George Pretyman, Bishop of. See
Tomline, George Pretyman
Lincoln's Inn, 4
Liverpool, Robert Bankes, 2d Earl of, xiv, 28,
57, 81, 85, 97–98, 111, 128, 138, 153, 175,
178, 185, 203, 204, 206, 207, 208, 220;
and Pittite reunion, 171, 191, 193; for
Grenville-Liverpool junction, 171–72, 180;
for Lord Grenville's support, 176–77; and

ministerial reshuffle (1821), 187, 188–89;
Lord Grenville opposed to junction, 190,
191–92; difficulties with Buckingham II
(1822–23), 197; views on Amherst's
successor, 202–3; and Buckingham's Indian
designs, 205; illness and death, 207
Londonderry, Charles Stewart, 3d Marquis of,
218
Londonderry, Robert Stewart, 2d Marquis of.
See Castlereagh, Viscount
Long, Charles (1st Baron Farnborough), 78–79
Louis XVIII, King of France, 7, 59
Lucan, Richard Bingham, 2d Earl of, 58, 81,
132, 221n; on Regency question, 147
MacDonald, James, 177; and Grenville-Foxite
split, 165
Mackintosh, (Sir) James, 31n, 177, 194, 194n;
relations with Lord Grenville, 129; and
Grenville-Foxite split, 165; on revived
Grenville-Foxite alliance, 178
Majorbanks, Campbell, 208
Malmesbury, James Harris, 1st Earl of, 54
Malta, 55, 57, 62
Malthus, Thomas, 154
Manners-Sutton, Charles (1st Viscount
Canterbury), 177
Mansfield, David William, 3d Earl of, 63, 70
Marengo, battle of, 12, 54
Melville, Henry Dundas, 1st Viscount. See
Dundas, Henry
Melville, Robert Dundas, 2d Viscount, 210;
and ministerial reshuffle (1821), 187;
Buckingham II's quarrels with, 197
Meyler, Richard, 29–30
Mildmay, Henry Carew, 29
Mildmay, Henry Paulet St. John, 69
Mildmay, Paulet St. John, 30
Minorca, 57
Minto, Gilbert Elliot, 1st Earl of, 53, 62, 70,
87, 90, 91, 132, 162, 221n; early career, 61;
anti-Pittite views, 66, 69; as Portland
Whig, 73; anti-Foxite views, 77; as a Whig,
123; and Holland House, 128
Mitchell, Austin, 220
Moira, Francis Rawdon, 2d Earl of (1st
Marquis of Hastings), 48, 91, 98, 111, 115,
188, 226; as leader of Prince's party, 51; and
ministerial negotiations (1803), 67; and
ministerial negotiations (1812), 152
Monson, John George, 4th Baron, 103, 132n,
221n
Morgan, George, 23